THE LACANIAN LEFT

Psychoanalysis, Theory, Politics

Yannis Stavrakakis

EDINBURGH UNIVERSITY PRESS

© Yannis Stavrakakis, 2007

Edinburgh University Press Ltd
22 George Square, Edinburgh

Typeset in Sabon
by Servis Filmsetting Ltd, Manchester, and
printed and bound in Great Britain by
Antony Rowe Ltd, Chippenham, Wilts

A CIP record for this book is available from the British Library

ISBN 978 0 7486 1980 1 (hardback)

The right of Yannis Stavrakakis
to be identified as author of this work
has been asserted in accordance with
the Copyright, Designs and Patents Act 1988.

Contents

Bibliographical Note	iv
Acknowledgements	vi
Introduction: Locating the Lacanian Left	1

PART I Theory: Dialectics of Disavowal

1. Antinomies of Creativity: Lacan and Castoriadis on Social Construction and the Political	37
2. Laclau with Lacan on *Jouissance*: Negotiating the Affective Limits of Discourse	66
3. Žižekian 'Perversions': The Lure of Antigone and the Fetishism of the Act	109
Excursus on Badiou	150

PART II Analysis: Dialectics of Enjoyment

4. What Sticks? From Symbolic Power to *Jouissance*	163
5. Enjoying the Nation: A Success Story?	189
6. Lack of Passion: European Identity Revisited	211
7. The Consumerist 'Politics of *Jouissance*' and the Fantasy of Advertising	227
8. Democracy in Post-Democratic Times	254
Bibliography	286
Index	312

Bibliographical Note

Page references are to the English translations of the works of Jacques Lacan, when these are available. In the case of the *Écrits* or Lacan's seminars, I used the following abbreviations:

E1977   Lacan, Jacques [1966] (1977), *Écrits: A Selection*, trans. Alan Sheridan, London: Tavistock/Routledge.

E2006   Lacan, Jacques [1966] (2006), *Écrits*, trans. Bruce Fink, in collaboration with Héloïse Fink and Russell Grigg, New York: Norton.

I   Lacan, Jacques [1953–4](1988), *The Seminar of Jacques Lacan, Book I: Freud's Papers on Technique, 1953–1954*, ed. Jacques-Alain Miller, trans. and notes John Forrester, Cambridge: Cambridge University Press.

II   Lacan, Jacques [1954–5] (1988), *The Seminar of Jacques Lacan, Book II: The Ego in Freud's Theory and in the Technique of Psychoanalysis, 1954–5*, ed. Jacques-Alain Miller, trans. Sylvana Tomasselli, notes by John Forrester, Cambridge: Cambridge University Press.

III   Lacan, Jacques [1955–6] (1993), *The Seminar of Jacques Lacan. Book III: The Psychoses, 1955–56*, ed. Jacques-Alain Miller, trans. and notes Russell Grigg, London: Routledge.

VII   Lacan, Jacques [1959–60] (1992), *The Seminar of Jacques Lacan. Book VII: The Ethics of Psychoanalysis, 1959–1960*, ed. Jacques-Alain Miller, trans. and notes Dennis Porter, London: Routledge.

XI   Lacan, Jacques [1964] (1979), *The Four Fundamental Concepts of Psychoanalysis*, ed. Jacques-Alain Miller, trans. Alan Sheridan, London: Penguin.

BIBLIOGRAPHICAL NOTE

XVII   Lacan, Jacques [1969–70] (1991), *Le séminaire, livre XVII, L' envers de la psychanalyse, 1969–70*, ed. Jacques-Alain Miller, Paris: Seuil.

XX   Lacan, Jacques [1972–3] (1998), *The Seminar of Jacques Lacan. Book XX: Encore, On Feminine Sexuality, The Limits of Love and Knowledge, 1972–3*, ed. Jacques-Alain Miller, trans. and notes Bruce Fink, New York: Norton.

XXIII   Lacan, Jacques [1975–6] (2005), *Le séminaire, livre XXIII, Le sinthome, 1975–6*, ed. Jacques-Alain Miller, Paris: Seuil.

Other published works by Lacan are cited in the text as dates only. References to his unpublished seminars are indicated by the date of the particular seminar in brackets. To avoid anachronisms, works by Lacan are listed in the Bibliography in the order of their first publication or composition. In the Bibliography the reader can also find the titles of the various papers from the *Écrits* to which reference is made in the text.

Acknowledgements

I have discussed both the idea of this book and the ideas in this book with numerous friends and colleagues. Many of them have also read earlier versions of some of the chapters. In this respect, I would like to thank Mark Bracher, Nikos Chrysoloras, Nicolas Demertzis, Kurt Hirtler, David Howarth, Andreas Kalyvas, Vassilis Lambropoulos, Christopher Lane, Lynne Layton, Akis Leledakis, Thanos Lipowatz, Chantal Mouffe, Nicos Mouzelis, Dany Nobus, Aletta Norval, Jina Politi, Pablo San Martin, and the *Umbr(a)* editorial collective. Likewise, exchanges with Yannis Triantafyllou and Themis Kanaginis have been extremely beneficial on many levels. Many thanks are also due to Jason Glynos, Alexandros Kioupkiolis and Peter Bratsis, who have read the whole manuscript and offered valuable comments. This book would not be the same without them. In Jason's case this was not the first time I have benefited from his friendship and intellectual powers, and thus I would like to express my long-term indebtedness. My teacher Ernesto Laclau has read most of the first part of the book in its final form and made helpful remarks; I want to thank him for all the stimulating exchanges we had since we first met in 1991 – apparent in Chapter 2 – and for his overall support. Thanks are also due to Slavoj Žižek, my other main theoretical interlocutor in Part I, for his co-operation in many projects over the years and for some heated but productive debates, always conducted in agonistic spirit (Chapter 3).

Bruno Bosteels, Nikos Bozatzis, Joan Copjec, Betina Davou, Thalia Dragonas, Julie Graham, Michael Gunder, Stephen Healy, Vicky Iakovou, and Ceren Ozselçuk have provided bibliographical help when it was most needed and I am grateful to them. I must not forget to thank the staff at Edinburgh University Press for their kindness and effective professionalism, and especially Manuela Tecusan for her meticulous copy-editing and my editor, Nicola Ramsey, for her unwavering support. I have tested her patience more than once and she has reacted with rare generosity and a firm commitment to this project. For the cover of the book I feel indebted to Theodosis Papanikolaou and Yannis Liveris, who devoted much energy and time to preparing

ACKNOWLEDGEMENTS

it. Finally, my family and especially my partner, Dora, have created the right environment to think and work in. Without them I might never have completed this project and, certainly, would not have enjoyed it as much.

In various places in the book, I have drawn on material from previously published articles: 'Theory and Experience: The Lacanian Negotiation of a Constitutive Tension', *Journal for the Psychoanalysis of Culture and Society*, 4:1, 1999, pp. 146–50; 'On the Critique of Advertising Discourse: A Lacanian View', *Third Text*, 51, 2000, pp. 85–90; 'Creativity and its Limits: Encounters with Social Constructionism and the Political in Castoriadis and Lacan', *Constellations*, 9:4, 2002, pp. 522–39; 'Re-activating the Democratic Revolution: The Politics of Transformation Beyond Reoccupation and Conformism', *Parallax*, 27, 2003, pp. 56–71; 'The Lure of Antigone: Aporias of an Ethics of the Political', *Umbr(a)*, 2003, pp. 117–29; 'Passions of Identification: Discourse, Enjoyment, and European Identity', in David Howarth and Jacob Torfing (eds), *Discourse Theory in European Politics*, London: Palgrave, 2005, pp. 68–92; (with Nikos Chrysoloras) '(I Can't Get No) Enjoyment: Lacanian Theory and the Analysis of Nationalism', *Psychoanalysis, Culture and Society*, 11, 2006, pp. 144–63; Jason Glynos and Yannis Stavrakakis, 'Encounters of the Real Kind: Sussing out the Limits of Laclau's Embrace of Lacan', *Journal for Lacanian Studies*, 1:1, 2003, pp. 110–28.

Acknowledgements are due to *Umbr(a)* and Joan Copjec for granting permission to quote from articles published in the journal, and especially from Slavoj Žižek, 'From "Passionate Attachments" to Dis-Identification', *Umbr(a)*, 1, 1998, pp. 3–17, and 'What Some Would Call ...: A Response to Yannis Stavrakakis', *Umbr(a)*, 2003, pp. 131–5; and to the *Journal for Lacanian Studies* and Dany Nobus for permission to quote from Ernesto Laclau, 'Discourse and Jouissance: A Reply to Glynos and Stavrakakis', *Journal for Lacanian Studies*, 1:2, 2003, pp. 278–85.

To my parents: Katerina and Dionisis

Introduction: Locating the Lacanian Left

The political Lacan

Over the last ten to fifteen years, psychoanalysis, and especially Lacanian theory, has emerged as one of the most important resources in the ongoing re-orientation of contemporary political theory and critical analysis. So much so is now acknowledged even in mainstream political science fora. For example, in a critical review essay recently published in the *British Journal of Politics and International Relations* – one of the journals of the UK Political Studies Association – and characteristically entitled 'The Politics of Lack', one reads that 'an approach to politics drawn from Lacanian psychoanalysis is becoming increasingly popular of late among theorists . . . Indeed, this approach to theorising politics is today second in influence only to analytical liberalism' (Robinson 2004: 259).[1] This in itself is quite astonishing; nobody could have predicted it ten years ago. Yet the most striking characteristic of this trend is that the work of Jacques Lacan is increasingly being used by major political theorists and philosophers associated with the Left.

Why is this so striking? Precisely because Lacan was a practising analyst without instantly noticeable leftist leanings, without even a declared interest in political life. This is not to say that he was apolitical. One can surely detect a certain (anti-utopian) radicalism in Lacan, although its political connotations have remained largely implicit. At the theoretical level, for example, his critique of American Ego-psychology is sometimes staged in quasi-political terms, implying a rejection of a 'society in which values sediment according to a scale of *income tax*' (Lacan 1990: 110) and of the 'American way of life' (XI: 127). In his famous Rome discourse (1953), his first psychoanalytic manifesto, Lacan explicitly criticises American capitalism and the affluent society, while later on he will associate his definition of 'surplus enjoyment' with Marx's conceptualisation of 'surplus value', thereby revealing the operations of enjoyment (*jouissance*) at the foundations of the capitalist order (XVII: 19).[2] But, like Freud, he was very sceptical of revolutionary politics. Paul Robinson has described Freud as a 'radical anti-utopian', meaning someone whose practice and theory, despite its distinct historical pessimism, refuses to adapt to the established political order (Robinson 1969: 3). Lacan's position is not far from that: psychoanalysis is simultaneously subversive of established orthodoxies and distrustful of utopian fantasies, with this distrust being crucial in sustaining its truly subversive edge.

We also know that Lacan had some experiences from the protest culture of his age. For example, in a letter to Donald Winnicott, written in August 1960, he refers to his wife's daughter, Laurence, noting that she 'has given us much torment (of which we are proud) this year, having been arrested for her political relations' and adding: 'we also have a nephew, who lived in my home during his studies as though he were a son, who has just been sentenced to two years in prison for his resistance to the Algerian war' (Lacan 1990: 77). During the May events, Lacan observes the teachers' strike and suspends his seminar; he even meets Daniel Cohn-Bendit, one of the student leaders (Roudinesco 1997: 336).[3] One way or the other, his name becomes linked to the events. No wonder then that, when his seminar is suspended at the École Normale (1969), the May 1968 climate returns: the director's apartment is occupied by protesters who are eventually removed by armed police.

However, the relation is not an easy one. In 1969, for instance, Lacan is invited to speak at Vincennes, but obviously he and the students operate at different wave-lengths. The discussion ends as follows:

> [T]he aspiration to revolution has but one conceivable issue, always, the discourse of the master. That is what experience has proved. What you, as revolutionaries, aspire to is a Master. You will have one . . . for you fulfil the role of helots of this regime. You don't know what that means either? This regime puts you on display; it says: 'Watch them fuck . . .'. (Lacan 1990: 126)

A similar experience marks his lecture at the Université Catholique de Louvain on 13 October 1973, when he is interrupted and eventually attacked by a student who seizes the opportunity to transmit his (situationist) revolutionary message. The episode, which has been filmed by Françoise Wolff, concludes with Lacan making the following comment:

> As he was just saying, we should all be part of it . . . we should close ranks together to achieve . . . well, what exactly? What does organisation mean

if not a new order? A new order is the return of something which – if you remember the premise from which I started – it is the order of the discourse of the master . . . It's the one word which hasn't been mentioned, but it's the very term organisation implies.

In any case, current efforts to explore the relevance of Lacan's work for critical political theory are not based on, and do not presuppose, any foundation in Lacan's biography,[4] although, at least to my mind, they need to register seriously his anti-utopian radicalism. What they entail is an articulation between critical political analysis and Lacanian theory which is not given in advance and, as we shall see, can be established in a variety of ways. Thus, to give only a few examples, Slavoj Žižek has put forward what he describes as an 'explosive combination of Lacanian psychoanalysis and Marxist tradition' in order to 'question the very presuppositions of the circuit of capital';[5] Alain Badiou has re-appropriated Lacan in his radical 'ethics of the event'; pointing out that 'Lacanian theory contributes decisive tools to the formulation of a theory of hegemony', Laclau and Mouffe have included Lacanian psychoanalysis on the list of contemporary theoretical currents which they consider as 'the conditions for understanding the widening of social struggles characteristic of the present stage of democratic politics, and for formulating a new vision for the Left in terms of radical and plural democracy' (Laclau and Mouffe 2001: xi).[6]

Obviously, Lacanian theory is not used in the same way by the authors in question. In Žižek's work, for instance, Lacan constitutes a constant and primary reference, while for Laclau and Mouffe his work is one reference among many others, albeit an increasingly privileged one. Nor is the Left understood by all these theorists in an identical fashion. For example, for Laclau and Mouffe the democratic revolution still functions as the ultimate framework for any politics of the Left, while for Žižek democracy seems to be a signifier that has lost all political relevance for a progressive political agenda – especially through its association with globalised capitalism and its instrumental application in the 'war against terror'. Yet the mere possibility of formulating these different positions clearly presupposes the slow emergence of a new theoretico-political horizon: this broad horizon is what I call the 'Lacanian Left'. This expression is proposed not as an exclusive or restrictive categorisation but as a signifier capable of drawing our attention to the emergence of a distinct field of theoretical and political interventions seriously exploring the relevance of

Lacan's work for the critique of contemporary hegemonic orders.[7] At the epicentre of this emerging field one would locate the enthusiastic endorsement of Lacan by Žižek;[8] next to him – at what some would call a more healthy distance – the Lacan-inspired insights of Laclau and Mouffe; at the periphery – negotiating a delicate balancing act between the outside and the inside of the field, often functioning as its intimate 'others' or adversaries – we would have to locate the critical engagement of thinkers like Castoriadis and Butler.

Without doubt, this field is heterogeneous. The designation 'Lacanian Left' does not refer to any kind of pre-existing unity or essence underlying all these diverse theoretico-political projects. In true Lacanian style, one could even declare that the Lacanian Left 'does not exist!', meaning that it does not impose itself on the theoretico-political domain as a homogeneous, full positivity. In fact, paradoxically, its own division is the best proof of its emergence, since – as everybody knows – there is only one test which can reveal – beyond any reasonable doubt, as they say – whether such a field does indeed exist or not. Wherever there is a Left there is bound to be a division between a supposedly 'real' Left and a 'false' Left, between revolutionaries and reformists. This seems to be exactly the case with our Lacanian Left. In Andrew Robinson's argument, for example, one will encounter such a distinction between a 'reformist' (Laclau, Mouffe and company) and a supposedly 'revolutionary' (Žižek) Lacanian political theory (Robinson 2004: 265). Not surprisingly, then, 'Lacanian Left' is a signifier continuously sliding over its potential signifieds. In that sense, talking about it partly entails constructing it, in the same way in which the emergence of something – any object of discourse – cannot be ontologically untied from the performative process of its naming.

Thus the crucial question is: how should this construction take place? Clearly, the aim is not to engage in some kind of totalising exercise guided by the fantasy of putting forward *the* new foundation for theory, analysis, and political praxis. Apart from being immodest and politically naïve, such an aim would be contradictory to anything useful that this distinct Lacanian type of theorising has to offer to our theoretico-political explorations. Taken in this sense, 'Lacanian Left' can only be the signifier of its own division, a division which is not to be repressed or disavowed but, instead, highlighted and negotiated again and again as a locus of immense productivity, as the encounter – within theoretical discourse – of the constitutive gap between the symbolic and the real, knowledge and truth, the social and the political. In his 1953 inaugural lecture at the Collège de France, while commenting on the Socratic position – a position favourably discussed by Lacan – Merleau-Ponty forcefully points out that it is only such an awareness of our lack in knowledge that makes us open to truth (Merleau-Ponty 1988). It is in this manner that we should also interpret Lacan's famous phrase from *Television*, offering the most impressive formulaic condensation of a variety of crucial insights originating from areas as diverse as philosophy (Merleau-Ponty is only one case in point), theology (especially apophatism, the *via negativa*), and mathematics (including Cantor's work and Goedel's theorem):[9] 'I always speak the truth. Not the whole truth, because there's no way to say it all. Saying it all is literally [materially] impossible: words fail. Yet it's through this very impossibility that the truth holds onto the real' (Lacan 1987: 7). To draw the political implications of this real, in its different modalities, will be one of the main aims of this book.

Theory, analysis, experience: encounters with the real

These last statements, which underlie the epistemological and methodological premises of this text, call for some elaboration. This is a book of theory and theoretically informed analysis; but what kind of theory? How can and how should theory position itself in relation to the experience it desires to analyse?[10] And how should it relate to the desire that stands at its own root as an experience? Here, the starting point can only be the constitutive tension between knowledge and experience, a tension that is neither epiphenomenal nor accidental. On a fairly simple level, the main purpose of knowledge and theory construction seems to be to approach and account for experience and then direct our praxis, that is to say, canalise experience and guide action along ethically sound, truthful, and legitimate channels. This is a very simple – almost simplistic – and neutral statement. It is a widely shared belief that 'the main reason for believing scientific theories is that they explain the coherence of our experience'. This is, in fact, a quotation from Alan Sokal and Jean Bricmont's now infamous book *Intellectual Impostures* (Sokal and Bricmont 1998: 55).[11] The problem is, however, that theoretical inquiry and scientific discourse continuously fail to account for, and understand, the totality of our experience, let alone to predict and direct human praxis. Even in Sokal and Bricmont's text, where the 'holy' integrity of science is defended at all cost, the aforementioned statement makes sense only when experience is reduced to scientific experiments and scientific theories to the 'best-verified ones'; this is again a quotation (ibid.). The problem here is, however, that, instead of entailing an encounter with the real, scientific experiments are often limited within an already domesticated field of experience, a field of measurements that are already paradigm-determined – that is to say, contaminated by the same theory they are called to verify (Kuhn 1996: 126).[12] Nevertheless, the verification they provide usually seems enough to sustain the fantasy 'that the scientific community knows what the world is like', the fantasy that 'verified' theories adequately represent the field of raw experience (p. 5). Besides, this is exactly what permits the word 'totality' to enter into the picture.

In this circularity of an already symbolised experience sustaining the fantasy of a closed and accurate order of theory is revealed the nature of what Thomas Kuhn calls 'normal science'. Needless to say, the constitution of this order is a predominantly political issue; it is not a coincidence that Kuhn's account of the historicity of science is articulated using a political vocabulary, thus revealing its direct relevance for political reflection. The fantasy of normal science rests 'on the power given to those who can move back and forth' between the reality of raw experience and our socio-political world. These *subjects supposed to know*, to use a Lacanian formulation[13], 'these few elect, as they themselves see it, are endowed with the most fabulous political capacity ever invented'. And what is this supposed capacity? *'They can make the mute world speak, tell the truth without being challenged, put an end to the interminable arguments through an incontestable form of authority that would stem from things themselves'* (Latour 2004: 14). One has to agree with Latour that 'we cannot pass this fairy tale off as a political philosophy like any other – and even less as superior to all others' (p. 15). Why? For one reason – and here I am advancing a Lacanian line of reasoning – because the circularity of this play between theory and experience, knowledge and truth, can be sustained only when something is excluded; what remains outside the equation is the unsymbolised or rather the unsymbolisable part of experience, what always escapes symbolisation and theoretical representation – in short, *the real* as distinct from reality. Theory can only appear as a truthful representation or adequation of experience if the field of experience is reduced to that which is already symbolised, at best, to what is symbolisable according to the prevailing rules of symbolisation: if, in Lacanian terms, the 'real' is reduced to 'reality' (which, according to Lacan, is constructed at the symbolic and imaginary levels, through the signifier and the image). What is disputed here, then, is not that knowledge can be truthful to reality; of course it can. Only this will be a reality already produced through the scientific rules of symbolisation; an already theorised reality. Knowledge can be truthful to the reality of our experience and still miss – foreclose, repress or disavow – the real of experience, what falls outside the grasp of this reality.

It is this exclusion that explains the *banality* of many scientific theories; and this is true in both natural and social sciences, provided one makes the appropriate 'translations' and modifications. The discourse of science is usually devoted to representing and accounting for this field of domesticated experience, the field of what could be called 'banal experience'.[14] One only has to go through a list of PhD titles and abstracts in our universities to become instantly aware of that. There are no surprises here, since the destabilising real is excluded: 'only the anticipated and usual are experienced, even under circumstances where anomaly is later to be observed' (Kuhn 1996: 64). Dealing with banal experience, with the rationalisations grafted on the automatism of natural and social reproduction, theory becomes part of the same banality. In fact, the more successful it is in representing reality – the reality of banal experience, the reality of what Latour calls 'matters of fact', risk-free objects which are supposed to have clear boundaries, a well-defined essence and properties (Latour 2004: 22) – the more banalised it becomes. Within the schema of normal science, all encounters with the real, with the 'anomalous' (what violates the paradigm-induced expectations governing normal science), are reduced to the 'expected' (Kuhn 1996: 55).[15]

This repression, however, can only be temporary. Sooner or later the real re-emerges and dislocates theory. Now 'matters of fact' become 'matters of concern', paradoxical objects which disturb any fantasy of absolute representation, control and predictability: asbestos, the perfect modernist substance, the magic material, turns into a nightmare of contamination; prions unexpectedly emerge to account for BSE where nothing of the sort was even imaginable in mainstream science (Latour 2004: 22–4). It is in such moments of disruption – of surprises and events (p. 79) – that experience qua 'encounter with the real', to use a Lacanian phrase, makes its presence felt. This can lead to a crisis of normal science and to a scientific revolution – although this dramatic impact is not always so visible, being retroactively absorbed by the various self-representations of scientific disciplines. In such encounters we come across a radical scientific impetus able to traverse the banality of normal science. The next moment, however, processes of sedimentation and normalisation begin anew. Now the 'return of the repressed' takes the form of an 'awareness of anomaly [which] opens a period in which conceptual categories are adjusted until the initially anomalous has become [again] the anticipated', initiating the hegemony of a new paradigm (Kuhn 1996: 64).

It seems that 'science, if one looks at it more closely, has no memory . . . it forgets the circuitous paths by which it came into being' (E2006: 738). Even Prusiner, the heretic who put forward the revolutionary prion hypothesis to explain CJD and 'mad cow disease', was eventually awarded the Nobel prize and his theories gradually acquired the status of a new orthodoxy, becoming increasingly resistant to questioning and dispute. However, the restoration of normality does not mean that the new paradigm is now safe. The reason is simple: isn't it founded on a similar banalisation of the real of experience? Isn't the real always exceeding its normalised representation? If this is the case, normal science is never safe. According to Kuhn's schema, it always remains susceptible to crises and scientific revolutions, to the forces of negativity and their partial positivisation/sedimentation into ever-new orders of (scientific) discourse. The conclusion flows almost naturally: contrary to a popular unconditional Enlightenment optimism, knowledge in general is never adequate; something always escapes. It looks as if theory is a straightjacket unable to contain our vibrant and unpredictable field of real experience. Scientific analysis is revealed as unable to map its frontiers. The real seems to be a *terra* which wishes to remain *incognita*.[16] Frustrated by its inability to articulate fully the truth of the real in knowledge, science prefers to forget its reliance on its traumatic encounter, it 'does-not-want-to-know-anything about the truth as cause' (E2006: 742).

Psychoanalysis as a discourse and a practice constitutes one of the privileged terrains from which it is possible to reflect on this constitutive tension between knowledge and experience, symbolic and real. In Jacques Lacan's words from his seminar on *The Four Fundamental Concepts of Psychoanalysis*, 'No praxis is more orientated towards that which, at the heart of experience, is the kernel of the real than psychoanalysis' (XI: 53). This becomes very clear when one examines, for example, the position of the psychoanalyst within the analytic setting. As Serge Leclaire has pointed out, a double and even contradictory requirement is imposed on the analyst.[17] On the one hand, the analyst 'must have at his disposal a system of reference, a theory' which permits one to 'order the mass of material' (Leclaire 1998: 14). On the other hand, however, when listening to the analysand's speech, the analyst has to be open to the singularity of this experience of listening and 'set aside any system of reference precisely to the extent that adherence to a set of theories necessarily leads . . . to privileg[ing] certain elements' and to sacrificing the 'floating attention' (pp. 14–15). For this reason, it appears that one of the most crucial problems faced by analysts in their everyday encounters is the following: 'how can we conceive of a theory of psychoanalysis that does not annul, in the very fact of its articulation, the fundamental possibility of its practice', of its openness toward the field of the patient's real experience? (p. 15). At a broader level, passing from psychoanalysis to analysis in general, how can we conceive of a theory which does not mortify or banalise the real in its attempt to master its representation, to analyse it?

Here Lacan may be of some help. Why? Precisely because, from the very beginning of his teaching, his aim was to articulate a theory, an orientation of analysis, based not on the reduction but on the recognition of the unrepresentable real. Again I quote from *The Four Fundamental Concepts*: '[W]here do we meet this real? . . . what we have in the discovery of psycho-analysis is an encounter, an essential encounter – an appointment to which we are always called with a real that eludes us' (XI: 53). But wait a minute, how can the paths of experience, belonging to what is impossible to be adequately represented in the domain of the symbolic (where theory is usually constructed and analysis practiced), the paths belonging to what Lacan names the real, acquire a place within a theory of psychoanalysis or within theory in general? Is not Lacan himself arguing that the real is radically incommensurable with our symbolic constructs?

It is true that the relation of knowledge to experience is only one of the modalities assumed by the relation between the symbolic (and the imaginary), on the one hand, and the real, on the other. The fact, however, that the symbolic can never master the real, that theory can never totally capture experience, does not mean that one should abstain from symbolising: Lacan is clearly against any such tabooing of the real. As Slavoj Žižek has pointed out, 'Lacan is as far as it is possible to be from any "tabooing" of the real, from elevating it into an untouchable entity exempted from historical analysis'; on the contrary, 'the only true ethical stance is to assume fully the impossible task of symbolizing the real, *inclusive of its necessary failure*' (Žižek 1994: 199–200, emphasis added). In the face of the irreducibility of the real of experience, we seem to have no other option but to symbolise, to keep on symbolising, trying to enact a positive encircling of negativity. But this should not be a fantasmatic symbolisation attempting to mortify the real of experience and to eliminate once and for all its structural causality. It will have to articulate a set of symbolic gestures (positivisations) that will include a recognition of the real limits of the symbolic, the real limits of theory, and attempt symbolically to 'institutionalise' real lack, the (negative) trace of experience, or rather of our failure to neutralise experience. Only thus might we be able to construct theorisations beyond the banality of normal science; only thus might we be able to explore new modes of positivisation, highlighting and not foreclosing the irreducible dialectics and continuous interpenetration between experience and knowledge, real and symbolic, time and space, negative and positive.

What is needed then is a reorientation of the way we construct our theories and conduct our analyses. Instead of repressing the recognition of their limits, of their ultimate failure to capture the real – this is the standard reductionist theoretical strategy – we can start incorporating this destabilising element within our theories. Instead of repressing the paradoxical relation, the tension between knowledge and experience that marks our lives, we would be probably better off acknowledging this tension, repeatedly inscribing the limits of theoretical discourse within its own symbolic fabric. In that sense, beyond the banality of normal science, a science which limits itself within the field of banal experience, Lacanian theory introduces the idea of a *permanent scientific revolution*. Furthermore, if epistemology can only be political – 'epistemology and politics . . . are one and the same thing', writes Latour (2004: 28) – this ethics of theorising has to be situated within its broader political background, one related to the legacy of the democratic revolution.

But is this (thoroughly political) mode of theorising possible, and how is it possible? According to Lacan it is. This is exactly because, right from the start, the real, although incommensurable, is not alien to the symbolic.[18] If the real is defined as that which resists symbolisation, this is because we can indeed experience the failure of symbolisation to master it. If the question is: 'How do we know that the real resists symbolisation in the first place?', the answer must be: 'Exactly because this resistance, this limit of symbolisation, is shown within the level of symbolisation itself.' Psychoanalysis is based on the idea that the real, the real of experience, is shown in certain effects persisting in representation, although it lacks any final positive representation per se. The limits of every discursive structure (of the conscious articulation of meaning, for example), the limits dividing the discursive from the extra-discursive, can only be shown in relation to this same discursive structure (through the subversion of its meaning). In Kuhn's vocabulary, 'anomaly appears only against the background provided by the paradigm' (Kuhn 1996: 65). Hence Freud's focus on the formations of the unconscious: dreams, slips of the tongue, symptoms, and the like – the places where ordinary conscious meaning is distorted or disrupted and negativity acquires a paradoxical and perplexing positive embodiment (both symbolic and affective). Furthermore, psychoanalysis argues that it is possible to enact the symbolic gestures, the modes of positivisation, that can encircle these moments of showing or resurfacing of the real; otherwise the 'talking cure' itself would have no effects at all. The question that remains open, of course, is what is the nature of these symbolic gestures. It is not so much a question of 'if' as a question of 'how'.

Now, it is clear that Lacan believes that, in the first instance, it is possible to escape from the illusion of theoretical closure and analytical reduction and approach the real by means of a study of paradox and bizarre representational structures such as those found in topology: the Borromean knot,[19] for example, is capable of showing a certain real (XX: 133). In his 1972–3 seminar, *Encore*, he makes it clear that the real can only be inscribed on the basis of an impasse of formalisation (XX: 93). It is through the failures of symbolisation – the play of paradox, the areas of inconsistency and incompleteness – that it becomes possible to grasp 'the limits, the points of impasse, of dead-end, which show the real yielding to the symbolic' (Lacan in Lee 1990: 171). Lacan's neologisms and statements like 'The Woman does not exist' or 'There is no sexual relation' attempt to reproduce this kind of paradoxical encircling of impossibility, this new orientation in theorising. As Nasio has put it, 'Lacan's formula "there is no sexual relation" is precisely an attempt to delineate the real, to trace or delimit the lack of the signifier of sex in the unconscious'. In that sense theoretical work is not reduced simply to stating 'here is the real that is unknown', but involves an attempt to delimit, to write the limits of, the real (Nasio 1998: 112).

This is, then, the Lacanian position, which underlies the epistemological and theoretical orientation of the present book.[20] Although we can never fully symbolise the real of experience in itself, it is possible to encircle (even in a metaphorical way) the limits it poses to signification and representation, the limits it poses to our theories. It is possible to become alert to the modes of positivisation these limits acquire beyond the fantasmatic reduction of negativity to positivity, of non-identity to identity, of the real to reality. Although it is impossible to touch the real, to master experience fully, it is possible to encircle this impossibility, exactly because this impossibility is always emerging within symbolisation, within a 'theoretical' terrain. This is not to say, of course, that such an encircling can ever be total; on the contrary, insofar as this strategy is also articulated at the symbolic level, it is doomed to fail. It remains, though, open to this failure, to the ontological trace of its own contingency. It assumes the responsibility of this limit, thereby highlighting the ethical dimension of the knowledge/experience dialectics. This has nothing to do, however, with some kind of nihilistic, even masochistic, acceptance of passivity and failure. Why? Not least because the registering of the limits of understanding allows for a better, or rather a different, type of understanding: 'one of the things we must guard most against is to understand too much ... it is on the basis of a kind of refusal of understanding that we push open the door of analytic understanding' (II: 265). Only through the assumption of this failure can theory remain open to the truth of experience. The point, in other words, is not to endorse the absence of knowledge, nihilistically celebrating its disintegration, but rather to adopt a position of *docta ignorantia*, 'a knowledge about the limits of knowledge, a profound awareness of the significance of not-knowing' (Nobus and Quinn 2005: 25). Which brings us back to Lacan's statement quoted earlier. It is impossible to speak the whole truth. Nevertheless, one needs to try. Not in the hope that he or she will eventually manage to say it all; on the contrary, fully assuming the failure of our own words to say it: it is through this very impossibility that truth holds onto the real. It is this solid orientation which, as we shall see throughout this text, underlies the continuous and often radical shifts marking Lacan's trajectory – with regard to his views on affect, desire, and so on.

Needless to say, this psychoanalytic truth encircled by knowledge is never defined on the basis of the adequation of language to reality. *It aims at orienting action*. Its aim, within the psychoanalytic setting, is to 'determine an act in the cure' (Nasio 1998: 116). At a more general level, its aim is an *act* proper, as opposed to activity. According to Žižek, activity 'relies on some fantasmatic support', while 'act involves disturbing – "traversing" – the fantasy' (Žižek 1998a: 13). From a Lacanian point of view, theory should be thought of as a resource enabling us 'to accomplish a more radical gesture of "traversing" the very fundamental fantasy', not only within clinical psychoanalysis, but 'even and also in politics' (p. 9). A resource, furthermore, creating and sustaining a space where such acts can be continuously re-conceived and re-enacted, a space permeated by a truly democratic ethos. And this is why such a mode of theorising is indispensable to the 'Lacanian Left'.

On the other hand, this is also why anybody reading this book in search of final answers and political blueprints is bound to be rather disappointed. This is an exercise in political theory and critical analysis and not a political manifesto. Even if the overall orientation of a Lacanian reformulation of political theory is thoroughly critical and enabling – critical of any established doxa and enabling the formulation of alternative visions and interventions – it cannot guarantee the emergence of the new. It can neither predict and command nor accomplish the act – any act, that is, beyond its own (limited) elaboration. Nothing would be more alien to psychoanalytic discourse, which locates itself beyond any naïve didacticism (academic or political) and remains suspicious of the discourses of the master and the university.[21] As Lacan makes abundantly clear, already from his first seminar: 'Do analysts have to push subjects on the road to absolute knowledge?' The answer is: 'Certainly not . . . Nor can we engineer their meeting with the real . . . It is not our function to guide them by the hand through life' (I: 265). The analyst is to enable a shift in the analysand's relation to desire and enjoyment – here conceived as another, more positive, modality of the real – through a practice that 'seems to be a break in the drum roll of being with common values' (Miller 2005: 22); but enacting – and continuously re-enacting – such a shift can only and should only be the result of the analysand's decision(s) and hard work.[22] In this vein, Lacan concludes his early text on the mirror stage with these words: 'psychoanalysis may accompany the patient to the ecstatic limit of the *"Thou art that"*, in which is revealed to him the cipher of his mortal destiny, but it is not in our mere power as practitioners to bring him to that point where the real journey begins' (E1977: 8).

This is what justifies the psychoanalytic doubts – present in both Freud and Lacan – about the possibility of effecting a miraculous change in society as a result of a direct application and implementation of pre-conceived ideals and theoretical insights through a singular radical act. During the May 1968 events, although Lacan will suspend his teaching, he initiates a debate in his seminar, in an effort to be 'worthy of the events that are taking place'. In this context, he will deal with a question apparently posed by many analysts at the time, making the following comment: 'What does the insurrection expect from us? The insurrection answers them: what we expect from you for the moment . . . this is the time to help throw some paving stones!' (seminar of 15 May 1968). The implication seems to be clear enough: the gap between theory and praxis is irreducible and this is not only a division between theorists and activists, it is a division internal to all of us, a constitutive division between our knowledge and our desire – if there is something that makes psychoanalytic *savoir* more appealing it is not its ability to bridge this gap but, on the contrary, to thematise and interrogate it in more clear terms. This is further clarified when Lacan concludes that 'the theoretician is not the one who finds the way. He explains it. Obviously, the explanation is useful to find the rest of the path' (seminar of 19 June 1968). It is the same strategy that informed Slavoj Žižek's reaction to the recent events in the French suburbs, in which one reads: 'So what can a philosopher do here? One should bear in mind that the philosopher's task is not to propose solutions, but to reformulate the problem itself, to shift the ideological framework within which we hitherto perceived the problem' (Žižek 2005c). Such a shift can often enable an alternative course of action, which, however, no philosopher-king (or psychoanalyst-king) can ever prescribe, predict or guarantee.

Hypotheses, chapters

So far, there has been no detailed study offering a mapping of the emerging Lacanian Left, no detailed examination of the convergences and divergences between the major figures active on this theoretical terrain and of their exact location in it, and no thorough evaluation of the importance of basic arguments circulating in this field in the analysis of concrete socio-political issues. This book aims at addressing this gap.

This will be first attempted through a series of critical readings in political theory and philosophy. These readings will occupy the first part of the book.[23] In the cases of Laclau and Žižek, the relevant chapters will also give me the opportunity to summarise and continue an ongoing dialogue on crucial issues related to the emergence and further development of the Lacanian Left. What is at stake, however, is not only a mapping of this uneven terrain but, in addition to that first step, a rigorous discussion of the importance of Lacanian argumentation *per se* for political theory and for the democratic politics of transformation. In this respect this text will also provide the opportunity to introduce the uninitiated reader, slowly but rigorously, to *some* of the most central aspects of Lacanian theory and to discuss their political implications. Here I will be passing from an account of the complex topology of *the* Lacanian Left as a general field to *my* rendering of the Lacanian Left as a set of concrete theoretical, analytical and critical orientations. Obviously, these two aspects of the book cannot be completely distinguished – they can only be adequately represented through the topological figure of a Moebius band.[24] My own orientations have been initially formulated through my encounter with the major figures active in this field, whose work I discuss in this book; at the same time, the readings presented here are conditioned by my idiosyncratic preoccupations as a political theorist and a Lacanian.

However, the reader will find here neither a comprehensive overview of Lacan's work and its relevance for the study of politics – something I have already attempted in *Lacan and the Political*[25] – nor global expositions of the intellectual projects discussed. In opposition to that earlier work, *The Lacanian Left* is not, strictly speaking, an introductory text, but a collection of essays targeting – in its first part – specific areas of the work of Castoriadis (the ambiguities of radical creativity and imagination), Laclau (the affective limits of discourse), Žižek (the status of the act in psychoanalysis and politics) and Badiou (the ethical and political implications of the event), which are central to a Lacan-inspired critical re-orientation of political theory and political analysis. Some of the crucial questions guiding my argumentation in the various chapters of this part of the book will be the following: Does the Lacanian Left which is currently brought into existence produce distinct effects at the intersection of theory and politics? What are the methodological, conceptual, theoretical and analytical forms these effects acquire in the various projects examined and how can we evaluate their current status and future prospects? Needless to say, the aim of such an evaluation is not to reduce the productive heterogeneity of the Lacanian Left, but to trace the ways in which certain themes remain central in its various instantiations and need to be further developed: the critical edge towards hegemonic orders and sedimented power relations; the need to theorise beyond fantasy in order not, of course, to guarantee, but to orient thought and action in politically innovative, enabling directions; the desire to illuminate the relation between representation and affect, the signifier and enjoyment, in political identification and social change; the importance of negotiating a course between negativity and positivity, between the limitations and the promise of political action, a course conscious of their irreducible dialectics.[26]

In the second part my focus will shift so as to encompass a set of concrete political issues of immense importance as we are entering the twenty-first century. How can Lacanian political theory interpret a variety of troubling phenomena – 'matters of concern' in Latour's vocabulary – that insist on frustrating our capacities for understanding and intervening? What does it have to say on the questions of nationalism, trans-national identities, consumerism? How does it respond to the de-democratising or 'post-democratic' trends in globalised capitalist societies? Can it combine an ethical attitude that reinvigorates modern democracy with a real passion for transformation, capable of stimulating the body politic without reoccupying the obsolete utopianism of the traditional Left? My central hypothesis here is that Lacanian theory, besides its important epistemological contributions, has a lot to offer on all these fronts. Not only does it provide a series of invaluable tools for the analysis of social and political reality – ranging from Lacanian semiotics and discourse theory to a theorisation of fantasy directly relevant to the critique of ideology – but it also introduces a new way to theorise the moment of the political along the lines indicated in the previous section of this introduction: as an encounter with the Lacanian real. Some of these themes have been discussed at length in *Lacan and the Political. The Lacanian Left* shares with that earlier text a desire to address an academic audience beyond the 'enlightened few' and encompassing all those who still value critical political analysis. It obviously builds on some of the arguments first presented there, but it primarily focuses on issues which have not been adequately covered in it but have been central to my work during the last five years.

Here I only want to highlight the most important of them, namely the role of enjoyment (*jouissance*) in political life, and especially in accounting for the longevity and pervasiveness of certain identifications and for the dialectics of social and political change. Beyond a registering of the real as the alienating and destabilising limit of signification and representation – an insight which remains important – it is also necessary to engage with its more positive modalities, present especially in Lacan's later work: with the real as *jouissance*. Throughout this book I will examine in detail how affect and enjoyment are conceptualised within the Freudian and the Lacanian corpus, as well as the ways these conceptualisations can be used in concrete political analysis. Gradually, an open-ended typology of *jouissance* will be constructed, able to guide the critical study of political phenomena. Moreover, the exact interface between the symbolic and the real of *jouissance* as two distinct but inter-implicated dimensions will be explored and its role in the formation of identities, in sustaining relations of power and in obstructing or facilitating real change will be discussed in detail.

Within this general framework, the opening chapter in the first part of the book aims at initiating a dialogue between Lacanian (political) theory and the social and political theory advanced by Cornelius Castoriadis. A follower of Lacan's seminar who subsequently rejected Lacanian theory, Castoriadis serves as a border figure, a frontier signpost, whose differentiation from the Lacanian corpus can help us draw a first delimitation of the terrain of the Lacanian Left. Strictly speaking, Castoriadis cannot belong to the Lacanian Left, but, standing at its periphery, can be instrumental in defining it. But this is not the end of the story. A closer look reveals a surprising proximity between the two projects on many levels. Crucially, they both seem to share a similar type of social constructionism. However, they draw quite different conclusions from this constructionism: Castoriadis stresses the importance of creativity while Lacan highlights the alienating dimension of every social construction. Furthermore, in order to safeguard a politics of radical imagination, Castoriadis ultimately disavows the alienating limits of human creation. The initially registered awareness of negativity is downplayed in favour of a romantic celebration of positivity. Here, the Lacanian Left follows a different direction. Instead of leading to political quietism or nihilism, a serious registering of the limits of creativity – the Lacanian real as an index of the negative – should be seen as a condition of possibility for a passionate and imaginative transformative politics and for the radicalisation of democracy.

Moving from the periphery to the core of the Lacanian Left, the second chapter will discuss the work of a theorist who has elevated this Lacanian conceptualisation of negativity into one of the most crucial dimensions of his multifaceted work. Laclau and Mouffe's publications, and even more so Ernesto Laclau's solo work – which will be my main focus – explicitly refer to a range of Lacanian terms of art and are extremely suggestive of many conceptual affinities even where there is no direct terminological cross-over. While acknowledging the insightful nature of these structural homologies, the second chapter will seek to probe the limits of such theoretical congruence. Lacan's category of the real will be the central probing tool here; its specific modality of *jouissance* offers a productive way of spurring on the dialogue between and among scholars inspired by Lacan and Laclau. My basic hypothesis will be that, although discourse theory does take on board and develops further the Lacanian conceptions of negativity, lack and signification and their political implications – exactly what is missing from Castoriadis' work – it has not tackled the Lacanian problematic of enjoyment, a problematic crucial in understanding the libidinal/visceral underside of identification processes. This situation has been changing recently, with Laclau endorsing the Lacanian logic of the real in its more positive aspects, by incorporating the category of *jouissance* into the conceptual apparatus of discourse theory, and with Mouffe focusing on the role of passion in democratic politics. I will obviously be discussing these developments. However, the terms of this confluence need further elaboration in order to reach a form capable of benefiting critical political analysis and the Lacanian Left.

My engagement with the work of Laclau aims at articulating an awareness of lack and of the limits of discourse (the Lacanian conceptualisation of negativity) with a more substantive dimension crucial for understanding political life: the axis of enjoyment (a more positive dimension in the Lacanian corpus). Such an articulation requires a delicate balancing act if one desires to avoid the dangers of theoretical essentialism, political voluntarism and wishful thinking. From this point of view, two major figures, absolutely central to the Lacanian Left, seem to be overstressing lately this positive axis at the expense of registering the negativity which is indispensable to Lacanian theory. The work of Alain Badiou (especially the idea of 'the event' and its ethical implications) and Žižek's thoughts on capitalism, 'the radical act', and the ethico-political example of Antigone, are often presented as integral parts of a Lacan-inspired radical political philosophy. The main theme examined in the third chapter will be the relation between negativity (the negative ontology of Lacanian theory) and the more positive, utopian and heroic political attitude recently implied by Žižek, while an excursus that follows will briefly deal with Badiou's stance on these issues. My main hypothesis is that in Žižek's recent work Lacanian negativity is ultimately disavowed and a positive politics of the event/act as miracle takes its place. Hence, the problem here is symmetrically opposite to the one associated with discourse theory and analogous with the one encountered in the work of Castoriadis. We reach then a full circle in this theoretical exploration of the Lacanian Left. The question, of course, is whether the circle is vicious or not. Does such an orientation have a place within the Lacanian Left? How does it relate to Lacan's teaching and to Žižek's earlier work? Is Badiou implicated in a similar disavowal or does he – paradoxically – remain more faithful than Žižek to the Lacanian dialectics between positive and negative?

This first part of *The Lacanian Left* is entitled 'Dialectics of Disavowal'. Operating within a field premised upon the registering of the positive/negative dialectics, each of the theorists associated with the Lacanian Left is obviously negotiating this dialectics on their own terms. There is, however, a clear pattern visible here. Depending on their diverse political priorities and theoretical preoccupations, Left Lacanians have typically stressed only one of the dimensions involved, downgrading the other. Against the background of a sophisticated constructionism, Castoriadis will stress the positive creative value of radical imagination, disavowing the negativity of alienation. Sharing a similar constructionist framework, Laclau does take fully on board the negative ontology of Lacanian theory – the real as negative – but is much more reluctant to engage with the positive aspects of the real as *jouissance*. Moving to the terrain of political praxis, Žižek's act and Badiou's event are also implicated in a similar dialectics of disavowal. It is surely a sign of both intellectual awareness and theoretical sophistication that none of these authors opts to exclude or silence – repress or foreclose – any of the dialectical moments involved. Nevertheless, this pattern of disavowal does jeopardise the theoretical integrity, the analytical scope and the political relevance of the Lacanian Left. Beyond any fantasies of arriving at a perfectly balanced theory and/or model of analysis, this dialectics of disavowal needs to be clearly thematised and a new orientation charted.

If the first (primarily theoretical) part is organised around a dialectics of disavowal, the second (primarily analytical) part is structured around a dialectics of enjoyment, focusing on the multiple ways in which the affective terrain of enjoyment interacts with other dimensions (such as the symbolic aspect of identification processes) in constructing and deconstructing, sustaining and dislocating discourses and identities. In this second part the preceding discussion of aspects of the Lacanian Left will culminate in the development of a coherent set of theoretical and ethico-political orientations applicable to the concrete analysis of a variety of social and political issues of central importance in the current conjuncture. Here the Lacanian orientation risks an encounter with the real of identification struggles in (late) modernity. This part will also differ from the previous one in chapter-length: chapters will be shorter and more empirically oriented. This obviously makes them more accessible to readers unfamiliar with psychoanalytic reasoning and with debates in contemporary political theory. Given the relative autonomy of the two parts – and of each chapter, for that matter – anybody tempted to start their reading from the discussions in Part II *should not give way on their desire*.

Thus, my fourth chapter will deal with the reluctance of post-structuralist critical political theory – including even Lacan-inspired approaches – to address the affective dimension of politics. Undoubtedly the stress on discourse and signification characteristic of post-structuralist theories has led to some of the most important developments in contemporary political analysis. Furthermore, this reluctance has not been without justification: politics and affect have often been linked in reductive ways, reproducing variants of humanist sentimentalism and a subjective essentialism which posits a deep emotional foundation of the human psyche. However, political analysis cannot be limited to the symbolic dimension of politics. There is also an affective dimension, although this has to be conceptualised in a way which avoids any essentialism of emotions, an approach that some have very aptly called 'emotionology' (Pupavac 2004: 36).

In this chapter it will be argued that the most promising way of conceptualising affect so as to expand the horizon of a post-structuralist style of political analysis is through an engagement with the Lacanian understanding of the relation between the affective and the discursive. In this effort the Lacanian concept of *jouissance* once more plays a pivotal role, carrying a variety of important implications for political analysis and progressive political critique. In opposition to what a quick reduction of Lacanianism to a mere moment in the semiotic structuralist/post-structuralist tradition would suggest, Lacanian theory not only introduces a variety of analytical tools capable of effectively accounting for the symbolic and imaginary aspects of political identification,[27] which remain essential; it also highlights the way our symbolic and imaginary representations are invested with the 'fantasmatic' and/or 'symptomatic' energy of *jouissance*, thus acquiring a resilience which explains their long-term fixity and the difficulties associated with displacing them and with socio-political change in general.[28] Thus, in opposition to post-structuralism – which focuses mostly on the fluidity of identity, and seems as a result unable to account rigorously for the resistances to social change and radical transformation – a Lacan-inspired approach is more adequately equipped to address this crucial problem: when things stick it is because, apart from offering a hegemonic symbolic crystallisation, they effectively manipulate an affective, libidinal dimension. The ideological *capitonnage* effected through a semiotic nodal point has to be supported by a knotting at the affective level of *jouissance* in order to stick. Symbolic power and authority finds its real support in the emotional dynamics of fantasy and (partial) enjoyment. Likewise, no social and political change can be effectively instituted if it is pursued merely at the level of knowledge, through transformations in consciousness. Here again the dimension of affect and libidinal investment is crucial. This is not to say that other factors (coercion, custom, economic and institutional dynamics, the *habitus*, etc.) play no role here. It is only to assert the importance of the often ignored or downgraded dimension of affect, libido and *jouissance*, which needs to be seriously taken into account and may also be deeply implicated in the functioning of these other factors. For example, can late capitalism's reliance on consumption be explained at a purely economic level, without taking into account desire and enjoyment? And is not some unconscious symptomatic *jouissance* usually behind the customary repetition of social acts and behaviours reproducing structures of subordination and obedience?

Chapters 5, 6 and 7 test all these hypotheses in the analysis of three concrete issues: national identification, European identity, and consumerism and advertising. Why has it proved so difficult to shift, modify or transform the national allegiance of the European peoples and encourage identification with Europe as a whole, with European identity? How can we effectively account for the recent rejection of the European constitutional treaty in the French and Dutch referenda? The reasons are obviously multiple, but these questions are not unrelated to the whole problematic of *jouissance*. The European project – a project crucial for the Left in terms of the global balance of power and of the egalitarian tradition, which still remains much more alive here than anywhere else in the world, with the possible exception of Latin America – has been put forward as part of a top-down, technocratic strategy which is devoid of any affective lure. Nationalism, on the other hand, and this is particularly the case with its most exclusionary and violent forms, has benefited enormously from a focus on the affective dimension of identity formation: on *jouissance* in its most obscene forms. In that sense nationalism's success as an object of identification, its ability to institute its discursive configuration as an imaginary horizon in modernity, and the failure of European identity to displace its force and function in an equally alluring way can be interpreted as two test-cases indicating that the hegemonic success and longevity of a discourse presupposes an efficient manipulation of enjoyment. When this is lacking – as in the case of European identity – the hegemonic project in question is likely to fail or encounter severe limitations.

That does not mean, of course, that it is impossible to shift long-term attachments. In Chapter 7 I shall argue that the enjoyment factor is not only important in explaining why certain discourses stick for long historical periods and others fail to attract; it also underlies successful projects of social, cultural and political change. A manipulation of enjoyment of this sort lies behind the enormous success of consumerism, the capacity of advertising discourse to hegemonise modern culture, and the difficulties encountered in fighting this seemingly irresistible trend and its political consequences – a failure of the leftist critique of consumer capitalism. It is commonplace today to argue that advertising and branding constitute hegemonic discursive tropes in late modernity. It is, moreover, the case that advertising discourse and political marketing are increasingly colonising the political space, which leads to a de-democratisation of liberal democratic institutions. At the same time, however, it is also obvious that up until now the critique of consumerism and advertising has failed to reach a degree of sophistication and rigour that would enhance its effectiveness and social relevance. An encounter with certain Lacanian insights – in particular the logic of desire and enjoyment elaborated in detail in the previous chapters – can benefit enormously the whole field of the analysis and critique of consumerism and advertising. Most importantly, it can illuminate the profound socio-political implications of consumer culture, whose hegemony seems to mark the passage from a *society of prohibition* to a *society of commanded enjoyment*.

In the concluding chapter I will put forward a Lacanian response to the de-democratising or 'post-democratic' trends in late capitalist societies. A Lacan-inspired re-activation of the democratic revolution – always alert to the continuous interpenetration of negative and positive, lack and excess – can combine a consistently democratic ethics of the political with a passion for real transformation, able to stimulate the body politic without reoccupying the dangerous utopian fantasies of the old Left. Nevertheless, the prospects of such a project also depend on its ability to couple its institutionalisation of lack with another, non-phallic *jouissance*, capable of gradually displacing or limiting dominant administrations of enjoyment (such as the ones which underlie national identification and stimulate consumption acts) and of opening up the space for the pursuit of a better future beyond utopian fantasies of wholeness and completeness.

Free associations

One last point before I bring this introductory chapter to a close. The syntagma 'Lacanian Left' inevitably entails many associations. I guess the most common among them will be that of the 'Hegelian Left'.[29] No doubt, Hegel has been one of the major influences on Lacan's early work, especially through the mediation of Alexandre Kojève.[30] Yet, although not completely accidental, this connection is not central to my argument. Simply put, I have not chosen this title in order to focus on the relation between the Hegelian and the Lacanian Left. At a first impression, one could even say that there is not much that is common between the two. Certainly, there are many differences. For example, the Hegelian Left is firmly located within a humanist framework associated with the major debates marking the period of its emergence. Lacanian theory, on the other hand, is grounded in what is usually described as an 'anti-humanism' typical of much French thought in the twentieth century.

On a closer look, nevertheless, a few similarities or analogies begin to emerge. Consider, for example, the following statement: the real, real being, is 'that which cannot be verbalised'. Who is the author of that? It could definitely be Lacan. As we have seen, he has consistently described the real as that which cannot be captured and represented using the symbolic and imaginary means involved in the construction of human reality. In actual fact, however, the aforementioned quotation comes from Feuerbach, one of the major figures associated with the Hegelian Left (Toews 1980: 366). This does not mean that Feuerbach was a Lacanian *avant la lettre*, nor does it justify any ideas of direct intellectual lineage connecting the Hegelian to the Lacanian Left. Admittedly, such analogies and similarities are largely superficial. But there are quite a few of them. Obviously, in both cases we are dealing with a major theoretical corpus (Hegel's or Lacan's), which can be interpreted in different political ways. In addition, in both cases the French influence is prominent. The development of the Hegelian Left has been significantly influenced in the 1830s by the French social thought of the period (Breckman 1999: 17). Similarly, the Lacanian Left – which is largely articulated in English-speaking political theory – is obviously grounded in the work of a Frenchman. Last but not least, both Lacanian psychoanalysis and the Hegelian Left have been victims of relentless persecution due to the radicalism of their respective views: Lacanians, by a psychoanalytic establishment keen on reproducing its banalised version of Freudianism; Left Hegelians, by the Prussian state (McLellan 1969: 27).

There are, moreover, a few further analogies which indicate an uncanny resemblance in certain respects. What has been crucial in shaping and crystallising the identity of the Hegelian Left was the polemics around Christianity (Kolakowski 1978: 84). As Toews has put it, 'the Left Hegelians demanded the emancipation of the state from the church, the creation of a completely secular, immanent human community' (Toews 1980: 361). A similar preoccupation with the legacy of Christianity is evident in authors central to the Lacanian Left – consider, for example, Žižek's numerous books and articles on Christianity – something not entirely surprising, given Freud's critique of religion and Lacan's statement that 'if religion triumphs it is a sign that psychoanalysis has failed', to which he added: 'the triumph of religion is more probable' (Miller 2004: 16). More importantly, as implied already in the subtitle – *Dethroning the Self* – of Warren Breckman's study *Marx, the Young Hegelians and the Origins of Radical Social Theory* (Breckman 1999: 19), the attack of Left Hegelians on Christian personalism had wider implications for the idea of selfhood in general, as well as for its social and political correlates:

> Thus, the radical Hegelians' campaign against Christian ideas of the person – their attempt to 'dethrone' the self, as the young Feuerbach put it in an audacious letter to Hegel in 1828 – leads us to the heart of their opposition to the conditions of their present. Hostility toward Christian personalism set Young Hegelian radicals against what was both the sovereign discourse of their day and a particular discourse on sovereignty. The controversy over sovereign personhood became a crucial vehicle for the discussion of state and civil society among the nascent intellectual left in the Germany of the 1830s and 1840s. (Breckman 1999: 19)

What we have here is, first, a passage from the individual level to the collective, an increased awareness of how our understanding of the former is directly relevant to our interpretations regarding the latter and to our attempts to change it. Secondly, we can also witness a process of politicisation: the critique of selfhood and Christianity leads to the rejection of a whole political order – the Prussian state – and of its processes of legitimation. What emerges in its place – and this is the third important moment – is an attempt to accept the radical disincorporation of power marking democracy (Breckman 1999: 301).

Surprisingly enough, these three moments can also be observed in the emergence of the field of the Lacanian Left. To begin with, Lacan's work disrupts the easy compartmentalisation into individual and collective, subjective and objective. He effectively deconstructs the essentialist opposition between these poles by registering the socio-symbolic conditioning of subjectivity and by addressing in a non-reductionist way the problem of the incomplete (lacking) constitution both of the subject and of the Other – a Lacanian term partly denoting socio-symbolic reality. This makes possible, among other things, a novel approach to political phenomena. If lack is clearly central to the Lacanian conception of the subject, it is because subjectivity constitutes the space where a whole 'politics' of identification takes place. The idea of the subject as lack cannot be separated from the recognition of the fact that the subject is always attempting to compensate for this constitutive lack at the level of representation, through continuous identification acts. This lack necessitates the constitution of every identity through processes of identification with socially available objects such as political ideologies, patterns of consumption and social roles. And vice versa: the inability of all identification acts to produce a full identity – subsuming subjective division – (re)produces the radical excentricity of the subject. In that capacity, the notion of the subject in Lacan does not only invoke lack but also all our attempts to eliminate this lack which, however, does not stop re-emerging. Such a standpoint also permits the development of a Lacan-inspired critique of political order and a new conceptualisation of radical democracy, of an ordering and ethos which incorporate and institutionalise a *savoir* of their own contingency, a knowledge of the constitutive lack around which the social is always constructed.[31] It is no coincidence that, in his analysis of the endorsement of democracy by the Hegelian Left, Breckman refers to Lefort's reading of democracy as a process of disincorporation where the locus of power remains empty and its permanent occupation by the body of the prince is precluded, something directly relevant for the Lacanian re-activation of the democratic revolution.

But this is where similarities end. The Hegelian Left proved unable to resist the temptation of replacing one form of embodiment for another, of substituting democracy's indetermination with a new humanist essentialism reintroducing the ideas of unity and perfectibility (Breckman 1999: 301–2). It is vital for the Lacanian Left to avoid this temptation, the temptation of an extreme positivisation/reduction of negativity. It is for this reason that radical democracy remains, for me, the most advanced political insight in terms of balancing an awareness of contingency and negativity with a positive institutional framework permitting and even encouraging concrete transformation. Interestingly enough, one of the most significant points of contention directly related to the emergence of the Hegelian Left has also been the dual, even contradictory legacy of the Hegelian system in terms of articulating negativity and positivity. As Kolakowski has put it, to Hegel's radical interpreters it seemed obvious that 'a philosophy which proclaimed the principle of universal negativism, treating each successive phase of history as the basis of its own destruction', was not compatible with an 'endorsement of a particular historical situation, or . . . [with the recognition of] any kind of state, religion, or philosophy as irrefutable and final' (Kolakowski 1978: 81). On the other hand, we need to take seriously into account Ziarek's point that authors like Mouffe and Lefort 'have little to say about the role of embodiment' and of 'libidinal investments underlying hegemonic formations in democratic politics' (Ziarek 2001: 138) – although Mouffe's recent work on passions in democracy seems partly to deal with this objection. Only a consistent and multifaceted engagement with the problematic of *jouissance* in Lacanian psychoanalysis – beyond the limited focus on fantasy in Ziarek's *Ethics of Dissensus* – can remedy this lacuna in radical democratic theory without falling back on the humanist essentialism that eventually mesmerised the Hegelian Left.[32]

However, apart from the Hegelian Left, there is one more association that the title of this book is bound to create, one even closer to its subject-matter; that of the 'Freudian Left'. Not only did a Freudian Left exist – in the work of people like Wilhelm Reich, Herbert Marcuse and others – but the Stanford historian Paul Robinson has also written a book with this very title. In fact, Robinson even draws a parallel between the Hegelian Left and the Freudian Left, both having become possible through the inherent difficulty in locating ideologically the diverse intellectual projects of Hegel and Freud respectively (Robinson 1969: 155).

Obviously, both the Freudian and the Lacanian Left share a common focus: to create a link between psychoanalysis and politics. Apart from this, however, the differences are more drastic than the similarities. In both cases, we can observe a strong differentiation from the conservatism of the apolitical Freudian establishment. Lacanian radicalism, though, is very far from the somewhat unsophisticated versions of Freudian radicalism. For example, as Robinson argues, the common denominator linking the three thinkers he includes in his study of the Freudian Left – Reich, Marcuse and Geza Roheim – is what he calls their 'sexual radicalism' (Robinson 1969: 4). Not only a theoretical interest in the central importance of sexual life and sexuation, but a (political) commitment to the promotion of sexual liberation. Many would argue that someone who married George Bataille's ex-wife must surely qualify as a 'sexual radical', but the fact remains that, for Lacan, no sexual liberation – whatever we mean by this term – could ever realise fantasies of sexual and social harmony or emancipation. What animated the theoretico-political desire of the Freudian Left is reduced by Lacan to a mere impossibility, and this is something that nobody operating within the Lacanian Left can ignore. For Lacan, 'there is no sexual relationship', no (sexual) harmony and emancipation, if by these words we denote the dawn of a limitless utopian future, beyond alienation and negativity.

Lacan would probably agree with Marcuse that Freud's radical socio-political message has been 'flattened out by the Neo-Freudian schools' (Marcuse 1966: 6). He would also endorse Marcuse's interest in Freudian metapsychology, in Freud's theorisations of drive and libido. When Marcuse argues that 'what started as subjection by force soon became "voluntary servitude", collaboration in reproducing a society which made servitude increasingly rewarding and palatable' (p. iii),[33] when he explains the attachment of the consumer to merchandise by recourse to the transformation of commodities into 'objects of libido' (p. ii), he is following a course parallel to the one Lacan's typologies of enjoyment have charted for the Lacanian Left, a course explored in detail in Part II. However, Lacan would never reduce this metapsychological orientation to a crude celebration of Freud's 'biologism' (p. 6), nor would he disengage positive from negative, valuing the 'Life instincts' against the 'Purveyors of Death' (p. i), and positing the utopian prospect of an 'abolition of repression' (p. 5).

The distance between the Freudian and the Lacanian Left becomes even more visible when one comes into contact with the work of Wilhelm Reich. Here, in his *Character Analysis*, the possibility of sexual liberation is founded on the delimitation of an essentialised, uninhibited and un-neurotic 'genital character structure', capable of what Reich calls 'orgastic potency', a surrendering to the involuntary convulsion of the total organism at the acme of genital embrace. Not unlike Marcuse, Reich rejects the duality of the drives, especially the Freudian conception of the death drive, and completely dissociates pleasure from pain – an un-Freudian move *par excellence*: he attributes biopathy and social irrationalism, the production of a 'neurotic character structure', to moral regulation, to a suppression emanating from the social world (Reich 1980). Social institutions induce a stasis, a damning-up of life-energy, leading to neurosis and sexual blockage. Although Lacan will eventually embrace – through his conception of *jouissance* – Freud's libido theory, he never questions Freud's central idea that it is not (social) suppression that produces repression but (primary) repression that makes (social) suppression possible and even necessary: 'Why couldn't the family, society itself, be creations built from repression? They're nothing less' (Lacan 1990: 28). The unconscious ex-sists, is motivated by the structure, by language, and in that sense repression and the superego (logically) pre-exist their crystallisation in 'discontents (symptom) in civilization' (ibid.). For this reason, to attribute the lack of (total) enjoyment to 'bad societal arrangements' can only be described as foolish (E2006: 695).

Reich's simplistic account ultimately rests on his theory of *Orgone*. It is the suppression of orgone, a life-energy related to orgasm and orgastic potency, that explains all personal problems and social ills. Moreover, this life-energy is conceived of with an exclusively heterosexual focus on a supposedly harmonious genitality and with a total neglect of the partial drives and of the polymorphous perverse basis of human sexuality. As if all that was not naïve enough, Reich was led to extend his conceptualisation of orgone in a post-mystical, all-encompassing way: as a Primordial Cosmic Energy, universally present and 'demonstrable' visually, thermically, electroscopically, and by means of Geiger–Mueller counters. This relation between psychic energy and cosmology, the natural world and the sciences, is elaborated in detail in Reich's book *Ether, God and Devil: Cosmic Superimposition* (Reich 1973), where orgone is elevated into a prime mover of the universe. Having entered such a delirious terrain, Reich even claimed to have the ability to produce rain through a manipulation of this cosmic energy. It is clear that his distance from the Lacanian Left could not be stressed enough. Notwithstanding certain common themes and preoccupations, the two orientations (Freudian Left and Lacanian Left) are ultimately incommensurable.

INTRODUCTION

The Hegelian Left has proved to be an 'ephemeral historical phenomenon' (Toews 1980: 356).[34] The same can probably be said of the Freudian Left.[35] Time only will tell what the fate of the Lacanian Left is going to be.

Notes

1. Ironically, it is not only Lacanian political theory that is becoming increasingly popular, but also the critique of Lacanian political theory. In another version of this article, published in *Theory & Event*, it is again stated that – to the great disappointment of the author of the article – 'among the plethora of radical theoretical perspectives, a new paradigm is slowly becoming hegemonic. Inspired by the work of Jacques Lacan, theorists are increasingly turning to the concept of "constitutive lack" to find a way out of the impasses of classical Marxist, speculative and analytical approaches to political theory . . . The challenge posed by this influential perspective is too important to ignore [apparently, to put it in lacanese, the theory of the real has emerged as the irreducible real in theory]. Its paradigmatic structure . . . is becoming the dominant trend in (ostensibly) radical theory' (Robinson 2005: 1).
2. For a detailed analysis of the relation between Lacan and Marx along these lines, see Žižek 1989.
3. It is no coincidence that Cohn-Bendit's photograph can be found on the front cover of Lacan's seminar XVII, *L'envers de la psychanalyse*.
4. Further biographical information sketching Lacan's relation to politics can be found in Roudinesco 1997 and Turkle 1992.
5. The quotation comes from the Foreword to Žižek's *Wo es War* series in Verso, which is reprinted in every volume.
6. Quoted from Laclau and Mouffe's statement in the *Phronesis* series. It is interesting to note that the reference to psychoanalysis was not included in the initial formulation of the statement. It was even absent from Žižek's first books published in this series. Its eventual addition testifies to the increasing centrality of psychoanalytic theory in Laclau and Mouffe's project from the early 1990s onwards.
7. As is well known, the political division between Left and Right emerged with the French Revolution and initially corresponded to the location of the various political groupings and deputies within the Assembly. Sitting to the left of the President were the most radical, anti-royalist and pro-democratic forces. Since then this horizontal division has functioned as a powerful metaphor, discursively organising the public sphere in a variety of contexts. Due to its formal/relational character, it has permitted the occupation of each of the two poles by very heterogeneous projects. Thus the Left has comprised, in different historical periods and spatial contexts, communist, socialist and liberal forces, as well as the

New Social Movements. It has also been historically associated with a variety of concrete proposals aiming to overthrow or transform the status quo – from public ownership of the means of production and state intervention/regulation of the economy to the expansion of rights, etc. The classical bibliographical reference on the Right/Left opposition is, of course, Bobbio 1996.

This political agenda is in need of radical reformulation and, to be sure, a lot of work is currently being done on this front. However, the present book is not about developing concrete policy proposals; Lacan would be an unlikely source for such an enterprise. Besides, something else is presupposed before one engages in the drafting of alternative policies: the legitimacy of critique and the plausibility (cognitive and affective) of the idea itself of an *alternative*. Today, all that seems to be in serious doubt. If the signifier 'Left' still retains any meaning, that will have to be primarily located here: emerging with the democratic revolution, it signals a democratic legitimation of antagonism and incarnates both the idea of a questioning of the status quo and the possibility of change. In opposition to what Roberto Unger has called 'the dictatorship of no alternatives' (Unger 2005), 'the Left' designates an attempt to restore and support the desire for a *democracy of alternatives*. Moreover, in order to avoid the nostalgic reoccupation of obsolete leftist themes, in order to be able to offer enlightening analyses of the dominant de-democratising trends and orient thought and action in innovative and appealing ways, this radical democratic orientation will have to draw on non-conventional theoretical/practical resources. Here is where Lacanian theory and the practice of psychoanalysis enter the picture. Besides, one should keep in mind that, as we read in the *Concise Oxford Dictionary of Current English*, 'the Left' also denotes an 'innovative section' of a philosophical school or theoretical tradition.

8. Given, however, the rapid and unexpected shifts in Žižek's positions and his drive to move continuously into more bizarre and unfathomable directions, one can almost predict that sooner or later a day will come when only one major self-transgression is left open to him: *a move beyond or even against Lacan*. In that sense, the mapping presented here does not preclude the future development of the theoretical projects examined, which can obviously follow a variety of different directions.
9. Miller is not exaggerating when he concludes that the 'whole of Lacan is in that paragraph' (Miller 1990: xix).
10. Theory and analysis are often conceptualised in terms of opposition. Theory is supposed to deal with the general, the abstract. It systematically articulates the basic principles of a scientific paradigm, the foundational ideas capable of explaining a set of phenomena, and so on. Analysis, on the other hand, is supposed to deal with the particular, with the concrete. Through a detailed examination of a delimited experiential

or conceptual field, it aims at capturing its elemental form, at separating its constituent elements and at mapping their modes of interaction. However, isn't it obvious that no theory can be sustained by staying at a purely speculative level, without some *rapport* with the particular? Both the etymology of ancient Greek *theoria* – which describes the act of seeing – and the meaning of the *syntagma* 'analytic theory' reveal this constitutive dialectic between experience, analysis and theory. Similarly, no analysis can take place at a purely empirical level, as if it was possible to arrive at an objective account of an unmediated encounter with the particular itself. No wonder, then, that 'discourse analysis' in Laclau and Mouffe's sense is marked by a strong theoretical profile. From this perspective, the two parts of this book should be seen as comprising two deeply interrelated gestures which, while functioning at different levels of generality and operating with different types of material, share the same epistemological and methodological orientation. The main parameters of this orientation are briefly sketched in the present section of the introduction.

11. I will not deal here with Sokal and Bricmont's comments on Lacanian theory. On this issue, see Glynos and Stavrakakis 2001.
12. For a general introduction to the often contradictory conceptualisations of 'experience' within Western modernity, see Jay 2005.
13. At this point, one should be aware of a crucial difference: while in psychoanalysis it is the analysand who invests the analyst with the supposed knowledge, a belief which is bound to be undermined as the treatment progresses, here it is the scientists themselves who often claim to embody this supreme knowledge, a knowledge of the whole, and – this is the crucial point – who insist on not allowing anybody (including themselves) to question the status of scientific discourse. Fortunately this does not always happen. Despite, however, some notable exceptions, fantasies of the whole remain operative in the 'scientific' background. Bruce Fink cites the example of the well-known Harvard professor of biology, E. O. Wilson, who, as his recent book *Consilience: The Unity of Knowledge* reveals, suggests that, 'using methods developed on the natural sciences, science will eventually be able to explain everything'. The conclusion is obvious: 'Have scientists left behind the fantasy of the whole? Not by a long shot!' (Fink 2002: 177).

If such a fantasy is believed to be indispensable in stimulating the desire of the scientist in normal science conditions, psychoanalysis aims at disturbing its smooth functioning, at questioning the *subject supposed to know*. It is here that the distance between academia and psychoanalysis is most fully revealed. As Lacan has formulated it in his unpublished seminar on the psychoanalytic act: 'I am not a professor, since, precisely, I put into question the subject supposed to know. This is precisely what the professor never puts into question because he is essentially, qua professor, its representative' (seminar of 22 November 1967). Can theoretical discourse escape this function of incarnation? And how? To start answering these questions is the aim of the following paragraphs.

14. Which is very different from arguing that banality is of no use. Besides, banality – from the banality of consumption to Hanna Arendt's 'banality of evil' – is an ever-present, unavoidable, and sometimes even necessary dimension of human life.
15. What is problematic here is not that theory attempts to symbolise the real, but that this attempt is founded on the banalisation of the real and on the non-recognition of the ultimate impossibility of its total representation.
16. We can get a first feel of this play between theory and experience through the distinction between space and time. Theoretical construction – constructing a theory or a philosophy of history, for example – always entails a certain spatialisation of the elusive temporality of experience, of the *event*. What theory attempts is to represent and fix in spatial terms something that is revealed in the continuous and unstoppable flow of temporality. In order to crystallise and make sense of experience, we need to reduce 'experiential' temporality to 'theoretical' space, to the space of a text. Which is not to say, however, that one should not explore the possibility of constructing spatial forms (topological, theoretical, institutional, artistic, urban, etc.) attempting to encircle the temporality of the real without neutralising it. In fact this is the direction my argumentation will follow.
17. Leclaire speaks about the psychoanalyst, but this predicament is shared by all forms of analysis.
18. I am summarising here an argument first presented in Stavrakakis 1999a: 82–90.
19. Topological structure involving three rings linked in such a way that, when one of them is cut, the other two are automatically released. Lacan uses this knot or chain to present the way the three registers of the real, the symbolic and the imaginary are linked together. This structure was included in the coat of arms of the Borromeo family, whence it gets its name.
20. More on Lacanian epistemology can be sought in Glynos and Stavrakakis 2002 and Nobus and Quinn 2005.
21. Which is not to say, however, that psychoanalysts have managed to avoid didacticism and power manipulations in their clinical practice and professional collectivities.
22. Any other position can only neutralise the potential of an analytic intervention. In a very 'Foucauldian' formulation, Lacan will even argue that 'to take the misery [of the analysand's predicament] onto one's shoulders . . . is to enter into the discourse that determines it, even if only in protest' (Lacan 1990: 13).

INTRODUCTION

23. My main interest in the material presented in this part is mainly limited to contemporary political theory and I will not provide a complete genealogy of the appropriations of Lacan by the Left in the 1960s and 1970s. Had I chosen to do so, I should have included lengthy chapters on important figures such as Louis Althusser – whose 1965 article 'Freud and Lacan' legitimised the communist interest in Lacan's work (Althusser 1999) – and Fredric Jameson – whose 1978 article 'Imaginary and Symbolic in Lacan: Marxism, Psychoanalytic Criticism, and the Problem of the Subject' (Jameson 1978) marked a similar legitimisation within leftist cultural theory in the Anglo-Saxon world. But such a historical account falls outside the scope of this project. The only exception is my engagement with Castoriadis' work. This choice is not totally arbitrary: very little has been written up until now on the relation between Castoriadis and Lacanian theory and my aim is to shed some light on this vexed issue. Most importantly, Castoriadis' work is chosen because it very clearly marks the extimate periphery of the Lacanian Left as it is currently developing.
24. This topological structure has attracted Lacan's interest because it destabilises commonsensical assumptions regarding the relation between the two sides of a given figure (and, more generally, between inside and outside, inclusion and exclusion), revealing that what initially looks like a two-sided space can be conceived of as a continuum with one side and one edge.
25. See Stavrakakis 1999a.
26. In this text the signifiers 'dialectic' and 'dialectics' are not used in a strictly technical manner, and definitely not in the Hegelian or Marxist sense. In most cases they will be employed to describe contingent patterns of dynamic interaction between (constitutive) factors or registers of experience. These interactions do not obey any immanent rules of development and escape all predetermined goals of synthesis. It is rather in this sense that Lacan refers to the dialectic of the subject and the Other and the dialectic between lack and desire or desire and the law. This is also the case with the dialectic between the Lacanian registers of the symbolic, the real and the imaginary. What is totally missing here is any reference to *Aufhebung*, any 'fantasmatic link with synthesis', since the Hegelian 'ideal progress' is replaced by 'the avatars of a lack' (E2006: 710). In this sense, if there is an affinity with a particular philosophical conceptualisation of dialectics, Adorno's 'negative dialectics' would probably be the most likely candidate to the extent that Adorno remains suspicious of identity and reconciliation and his argument is articulated on the basis of a 'consistent consciousness of non-identity' (Adorno 1973: 5). Negative dialectics pushes thinking to think against its own closure, against the reduction of our experience of the 'nonidentical', a term structurally equivalent to the Lacanian real.

27. See, in this respect, Stavrakakis 1999a, especially chs 2 and 3.
28. Bruce Fink is right when he points out that structural linguistics, which initially served as a model for Lacan's recasting of psychoanalytic research, restricts its attention to the level of signification and representation, the subject of the signifier (Fink 2004: 144). There is, however, another equally important dimension, the subject of *jouissance*, which should not be ignored. This is a call Fink addresses not only to psychoanalysis but also to areas such as economics, sociology and political science: 'many other fields in the humanities and the social sciences have to come to terms with these two faces of the subject in theory building and praxis' (p. 147).
29. The phrase usually denotes a group of intellectuals that disputed the conservative interpretation of Hegel's work within the Prussian state and sought to reformulate his legacy in a progressive direction, even if this meant turning Hegel 'upside down'. Ludwig Feuerbach, Bruno Bauer, David Strauss, Max Stirner and the young Marx have been categorised as Left Hegelians, although membership to the group depends on the criteria that one utilises.
30. As is well known, 'Lacan was only one of the many who were captivated by his teachings' (Roudinesco 1997: 99). In fact, it seems that Kojève and Lacan had even agreed to co-author a book with the provisional title *Hegel and Freud: Attempt at a Comparative Interpretation*, although the project was never realised (p. 105). At any rate, a genealogy of Lacan's conceptualisations of the real, the 'I' and 'Desire' would have to pay special attention to Kojève's seminars (Kojève 1980).
31. All these points are elaborated in great detail in Stavrakakis 1999a.
32. A large part of Chapter 8 is devoted to this issue.
33. A theme that preoccupied many members of the Frankfurt School from the 1930s onwards.
34. Obviously, Marx's impact is not taken here into account, since his contribution extends far beyond his association with the Hegelian Left in his early career.
35. Although points from its agenda have been inherited by Deleuze and Guattari's anti-psychoanalytic – but often respectful towards Lacan – work.

Part I

Theory: Dialectics of Disavowal

1

Antinomies of Creativity: Lacan and Castoriadis on Social Construction and the Political

I am autonomous only if I am the origin of what will be and I know myself as such.

Cornelius Castoriadis

The radical heteronomy that Freud's discovery shows gaping within man can never again be covered over without whatever is used to hide it being profoundly dishonest . . .

Jacques Lacan

Hostility overcome

Of all the theorists examined in this book, Cornelius Castoriadis is neither the most well-known nor the closest one to Lacan's legacy. However, the decision to put this chapter first is not entirely arbitrary.[1] From a historical point of view, Castoriadis was one of the first major political and social theorists of the Left – a founding member of the famous *Socialisme ou barbarie* group – to engage so closely with Lacanianism, and already in the 1960s.[2] More importantly, exactly because he was gradually led to a violent rejection of Lacanian theory, his work can function as an external frontier, helping us to delimit the emerging terrain of the Lacanian Left. However, and this is indicative of the force of Lacan's work, this external limit is by no means radically external. To determine clearly what is at stake, from the point of view of political theory, in the clash between what the names of Castoriadis and Lacan stand for, presupposes an understanding of what they both share – rather, of what Castoriadis retained from Lacan's theoretical apparatus even after taking his distance from Lacanian circles. And this is quite a lot. Yet there is also another important reason which justifies the location of this chapter. Due to the nature of the issues discussed in it (social construction, radical imagination, alienation, creativity and the political), it can partly function as a more or less straightforward initiation both to some of the defining characteristics of Lacanian theory – simultaneously dispelling some of the most popular misconceptions regarding Lacan's work – and to the central themes of this book, including the relation between negative and positive in politics and political theory.

In any case, the lack of any serious dialogue between Lacanian political theory and the work by, or inspired by, Cornelius Castoriadis is perhaps one of the most striking characteristics of contemporary 'non-conventional' political theory. I am stressing the word 'serious' because until now the strategies of each side vis-à-vis the other have been, to say the least, unproductive, if not downright hostile. Castoriadis himself, after distancing himself from the École Freudienne, has embarked on a vicious attack on Lacan, which can hardly be justified on any grounds (clinical, theoretical, even personal). How is it possible to accept as plausible arguments sentences or views like the following: 'Yes, Lacanianism is a monstrosity' (Castoriadis 1984: 48); or descriptions of Lacanianism as 'psychosis, abasement, contempt, enslavement, perversion', which, following Roustang, Castoriadis uses without any hesitation (p. 104)? And what about the idea that certain of Lacan's 'sophistries' take 'psychoanalysis back sixty-five years' (p. 107)? Besides this avalanche of *ad hominem* arguments, both Castoriadis and some of his supporters or commentators have persistently failed to engage in a constructive way with Lacanian theory and remain stuck in reiterating the same old – unfounded, I fear – criticisms. To give only one example, let me refer to a relatively recent article by Joel Whitebook, in which he reiterates Castoriadis' views on the supposedly crippling structuralism which robs Lacanian theory of any theoretical plausibility and progressive political relevance:

> His [Castoriadis'] theoretical critique of *le maître* follows more or less *mutatis mutandis* from his criticisms of classical structuralism. If we disregard the *ad hominem* considerations – namely, that Lacan was aristocratic, authoritarian, anti-democratic, misogynist and openly contemptuous of the idea of emancipation – his theories were also intrinsically anti-political on their own. For, like classical structuralism on which he drew, they systematically denied the possibility of anything new emerging in history and excluded the margin of freedom necessary for any sort of autonomous political action. More specifically, his hypostatization of the determinative powers of language – conceived as a machine-like 'circuit' – was every bit as a-historical as the most biologistic doctrines of Freud. (Whitebook 1999: 346–7)

Whitebook is neither the only one nor the most violent in rearticulating such a view of Lacanian theory; in fact, elsewhere – in the third chapter of his *Perversion and Utopia* – he articulates a very intelligent and thorough reading/criticism of certain aspects of Lacanian theory (Whitebook 1995).[3] No doubt, such a standpoint – I am referring to the quotation above – is consistent with Castoriadis' own views. Castoriadis was the one to argue that 'linguistic structuralism, an illegitimate extrapolation of *some* aspects of the organisation of language as a *code*, was pressed by Lévi-Strauss into the service of ethnology, and by Lacan into the service of psychoanalysis' (Castoriadis 1984: 100). Nevertheless, such a conclusion can only be based on a rather selective evaluation of Lacan's teaching, a reading which ultimately fails to take into account some of the most simple and well-documented principles of Lacanian theory.

Already in 1956, well before the structuralist boom, Lacan does indeed speak of the importance of the notion of 'structure'. He starts his seminar of 18 April 1956 with the following statement: 'The notion of structure by itself deserves our attention. Given the manner in which we efficaciously apply it in analysis, it implies a number of coordinates, and the very notion of coordinate is part of it. A structure is in the first place a group of elements forming a covariant set' (III: 183). This sounds like an easy vindication of the Castoriadian view – but only if we ignore the very next sentence, in which Lacan is distinguishing structure from totality, implying a critique of the idea of a closed structure: 'I said a *set*, I didn't say a *totality* . . . But the notion of totality only comes into it if we are dealing with a closed relation . . . On the other hand it is possible to have an open relation' (III: 183). By the early to mid-sixties it becomes explicitly clear in Lacan's seminar that he is not considering his project as associated in any way with structuralism. In his seminar on *The Logic of Fantasy*, when commenting on his experience of the notorious Johns Hopkins structuralist conference, he concludes that the structuralist ear is after all revealing itself as being a little deaf! (seminar of 30 November 1966). Can one imagine a more telling criticism coming from a psychoanalyst?

But let's move beyond Lacan's own image of himself. In fact Lacan's project can be seen as radically reformulating classical structuralism as well as the Saussurian picture of signification: he introduces a conceptualisation of the symbolic which is not that of a closed circuit but that of an always lacking and incomplete ensemble. This is what he describes as 'the lack in the Other'. This is what he has in mind when, again in *The Logic of Fantasy*, he points out that language cannot constitute a closed set, that there is no universe of discourse (seminar of 16 November 1966).⁴ Furthermore, it is this lacking character of sedimented meaning that makes possible the emergence of the *subject*⁵ and the continuous (partial) recreation of identity (individual or collective) through new identification acts. Besides, the last twenty years of Lacan's teaching have been consistently devoted to the search for what accounts for this lack in the symbolic realm. Hence the importance of the register of the real and of enjoyment (*jouissance*) in Lacanian theory, both these two (interconnected) concepts making abundantly clear the huge distance between Lacan and the structuralist omnipotence of closed linguistic structures. In fact it is this constitutive and unbridgeable gap between the symbolic/imaginary nexus (the field of social construction and institution) and the always escaping real which also makes history possible: if it was feasible for a particular social construction to symbolise fully the real, then history would come to an end, together with the permanent play between human creativity (desire) and social dislocation (lack).⁶

This is not to say, however, that most Lacanians followed a more open attitude towards a dialogue with Castoriadis or his followers. Unable to bypass the aforementioned deleterious comments and misconceptions, they decided to condemn to oblivion this *un nommé Cornélius Castoriadis*, as Lacan himself refers to him (XVII: 171), surrounding his work in a veil of silence. It is the starting point of this chapter that something important was missed in this unfortunate reciprocation. And this is because, even if a dialogue between the two on clinical issues would be almost impossible, a dialogue between Lacanian political theory and the social theory advanced by Castoriadis and his commentators is possible and might even prove to be quite a fruitful enterprise. What I will try to argue here is that Castoriadis' insistence on the creative role of imagination should not be considered as something antithetical to Lacanian theory and the Lacanian Left: it is certainly not alien to the Lacanian conception of desire and to Lacan's theory of signification. Moreover, it does stress a dimension which radical critique and transformative political action cannot afford to ignore. In fact, it is possible from a Lacanian point of view to interrogate and illuminate further this creative/instituting dimension and its ethico-political implications. But it is also possible to articulate a coherent account of the limits of imagination (the alienating side of human construction), limits which should not be downgraded, as is usually the case in some of Castoriadis' works and in a more or less romantic reading of his prolific output. In that sense the

Lacanian Left would clearly benefit from a dialogue with Castoriadis and the same might apply to Castoriadians, provided that both sides manage to overcome what seems to be an almost instinctive dislike of each other. In the course of this chapter I hope to show the – surprisingly – considerable proximity of the two projects while at the same time highlighting the distinct character of each of them.

Hopefully, the result of this exercise will be to minimise mutual suspicion and to open up the space for a more constructive exchange. Besides, even Castoriadis himself, in the same text that constitutes his most virulent attack on Lacan, does not refrain from acknowledging the latter's important contribution in breaking up the conformism, rigidity and intellectual poverty of official psychoanalysis.[7]

> Although his undertaking already bore the signs of the deep ambiguities which were to be resolved, as time passed, in the manner which has been described, nonetheless it has been his merit not only to have been the stone which broke up the stagnation of the pool, not only to have disturbed institutionalised drowsiness and shaken up pseudo-'specialist' cretinism by his appeal to disciplines 'external' to psychoanalysis, but also to have revitalised the reading of Freudian texts, to have restored to life their enigmatic movement, and to have introduced some substantial extensions into psychoanalytic research. Lacan's decisive contribution, during this early period, was that he forced people to think . . . (Castoriadis 1984: 99)

Let's see, then, whether Lacan can still make us think, let's see whether, in the first instance, he can make us think productively vis-à-vis some of the most pressing problems in contemporary social and political theory.

Constructing the social

I will start this exploration with something very basic from Castoriadis' and Lacan's ontological apparatus, an element that seems to be common to both and which explains to a certain extent the topicality of their work. I am referring to what could be called their *social constructionism*. In Castoriadis' work, for example, it is clear that the human world, reality itself, in all its different forms, is socially constructed. According to his view, 'society creates its world; it invests it with meaning; it provides itself with a store of significations designed in advance to deal with whatever may occur' (Castoriadis 1991c: 151). In 'Radical imagination and the social instituting imaginary', he further argues that 'society is creation, and creation of itself: self-creation': society is self-creation and each and every different society is a specific creation, the emergence of a new and distinct *eidos* within the generic *eidos* of society (Castoriadis 1997a: 332–3). Everything that constitutes our human world is, then, the product of social construction. The self-institution of society entails the construction of the human world, including the creation of 'things', 'reality', language, norms, values, ways of life and death, 'objects for which we live and objects for which we die' (Castoriadis 1991b: 84). Furthermore, this process of social creation or construction is a radical process (it is a creation *ex nihilo*, something to which I shall return), thus being directly related to what Castoriadis calls the 'radical instituting imaginary'. It is also continuous: 'Society is always historical in the broad, but proper sense of the word: it is always undergoing a process of self-alteration' (Castoriadis 1997a: 333).

Two further points are extremely important here. First of all, this process of social construction is also what creates the individual. The social–historical is what 'shapes' individuals. As it is expressly stressed in 'The Greek *Polis* and the creation of democracy', it is the self-instituting society that entails, 'first and foremost', the creation of human individuals in which the institution of society is, of course, embedded on a massive scale (Castoriadis 1991b: 84). This issue, which relates to the whole process of socialisation, will be one of the main foci of my argumention in this chapter. Second, society always attempts to cover the traces of its contingent institution. One of the ways it tries to do so is by presenting itself as the product of a pre-social or extra-social, and thus eternal and unchanging, or foundational, source: Gods, heroes or ancestors are the most likely candidates for it (Castoriadis 1991c: 153) and, more recently, the so-called 'laws of nature' or the 'laws of history'.

What would be Lacan's position here? Is Lacan articulating a similar constructionist argument? In Lacan it is indeed the case that reality is always precarious and not some kind of pre-social given (III: 30), although this is usually repressed in a variety of social forms. From a psychoanalytic point of view, reality, the human world, is 'upheld, woven through, constituted, by a tress of signifiers'. Reality always implies the subject's integration into a play of significations (III: 249). The whole of human reality is nothing more than a *montage* of the symbolic and the imaginary (seminar of 16 November 1966), an articulation of signifiers which are invested with imaginary – fantasmatic – coherence and unity. As it is very boldly pointed out in *Encore*, 'every reality is founded and defined by a discourse' (XX: 32). Furthermore, in Lacan's seminar on *The Psychoses*, it is made abundantly clear that this constructionism is not only of psychoanalytic, that is clinical, relevance but – like Castoriadis' argument – implies a general epistemological, philosophical view. Here the psychoanalytic theorist reveals something that should have been obvious to every philosopher:

> On reflection, do we need psychoanalysis to tell us this? Aren't we astounded that philosophers didn't emphasize ages ago that human reality is irreducibly structured as signifying?
>
> Day and night, man and woman, peace and war – I could enumerate more oppositions that don't emerge out of the real world but give it its framework, its axes, its structure, that organize it, that bring it about that there is in effect a reality for man, and that he can find his bearings therein. (III: 199)

It follows – and this is another crucial similarity between Lacan and Castoriadis – that the social individual, the social subject, is also something emerging within the field of social construction. Already in his doctoral thesis (1932) Lacan was aware of this irreducible dialectic between the social and the individual. Later on he was to devote a very large part of his teaching to demonstrating the 'priority of social discourses, of language, over the subject' (Copjec 1994: 53). The subject of the signifier, the social subject, is surely one of the nodal points of the Lacanian problematic and a particular aim of this problematic is to register the signifying dependence of the social subject (XI: 77).[8] Any identity is constructed through a variety of identifications with socially available objects, that is to say, images and signifiers. Both subjective and social reality are articulated at the symbolic and imaginary level.[9]

It becomes plausible to conclude, then, that a certain social constructionism (with regard to both social reality and individual identity or individual identifications) seems to be shared by Lacan and Castoriadis. Yet what are the specific characteristics of their respective constructionisms? Let's take a closer look. My impression is that what is also shared is the idea that constructionism cannot be absolute.

Castoriadis, for his part, is very keen to stress that the social creation or construction of reality through human signification should not be perceived as intellectualistic. As he points out, whenever he speaks about 'social imaginary significations' he is not speaking about 'intellectualistic' or 'noematic' contents. These significations organise, articulate and vest with meaning the world of each and every society by leaning each time upon the intrinsic organisation of the first natural stratum (Castoriadis 1991a: 42):

> The construction of its own world by each and every society is, in essence, the creation of a world of meanings, its social imaginary significations, which organize the (presocial, 'biologically given') natural world, instaurate a social world proper to each society (with its articulations, rules, purposes, etc.), establish the ways in which socialized and humanized individuals are to be fabricated, and institute the motives, values, and hierarchies of social (human) life. Society leans upon the first natural stratum, but only to erect a fantastically complex (and amazingly coherent) edifice of significations which vest any and every thing with meaning. (Castoriadis 1991a: 41)

In other words, Castoriadis' constructionism is not of a relativist or solipsist kind. Not only is extra-discursive, pre-social nature the subject-matter of social institution; it also poses limits and creates obstacles to human construction (Castoriadis 1978: 336).

A similar argument is put forward by social and political theorists related to the Lacanian Left. Ernesto Laclau and Chantal Mouffe are a good case in point.[10] They have consistently argued that their discourse theory (which, as we shall see in the next chapter, also involves a similar type of constructionism) is not equivalent to idealism. According to Laclau and Mouffe, to argue that all objects are constituted as objects of discourse has *nothing to do* with whether there is a world external to thought. Events like earthquakes or the falling of a brick certainly exist independently of our will. However, whether their specificity as objects will be constructed in terms of 'natural phenomena' or 'expressions of the wrath of God' depends upon their discursive articulation. What is denied here 'is not that such objects exist externally to thought, but the rather different assertion that they could constitute themselves as objects outside any discursive conditions of emergence' (Laclau and Mouffe 1985: 108). In other words, we have to do with two distinct orders of phenomena: discursive being and natural existence. Stressing the importance of the first for human societies does not dispute the irreducibility of the second.

But one can also have a strictly Lacanian tack to this problem. The aforementioned distinction between discursive being and extra-discursive existence seems to be analogous to the crucial Lacanian distinction between 'reality' and the 'real'. As we have seen in the introduction, reality here corresponds to the constructed identity of objects, whereas the real names what is not part and parcel of social construction, what is *impossible* to inscribe in its totality into any articulation of reality. More precisely, reality is what societies construct utilising their symbolic and imaginary resources:

> Cancelling out the real, the symbolic [which has the dominant role here] creates 'reality', reality as that which is named by language and can thus be thought and talked about. The 'social construction of reality' implies a world that can be designated and discussed with the words provided by a social group's (or subgroup's) language. (Fink 1995: 25)

The real, on the other hand, is what remains outside this field of representation, what remains impossible to symbolise: 'What cannot be said in its language is not part of its reality . . . The real, therefore, does not exist, since it precedes language; Lacan reserves a separate term for it, borrowed from Heidegger: it "ex-ists". It exists outside and apart of reality', both in the sense that it is there before the articulation of social reality, before the socialisation of the human infant, and in the sense of something which 'has not yet been symbolized, or even resists symbolization' and thus exists 'alongside' our socially constructed reality (Fink 1995: 25). In fact, the gap between the real and reality is unbridgeable, but this is also what stimulates human desire, the unending (ultimately failed) attempts of reality to colonise and domesticate the real, to represent it fully.[11]

One can conclude then that both Castoriadian constructionism and the constructionism characteristic of the Lacanian field are very cautious not to collapse into some kind of solipsist argumentation. In fact, it seems that they also propose a very similar articulation or interaction – in actual fact, a relation of tension, incommensurability or gap – between real and reality (Lacan), natural world and social imaginary significations (Castoriadis).[12]

The importance of constructed reality and meaning in general for humans is what accounts for what Castoriadis calls the 'defunctionalization' of the human psyche, a defunctionalisation which makes possible 'the detachment of the representation from the object of biological "need", therefore the cathexis of biologically irrelevant objects' (Castoriadis 1997a: 328). For Castoriadis, it is clear that human societies are marked by this priority of meaning over biological need. In *The Imaginary Institution of Society* he asks the following question: 'Is it not obvious that, once we leave the company of higher apes, human groups provide themselves with needs that are not simply biological?' The biological needs of a living organism are very well known; the same applies to the functions to which they correspond. But this is the case only because the biological organism does not exceed the sum of the functions it performs, all those functions that make it a living organism: 'A dog eats to live, but one could just as well say that it lives to eat: for it (and for the species, dog) living is nothing but eating, breathing, reproducing and so on. But this is meaningless with respect to a human being or to a society.' And this because human societies have to articulate all these needs and can only deal with them within 'a symbolic network', which is first encountered in language (Castoriadis 1987: 116–17). Moreover, this symbolic dependence is also what creates new 'afunctional' or even 'antifunctional' needs (Castoriadis 1997b: 357).

Such a picture is definitely congruent with our everyday experience. For example, we know that procreation presupposes sexual intercourse, but that does not reveal much about the vast alchemy of desire and sexuality marking human behaviour. As it was successfully pointed out a few years ago in a title for the *Observer Review*: 'Birds do it, bees do it, and rabbits are at it, well, as rabbits. But none of them dress up in rubber.' One cannot but be struck, furthermore, by the proximity of the Castoriadian view to the very well-known Lacanian distinction between need, demand and desire. In Lacan, the level of need and of its unmediated natural – instinctual – satisfaction is initially shared by all, human and non-human, animal life. Humanity, however, by virtue of the symbolic character of society, is forced – and/or privileged – to lose this direct, unmediated relation to need. Entering into the symbolic, into the world of language, the speaking subject loses for ever all unmediated access to a level of natural needs and of their quasi-automatic satisfaction. Every need has to be articulated in language, in a demand to the Other (initially, the mother), who is invested with the power to satisfy or frustrate them. In that sense, on top of expressing biological need, demand also functions as the vehicle through which the subject is implicated in a relation of dependence to the Other, whose recognition, approval, and love thus acquire a supreme value. Not only is this second dimension, that of demand (for unconditional love), ultimately impossible to satisfy, but exactly because it contaminates the first one, human needing is irreversibly derailed. As it is revealed in 'The signification of the phallus' and in 'The subversion of the subject and the dialectic of desire in the Freudian unconscious' (E2006), it is this difference between need and demand that introduces the dimension of desire:

'desire is neither the appetite for satisfaction [need], nor the demand for love, but the difference that results from the subtraction of the first from the second, the phenomenon of their splitting (*Spaltung*)' (E1977: 287).

In Lacanian theory desire is thus constitutive and not secondary. Human life is structured around desire. In fact, reality itself is articulated around desire in the sense that the emergence of reality (as incommensurable with the real) presupposes the loss of our unmediated access to real need, it presupposes the imposition of the symbolic. By imposing a gap between pre-symbolic need and demand, symbolic castration permits or/and forces humans to pursue their desire within a socially constructed reality. This also explains why, according to Lacan, socially conditioned desire constitutes the alienated, 'extimate' (that is, 'externally intimate' in his language) essence of our reality – but not, strictly speaking, 'the very essence of man', as Spinoza thought. Although Spinoza's statement retains an emblematic status, highlighting the importance of desire – something far from self-evident, as we shall see in Chapter 7 – Lacan points out that this reference to man cannot be retained within an atheological discourse (seminar of 16 November 1966). This is important because it leads directly to Lacan's rejection of humanism, psychologism, and subjective essentialism. It also explains why, in opposition to Castoriadis, Lacan has remained deeply suspicious of the idea of 'autonomy', especially in its 'autonomous ego' version. *Desire is always the desire of the Other*; it is conditioned by its symbolic dependence, the implication being that it is, by definition, unsatisfiable and alienating. The price for gaining access to reality (predominantly symbolic reality, socially constructed reality) is the sacrifice of the real of need. We are forced to look for it within the symbolic, soon to realise that no identification, no social construction or relation, no Other, can fully restore or recapture it for us. But it is exactly this impossibility, this lack in the Other, which keeps desire – and history – alive. We never get what we have been promised, what we were expecting from the Other, but that's exactly why we keep longing for it. Alienation is thus revealed as the other side – but also, and more crucially, the condition of possibility – of desire, of human creation and historical action.[13]

It is here, I suspect, that Lacan and Castoriadis start parting company. Starting from analogous versions of constructionism they are led to quite different conclusions. Although they both acknowledge the gap between the real and reality, between natural stratum and social imaginary significations, the conclusions they draw from that are very different: Castoriadis is led to celebrate the *creativity* of the human subject and human society, while Lacan is led to stress the constitutive *alienation* of human experience. How can we account for this paradox, and what are its consequences for contemporary ethico-political thinking and the Lacanian Left? These questions will animate my argumentation in the rest of this chapter.

The limits of constructionism: creativity and alienation

From the outset it must be emphasised that, for Lacan, creativity, construction, and alienation are two sides of the same coin. In actual fact Lacan was very interested in pursuing questions of creativity. Everyone knows, for example, that he was permanently engaged in exploring literary and artistic creation in order to open new avenues for psychoanalytic research. Indeed, some of his most famous seminars deal with the works of Sophocles, Poe, Joyce, Shakespeare, etc.[14] Of course, the objection usually is that he understood this creative force of humanity as secondary, as severely limited by some kind of structuralist conformism. What is Lacan replying, for example, to the idea of *ex nihilo* creativity put forward by Castoriadis? Well, it might surprise a few people, but Lacan would probably agree with this *ex nihilo* character of human symbolisation as a whole (after all, he devotes a whole session of his seminar – 27 January 1960 – to discussing this topic, a session which is entitled 'On creation *ex nihilo*' and forms part of his *Ethics of Psychoanalysis* – VII: 115–27).[15]

He seems, however, much more alert than Castoriadis to the price involved in human creativity, which he also takes into account. He does that by avoiding a simple replacement of the religious conception of creation *ex nihilo* by a subjectivist conception. As Chaitin has very cogently observed, Lacan's view on creativity 'differs from that of romanticism and humanism in that, instead of transferring the creative power from God to the autonomous subject, Lacan has moved it onto the signifier itself' (Chaitin 1996: 64–5). Yes, for Lacan human creativity is the only way we can attempt to recapture the lost/impossible real – the *jouissance* sacrificed upon entering the social world of language, upon articulating need in demand. But, since this attempt can only take place through symbolisation, through symbolic articulation (and imaginary representation), and since, furthermore, the symbolic is not a closed order but an inherently lacking space, ultimately incapable of bridging the gap which separates it from the real, human creativity also entails a profoundly alienating dimension.[16] There is no creation without alienation – there is no construction which is not, to some extent, alienating. In that sense there is no point in glorifying creativity; by its own measure, by the mere fact that creation relies on a medium which is unable to realise our fantasies of wholeness and autonomy, creativity loses all its romantic and humanist gloss. That is why, instead of the creative psyche or the autonomous subject, Lacan stresses the theme of lack. The subject is lacking exactly because it is unable to recapture her lost/impossible real fullness through symbolic creation or imaginary representation, because 'individual autonomy is continually deferred by its dependency on language and speech' (Barzilai 1999: 101). It is this deferral, however, that keeps desire alive and socio-political creation open.[17]

Unlike Lacan, Castoriadis looks determined to ignore or downplay this alienating dimension of creativity, of social construction. Although on a first impression he seems aware that every new social creation is quickly transformed into a new – alienating – establishment (this is one of the possible meanings of his distinction between the 'instituting' and the 'instituted'), nevertheless he compromises the importance of this distinction through the ambiguity of his position and through the fact that he eventually seems to understand meaning – and also creativity or radical imagination in general – as emanating from some kind of overdetermining source, identified with what he calls the 'psychic monad'. As Habermas has put it – admittedly with some degree of exaggeration – 'the psychic streams of the imaginary dimension have their source in the springs of each's own subjective nature' (Habermas 1987: 333). Castoriadis' explanation of social praxis is 'compelled to begin from the premise of isolated consciousness' (ibid.). It is possible and instructive to trace both the origins and the theoretical side-effects of such a strategy; and here, I suspect, the premises of my argument will be quite different from the ones put forward by Habermas.

Paradoxes of socialisation

My starting point will be Castoriadis' view of socialisation. The same pattern we saw in the last section is, in fact, repeating itself now. Castoriadis starts with a series of observations and insights which are remarkably close to, if not originating directly from, Lacanian theory – or from an interpretation of Freud which is very close to the Lacanian one. Consider, for instance, the following quotation:

> From the psychical point of view, the social fabrication of the individual is the historical process by means of which the psyche is coerced (smoothly or brutally; in fact, the process always entails violence against the proper nature of the psyche) into giving up its initial objects and its initial world (this renunciation is never total, but almost always sufficient to fulfil social requirements) and into investing (cathecting) socially instituted objects, rules and the world. (Castoriadis 1991c: 148)

Lacan could very well – and indeed *has* – put in similar terms his view of the alienating imposition of the socio-symbolic field. The fact that they both use terms like 'imposition' or 'superimposition' to refer to socialisation is indicative in this respect (Castoriadis in Urribarri 1999: 385; III: 96). Lacan would definitely agree with Castoriadis that 'the social side of this process concerns the whole complex of institutions in which the human being is steeped as soon as it is born and, first of all, the Other – generally, but not inevitably, the mother – who, already socialized in a determinate manner, takes care of the newborn and speaks a determinate language' (Castoriadis 1991c: 149). This sentence, with its explicit reference to what seems to be Lacan's Other, could easily originate from one of Lacan's seminars. In general, Castoriadis' view of socialisation is very close to the Lacanian view of the (social) process in which the pre-symbolic real, 'the infant's body before it comes under the sway of the symbolic order', 'is subjected to toilet training and instructed in the ways of the world': through socialisation, 'the body is progressively written or overwritten with signifiers; pleasure is localized in certain zones, while other zones are neutralized by the word and coaxed into compliance with social, behavioural norms' (Fink 1995: 24).[18]

The differences emerge when one inquires into the 'proper nature of the psyche', in Castoriadis' terms, and into the implications of what he calls the 'never total' imposition of the symbolic. What Castoriadis understands by the 'proper nature of the psyche' is a monadic core, a unitary and self-enclosed subjective circuit pre-existing socialisation, a psychic monad which, as we shall see, 'is far from being immune from criticism' (Whitebook 1995: 164). Castoriadis' description of socialisation can very easily lead to the conclusion that this original pre-symbolic state is radically different from, or incommensurable with, the socio-symbolic field, the field of (social) meaning. This is Whitebook's interpretation when he stresses that, 'owing to this monadic core, all socialization comes from the outside and is necessarily violent' (Whitebook 1999: 334). If one considers Castoriadis' view of socialisation together with his acceptance, at one point, that the monad is 'unsayable' (Castoriadis 1997a: 331) or 'unrepresentable' (Castoriadis 1978: 425), that 'nothing is lacking' at this stage – terms which are almost identical with definitions of the pre-symbolic real in Lacan[19] – one is easily led to the conclusion that what exists before the imposition of the symbolic is something radically different – 'heterogeneous', to use Castoriadis' exact word – from the symbolic, from the forces of language and socialisation. This is what leads Habermas to argue that Castoriadis posits a metaphysical opposition between the psyche and society, that he 'cannot provide us with a figure of the mediation between the individual and society' (Habermas 1987: 334). Without agreeing entirely with the premises of Habermas' criticisms, Whitebook also considers Castoriadis' position ultimately incoherent (Whitebook 1999: 335).

The problem, however, is where exactly the incoherence lies. From a Lacanian point of view, to highlight the radical gap between the pre-symbolic real state and subjective identity as conditioned by socialisation, a gap that stands at the root of the ontological imbalance marking human life, does not entail any theoretical or analytical incoherence. In Lacanian terms, this pre-social state of the infant's body can only be approached by means of the concept of the real; it is impossible to describe it in any fully positive way, precisely because any description can only take place through language and discursive meaning and this real state is located before the imposition of the symbolic.[20] I suspect that the incoherence, the essential ambiguity of Castoriadis' work lies in the fact that, although on the one hand the psychic monad and the social meanings imposed through socialisation seem radically incommensurable, on the other hand there is something very important linking the pre-symbolic psychic monad and the socio-symbolic meanings, something rather ignored by both Habermas and Whitebook. It is here that Castoriadis follows a course radically different from the one chosen by Lacan. All this is evident in Castoriadis' reply to Whitebook: although he claims that there is 'ontological alterity' between the monadic universe and the 'diurnal universe of signs', of shared significations, he nevertheless insists that there is something in the psyche that renders it capable of language and amenable to socialisation, something associated with the fact that, 'from the outset, the psyche is in *meaning*' (Castoriadis 1997d: 377).

Paradoxically, then, although the psychic monad exists before the imposition of meaning (insofar as meaning is socially produced), it is nevertheless a *meaningful* state. As Castoriadis puts it, 'this mode of originary being of the psyche . . . is the first matrix of meaning'. The paradox is, of course, as Castoriadis himself ascertains, that this 'proto-meaning realizes by itself, just where meaning obviously cannot yet exist, total meaning' (Castoriadis 1987: 299). This 'meaning of meaning', as Castoriadis calls it, refers to 'the coincidence of self-image with the representation of a satisfied desire and with the representation of all that is' (Urribarri 1999: 379). The proto-meaning is what characterises an inherent and irreducible ability to create representations: 'the radical imagination pre-exists and presides over every organization of drives, even the most primitive ones' (Castoriadis 1987: 287). In this original monadic state, then, this proto-meaning understood as radical imagination is 'all that operates within a psyche totally enclosed upon itself' (Leledakis 1995: 111). This self-enclosed monadic core is ruptured by the pressure entailed in somatic need and by the presence of other human beings (the Other in Lacan), as the psyche's continued existence in a monadic state is antagonistic to biological and psychic survival (Urribarri 1999: 379). As a result, the 'initial, monadic meaning' is disrupted through socialisation and replaced by the meaning supplied by society: 'Socialisation is the process whereby the psyche is forced to abandon (never fully) its pristine solipsistic meaning for the shared meanings provided by society' (Castoriadis 1997a: 331). In order for the psyche to be socialised, it has to abandon its own meaning and assume the meaning (orientations, actions, roles) of society (p. 334). This is how Castoriadis summarises his own position:

> What, then, is there 'in common' between psyche and society, where is the 'mediation' or the 'point of identity'? For both, there is and there has to be nonfunctional meaning . . . But this meaning is . . . of another nature in each of the two cases. Psyche demands meaning, but society makes it renounce (though never completely) what for the psyche is its proper meaning and forces it to find meaning in the S.I.S. and in institutions. (Castoriadis 1997d: 379)

It is here that a fundamental difference from the Lacanian orientation emerges. While in Lacanian theory the two states are incommesurable, marked by the constitutive gap between the real and the symbolic, Castoriadis seems to disavow this gap, to disavow the constitutive alienation marking subjectivity (including all human creations) within the social world. He introduces a sense of continuity – continuity of meaning – which becomes in his schema a somewhat essentialist ground or source of creativity. In Castoriadis' view – an admitedly ambiguous view, which explains why Whitebook can offer an opposite interpretation to the one I am advancing – the replacement of primal representations by the ones acquired through perception and the external, socially constructed environment 'is facilitated by the fact that the two levels of representations are considered as sharing essentially the same modality' (Leledakis 1995: 132). From a Lacanian perspective the incoherence here is obvious: by stressing the continuity between pre-symbolic and socio-symbolic meaning, in fact by introducing the essentialist idea of a paradoxical original (pre-symbolic) proto-meaning and positing it as the source of creativity, of an original radical imagination, Castoriadis is led towards a romantic and vitalist Cartesianism which fails to account in a coherent way for the dialectics of desire marking human life. By highlighting his 'meaning of meaning', the prototype of creativity that is the psychic monad, Castoriadis seems to be revealing to us the true face of 'the Other of the Other', the lost prototype of meaning to which every new meaning subsequently refers, the *immanent* guarantee of truth in the real, which is posited as always already *in meaning*. Although – to be fair to his argument – Castoriadis falls sort of providing a complete positivisation (imaginarisation) of the pre-symbolic real, there is little doubt that, starting from a quasi-Lacanian account of socialisation, he is eventually led to exactly the opposite conclusions from Lacan, at the same time contaminating his theory with a strong metaphysical, essentialist and immanentist element.

This conclusion can be further corroborated by an examination of the Castoriadian account of the state of affairs following socialisation. From a Lacanian point of view, the fact that the imposition of the symbolic is never total can only mean that the real, being ultimately incommensurable with the symbolic, resists symbolisation and persists alongside our socio-symbolic identifications. In fact it not only persists but also interacts with the socio-symbolic field in a variety of ways, which will be explored throughout this book. First of all – and this does not exhaust the modalities of the real in Lacanian theory – it persists through the continuous resurfacing of negativity, through the dislocation of subjective and social identities. By encircling these encounters with the real, Lacan seems to register the importance of a moment that, in social and political theory, could only be described as the moment of the political *par excellence*. Thus, far from entailing anti-political implications, Lacan's insistence on the persistence and irreducibility of the real, a real which poses limits to human construction, to our creativity and autonomy, but at the same time constitutes the condition of possibility for any creative political reconstruction, constitutes an opening towards fully acknowledging the constitutivity of the moment of the political. The political here is crucial in relating creativity to alienation, construction to dislocation – and vice versa. It refers to the moment of failure of a given identity or social construction; a failure which not only dislocates the identity in question but also creates a lack, stimulating the desire for a rearticulation of the dislocated structure, stimulating, in other words, human creativity, becoming the condition of possibility for human freedom. Unable to accept the argument that desire and creation are conditioned by dislocation and by the lack of the real, Castoriadis posits an always already meaningful, immanent proto-creativity:

> Castoriadis maintains that the answer to the paradox of representation cannot be found 'outside representation itself' and that an 'original representation' must be posited that, as a schema of 'figuration', would 'contain within itself the possibility of organizing all representations' and, as such, would be the condition of possibility of all further representations in the psyche. (Whitebook 1995: 171)

But let us take one step at a time. Castoriadis' fascinating and inspiring work is complex and at times ambiguous, and so it is important to reconstruct his argument in detail. At first it seems that he is himself moving in a direction similar to that of Lacanian theory:

> Considered in itself, therefore, the instituting ground-power and its realization by the institution should be absolute and should shape the individuals in such a fashion that they are bound to reproduce eternally the regime which has produced them . . . If this finality were strictly fulfilled, there would be no history. We know, however, that this is not true. Instituted society never succeeds in wielding its ground-power in an absolute manner . . . Seen as absolute and total, the ground-power of the instituted society and of tradition is therefore, sooner or later, bound to fail. (Castoriadis 1991c: 151)

Every instituted social form, every symbolic/material creation, is always limited. Limited by something which seems to resemble the Lacanian real:

> the world qua 'presocial world' – a limit for any thought – though in itself signifying nothing, is always there as inexhaustible provision of alterity and as the always imminent risk of laceration of the web of significations

with which society has lined it. The *a-meaning* of the world is always a possible threat for the meaning of society. Thus the ever-present risk that the social edifice of significations will totter. (Castoriadis 1991c: 152)

What Lacan would call an encounter with the real, what one could interpret as the moment of the political, takes in Castoriadis the form of a 'shock'. If encounters with the real can dislocate our constructions of reality, leading at the same time to new symbolisations, shocks, according to Castoriadis, create the need for new representations, representations of what Lacan would call the unrepresentable real, and which Castoriadis calls the 'ultimately undescribable X "out there"': 'The ultimately indescribable X "out there" becomes something definite and specific for a particular being, through the functioning of its sensory and logical imagination, which "filters", "forms", and "organizes" the external "shocks"' (Castoriadis 1997a: 327).[21]

Up until here, then, Castoriadis and Lacan seem to be, once more, in agreement. From now on, however, they part company again. And this is because Castoriadis introduces something else, a *supplement* contradicting the logic exposed up to now. While Lacan views the inside and the outside as two intertwined dimensions (thus coining the term *extimité*), Castoriadis introduces a sharp distinction between the inside and the outside. According to his view, 'we do not have to do only with representations provoked by external "shocks". In relative (and often absolute) independence from these, we do have an "inside"'(ibid.). Whereas when speaking about the outside he seems to accept the Lacanian schema of a gap between the real and the symbolic, a-meaning and meaning, when discussing the inside he sees no gap at all. The inside is homogeneous, described as 'a perpetual, truly Heraclitean flux of representations *cum* affects *cum* intentions' (ibid.). There is no a-meaning here; everything is reduced to a field of (different) representations. This homogeneity is sustained despite the fact that the inside comprises two completely different moments. It comprises, first, what constitutes the human infant before the imposition of the symbolic, what Lacan would describe as a pre-symbolic *real* state.[22] Second, it comprises the subject as it is produced through socialisation, through, that is to say, the imposition of the symbolic order. It seems that, for Castoriadis, despite the crucial differences between these two states, there is also a crucial continuity. As we have already seen, both states are related to the level of meaning (even if different types of meaning are involved).

In Lacanian theory the two states are incommensurable.[23] In Castoriadis' work, though, the gap between them is annulled whenever we are dealing with relations of interiority. A continuity of meaning is introduced which becomes, in his schema, the undisputable ground or source of creativity. Although he sees socialisation as entailing the replacement of the original monadic meaning by social meanings, he argues that the 'constitution of the social individual does not and cannot abolish the psyche's creativity, its perpetual alteration, the representative flux as the emergence of other representations' (Leledakis 1995: 113). As we have seen, the subject's original monadic creativity cannot be eliminated, wholly replaced by social meanings; the monadic meaning, source of creativity, is never fully abandoned or repressed, the imposition of the symbolic is never total, the renunciation of the psyche's proper meaning is never completely effected. As Urribarri has put it, 'the idea of the monad as original mode of being of the psyche remains, even after its breakup, the background polarizing subsequent psychical life' (Urribarri 1999: 380).

The problems with maintaining such an – ultimately inconsistent – position must have become by now clear. The difference with Lacan is not only that in his theory the original state belongs to the register of the real, the pre-symbolic real, while for Castoriadis we have to do with an original meaning ('the proto-meaning of the psychic monad'), a primordial symbolisation/imaginarisation, the 'Other of the Other'. It is also that what in Lacan ultimately remains in the field of unrepresentability and can only thus function as the (absent) cause of desire and creation becomes in Castoriadis a lost (but, in principle, representable) point of reference. Only thus can it function as a meaningful prototype. Only thus is it possible to prioritise an essentialist, subjectivist creativity and to avoid acknowledging the constitutive alienation which marks human life, the fact that desire and creation are marked by an irreducible dialectics between positive and negative and cannot make sense without it.

Encountering the political

To conclude this chapter, what is taking place here is a *disavowal* of the real, which is at the same time recognised as the *limit* in relations of exteriority but is forgotten when dealing with relations of interiority. The only explanation for this inconsistent and contradictory position – positing a continuity of the subjective space as a space of meaning, a space marked by the proto-meaning of the psychic monad – seems to be Castoriadis' desire to guarantee at all costs the prospects for a politics of radical, totally unrestrained imagination. It is not that Castoriadis completely excludes the possibility that something can go wrong. He simultaneously registers and forgets this alienating prospect, avoiding to reflect on its implications for political creativity and imagination. This is precisely why the psychoanalytic category of *disavowal* is a fitting description of his position.[24]

Here the affinities between Castoriadis' work and the immanentism of Negri are also revealed. Consider, for example, this quotation – it is Negri but could very well be Castoriadis:

> I cannot conceive of time other than as *kairos*, and so never as corruption and death . . . to think that temporality could have 'destruction' as its name is meaningless, because the temporality that we experience and that we live through is that of *kairos* and of the creative act that constitutes it – and only that. In being, 'all is created and nothing is destroyed' within the immediacy of the present. (Negri 2003: 164)

Castoriadis' vitalist focus on creativity and on its grounding in an immanent space of meaning underlying human life finds a clear ally in Negri, who identifies immanence with the dynamism of life: 'Generation is irreducible: the horrible fairy-tale that considers corruption and destruction as its necessary complements is merely the illusion of an immobile world, of a cosmos that adds up to zero, of a being deprived of love' (p. 187). Against this, Negri paints a more rosy picture: 'once generated, being is no longer inclined towards death, and generation holds for eternity' (p. 212).[25] Similarly, in Castoriadis' schema the ontological moment of social construction is not related to our encounters with the political, to the moment of social dislocation and subjective alienation and lack, but to a primordial source of human creativity associated, in certain respects, with the pre-symbolic psychic monad. In what he calls 'a parenthesis of hatred', Lyotard speaks of 'the great cesspool of consolations called *spontaneity* and *creativity*,' over which he broke, in 1964, with Castoriadis, 'who, rightly bored with reassessing historical, dialectic and diarrhoetic materialism, nevertheless proposed to put in its place the abominable super-male thing of generalised creativity . . . against alienation, this always active creativity. Every-where and always, creativity' (Lyotard 1993: 116). Thus Castoriadis is ultimately led to adopt what dangerously flirts with an essentialist and subjectivist view: 'Castoriadis' notion of imagination remains within the existentialist horizon of man as the being who projects its "essence" in the act of imagination transcending all positive being' (Žižek 1999: 24). Only the Cartesian tradition could lie behind such an imaginary 'super-subject' of the self-instituting society (Simopoulos 2000: 583), and this Cartesian association is pointed out even by supporters of Castoriadis' views (Whitebook 1999: 333). Ironically, the Cartesian element is coupled with a clearly romantic idealisation of human imagination and creativity reminiscent of a Coleridge.[26]

The moment of the encounter with the political, the moment when the limits of human creativity and autonomy become visible – limits which are due to the fact that we are always attempting to recapture the impossible real through our inadequate symbolic means, due to the radical distance between pre-symbolic and post-symbolic states – is disavowed by Castoriadis in favour of the autonomy of an essentialised subject. It is not surprising, then, that Castoriadis was adverse to the use of the concept of the political in theoretical discourse, especially when discussing the institution of the social. In 'Power, politics, autonomy' he argues very clearly that the gains to be made by associating 'the political' with the overall institution of society 'are hard to see, but the dangers are obvious' (Castoriadis 1991c: 158).[27] Frankly, the only danger I see is the danger of exposing the essentialism of Castoriadis' theoretical apparatus, which is, however, impossible to conceal. His disavowal of the political serves only to legitimise the following conclusion: it is not Lacanian theory which is anti-political; what is anti-political, and here I fully endorse Paul Ricoeur's position, is something else, something very close to Castoriadis' heart: it is 'the theory of autonomy [which] is anti-political by principle' (Ricoeur 1986: xii).

Does that mean, however, that the radical politics promoted by Castoriadis is reduced to a mere impossibility? Is some kind of reactionary or cynical conformism the only political option left? More specifically, what could be the future of the democratic politics of transformation after recognising the real limits to creativity, after acknowledging the continuous interpenetration between positivity and negativity, creativity and alienation? Castoriadis is obviously afraid that registering the irreducible force of alienation, antagonism and dislocation, can endanger the prospects of radical change – of imagining a better future – and discourage political participation. Lacanian theory does not share this fear. Apart from leading to a theoretically contradictory position, the (utopian) disavowal of negativity and alienation can also disorient radical politics, which always involves an impure (re)negotiation of the ever-present link between creation and alienation: it cannot hope to eliminate exclusion and antagonism but can continuously displace and redraw their frontiers. Lacan's first answer to these questions is his elaboration of the category of the *point de capiton*, the 'nodal point' in Laclau and Mouffe's vocabulary. The *point de capiton*, a concept which originates in the Lacanian understanding of psychosis, is used to describe the signifier which, in every chain of signification, serves as reference point, the 'anchoring point' uniting a whole set of signifiers.[28] For example, it is always a *point de capiton* that puts together an ideological discourse; the 'class' in Marxism or 'nature' in Green ideology. The 'new' in politics is always related to the emergence of a new signifier, a new ideal which comes to occupy the place of the organising principle of a discursive field and of associated subjective identities.[29] In opposition to any conformism, structuralist or other, Lacan never denies the possibility of a radical rearticulation of the predominant symbolic order. As Žižek has put it, 'this is what his notion of the *point de capiton* (the "quilting point" or the Master-signifier) is about: when a new *point de capiton* emerges, the socio-symbolic field is not only displaced, its very structuring principle changes' (Žižek 1999: 262).

Furthermore, this rearticulation is radical because it involves 'the intervention of the Real of an act' (ibid.). However, it neither springs from nor is guaranteed by any primordial essence or source of representation. More importantly, such a rearticulation becomes possible through the contingent dislocation of a pre-existing discursive order, through a certain resurfacing of the traumatic real which shows the limits of the social; the moment of the political creates a lack in the discursive structure and only thus can it stimulate the desire for a new articulation.[30] *It is also something which mostly surprises its agent itself*. After an act of this sort the reaction usually is: 'I myself do not know how I was able to do that' (Žižek 1998a: 14). In Lacanian political theory, *ex nihilo* does not imply any association with the remnants of primordial subjectivity in the sense of positing a supposed proto-meaning of the psychic monad. It invokes something radically transforming both for the symbolic order and for subjectivity itself, beyond any imaginary voluntarism: 'the act as real is an event which occurs *ex nihilo*, without any fantasmatic support. As such . . . it is also to be opposed to the subject' (ibid.).

It follows that, within such a context, the role of political theory can only be to encourage the creation and institutionalisation of political arrangements which make possible the continuous rearticulation of the socio-symbolic field, through the real acts of *capitonnage*. These arrangements can only be associated with the democratic revolution. Democracy is primarily 'about the permanent creation of the new' (Unger 2005: 156), and about ensuring 'everyone's power to share in the permanent creation of the new' (p. 23). Yet, if today the radicalisation of democracy is perhaps the most pressing task for a progressive politics and for the Lacanian Left, this radicalisation can be based neither on some kind of romantic foundationalism nor on any subjective essentialism. If democracy is marked, in Lefort's classical definition (to which I shall return), by the negative, the emptiness in the locus of power, an emptiness making possible the creative rearticulation of the social order, then the radicalisation of democracy can only pass through what today emerges, in a variety of politico-theoretical projects, as a self-critical, anti-essentialist and pro-democratic ethos.[31]

This is not, however, the end of the story. In fact, it is only the beginning. This is why, when linking the Lacanian real with the disruptive moment of the political, I stressed the fact that this linkage offers us only a first indication of what takes place at the intersection of the real with the symbolic. This is also why, when discussing the political importance of Lacan's *capitonnage*, I indicated that this can only be a first formulation of what is at stake in political identification. So, what else does the real imply? What else is at stake in political struggles? All that will be explored in the following chapter. What is certain is that it will have nothing to do with Castoriadis' idealised prototypes of imagination.

Notes

1. Nor can it be (solely) attributed to an expression of sublimated nationalism based on our shared Greek origin.
2. He is also the only one of the theorists examined in Part I who became a practising psychoanalyst.
3. For another example, see A. Elliott's work, in which one finds the following conclusion: 'Lacan's emphasis on the inescapability of alienation within the signifier, his characterization of desire as "lack" structured around the symbolic order, his reconceptualization of the unconscious within a universal and ahistoric structure of language – these and other related aspects of his theory would seem to forestall, rather than promote, critical social inquiry' (Elliott 1992: 163). Elliott seems to have softened his view of Lacanian theory lately, although not to a substantial degree. See, for his more recent position, Elliott 1999. I have

already dealt with some of his criticisms in Stavrakakis 1999a, especially chs 3 and 4.
4. Moreover, this is also what permits Jacques-Alain Miller to point out, in an encyclopaedic article written in 1979, two years before Lacan's death, that, although structure is important for Lacan, he is clearly not a structuralist, since the structure characteristic of structuralism is coherent and complete, while Lacan's structure is antinomical and lacking (Miller 1981). Hence the current appropriation of Lacanian theory by many post-structuralist authors.
5. A concept which was deprived of any meaning in structuralism, in opposition again to Lacanian theory, within which it is assigned a prominent place. In that sense to blame Lacan for the 'death of the subject' (Curtis 1999: 326) can only be treated as a slip of the tongue.
6. The idea that Lacanian theory is, by nature, anti-historical is, of course, a common criticism. It has even been shared by Stuart Hall, who argues that 'the transhistorical speculative generalities of Lacanianism' deny its usefulness in the analysis of historically specific phenomena (Hall 1988: 50–1). Lacanian theory is thus declared unable to provide a plausible understanding of history or politics.

At first glance, this critique sounds justified. Isn't psychoanalysis always implying a negation of history, with its acceptance, for example, of the universality of the Oedipus complex? However, as Dylan Evans has shown, a close reading of Lacan's texts reveals that structures and features like this are presented by Lacan as arising at specific moments in history: 'By grounding psychic structure in historical processes, Lacan makes it clear that no account of subjectivity, psychoanalytic or otherwise, can claim an eternal ahistorical validity' (Evans 1997: 142). Already in 1946, in his 'Presentation on psychical causality', Lacan suggested that 'the Oedipus complex did not appear with the origin of man (assuming that it is not altogether senseless to try to write the history of this complex), but at the threshold of history, of "historical" history, at the limit of "ethnographic" cultures. It can obviously appear only in the patriarchal form of the family as an institution, but it nevertheless has an indisputably liminary value' (E2006: 150). Simply put, Lacan is open to historical analysis. Furthermore, as Joan Copjec and Slavoj Žižek have shown, he introduces a novel conception of historicity, directly relevant for political analysis (Copjec 1994; Žižek 1992).

More recently, in a collective volume written by Judith Butler, Ernesto Laclau and Slavoj Žižek, Butler raises the same issue by referring to the 'ahistorical recourse to the Lacanian bar' only to receive the following answer by Laclau: 'I do not see any validity in Butler's claim that the notion of a structural limit – conceived in this way – militates against the notion of historical variation. It is precisely because there is such a structural limit that historical variation becomes possible'

(Laclau in Butler et al. 2000: 185). On the question of Lacan and history, also see Stavrakakis 1999b.
7. Something that gives the opportunity to David Fel, in one of the very few published articles that attempt a parallel reading of Lacan and Castoriadis, to argue that, 'in spite of the fundamental differences, the alternative readings of Freud offered by Castoriadis (1987) and Lacan are similarly motivated by the desire to restore Freud's radical view of the unconscious . . . in the face of subsequent neo-Freudian and ego-psychological revisions' (Fel 1993: 161). Unfortunately, exploring the relation between the interpretations of Freud put forward by Castoriadis and Lacan largely falls outside the scope of this chapter. It constitutes, however, a promising area for further research.
8. Of course this is not the only such nodal point. As we shall see in the next chapter, apart from the subject of the signifier, one needs to take into account the subject of *jouissance*.
9. Needless to say, the 'imaginary' is invested with quite different meanings in Castoriadis and Lacan. In this chapter, largely due to space limitations, judgement is suspended on the plausibility of Castoriadis' definition. In any case, I don't consider this issue to be of crucial importance, provided that one makes the appropriate 'translations' when necessary.
10. One of the reasons I am referring here to these two theorists is the almost uncanny resemblance between their theoretical trajectory and the structure of their *Hegemony and Socialist Strategy* (Laclau and Mouffe 1985) and Castoriadis' *Imaginary Institution* (Castoriadis 1987). Both books start with an exhaustive critique (or deconstruction) of various Marxist themes before embarking on a post-Marxist theoretical journey. However, at least to my knowledge, no parallel reading of the two projects has been undertaken yet.
11. In that sense the frontiers between the real and the imaginary/symbolic nexus are being continuously displaced as long as humans follow their desire fully to symbolise the escaping real. This continuous displacement, however, is not capable of bridging the ontological gap between reality and the real, the discursive and the extra-discursive in the vocabulary of discourse analysis, thus falsifying all predictions of the end of history. It is in this vein that Žižek argues that the only way to save a sense of historicity from collapsing to historicism, into a conception of linear succession of historical epochs, is to construe these epochs as a series of ultimately failed attempts to represent and fully control the impossible real, to fulfil our desire.
12. This analogy between the real and the natural world does make sense simply because the real, together with other Lacanian concepts, does not pertain solely to psychic/subjective life but 'applies as much to a child's body as to the whole universe' (Fink 1995: 24). This is hardly surprising for a concept which Lacan seems to appropriate from the work of

the French philosopher of science Émile Meyerson, but may also be traced back to Kojève's seminars on Hegel.

13. In that sense the fact that desire 'seeks after an impossibility', that it is always, by constitution, contentless, that it is 'the desire of the Other', does not mean that desire is articulated with reference to the locus of a supposedly (closed) Other, as if the Other's desire is out there, fully constituted and ready for us to copy: 'Lacan's answer to this mistaken interpretation of his formula is simply that we have no image of the Other's desire . . . and it is this very lack which causes our desire' (Copjec 1994: 36, 55).

14. His very strong interest in questions of origins and creation is also – amusingly – revealed in the fact that he owned the notorious nude painting by Gustave Courbet entitled *L' origine du monde* – now hanging at the Musée d' Orsay in Paris. For the full story of Lacan's relation to this painting, see Barzilai 2000.

15. This theme returns again in other seminars. See for example his seminar on *The Object of Psychoanalysis* (1965–6), and especially the session of 8 December 1965.

16. To return to the preceding discussion on need – which is relevant here since it concerns one of the sources of this alienating dimension – Lacan observes that it is due to the fact that we speak, due, that is to say, to our symbolic dependence, that we are subject to a 'deviation' of our needs, in the sense that, 'in so far as needs are subjected to demand, they return to [us] alienated' (E1977: 286). Alienation, however, is not only linked with the symbolic but also with the imaginary. As it is clear in Lacan's conception of the mirror stage, the imaginary identity acquired through identification with the mirror image entails a profoundly alienating dimension (E1977: 2).

17. I will return to this Lacanian understanding of creativity towards the end of the present chapter.

18. As we will see in detail in the next chapter, this process is not without remainders, remainders with important subjective as well as social and political implications:

> As we become human, we lose something. Our needs are alienated in the language systems of our care-givers. We stop stimulating our body surface to produce enjoyment, we learn the rules of bodily conduct and cleanliness, we are taken up in the universe of signs with all its laws and prohibitions. A void, or emptiness, is thus created. Our enjoyment will then take refuge in edges, in erogenous zones which are like leftovers, remnants. The activity of drives aims at recuperating some of this enjoyment that has been drained from the body. (Leader 2002: 58)

19. This is what probably leads someone like Elliott to argue that 'Castoriadis' starting position – that is, that the psyche is initially closed

in upon itself – ultimately puts him in a position connected with the Lacanians', albeit he is led to this conclusion for the wrong reasons (Elliott 1999: 61).
20. As a result, anything we can say about it can only have the status of a hypothesis, a fiction (XI: 163) or even a myth. Lacan is not against the formulation of such myths insofar as they are designed to encircle the impossibility, the lack, that stimulates their construction. This is how he constructs his own myth of *lamella*, of libido as 'pure life instinct, that is to say, immortal life, or irrepressible life', life before sexuation and symbolisation (XI: 198). Here real and unreal are joined. Lamella is unreal, it is pure fiction, a mythical construction. Moreover, it is presented exactly like that. But this is an unreal 'in direct contact with the real' (E2006: 718). It simultaneously points to the necessity of positing a pre-symbolic real and registers the impossibility of its representation in meaning: 'This organ is unreal. Unreal is not imaginary. The unreal is defined by articulating itself on the real in a way that eludes us, and it is precisely this that requires that its representation should be mythical' (XI: 205).
21. It is very revealing that Žižek occasionally uses similar expressions to refer to the Lacanian real.
22. A real which, in opposition to Castoriadis' view, should be taken in its totality, 'both the real of the subject and the real he has to deal with as exterior to him' (VII: 118).
23. Which does not mean, of course, that they do not enter into a variety of relations, as we shall discover in the next chapter. The question is whether in order to conceptualise these relations it is necessary to posit a commonality of meaning or not. Here Lacan's answer is very different from the one of Castoriadis as well as from the one Laclau will initially give.
24. More on the status of disavowal can be found in Chapter 3.
25. In fact, the similarities do not end here. For example, the homology between Castoriadis' opposition between *instituted* and *instituting* and the opposition between *constituted* and *constituting* in Hardt and Negri's *Empire* should not pass unnoticed.
26. Creative imagination constitutes one of the central axes of the Romantic *Weltanschauung*. To oppose Enlightenment alienation, the romantic subject invests in what is presented as a primarily imaginary force, a force of creative energy which pre-dates the real (Rozanis 2001: 134). Although psychoanalysis developed on a terrain prepared by the romantic critique of objectivist science as neglecting the dark forces of the unconscious (Berlin 2002: 215), neither Freud nor Lacan will adopt a romantic stance vis-à-vis science or formalisation.
27. This does not mean that a re-introduction of the concept of the political within a theoretical framework influenced by Castoriadis is impossible. For a brilliant example of such an attempt, see Kalyvas 2000.

28. Lacan's invention of the *point de capiton* also uses the notion of assembling opposites in a new unity, derived from Heidegger's article 'Logos', which Lacan translated for the first number of the journal *La Psychanalyse* in 1956 (Chaitin 1996: 65).
29. For an example of the use of the Lacanian logic of *capitonnage* in political analysis, see my account of the discursive articulation of Green ideology in Stavrakakis 1997a.
30. For an analysis of the emergence of a concrete ideological form along these lines, see my analysis of the emergence of Green ideology in Stavrakakis 2000b.
31. Notwithstanding all the aforementioned problems, such an ethos is not alien to Castoriadis' conceptualisation of democracy, something I will be discussing in the final chapter of this book.

2
Laclau with Lacan on *Jouissance*:
Negotiating the Affective Limits of Discourse

The discursive appropriation of Lacan: accomplishments and limitations

If Castoriadis constitutes the (extimate) frontier of the emerging Lacanian Left, two of its pivotal figures are certainly Ernesto Laclau and Chantal Mouffe. For a start, they have both exhibited, again and again, their increasing readiness to take on board many crucial Lacanian insights in their innovative analysis of political discourse and in reorienting the political theory of the Left in the direction of a 'radical and plural democracy'. In their joint work, theoretical affinities with Lacanian thought are evident from at least the time of *Hegemony and Socialist Strategy* (Laclau and Mouffe 1985), if not earlier. This is not to argue, of course, that during the mid-eighties Lacanian theory is already the main theoretical reference in the work of Laclau and Mouffe or in that of Laclau alone. The relative importance of Lacanian argumentation was to increase in Laclau's subsequent work – partly due to the whole dialogue that took place after 1985 between Laclau, Žižek and others – leaving a distinctive mark on his theoretical trajectory, most notably in *New Reflections on the Revolution of our Time* (Laclau 1990), and in *Emancipation(s)* (Laclau 1996). Since then, such affinities have been subject to further exploitation, culminating in *On Populist Reason* (Laclau 2005). It is true that, in terms of their solo work, Laclau has devoted much more space and effort to discussing Lacanian theory than Mouffe. Accordingly, this chapter will primarily focus on his work. From the outset, however, it has to be emphasised that no global overview of Laclau's approach will be articulated; that would exceed the scope of the present book.

I have dealt elsewhere in genealogical detail with the conceptual and theoretical affinities between Lacanian theory and Laclau's (and Mouffe's) work.[1] First of all, there is often a straightforward terminological cross-over. Think, for example, of terms like suture, identification, and the subject of lack. But there is also an apparently close conceptual affinity, even when the names of concepts are not shared. Think, for example, of the nodal point, the empty signifier, the radically excluded, the impossibility of society, or the notion of an outside that is constitutive of the inside (roughly corresponding to the Lacanian concepts of the *point de capiton*, the master signifier, the *objet petit a*, the lack in the Other, and *extimité*). Indeed, conceptual affinities such as these make up a fairly extensive reservoir, from which especially Laclau does not hesitate to draw in elaborating further his discursive approach to political analysis.

Laclau himself has explicitly acknowledged a strong Lacanian influence upon his work. As he clearly points out in a 1993 interview, although 'Lacanian theory played an important role in my theoretical trajectory at least from the beginning of the eighties . . . this influence has increased during these last years' (Laclau 1993: 58). This has led him to a very important redefinition of some of the categories of his theory of hegemony: one can think of the shift from a conception of subjectivity in terms of 'subject positions' to acknowledging the importance of understanding subjectivity in terms of the subject as lack, a redefinition put forward in *New Reflections*. Moreover, he has also actively defended his Lacanian 'turn' in the most uncompromising terms. In his 2000 exchange with Judith Butler and Slavoj Žižek, he finds himself 'allied with Žižek against Butler in the defence of Lacanian theory' (Laclau in Butler et al. 2000: 281), concluding that Butler's 'objections to incorporating the Lacanian Real into the explanation of hegemonic logics are not valid' (p. 182). As we shall see, his support of Lacanian theory has recently become even more explicit. The same applies to Mouffe who, in *The Democratic Paradox*, concludes her argument with an endorsement of Lacanian ethics as crucial for agonistic pluralism and radical democracy (Mouffe 2000: 129–40).

What has to be stressed here is that the relation between discourse theory and Lacanian psychoanalysis is twofold, and this is what makes the situation entirely different from the one discussed in the previous chapter, simultaneously locating Laclau's project at the forefront of the theoretico-political adventure of the Lacanian Left. In what sense is it twofold?

1. On the one hand, of course, Laclau (and Mouffe) share the constructionist profile characteristic of the arguments of Lacan (and

Castoriadis). In the most general terms, the problem of identity is not a problem of people discovering or recognising their true, essential identity but rather of *constructing* it (Laclau 1994: 2). Modernity, and especially late modernity, with its increased awareness of contingency, reveals the socially and politically constructed character of all and every identity: 'The more the "foundation" of the social is put into question, the less the sedimented social practices are able to ensure social reproduction' and the more we recognise that 'a dimension of construction and creation is inherent in all social practice. The latter do not involve only repetition, but also reconstruction' (pp. 3–4).

It is worth noting at this point that what has often been misconceived or downplayed in the various readings of Laclau and Mouffe's work – especially when it is mistakenly linked with a postmodern conception highlighting the fluidity of identity – is their persistent attempts to account for the ways in which societies, groups and subjects try to inject some kind of (relative) fixity in their identity constructions. Hence the introduction of a whole theoretical and conceptual apparatus capable of helping us to map this terrain of social construction and political institution, an apparatus elaborated at the intersection between discourse theory and psychoanalysis.

An early example of such conceptual cross-fertilisation is the already-mentioned 'nodal point', as developed in *Hegemony and Socialist Strategy*. The nodal point, with its distinct Lacanian origins, functions as a central category in discourse theory, designed to explain how meaning achieves a (partial) fixation without which social and political discourse would surely disintegrate into psychotic rumbling and no political institution would be possible:

> Any discourse is constituted as an attempt to dominate the field of discursivity, to arrest the flow of differences, to construct a centre. We will call the privileged discursive points of this partial fixation, *nodal points*. (Lacan has insisted on these partial fixations through his concept of *points de capiton*, that is, of privileged signifiers that fix the meaning of a signifying chain. This limitation of the productivity of the signifying chain establishes the positions that make predication possible – a discourse incapable of generating any fixity of meaning is the discourse of the psychotic). (Laclau and Mouffe 1985: 112)[2]

A similar appropriation is performed vis-à-vis other Lacanian concepts such as 'metaphor' and 'metonymy' (the two different axes along which every partial fixation of meaning is crystallised), which are used in a theoretically sophisticated account of how political space is represented within discourse (following the logics of 'equivalence' and 'difference').[3]

2. On the other hand, however, and in opposition to Castoriadis' ultimate disavowal, Laclau and Mouffe also accept the crucial idea that human creativity and construction have precise limits – which are, moreover, not purely prohibitive and castrating but also enabling, internal to the continuous (re)construction of social and political identity. Hence, in Laclau's work, *dislocation* constitutes the ultimate ontological horizon of human construction and discourse (Laclau 1990). But the lack produced by dislocations is not purely negative; it is also productive: 'one needs to identify with something because there is an originary . . . lack of identity' (Laclau 1994: 3). This acceptance of a (productive) negative ontology is what brings Laclau so close to the Lacanian problematic in one of its essential and most revealing aspects. For in Lacanian theory, Laclau's 'discourse' – roughly equivalent to Lacan's symbolic, the order of the signifier – is similarly revealed as lacking: it attempts the impossible, that is to say, the representation of something ultimately unrepresentable. Both at the subjective and at the objective level there is always a real which escapes our attempts to master it, to represent it, to symbolise it. It is the impossibility of mastering this real, which splits subjective and objective reality, that creates and sustains desire.

Simply put, lack not only marks the Lacanian subject, it also splits the big Other, our socio-symbolic reality (Žižek 1989: 122). This is 'the big secret of psychoanalysis', as Lacan calls it already in his 1958–9 seminar. And isn't this what Ernesto Laclau calls the ultimate 'impossibility of society'? In this regard, Lacanian psychoanalysis is indispensable for discourse theory to the extent that it reveals how understanding social reality is equivalent to understanding not what society is, but what prevents it from being (Laclau 1990: 44), thus elevating its (re)creation into the prime object of socio-political desire. It is at the moment of this prevention, which simultaneously generates new attempts to construct this impossible object – society – that 'the moment of the political' is surfacing and resurfacing again and again. A moment which takes the form of rupture, crisis, dislocation and leads to new attempts at discursive stabilisation, to new discursive constructions, ideologies, political discourses, social movements and practices. We have here, then, two distinct orders of phenomena: on the one hand we have a *real* whose unrepresentability dislocates our subjective and objective identities, and, on the other hand, we have socio-political *reality*, a field of construction which attempts to master this real. Furthermore, the dialectics between the two, between positive and negative, is irreducible and leads to no moment of sublation.[4]

All that is extremely important and goes a long way towards constructing a comprehensive framework for making sense of social and political life. Moreover, it has been fruitfully applied in the analysis of a multitude of concrete socio-political issues (Laclau 1994; Howarth et al. 2000; Howarth and Torfing 2005). This does not mean, however, that it does not have its (very precise) limits. It is bound to have, as all frameworks do. According to the Freudian/Lacanian ethics of theorising discussed in the introduction, one is obliged to explore, re-negotiate and then traverse these limits, since a theory can only be productively developed on the basis of probing the resistances (internal and external) to its own construction. This is what legitimises the permanent striving of theoretical discourse to displace them again and again. But where exactly is the limit located here? I think it primarily involves a conceptualisation of the Lacanian real in predominantly negative terms; it concerns, in other words, the particular way Lacan's negative ontology is registered within discourse theory. As Jeremy Gilbert has put it, although the category of the 'real' provides a way to understand what is not in meaning (but, nevertheless, functions as the cause and the impossible object of meaning), it remains 'a definitively undifferentiated and undifferentiable category which effectively consigns all that is not experienced within the realm of meaning to the category of the unknowable' (Gilbert 2004). From his point of view the crucial question is the following: *isn't there anything else we can say about this unknowable real, any other way of illuminating its causal powers and its inter-relation with discourse?* These are perfectly legitimate questions, which emerge not only from Gilbert's side but almost every time one engages in the analysis of concrete political phenomena. However, and that might surprise Gilbert, psychoanalysis has a lot to contribute on this front: it is here that Freud's affect and Lacan's *jouissance* as a modality of the real order come into play. But is this a direction that Laclau is willing to explore? To try to answer this question will be the main aim of this chapter.

Enter affect and jouissance!

To be sure, Laclau's work has been crucial in developing the social and political relevance both of Lacanian constructionism and of Lacan's negative ontology. His work has been paradigmatic in simultaneously highlighting the political workings of the symbolic and in registering the real limits of signification. However, this should not be interpreted as a sign of limitless convergence or fusion between Laclau and Lacanian theory. Although discourse theory, overcoming Castoriadis' reluctance, does take on board and develops further the Lacanian conceptions of negativity, lack and signification and their political implications, it has not managed – until recently at least – to incorporate the Lacanian problematic of enjoyment, a problematic crucial in understanding the libidinal/visceral dimension of identification processes. What I am, of course, touching upon here is a more general problem related to the neglect of the affective dimension of identity in theoretical approaches influenced by the structuralist/poststructuralilst tradition. Although Lacan himself developed his project in close dialogue with this tradition, he eventually came to acknowledge that Freud's metapsychological insights – pointing to the importance of libidinal energy, the importance of the drive – need to be taken into account if one wants to arrive at a more thorough understanding of human reality. And this is bound to include social and political phenomena.

If in Freud this whole metapsychological problematic is related to the question of affect and psychic energy, Lacan will reformulate this issue along the lines of his conceptualisation of the real, which will be gradually defined not only in negative terms (as the alienating limit of construction and signification) but also in terms of *jouissance*, of a paradoxical enjoyment that cannot be fully represented in meaning, that is not made of meaning (as Castoriadis would have wanted it), but, nevertheless, does invest meaning and thus does make some sense. As Bruce Fink has put it, 'there is a kind of basic equivalence between affect and *jouissance* (in Freud's terms, between affect and libido or libidinal discharge)' (Fink 1997: 215).[5] Here, the Lacanian distinction between the plane of the signifier – the symbolic – and *jouissance* – as a positive modality of the real – parallels, to some extent, the Freudian one between representation and affect:

> The subject of representation can be associated here with the unconscious, and thus with the articulation and development of unconscious desire – Lacan's subject of desire or desiring subject – whereas the subject of affect or 'emotive' subject is the subject of *jouissance*, or 'enjoying subject'. For as clinicians quickly learn, where there is affect, there is *jouissance*. (Fink 1997: 212)[6]

Thus, from a Lacanian point of view, assuming the distinction between the plane of the signifier and real *jouissance* and exploring their complex relation and interpenetration becomes crucial in accounting for a dimension of politics, which is rather extimate to representation and meaning. From the point of view of discourse theory – and post-structuralism in general – what is primarily and crucially at stake here is the status of *jouissance* as a modality of the real order. Is Laclau willing to consider this link between the real and *jouissance*?

But let us take things from the beginning, assuming – for the sake of clarity – the unavoidable risk of some repetition. There are a lot of points in Laclau's work where one can find direct references to, or analogies drawn with, the category of the real in Lacanian theory. A good starting point in probing the relation between Laclau and Lacan in this area is the category of the real conceived negatively, as the limits of signification. Theoretical affinities are strongest here, sharing as they do what I have already described as a negative ontology. Gradually, however, the affinities become less clear and potentially divergent. This is the case, for example, when one turns his or her attention to the means by which the real is positivised for the social subject; and second, to the means by which the real provides a kind of positive satisfaction or enjoyment. It is worth examining in some detail Laclau's appropriations of Lacanian theory under this light before evaluating some of his recent views in terms of the positive/negative dialectics within the Lacanian Left.

Negative and positive real

NEGATIVE DIMENSIONS OF THE REAL: THE LIMITS OF DISCOURSE AND THE INDEX OF DISLOCATION

We have already seen how Laclau's work aims at showing the discursive nature of social objectivity: it understands human reality as socially constructed and articulated in discourse, something also shared by Lacan and Castoriadis. Neither Laclau nor Lacan, however, are content with this banal constructionism – and the same, as we saw in the previous chapter, equally applies to Castoriadis.[7] Such a position can only be the starting point for a complex understanding of human experience. Indeed, they are all interested in showing that human construction is never able to institute itself as a closed and self-contained order. There is always something which frustrates all efforts to reach an exhaustive representation of the world – whether natural or social. One can approach this constitutive frustration by speaking of the 'limits of discourse', often associated with notions like 'incompleteness of identity' (post-structuralism), 'impossibility of society' (Laclau) or 'the lack in the Other' (Lacan).

As we have already seen in the introductory chapter with reference to Kuhn, Freud, and Lacan, from a psychoanalytic point of view, the limits of every discursive structure (of the conscious articulation of meaning, for example) can only be shown in relation to this discursive structure itself (through the subversion of meaning). This relation of tension is not unlike the one between the real and reality in Lacanian theory. Although the real is *ex definitione* irreducible to the field of construction and representation, it nevertheless shows itself in the first instance – and indirectly – through the kinks and inconsistencies of the latter's functioning: 'As essentially unthinkable and unrepresentable, the real can only be conceived negatively, in terms of disturbances of the imaginary and the symbolic' (Boothby 2001: 295). This psychoanalytic idea of distortion or disruption as a (negative) index of the real has been progressively endorsed by discourse theory as its emphasis shifted from the status of signification and discursive articulation to exploring the limits of signification. This is what Laclau had to say on the question of the limits of a signifying system in 1996:

> it is clear that those limits cannot be themselves signified, but have to show themsleves as the *interruption* or *breakdown* of the process of signification. Thus, we are left with the paradoxical situation that what constitutes the condition of possibility of a signifying system – its limits – is also what constitutes its condition of impossibility – a blockage of the continuous expansion of the process of signification. (Laclau 1996: 37)

In fact, it can be argued that his concept of 'dislocation', first developed in *New Reflections* following Žižek's critique of the concept of antagonism, seems to be designed to account for exactly such a breakdown or radical interruption of signification, what one could describe in Lacanian terms as 'encounters with the real': while 'antagonism' falls on the side of the imaginary–symbolic order of reality (denoting the relation between different but already articulated discursive projects fighting for hegemony), 'dislocation' falls on the side of an encounter with the real order. It may not be a coincidence that Boothby joins Laclau in explicitly referring to 'dislocations' – together with misalignments and catastrophes (in the mathematical sense) of the structures of representation – as the crucial evidence indexing our encounters with the real (Boothby 2001: 295). On this view, dislocation becomes *an index of the negative dimension of the real as limit of discourse*. Laclau even goes on to link his treatment of the issue explicitly with the Lacanian problematic of the real:

> we are trying to signify the limits of signification – the real, if you want, in the Lacanian sense – and there is no direct way of doing so except through the subversion of the process of signification itself. We know, through psychoanalysis, how what is not directly representable – the unconscious – can only find as a means of representation the subversion of the signifying process. (Laclau 1996: 39)

POSITIVE DIMENSIONS OF THE REAL I: EMPTY SIGNIFIERS AND *OBJETS PETIT a*

One must not forget, however, that in Lacanian theory the real is not only associated with moments of disruption, with traumatic or dislocating experiences. First of all, *the real-in-itself cannot be disruption or lack*. Disruption is certainly one way of showing the constitutive inability of the symbolic to represent the real, of demonstrating the symbolic order's lack of resources. But that can only mean that the real should rather be thought of as a 'lack of lack' (XI: ix). Moreover, for Lacan, this lack in the symbolic is not simply a lack of symbolic resources. Rather, it also has to be acknowledged as a lack of the real; more precisely, as a lack of the real *jouissance* castrated through socialisation: 'the lack inscribed in the signifying chain through which the Other, as the only possible site of truth, reveals that it holds no guarantee, is in terms of the dialectic of desire a lacking in *jouissance* of the Other' (Lacan and the École Freudienne 1982: 117). In this sense the lack in the Other is a lack of a pre-symbolic real enjoyment or satisfaction which – at least in its fullness, as the lack of lack – always presents itself as lost, as the part of ourselves that is sacrificed when we enter the socio-symbolic system – a system that, as we have seen in the previous chapter, regulates the discursive articulation of human reality. Last but not least, in order for the social world to retain any consistency and appeal, this lack of the real, the negative mark of symbolic castration, needs to be positivised (imaginarised). To stimulate the desire for identification, for social and political life, to imaginarise lack, is the function of *fantasy*. Fantasy attempts this by offering us what Lacan calls the *objet petit a*, the object-cause of desire, embodying, in a double movement, the lack in the Other together with the promise of its filling, the promise of a miraculous encounter with castrated *jouissance*. At the imaginary level then – or rather at the level of an imaginarised real – the limits of the symbolic are positivised in the form of *objets petit a*: '*Objet [petit] a* is a kind of "positivization", filling out, of the void . . .' (Žižek 1993: 122). It incarnates 'simultaneously the pure lack, the void around which the desire turns and which, as such, causes the desire, *and* the imaginary element which conceals this void, renders it invisible by filling it out' (Žižek 1994: 178–9).

What is Laclau's position vis-à-vis these important aspects of Lacan's conceptualisation of the real and its fantasmatic positivisations? It is possible to argue here that Laclau's work takes a direction which brings him very close to the Lacanian approach. As briefly mentioned, Laclau's dislocation, any encounter with the real that disrupts a given discursive field, is not only something traumatic – an experience of negativity – but also the condition of possibility for social and political creation and rearticulation. In other words, dislocation also has a productive dimension. As far as the nature of dislocations is concerned, therefore, it is clear in *New Reflections* that dislocations are, at the same time, traumatic/disruptive and productive. They are traumatic in the sense that 'they threaten identities', but they are also productive in the sense that they serve as 'the foundation on which new identities are constituted' (Laclau 1990: 39). Dislocation qua encounter with the impossible real functions as both the limit and the ontological condition of identity formation.[8]

In particular, for Laclau, this dual nature of dislocation is positivised in what he calls an 'empty signifier'. If our continuous experiences of dislocation reveal that the full closure of the Other is impossible, that the real is ultimately unrepresentable, that lack is an irreducible characteristic of socio-political reality, this does not mean that positivisation in terms of closure, fullness or full representation disappears from political discourse. Politics comprise all our attempts to fill in this lack in the Other: 'although the fullness and universality of society is unachievable, its need does not disappear: it will always show itself through the presence of its absence' (Laclau 1996: 53). And this is precisely where Laclau's category of the empty signifier becomes relevant:

> In a situation of radical disorder 'order' is present as that which is absent; it becomes an empty signifier, as the signifier of this absence. In this sense, various political forces can compete in their efforts to present their particular objectives as those which carry out the filling of that lack. To hegemonize something is exactly to carry out this filling function. (Laclau 1996: 44)

Laclau suggests, moreover, that signifiers other than 'order' – signifiers like 'unity', 'revolution' and so on – can function in a similar way: 'Any term which, in a certain political context, becomes the signifier of the lack, plays the same role. Politics is possible because the constitutive impossibility of society can only represent itself through the production of empty signifiers' (ibid.). Clearly, therefore, there is an immediate theoretical affinity holding between Lacan's positivisations of the real through the fantasmatic *objet petit a* and Laclau's positivisation of the limits of signification in terms of 'empty signifiers'. What both gestures have in common is the acknowledgement of the need to index these limits positively in the psychic economy and the discursive identity of the social subject.[9]

What is less clear, however, is whether Laclau is also willing to take into account other important ways – beyond imaginarisation – in which the real becomes positivised within Lacanian theory. These other ways – delicately negotiating the relation between negativity and positivity – refer to the whole problematic of psychic energy and affect in Freud and its radical Lacanian reformulation in terms of a vast and complex typology of *jouissance*. Indeed, *jouissance* is almost entirely missing from Laclau's corpus.[10] A plausible hypothesis is that this is due to the overall mode of Laclau's embrace of the Lacanian real – an embrace framed in formal, structural, rather than substantive terms. For, as Jacques-Alain Miller has recently put it, '*jouissance* presumes the body; *jouissance* needs the body as its support, thus Lacan called it a substance. In Aristotle's tongue it's *ousia*; where *ousia* is, so is substance' (Miller 2000a: 13). So if the decision to forego any discussion of *jouissance* is a conscious decision on Laclau's part, there is no doubt that prima facie objections could be summoned to support this decision. For in talking about *jouissance* one is always walking on the threshold of essentialism. Indeed, 'there is no exaggeration in positing Lacan's teaching as being animated by the difficulty of thinking about the subject as lack-in-being, that is, as a certain kind of non-being, together with *jouissance* as substance' (ibid.) – an especially poignant and potentially productive difficulty for anyone working within the broad field of anti-essentialist political theory. However, one should not forget that, even if thinking about the real qua *jouissance* seems to flirt with a certain essentialism, it nevertheless remains 'essentially' unrepresentable and always in a state of irresolvable tension with the socio-discursive field. Hence the whole issue seems to hinge on the particular advantages, insights, or problematisations the category of *jouissance* can offer to a discursive approach to politics such as the one advanced by Ernesto Laclau, and more generally to the Lacanian Left. The analytical advantages will be illustrated throughout Part II, but they are not the only ones.

First of all, it is necessary to point out that the category of *jouissance* and Lacan's continuous engagement with the field of enjoyment in both his clinical and his theoretical work should not be treated as a mere supplement, as some kind of optional conceptual extra that can easily be bracketed, leaving intact and ready for appropriation the rest of Lacan's theoretical edifice (mainly his theorisation of signification, symbolic articulation and their limits). This is not because of any kind of old-style essentialism. The problem is that, without taking into account enjoyment, the whole Lacanian framework loses most of its explanatory force. All things considered, *jouissance* emerges as the central hypothesis of Lacanian theory. For example, what can possibly account for the constitutivity of desire (both in personal life and in the variety of political identifications) if the absence/castration of *jouissance* is not accepted as its cause? Furthermore, such enjoyment helps us answer in a more concrete way what is at stake in socio-political identification and identity formation, suggesting that support for social fantasies is provided by a promise of recapturing a lost/impossible *jouissance* as fullness, while partially rooted in the *jouissance* of the body. A similar mechanism may explain the persistence of social symptoms insofar as, according to Lacan, a symptom always implies a paradoxical unconscious satisfaction in pain. In Part II of this book I will have the opportunity to show how insightful all these concepts and logics can be in analysing crucial issues such as nationalism, European identity and consumerism.

POSITIVE DIMENSIONS OF THE REAL II: FROM FANTASY TO SYMPTOM

Indeed, throughout this book a variety of different typologies of *jouissance* will be sketched – based on different formulations present in the Lacanian corpus and able to guide the analysis of concrete political phenomena. At this point I will be sketching a first typology in terms of *fantasy* and *symptom* as two distinct modalities of *jouissance*: 'these two modes have this difference, even opposition. One [the symptom] is *jouissance* under the genre of displeasure, while the other [the fantasy] is *jouissance* – which is not less paradoxical – under the genre of pleasure' (Miller 2005: 17). As we have already seen, what Lacan sees in *jouissance* is an initially surprising confluence of satisfaction with its own negation: *jouissance* is pleasure in displeasure, satisfaction in dissatisfaction.[11] And we have already touched upon what Miller qualifies as one of the two modes, that of fantasy.[12] Here, in this particular modality, '*jouissance* is accommodated to pleasure' (p. 24). But this is not ordinary pleasure. It is an imaginarisation of enjoyment as fullness, which promises to bring back something irretrievably lost through socialisation. This, however, is the first part of the equation, the part of satisfaction. What must be stressed here is that this satisfaction is not directly experienced in fantasy – it is only implied. What is experienced is its promise, embodied in the object-cause of desire. But the object can only incarnate enjoyment insofar as it is lacking; as soon as we get hold of it all its mystique evaporates! This is the second part of the equation, the part of dissatisfaction and frustration. In that sense, one could argue that in fantasy the *presence of an absence* (the object-cause of desire, the empty signifier) represents and, at the same time, masks the ultimate *absence of presence* (of a pre-symbolic *jouissance* as fullness, as lack of lack).

And what about the second mode: *jouissance* as symptom? Here the idea of a satisfaction in dissatisfaction can be traced back to the Freudian intuition that displeasure can paradoxically procure a certain type of satisfaction. This seems to be the idea behind Freud's concepts of 'negative therapeutic reaction' (an often radical sticking – impossible to shift or fully interpret – of an analysand to his painful symptomatic reality) and of 'primary and secondary gain from illness' (a direct or indirect satisfaction one acquires from his neurotic symptoms) (Laplanche and Pontalis 1988: 182–4). Through the elaboration of his category of *jouissance*, Lacan is the first major psychoanalytic theorist to elevate these ideas into a cornerstone of the conceptual, theoretical and clinical apparatus of psychoanalysis. This is straightforwardly the case when we examine both the clinical and the social dimension of the symptom.

Let us first examine its clinical status. Although symptoms are initially thought and experienced as trouble, anomaly, deviation, constraint, that is to say, as problems, psychoanalysis reveals that they may also be viewed as solutions, symptomatic solutions to the deeper division of speaking beings that have to deal with the constitutive lack of *jouissance*:

> This symptomatic solution can be more or less uncomfortable for the subject, more or less common, but in any case it responds to the lack which is at the core of language . . . there is no subject without a symptom . . . It is through the symptom that everyone has access to his or her jouissance, supplying the lack proper to language with the forgeries of the unconscious. (Soler 2003: 90)

It is in that sense that the analysand enjoys 'the very conditions that he or she is complaining about' (Hoens and Pluth 2002: 10). There is a painful pleasure to which the subject is attached despite him or herself. The symptom clearly satisfies something in the subject: 'the subject would not be riveted to this symptom if it were not a mode of *jouissance* for him. To speak of the *jouissance* of the symptom is a paradox since it presents itself under the genre of displeasure. We are now tied to this paradox, thanks to Lacan's injection in our conceptualization, of the term of *jouissance* as distinct from pleasure' (Miller 2005: 23).

What is the socio-political relevance of this clinical insight? There is no doubt that in social and political life we also experience constraining and disabling attachments and dependencies from which it is very difficult if not impossible to distance ourselves. In Chapter 4 we will see how attachment to power and authority itself is marked by such a dimension. Indeed, we even encounter cases in which subjects fully acknowledge the contingency of their situation and see how things could be otherwise, how an even minor change (in behaviour, attitude, and so on) would lead to a different life, visited less by suffering. Yet they cannot help themselves, they cannot stop repeating the same pattern. Why? As should be clear by now, Lacan's answer is to be found in this strange word: *jouissance*, the *jouissance* of the social symptom. In fact, terms such as 'social symptoms' or 'contemporary symptoms' have emerged within psychoanalytic literature, indicating the social and political relevance of the notion of symptom in accounting for identification processes and in highlighting the social conditioning and constitution of particular subjective formations: practices of *jouissance* ranging from toxicomania, anorexia and depression to ideology and consumerism – 'where *jouissance* regulates the social order' (Britton 2004: 54–8) – many of which will be explored in detail in the second part of this book. The reason why a (social) symptom persists, the reason why it proves impossible to get rid of something we consciously experience as painful and disturbing, is that, on another level, we procure a certain (primary or secondary) gain, a certain enjoyment (as opposed to conscious pleasure) from it. It is '*jouissance* [which] accounts for the fact that . . . the symptom ['which is not merely subjective, but manages 'a social bond and a manner of living which may be described as a lifestyle'] lasts' (Porcheret 2000: 141–2).

It is important to note two things at this point. First of all, this understanding of the symptom signals a shift in focus from the symbolic of discourse – from 'discourse' in discourse theory's sense, where it is primarily associated with networks of meaning – to the real of *jouissance*. Lacan himself will illustrate this shift in his latter work by introducing the concept of the *sinthome* (XXIII). Previously, the symptom was understood as a purely symbolic knot, to be deciphered and interpreted. Thus, in his seminal Rome discourse, Lacan explicitly states that an analysis of language is enough to resolve a symptom, since 'the symptom itself is structured like a language' (E1977: 59). In his latter work, however, Lacan will emphasise another aspect: the language of the symptom is incarnated in the body, embodied; it invokes, organises and regulates *jouissance* (Soler 2003: 87). In Slavoj Žižek's words, 'sinthome is a central signifier penetrated with enjoyment, its status is by definition "psychosomatic"' (Žižek 1989: 76). Resistance to linguistic interpretation demonstrates that the symptom cannot be reduced to its symbolic dimension: the symptom as a symbolic construction is articulated around a kernel of real enjoyment (Verhaeghe and Declercq 2002: 60). It is this root of the symptom in the real of *jouissance* that obstructs therapeutic effectiveness (ibid.). Working exclusively on the symbolic material of a symptom does not touch its relation with the drive and undermines the success of the treatment. That was the final conclusion of both Freud and Lacan (p. 61). The term '*sinthome*' signifies this disturbing real aspect of the symptom beyond its linguistic articulation.

Second, this shift from the symbolic to the real of *jouissance*, from symptom to *sinthome*, has some very serious implications on the way Lacanian theory conceptualises processes of both psychic and social ordering. During the predominantly linguistic (structuralist/post-structuralist) phase of Lacan's teaching, what is supposed to confer a (relative) stability to our discursive constructions of reality is the function of the *points de capiton*, signifiers which work as points of reference for the articulation of networks of meaning. At the level of subjective structuration, such is the role of what Lacan calls the Name-of-the-Father. At the socio-political level this role is assigned to Laclau and Mouffe's nodal points, a category which – as we have seen – is conceptualised with direct reference to Lacanian theory. As soon as the focus shifts from language to enjoyment, this function passes from the Name-of-the-Father to the *sinthome*, which now becomes the element that holds human reality together and anchors it onto the real of *jouissance*. It is the *sinthome* which is thus acknowledged as the foundational moment of symbolic reality (Hoens and Pluth 2002: 12–13). The implication for the type of socio-political analysis articulated here, for the Lacanian Left, is that it now becomes necessary to explore the affective aspect of the nodal point, to formalise its link to the real of *jouissance*. And this link, amply present in our experience and in the difficulties of effective socio-political critique, crystallised in contemporary forms of voluntary servitude, cannot be reduced to a discussion of the imaginarised real present in fantasy constructions and incarnated in empty signifiers. The success of a nodal point is not wholly attributable to its ability to effect discursive closure and to embody the promise of an imaginarised *jouissance*; it also depends on its ability to manipulate a certain symptomatic enjoyment – on its capacity to function as a social *sinthome*. And it is this function which explains its fixity: 'Lacan's insight here is that of the full ontological weight of "stuckness": when one dissolves the sinthome and thus gets fully unstuck, one loses the minimum consistency of one's being' (Žižek 2005b: 152). Accordingly, a critique of an ideological system of meaning cannot be effective if it remains at a purely deconstructive level; it requires a mapping of the fantasies supporting this system and an encircling of its symptomatic function. If, at the clinical level, 'to know how to handle, to take care of, to manipulate . . . to know what to do with the symptom . . . is the end of analysis' (Lacan in Verhaeghe and Declercq 2002: 65), then to know where to find and what to do with the social *sinthome*, with the *jouissance* implicated in particular socio-historical configurations, could be the goal at the level of political analysis.

In that sense, the importance psychoanalysis attaches to the notion of the real qua *jouissance* – in its different forms, fantasmatic and symptomatic – is not purely theoretical, it is primarily grounded in the need to reflect seriously on, and to deal effectively with, the difficulties involved in effecting subjective and social change. Here, psychoanalytic theory suggests that analyses of the discursive, deconstructive or interpretative kind, though perhaps a necessary prerequisite, are often not sufficient to explain attachment to particular objects of identification, let alone to effect a displacement in the social subject's psychic economy. Undoubtedly, the structures of fantasy and symptom define modes of *jouissance* that often resist all interpretive/deconstructive strategies. If psychoanalytic intervention (and, by extension, political intervention) is to have any effect in these cases, it must aim between the lines, so to speak, even beyond the ineffable *objet petit a*, at the whole field of real *jouissance*. It must aim at 'traversing the fantasy' and 'identifying with the symptom'.[13] This is ultimately what is at stake in working with a concept such as that of the Lacanian real. An articulation of this problematic of the real qua *jouissance* with Ernesto Laclau's discourse theory would enhance our understanding not only of ideological processes, but also of the conditions of ethically relevant and politically efficient ideology critique.[14] This is why such an articulation is absolutely crucial for the Lacanian Left. And this is why it will also inform the analyses of concrete political phenomena contained in the various chapters of the second part of this book.

Laclau on jouissance: *crossing the Rubicon?*

Part of my argumentation so far in this chapter has drawn on, and deepened, arguments first put forward in an article co-authored with Jason Glynos and published in the *Journal for Lacanian Studies* (Glynos and Stavrakakis 2003). One of the central aims of that text was to push Laclau to reflect directly on these issues and to state clearly his position on the question of *jouissance* as a political factor. On that front it has been quite successful. It has provoked not only one but – as I will claim – at least two lines of response from Ernesto Laclau. The first can be found in the same journal where our initial article was published (Laclau 2003). A second, somewhat different line is discernible in some supplementary remarks present in his overall reply to a set of texts included in the recently published *Laclau: A Critical Reader* (Critchley and Marchart 2004). While this volume reprints verbatim our initial text and Laclau's reply from *JLS* becomes part of his general reply to the articles of the volume, nevertheless some new relevant comments are added towards the end of his reply, comments that seem to add a new angle to the discussion. Needless to say, these two lines of response are of direct relevance to the critical approach presented in the preceding sections of the present chapter. Hence, discussing them in detail will make it possible to reflect on the way Laclau's views on the inter-implication of discourse and real *jouissance*, discourse theory and psychoanalysis, are currently developing.

The most profound characteristic of Laclau's reply in *JLS*, what makes this text absolutely central for any exploration of the Lacanian Left, is the unequivocal and straightforward embrace of the Lacanian category of *jouissance*. This happens for the first time and indicates a further willingness to work seriously with reference to a conceptual and theoretical constellation which is deeply and clearly marked by its Lacanian orientation. To my mind, there is no doubt that, in terms of Laclau's theoretical trajectory, the embrace of the crucial Lacanian concept of *jouissance* signals a passage from a largely eclectic use of Lacanian insights to a committed engagement with the Lacanian corpus. Notice, for example, the unequivocal terms of Laclau's acceptance of the relevance of *jouissance*: 'I do not disagree with practically anything they [Glynos and Stavrakakis] say concerning jouissance and its relation to the symbolic' (Laclau 2003: 278). In fact, Laclau goes on to argue that this dimension has not been absent from his work: 'what they claim is a dimension absent from my work, I see, on the contrary as very much present in it – although, admittedly, sometimes in a rather sketchy and inchoate way' (ibid.). From now on, however, one can observe two different directions in which his argument evolves. I will first try to highlight what is at stake in these two directions before entering into a dialogue with them.

1. The first direction centres around an exposition of the *ontological* character of Laclau's concept of discourse, which is presented as an all-encompassing category, already incorporating the logic of *jouissance*. It is worth quoting the relevant passage at length, to do justice to the kernel of Laclau's argument:

   Let us return at this point to the main criticism of Glynos and Stavrakakis, which concerns the unilateral emphasis that I would supposedly have given to the discursive at the expense of enjoyment. My answer is that by discourse I do not understand something restricted to the linguistic conceived in its narrow sense, but a relational complex of which enjoyment is a constitutive element. Let us think for a moment in the symptom. We have in the process of its formation a dimension of repression by which affect is withdrawn from representation and attached to a substitutive representation. Jouissance results from the experience of satisfaction/dissatisfaction which crystallises in the symptom. It is clear that linguistic representation is not an 'other' vis-à-vis jouissance, but an internal component of jouissance itself . . . Conversely, for the reasons that I have indicated above, language itself cannot function without cathexis (ie. affective unevenness). It is this sequence of structural/relational moments which includes both linguistic and affective components that I call *discourse*. It is worth stressing that, since *Hegemony and Socialist Strategy*, we have always criticised the distinction between the discursive and the extra-discursive as an untenable dualism. Discourse involves both words and the actions to which those words are linked, as in Wittgenstein's language games. It would obviously be absurd that we criticise the dualism words/actions but that we, however, excluded affects from those relational complexes. Moreover some of the categories that I employ, as 'radical investment', would be unintelligible without the notion of jouissance. (Laclau 2003: 283)

I consider Laclau's strategy of trying to re-conceptualise discourse with *jouissance* and affect as one of its crucial internal moments not only as entirely legitimate but also as extremely productive. It is very difficult, though, to recognise in this re-conceptualisation some sort of *retroactive* quality. For it seems as if Laclau is arguing that *jouissance* was always already part and parcel of the concept of discourse. But how could this be so, given the fact that the word *jouissance* was hardly ever mentioned in his work before? The fact that it has not been excluded – or that, with hindsight, it would be absurd to exclude it – cannot count as proof of inclusion, especially in the absence of any other equivalent term. The fact remains that this dimension was not properly thematised (as was, for example, the dualism words/actions he mentions). This is in no way a mortal sin for discourse theory – very simply, intellectual priorities and theoretico-political stakes at the time neither permitted nor encouraged this thematisation. At best, then, one can accept that Laclau has conceived of discourse in a way that does permit – now, in our theoretico-political present – a grafting of the problematic of affect and *jouissance* through the dialectics of investment. This grafting, however, is not a *fait accompli*. It requires substantial further theoretical effort and conceptual innovation – especially since, as he acknowledges himself, the problematic of affect and *jouissance* has hitherto been incorporated into discourse theory in a 'rather sketchy and inchoate way'.[15]

The crucial question is how this effort should proceed. It is here that Laclau rightly locates a difference between our approaches:

> In that case, if there is such a considerable common terrain between both approaches, what could have led Glynos and Stavrakakis to think that I have left aside the whole side of affect in Lacanian theory? I think that the explanation is to be found in the fact that, for them, signification and jouissance, although closely interconnected in their operation, are conceptually distinguishable dimensions – or, at least, distinguishable to a larger extent than I am prepared to accept. (Laclau 2003: 280)

Let us examine more closely what is really at issue here. The question is how *jouissance* and signification/representation are related. This is, admittedly, a tricky area. Does that, however, justify Laclau's strategy to, in effect, 'neutralise' his registering of *jouissance* through its retroactive absorption into a concept of 'discourse' which remains intact? For the kernel of his first line of response seems to lie in *insisting that both dimensions are internal to discourse and thus, more or less, co-extensive.*[16] They cannot be observed independently of one another and, consequently, they cannot be theorised independently of each other: 'If this is so, however, the only possible conclusion is that the dimension of affect is not something to be added to a process of signification but something without which signification, in the first place, would not take place'. And what about the other side? 'Is affect something that we could conceive as independent from the signifying side of the equation?' (ibid., p. 282). Laclau answers in the negative: 'there is no signification without affect; but, at the same time, there is no affect which is not constituted through its operation within a signifying chain' (p. 283). This position is then formulated in the most radical terms: '*What I want to question is the idea that here we are really dealing with two sides*' (p. 282, emphasis added).

2. I have the impression that Laclau himself is aware of the ultimate untenability of this position. This is perhaps why in certain places of his original reply he introduces another line of response. This becomes clear, for example, when, having already stated that he does not think we are dealing with two sides, he goes on to argue that 'the link between the two sides is somehow more intimate than they [Glynos and Stavrakakis] allow for' (p. 281). Now the distance between our respective arguments is minimised, becoming a difference in emphasis:

> In conclusion: I do not think that my views are ultimately that distant from those presented by Glynos and Stavrakakis. The nuance separating us is to be found in that, while the three of us agree that there is a constitutive relational moment linking the linguistic and the affective, they have concentrated on the *duality* as such, while my attention has been mostly directed to the *relation* which makes that duality possible. (Laclau 2003: 281)

This obviously makes things very different, introduces a productive affinity, and opens the road for an approach which will attempt to elaborate these issues further, along the line of accounting both for the distinct character of and for the irreducible link between the two registers.

This is a line of argument which is also present in another text, Laclau's extensive reply to a series of critical papers in *Laclau: A Critical Reader*, in which he sets the future research agenda for discourse theory in the most unambiguous and rigorous terms. Here he does acknowledge that 'something of the order of hegemony and rhetoric takes place which could not be explained without the mediating role of affect'. In the same text he introduces a crucial and novel distinction between the *form* and the *force* of a discourse:

> For what rhetoric can explain is the *form* that an overdetermining investment takes, but not the *force* that explains the investment as such and its perdurability. Here something else has to be brought into the picture. Any overdetermination requires not only metaphorical condensations but also cathectic investments. That is, something belonging to the order of *affect* has a primary role in discursively constructing the social. Freud already knew it: the social link is a libidinal link. And affect, as I have earlier pointed out in this essay, is

not something *added* to signification, but something consubstantial with it. So if I see rhetoric as ontologically primary in explaining the operations inhering in and the forms taken by the hegemonic construction of society, I see psychoanalysis as the only valid road to explain the drives behind such construction – I see it, indeed, as the only fruitful approach to the understanding of human reality. (Laclau 2004a: 326; also see Laclau 2005: 110)[17]

What we have here is, first of all, a rather radical shift from Laclau's initial position (although the part about co-substantiality slightly blurs the picture). And we have to be clear on this: the two positions are mutually exclusive; either we are dealing with two dimensions or not. But we also see the beginning of an effort to reflect theoretically on the way the relation between the two dimensions should be elaborated – hence the introduction of the distinction (and interconnection) between form and force. This is a crucial issue regarding the location of discourse theory within the Lacanian Left, and thus it is worth discussing in some detail the pros and cons of these two lines of response. Needless to say, I think that the second one is by far the most promising of the two, and there is a score of reasons to support this choice.

Acknowledging the shift: affect and jouissance *in Lacanian theory*

First of all, I see no problem at all in openly acknowledging that prior theorisation within discourse theory has neglected to a considerable extent the dimension of affect and *jouissance* – and I am not excluding myself from this. In fact, such a clear acceptance has two advantages. First of all, it is exemplary of the way the ethical status of theorising is viewed from a Lacanian perspective: as something inherently limited, continuously obstructed by a desire not to know, by a 'conformist' desire for ignorance. Theorisation is able to advance only through efforts to overcome this resistance by entering into a continuous and tortuous negotiation of its own limits, a stance paradoxically conferring on it the possibility of 'permanent renewal' beyond any defensive attitude. It is also the case that, without accepting and encircling the ever-present limitations of any given theoretical terrain, it is impossible to move forward in any really productive way. And we need to move forward: 'to continue to remain in semiotic thought is to languish in religious melancholy and to subordinate every intense emotion to a lack and every force to a finitude' (Lyotard 1993: 49). Regardless of whether one accepts *in toto* Lyotard's provocative formulation from his impressive *Libidinal Economy*, he does touch on something important; what is also significant is his use of the word 'force', which also resurfaces in Laclau's second line of response.[18]

In this respect, beyond any mechanistic imitations, it might be possible to learn something from the boldness characteristic of the theoretical trajectories of both Freud and Lacan. As for Freud, anyone with even a limited familiarity with his writings cannot but be astonished by the numerous acknowledgements of failure of past theories and hypotheses – even of whole books, starting with his *Project for a Scientific Psychology*; by the open negotiation of shifts and the continuous experimentation with new insights; by his determination to overcome even his own resistances to the disturbing knowledge psychoanalysis unveils. Lacan's dealings with the issue of affect presents a similar picture. I am saying this because, to some, the choice of Lacanian theory as offering the proper direction in an exploration of the affective dimension in political life – a view informing both Laclau's argument and the positions put forward in this book – will undoubtedly sound bizarre. Is not Lacanian theory part of the original problem?

It is true that Lacan has been renowned for his dislike of 'affect' as a psychoanalytic category. In fact, this is one of the most commonplace criticisms directed against his work: 'his focus on linguistics and logic is thought to lessen the importance of the affective dimension and to lead to a sterile analysis from which anger, shame, pity, indignation, envy and jealousy have been banished' (Gallagher 1997: 111). Perhaps the most elaborate critique of Lacan along these lines can be found in André Green's *Le discours vivant*, where Lacan's work is presented as the paradigmatic case of a rejection of affect, not only because affect has no place in it, but because, in Green's view, it is explicitly banished from it (Green 1999: 99).[19] Cornelius Castoriadis, a good friend of Green, was also of the view that Lacan reduced 'what can best be described as the energetics, the affectations of the subject to an (ultimately linguistically) representable form' (Williams 1999: 111).[20] This critique is not totally unfounded. In fact, already in his first seminar (1953–4), Lacan speaks of affects as 'imaginary references' (I: 107), before engaging in the following exchange with Serge Leclaire:

> Leclaire: . . . It is quite clear that the terms affective and intellectual are no longer common currency in the group we make up.

Lacan: A good thing too. What can one do with them?
Leclaire: But that's the point, that is one thing which has been left hanging a bit since Rome.
Lacan: I believe I didn't make use of them in that famous Rome discourse, except to expunge the term *intellectualised*.
Leclaire: Exactly, both this silence, and these direct attacks on the term affective did have an effect.
Lacan: I believe this is a term which one must completely expunge from our papers. (I: 275)

This sounds pretty straightforward. Of course, it could be argued that Lacan's target is not the affective dimension per se. His target instead is a particular understanding of affect, an understanding conditioned by what he calls 'the notorious opposition between the intellectual and the affective', where the affective is taken as a kind of ineffable quality which has to be sought out in itself. For Lacan, by contrast, 'the affective is not like a special density which would escape an intellectual accounting. It is not to be found in a mythical beyond of the production of the symbol which would precede the discursive formulation' (I: 57). Hence Lacan's final warning: 'I urge you, each of you, at the heart of your own search for the truth, to renounce quite radically . . . the use of an opposition like that of the affective and the intellectual . . . This opposition is one of the most contrary to analytic experience and most unenlightening when it comes to understanding it' (I: 274). Here the similarities with Laclau's first line of reasoning are astonishing. In effect, what we have in both cases is a neglect or rejection of affect as a distinct psychic or political dimension. There is a resistance to any kind of duality — even a relational one — and, ultimately, a subsumption of the affective within the symbolic/discursive. As we have seen, in Laclau this subsumption proceeds through his all-encompassing conceptualisation of discourse. In Lacan, it follows directly from what he called his *Return to Freud*. In this early phase of his teaching, Lacan's priority is to highlight the signifying mechanisms involved in Freud's account of the creation of human reality (such as condensation and displacement, etc.) and to reformulate them along the lines of linguistics and structuralism. His main effort is to stress the constitutivity of the symbolic in human life. It is during this period that he articulates his famous motto that 'the unconscious is structured as a language'. Most of his energy is directed in demonstrating the linguistic/semiotic aspects of the Freudian revolution. And what guides this whole enterprise is clearly the reduction of Freud's *Lust* to meaning (Miller 2002a: 41). This is also what, during the same phase, underlies the reduction of the terrain of affect and enjoyment to the problematic of a signifier, that of the phallus. Fortunately, both for Lacan and Laclau this is not the end of the story.

In fact, as Cormac Gallagher has argued (Gallagher 1997: 113), Lacan's renunciation of the term in some parts of the 1953–4 seminar is only 'a provisional and temporary one'. Gallagher points out that affect has been one of the main preoccupations of Lacan's theorisation both before and after his first seminar. Before, in his writings on the family complexes for the *Encyclopédie Française* (1938), and after, in the whole seminar he devoted to discussing anxiety (1962–3), what he called 'the only affect that does not deceive'.[21] If the accusation is that Lacan 'scotomised' the consideration of affect, then this seminar proves, beyond any doubt, that the accusation is unfair (Harari 2000: xvi).

But even before the *Anxiety* seminar we have the transitional one on the *Ethics of Psychoanalysis* (1959–60), where Lacan's discussion of 'the Thing', Freud's *das Ding*, will break the monopoly of signification: 'With this field that I called the field of *das Ding*, we are projected into . . . something moving, obscure and without reference points owing to the lack of a sufficient organization of its register, something much more primitive . . .' (VII: 103). This opaque field is associated with 'analytical metaphysics' notions concerning energy' (VII: 102). At this stage, however, Lacan refrains from linking affectivity with this field of the real beyond signification: 'now it is not a matter of denying the importance of affects. But it is important not to confuse them with the substance of that which we are seeking in the *Real-Ich*, beyond signifying articulations of the kind we artists of analytical speech are capable of handling' (VII: 102). Recourse to affectivity is thus, once more, deemed 'confused' and misleading. There is, however, an important differentiation to be made in terms of the exact grounds on which affectivity is rejected. This time it does not happen because stress on affects is distanced from a registering of the all-encompassing field of signification or denies its value – as his earlier rejection seemed to imply. Interestingly enough, affectivity is rejected for precisely the opposite reasons, namely because it is not distanced enough, because of 'the conventional and artificial character' of affects (VII: 102). With the introduction of a distinction between emotion and affect this picture will be further and decisively modified, leading to the final position to be found in the *Anxiety* seminar: 'What is anxiety? We have ruled out its being an emotion.

And to introduce it, I would say: it is an affect' (seminar of 28 November 1962). The following year, in his interrupted seminar on *The Names-of-the-Father* (seminar of 20 November 1963), Lacan will re-state once more this new position, making clear the association between the affective and the field of libidinal energy at the frontiers of symbolic mediation:

> *anxiety is an affect of the subject* . . . In anxiety, the subject is affected by the desire of the Other. He is affected by it in a *non-dialectizable* manner, and it is for that reason that anxiety, within the affectivity of the subject, is what does not deceive . . . That characterization is in conformity with the first formulations Freud gave anxiety as a *direct transformation of the libido*. (Lacan 1990: 82, emphasis added)[22]

Almost ten years after this formulation, in section IV of *Television*, Miller directly asks him about the place of affect within his theory in its relation to language: 'What is said in opposition to you, in various forms, is: "Those are merely words, words, words. And what do you do with anything that doesn't get mixed up with words? What of psychic energy, or affect, or the drives?" ' (Miller in Lacan 1990: 17). Lacan's answer is to stress that, contrary to what the position of the *International Psychoanalytical Association* reiterated here by Miller conveys, this accusation is false on account of his devoting a whole year's seminar to *Anxiety* as an affect, which proves 'sufficiently that affect is not something I make light of' (Lacan 1990: 21; also see XVII: 168).[23]

How should one interpret this radical shift in Lacan's evaluation of affect? I think its cause should be located in the failure of the signifying reduction implicit in Lacan's initial strategy of a predominantly structuralist *Return to Freud*. It is fair to say that, although central to his teaching in the 1950s and 1960s, the priority of meaning over enjoyment and affect never stopped troubling Lacan. But why? Obviously not because of some bizarre fixation on affectivity, since, as we have seen, he did nearly everything he could to downplay and even eliminate it as a separate register. Why then? Precisely because this priority of meaning does not stop producing a certain remainder, something which reveals its partial character and also indicates the need – both theoretical and clinical – to reflect seriously on enjoyment as something distinct, irreducible to meaning, to the symbolic. It is here that Lacan returns to reflect on the central idea of Freudian metapsychology, that of a disjunction between the level of somatic excitations and that of their representation in the psyche: 'There is always a remainder, an irrecoverable left-over, a portion of the body's energies that fail to receive adequate registration in the battery of *Triebrepraesentanzen*. The processes of psychical binding never succeed in exhausting the somatic reservoir of unbound energies' (Boothby 2001: 286–7). Replacing the phallus with the *objet petit a* – one of the names given to this remainder – is only one of the ways in which Lacan initiated this quest in the latter part of his teaching.[24]

Undoubtedly this quest takes place on a very tricky terrain. For a start, there is the ever-present danger of dualism – both Lacan and Laclau are justified in their determination to avoid that. In Lacan's case, however, this does not presuppose discarding the (relational) *duality* in question but operating a shift in its conceptual parameters. This is, simply put, the reason behind Lacan's conceptual transition from the somatic to the real (Grigg 1994: 161). This transition also suggests a way of overcoming the problems of Freudian metapsychology. For the relation between libidinal energy, the somatic frontier of the drive, and representation, as well as the modus operandi between them, is not always clear-cut in Freud. One can notice, for example, the differences in his account from *Instincts and their Vicissitudes* to his study on *Repression* (Freud 1991b and Freud 1991c; also see Shepherdson 1997: 142).[25] What is crucially at stake here is the relation between the two registers, the extent to which energy/libido is co-extensive with, or antithetical to, representation. While the account presented in the prior text – and in others – tends to emphasise their constitutive interrelation (Shepherdson 1997: 143) or, at any rate, refrains from drawing a clear distinction between drive's somatic force and its psychic representative (Strachey 1991: 108), in *Repression* – as well as in *The Unconscious* and other texts – a much sharper distinction between the two is elaborated. Even though the second approach had the predominant influence – and rightly so – one has to agree with Shepherdson's conclusion: what we have is not any kind of simple division, a dualism, but a more complex and tangled relation, 'one in which it is still possible and necessary to differentiate', to follow up separately both sides (affective energy and representation) but only in their extimate relation (Shepherdson 1997: 143).

At this point one is bound to encounter another difficulty, what could be called the (epistemological) problem of the *before*, one that has also been touched upon in the previous chapter. How is it possible to talk about the before of representation? Certainly there is such a pre-symbolic, extra-discursive before. Lacan is absolutely clear on that: 'I am not at all trying to deny here that there is something which is before, that, for example, before I become a self or an It, there is something which the It was. It is simply a matter of knowing what this It is' (Lacan in Boothby 1991: 62). And, of course, we can only get an idea of what it is through representation, by losing this before in its unmediated primacy. Lacan introduces here the analogy between pre-symbolic real energy and the operation of a hydroelectric dam. As Richard Boothby observes, it is impossible to specify and calculate the energy of the river without referring to the structure of the dam that will obstruct and redirect its flow. We can and should presuppose the *force* of the river, but that force is not accessible to us in any meaningful way without the mechanism of the dam, without, that is, erecting an obstacle with relation to which force will be felt. This is Lacan's point:

> To say that the energy was in some way already there in a virtual state in the current of the river is properly speaking to say something that has no meaning, for the energy begins to be of interest to us in this instance only beginning with the moment in which it is accumulated, and it is accumulated only beginning with the moment when machines are put to work in a certain way, without doubt animated by something of a sort of definite propulsion which comes from the river current. (Lacan in Boothby 1991: 62)

The paradox here is related to the necessity of presupposing a pre-symbolic energetic substratum, a before of representation and symbolisation, which, however, cannot be articulated in meaning without reference to the matrix within which it is invested or which represses it. In other words, to presuppose psychic energy is unavoidable, but also by necessity indeterminate (Boothby 1991: 62–3; also see Boothby 2001: 147). In Lacan's own terms, the metapsychological presupposition 'is in truth completely impossible . . . But one cannot practice psychoanalysis, not even for one second, without thinking in metapsychological terms' (Lacan in Boothby 1991: 62–3).

Lacan offers a two-pronged solution to this paradox. Surely, insofar as we are destined to access the limits of discourse (affect and *jouissance*) through the traces they leave within discourse and representation, our focus is necessarily limited to an exploration of their constitutive relation. However, and this is the crucial point, the irreducible impossibility of a castrated pre-symbolic positivity, the X of the real, also has to be registered and encircled, even if this entails the risk of introducing a certain metaphysical element. The fiction, the hypothesis, of the pre-symbolic, extra-discursive real – as well as Freud's *das Ding* and the Lacanian myth of the *lamella* – is necessary if we want to make sense of all the phenomena in which discourse interacts with what exceeds its terrain: from identification to *lalangue*, from fantasy to *sinthome*. Otherwise the (often indeterminate) specificity of the two interconnected dimensions is bound to be lost (as in Laclau's first line of response) and the conditions of possibility for their interpenetration greatly obscured.

Lacan's radical gesture here is to traverse the fantasy of an *all-encompassing symbolic*. He knows that, in order to make sense of what escapes symbolisation, in order to account for the remainders of this process, he has to entertain, conceptually, the possibility of an almost complete reversal; he has to traverse his own universe of discourse, to turn his teaching upside down. This is a risk Lacan is perfectly willing to take.[26] He also knows that this remainder can be effectively produced and accounted for only after we have explored and traversed the linguistic field itself. This reversal requires an exhaustion of language: we need to immerse ourselves in the most extensive conceptualisation of language, to take into account the multitude of ways in which it determines/produces our reality in order to be able to envisage what is beyond language but – still – in relation to language. If in animals no distance between *jouissance* and the biological/instinctual body can be observed, in humans, language, the signifier, changes the picture completely. *Jouissance* cannot be reduced to natural processes and, thus, only after exhausting the linguistic field can one properly speak of *jouissance* (XVII: 37). There is no paradox here: we can only move beyond language insofar as we have reduced everything to language; if this signifying reduction leaves real remainders, then these need to be accounted for in the most thorough way, even if this involves a radical reversal.

What are the terms of this reversal with reference to Lacan's account of language? Miller has put it in the most vivid terms: 'Lacan, who anointed language, qualified it in his later teaching as chatter, blahblah, and even as a parasite of human beings . . . he downgraded his concept of language, and also that of structure, now not carried to the level of the real' (Miller 2002c: 23). Indeed the real, especially through the Lacanian typologies of *jouissance*, becomes 'the Lacanian analog of the raw force or *Drang* of the Freudian drive' (Boothby 2001: 287). Together with, but also beyond, the signifying level, it is now important 'to look for the real [*jouissance*]. Look for the real, try to bypass under meaning, to bypass constructions, even the elegant ones, even the probing ones, especially if they are elegant. It is what Lacan assumed and demonstrated in his later teaching' (Miller 2002c: 42). Now it is *jouissance* which acquires a certain conceptual and causal priority over the signifier; not only are the two planes distinct and even antithetical but *jouissance* is also theorised as what relegates the symbolic to the status of an imaginary *semblant* (p. 47).

Only now, having passed through a first major stage, at which the symbolic is primary, and through a second stage, at which this fantasy is traversed and the real restored in its equally causal powers, is it possible to reach an adequate understanding of the interpenetration of the two domains. Only now does it become possible to re-conceptualise signification along the lines of *signifiance*, *jouis-sens* and *lalangue*. These are three of the many Lacanian neologisms which aim to convey paradoxical fields in which the limits between language and *jouissance* become blurred, with meaning and affect, symbolic structure and *jouissance*, contaminating each other at the most profound level (Miller 2000b). The status of the Lacanian category of *lalangue* is indicative in this respect. It indicates, it encircles, the force of a non-linguistic language, a language *before* and *after* language. In its pre-symbolic form this relates to the babbling of the infant, a phenomenon situated at the frontier between language and *jouissance*, need and demand (Christidis 2002: 107). In the first instance, *lalangue* designates the 'primary chaotic substrate of polysemy out of which language is constructed' (Evans 1996: 97): language is without doubt made of *lalangue* (XX: 139). Furthermore, symbolic castration, accepting the laws of the symbolic, never manages fully to process and symbolise this real dimension of *lalangue*. Something persists within our socio-symbolic world, a remainder that resurfaces in a variety of formations at the borders of acceptable discourse: in the private language of lovers, in some versions of poetic and prophetic discourse, in the paroxysmal language of magic (What does 'abracadabra' mean?) (Christidis 2002: 101–15, 134). In that sense, *lalangue* refers to the non-communicative, affective aspects persisting within language which, by using ambiguity and homophony, produce a certain *jouissance* beyond meaning (Evans 1996: 97): it 'affects us first of all by everything it brings with it by way of *effects that are affects*' (XX: 139, emphasis added).

Taking the risk: challenges for discourse theory

Accepting these paradoxes of the real is a prerequisite to avoiding both a reification or essentialisation of affect and a signifying reductionism.

What such a move enables is a rigorous consideration of affect and discourse together, as two distinct but interpenetrating fields. A proper analytic understanding of affect must focus, first, on the proper (theoretical and clinical) delimitation of affect – distinguishing it from what Lacan calls 'affective smoochy-woochy' – and, second, on the interrelation between the affective domain and that of signification and meaning. The former has to be seen as shifted and directed by the symbolic order, by the order of representation, which is in turn limited and distorted by its pressure, by the persistence of the drive and the irreducibility of enjoyment. It seems, then, that we have been doing some progress. In fact, we have ended up in a position very similar to Laclau's second line of response: *there are indeed two sides but these can only be explored in their mutual relation*. Undoubtedly so; but it is important to emphasise once more that the relation loses all its meaning without the risk of positing the two sides as ontologically extimate to each other. This is why Lacan's complex trajectory vis-à-vis the exact formalisation of the dialectics between real and symbolic is so crucial here. Traversing the fantasy of an all-encompassing symbolic, Lacan assumes the impossible risk of positivising the real, which includes the necessary limitations, or even the failure, of this process – limitations imposed by our entrapment within the symbolic (but a symbolic that is, in its turn, split by a real division). *It is the failure to reduce real to symbolic and symbolic to real and the assumption of both these irreducible moments that permits a new insight into their complex modes of interaction.*

This is a risk that Laclau does not seem willing to take.[27] Again – and here I risk a certain repetition – I am not saying that there are no plausible reasons for such a reluctance. In his *JLS* reply he does mention two dangers related to the question of essentialism – indirectly verifying my initial hypothesis. The first one is that 'if affect is seen as a foreign intrusion within the linguistic, the latter will be seen as capable of a closure of its own if that interruption did not take place – however inevitable the interruption is. That is the best road to end in a purely essentialist/structuralist conception of language' (Laclau 2003: 284). However, affect and *jouissance* are not experienced merely as intrusions but also as investments which infuse signification, fortifying meaning and discourse. In any case, I cannot see how insistence on their distinct character leads to an essentialist/structuralist conception of language. Surely, if the mutual interruptions and inter-implications are inevitable – and here I am in full agreement with Laclau – then neither language nor *jouissance* can be presented as self-enclosed essences. Language is always incapable of subsuming an irreducible (affective) remainder of symbolisation which contaminates and disrupts in a variety of ways its supposedly normal functioning. The capability of a closure of the symbolic is already denied by the whole Lacanian conceptualisation of the constitutive lack in the Other – but, and this is the crucial step, this lack has to be acknowledged in its unequivocal real dimension, as a lack of *jouissance* that kicks off a whole dialectics of interruptions/interimplications between *jouissance* and language, affect and representation.[28] At the same time, although this real remainder and its hybrid implications within the symbolic presuppose an extimate real, this real is by definition impossible to represent in its totality: the means are lacking within the field of representation.

This clarification also deals with the second danger mentioned by Laclau, which is symmetrical to the first: 'there is the parallel danger of essentialising the operations of the unconscious making of the latter a fully fledged agency . . . While Lacan certainly presents the unconscious as that which interrupts the normal flow of events, he never makes an agency of the unconscious' (Laclau 2003: 284).[29] What seems to be implied here is the symmetrically opposite danger of a denigration of language. In his *Neuropolitics*, William Connolly deals with exactly this objection:

> Does attention to the role of affect in the mobility of thought denigrate the role of language? Not at all. First, linguistic distinctions, in the largest sense of the idea, are differentially mixed into affective states at each level of complexity, even if they do not exhaust them . . . Affect would be more brutish than it is without language. It would thus not be able to play the critical role it does in the consolidation of culturally imbued habits and regularities. (Connolly 2002: 71)

In short, to argue that we are dealing with two conceptually – and even ontologically – distinct orders of phenomena does not entail the further step of concluding that these two orders can only be thought of as self-enclosed essentialist entities.

If there is a danger of essentialism here, this could only result from the all-encompassing conception of discourse put forward by Laclau in his first line of response. In fact, what is most surprising is that it is even possible to detect traces of an immanentist logic in this conception – surprising because Laclau has been one of the most efficient critics of the ultimately anti-political *cul-de-sac* of immanentism as it is articulated, for example, in the work of Hardt and Negri.[30] For a failure to theorise in a distinct and rigorous way the two sides of the duality (discourse and affect) leads to a situation in which everything becomes an internal moment of discourse and loses any distinct presence. The development, the contingent history of a discursive ensemble, becomes the result of an endogenous dynamic, especially since the extra-discursive remains outside our field of reflection. Notice, for example, the following quotation:

> That is why I have extracted some categories – such as discourse – from any regional connotation and I have attempted to give to them a more primary ontological role. The complexes that I call 'discursive' include both affective and linguistic dimensions, and, *ergo*, they cannot be affective or linguistic. This is an intellectual strategy that I am prepared to defend.
>
> So, the crucial task is to think the specificity of discursive formations in such terms that the interaction between the various instances and registers loses its purely casual and external character and becomes constitutive of the instances themselves. This clearly requires a new ontology. I see the psychoanalytic revolution as an immense widening of the field of objectivity, bringing to consideration kinds of relations between entities which cannot be grasped with the conceptual arsenal of classical ontology. I see as our main intellectual task to rethink philosophy in the light of this project. (Laclau 2003: 283–4)

Although I am obviously in full agreement with Laclau on the importance of the psychoanalytic revolution, I can't see how such a quasi-immanentist, all-encompassing conceptualisation of discourse can follow from or be made compatible with the Lacanian orientation in its diachronic development. For, as we have seen, from a Lacanian point of view, even if discourse designates the terrain in which *jouissance* (the real) and meaning (the symbolic) encounter each other[31] – producing a variety of articulations – this does not presuppose a reduction of both these distinct dimensions to internal moments of discourse, now transformed into an immanent category. All the categories comprising the Lacanian triad – imaginary, symbolic, real – are ontological but none is all-encompassing or immanent. Without accepting this (relational, even failed) transcendence, the extimate relation of each one vis-à-vis the others, it is impossible to make sense of human (and political) reality.

Simply put, what is at stake here is whether the relation between the symbolic and the real, representation and affect, the signifier and *jouissance*, is one of *imminence* or *immanence*. This is very well exemplified in the recent work of two American Lacanians, Joan

Copjec and Bruce Fink. Fink does register the fundamental distinction between the two orders, 'representation and language (*savoir*) versus affect, libido, and jouissance (truth as jouissance)' (Fink 2004: 110). It is this polarity that permits the formulation of two distinct modalities of subjectivity, the subject of the signifier and the subject of *jouissance* (p. 124). That, of course, does not mean that the two orders are completely dissociated. Although affect can indeed be described metaphorically as an amorphous substance, an indeterminate state which is given meaning – symbolised – *après coup*, this, however, does not mean that it is more real than speech, or that it is possible to have some direct, unmediated access to it (p. 51). The 'symbol is imminent in affect', but there is no easy alliance between them (ibid.). Imminent yes, but is it also *immanent*? This, as we have seen, would probably be contrary to the overall Freudian–Lacanian orientation. But isn't exactly this what Copjec is proposing when she points out that the relation between the signifier and *jouissance* should not be treated as antinomic, specifying that – and this is the crucial point – affect is not something added to representation 'but a surplus produced by its very function, a surplus of the signifier over itself' (Copjec 2006: 94)? It is very difficult to see how an all-encompassing, immanentised 'discourse' and a conception of the signifier as 'alchemistically' producing an affective surplus out of its own immanent functioning can be reconciled with the Lacanian programme – or with discourse theory, for that matter.

More importantly, the problems here are not purely philosophical but also analytical and political. To view discourse and the signifier in such an all-encompassing way, to view affect and representation as co-extensive, to deny that there are two sides at play here, makes it very difficult to theorise in any productive way the interrelation between them. For example, how would it be possible, within such a framework, to differentiate between discourses which successfully function as objects of investment and discourses which fail to interact with *jouissance* in a successful (hegemonic) way? A concrete example of such an opposition will be presented in the second part of this book through the examination of the differences in the libidinal investment characteristic of nationalist identifications and identifications with 'European identity', differences which may explain the salience and relative durability of the former and the weakness of the latter. In other words, my worry is that to downplay the distinct character of the two registers may lead to the bizarre conclusion that all discourses are cathected to the same extent or that differences in cathexis are ultimately insignificant. Even if one accepts that there is no articulated discourse totally devoid of affective substance – since the desire to articulate something must surely presuppose a minimum of affective investment – would that mean that all discourses are isometrically cathected? Or that they are bound to appeal equally to everybody?

This is a problem that has also preoccupied the psychoanalytic clinic. Here, the crucial question is why and how some drives are fixated for some subjects and not for others. How come, for example, 'the Rat-man's anal drive was fixated and not his oral drive? How come it was Dora's oral drive and not her anal one?' Lacan's answer is that a *jouissance* of the body is involved in these stopping places (Declercq 2004: 244). A similar question can be posed with reference to the signifying architecture of a neurosis: How is it possible to explain why certain specific signifiers and not others determine each time the structuration of a neurosis? Why, for example, is it the word 'horse' that forms Little Hans' anxiety? Freud's intuition was that specific signifiers are chosen because 'they hook up with the drives fixated for these subjects'. For Lacan too, it is again the real of the body that (partially) overdetermines which particular master signifiers will condition the formation of a neurosis (ibid., p. 245). Here, 'perception, interpretation, normalisation, etc. are processes that are highly selective and biased by jouissance' (p. 246).[32] Ahmed has also reached a similar conclusion: 'some words stick because they [historically] become attached through particular affects' (Ahmed 2004: 60).

Any intelligent account of circulation and interpenetration between affect and Laclau's discourse requires registering their distinctiveness, simply because without it no consistent account can be formulated not only of fixation but also of repression – and we have seen how Laclau's own argument relies on such a conceptualisation of repression. Besides, without it there can be neither 'affective unevenness' nor 'differential cathexis' (Laclau 2003: 282–3; Laclau 2005: 119). Now, the exact relation between representation and affect within the framework of repression, especially the question whether what is repressed is affect or representation or both, has never stopped preoccupying Freud. He has experimented with different solutions and his views seemed to change with the passage between the different topographies. The dominant view in his work seems to be that repression does not touch affects directly but only the ideational representatives of the drive. Affects, however, are *displaced and transformed* as a result of repression. As Lyotard has put it, 'in

Freud, the affect is well and truly the name borne by energy itself in its investments and displacements when it operates on "representations"' (Lyotard 1993: 186). In that sense, the whole schema of repression is directly related to the energetic metaphor at the kernel of Freudian metapsychology: 'The key concept that underlies the whole system of metapsychological ideas is that of psychical energy. The notion of a mobile energy, capable of variable investments or "cathexes" and susceptible of transfer along a chain of associated representations, remained throughout Freud's career his single most important theoretical construction' (Boothby 2001: 4). In fact, the energetic metaphor is crucial in permitting psychoanalytic theory to postulate the *transmission* of psychic value between a variety of very different representations and to conceptualise a surplus of energy excluded from the symbolic system of representations (p. 147).

How does repression work, then? Let me offer a brief – and necessarily incomplete – sketch. When we encounter something incompatible with the reigning mass of representations in the ego, the latter tries to maintain its integrity by driving the event out of consciousness. Defence (repression) 'takes place via a withdrawal of the affect (quantum of energy) from the event's psychical representation, through which the event itself is transformed into an unconscious memory trace, while the affect is displaced to another representation' (Nobus 2000: 23). In repression, in other words, *affect and thought are detached from each other*. While, however, the representation is directed to the unconscious, affect remains. Clinicians often encounter patients voicing a variety of complaints (anxiety, sadness, depression, guilt, etc.) without being able to locate what exactly triggered such feelings: 'Affect often remains when the thought related to it is repressed, and the troubled individual tends spontaneously to seek ad hoc explanations for it, attempting to understand it in some way or other' (Fink 1997: 113). In Lacan's own words from the *Anxiety* seminar, 'What on the contrary I did say about affect, is that it is not repressed; and that is something that Freud says just like me. It is unmoored, it goes with the drift. One finds it displaced, mad, inverted, metabolised, but it is not repressed. What is repressed are the signifiers that moor it.' (seminar of 14 November 1962; also see XI: 217, XVII: 168, and Copjec 2006: 93). Indeed, this is very close to Freud's position in *Repression*: 'The general vicissitude which overtakes the idea that represents the instinct can hardly be anything else than that it should vanish from the conscious if it was previously conscious' (Freud 1991c: 152).[33] As far as the energy linked to the repressed idea is concerned, this, in Freud's view, can have a variety of possible vicissitudes: although its suppression is not excluded – corresponding to a successful repression and thus positing affect and representation as more or less co-extensive domains following parallel tracks, as in Laclau's first line of argument – in all other cases the two are dissociated and follow different courses, something vindicating the preceding critique of Laclau's position (Freud 1991c: 153). Typically, a certain transformation takes place that permits the expression of affect either through feelings (anxiety) that get retroactively symbolised or through the formation of symptoms: when a component of the repressed event (the affect) is attached to an element of the repressive structure (the substitute representation), it often produces a compromise symptomatic formation in a way which the subject cannot consciously understand (but can nevertheless enjoy in a distorted way, acquiring the 'satisfaction in dissatisfaction' which Lacan calls *jouissance*) (Nobus 2000: 24).[34]

Displacements, transformations, investments, cathexes, transfers, exclusions, detachments, inversions, metabolisms: so many forms of relation between affect and representation, *jouissance* and discourse. Can these – and their political implications – really be explored without a clear sense of the two dimensions at stake and of the conditions of possibility for their adequate – even if ultimately indeterminate – formulation? To conclude this chapter, questions like that clearly prioritise Laclau's second line of response, but this will never be solidly formulated without traversing the fantasy of an all-encompassing discourse. Lacan's radical gesture has to be kept in mind. Perhaps discourse theorists should consider treating 'discourse' the same way Lacan eventually treated not only language but also 'desire', traversing the conceptual nodal point of his early work. For Lacan admits that *jouissance* is 'a notion . . . that has always been implied in our reflections on desire [remember Laclau's claim that affectivity and *jouissance* were always part and parcel of his category of 'discourse'] but that deserves to be distinguished from it, and which can only be articulated after one is sufficiently imbued in the complexity that constitutes desire' (Lacan in Braunstein 2003: 102). If we want to examine how hegemonies are sustained, how identifications stick and political discourses get sedimented – obstructing or enabling social change – we need to take into account form and force, symbolic structuration and *jouissance*. This is not only a question of theoretical sophistication and analytical clarity, but also of critical awareness and theoretico-political strategy. Discourse theory has made enormous progress on this front, with Laclau gradually embracing and employing the category of the real in a variety of its modalities, including – very recently – that of *jouissance*. However, more needs to be done and Lacan's boldness in drawing the various implications of *jouissance* needs to be seriously considered and perhaps used as a source of inspiration in traversing the fundamental fantasy of discourse theory and risking a journey into new theoretical and analytical directions.

In this journey discourse theory will not be alone. For example, here Žižek and Laclau – notwithstanding their recent disagreements and heated exchanges – seem to share common ground. Laclau's distinction between form and force – as well as that of Castoriadis between *vis formandi* and *libido formandi* – parallels to a certain extent the Žižekian reformulation of the critique of ideology as a twofold strategy:

> At first sight it could seem that what is pertinent in an analysis of ideology is only the way it functions as a discourse, the way the series of floating signifiers is totalized, transformed into a unified field through the intervention of certain 'nodal points'. . . . in this perspective, the enjoyment-in-signifier would be simply pre-ideological, irrelevant for ideology as a social bond . . . [however] the last support of the ideological effect (of the way an ideological network of signifiers 'holds' us) is the non-sensical, pre-ideological kernel of enjoyment. In ideology 'all is not ideology (that is, ideological meaning)', but it is this very surplus which is the last support of ideology. That is why we could say that there are also two complementary procedures of the 'criticism of ideology':
>
> – one is *discursive*, the 'symptomal reading' of the ideological text bringing about the 'deconstruction' of the spontaneous experience of its meaning – that is, demonstrating how a given ideological field is a result of a montage of heterogeneous 'floating signifiers', of their totalization through the intervention of certain 'nodal points';
>
> – the other aims at extracting the kernel of *enjoyment*, at articulating the way in which – beyond the field of meaning but at the same time internal to it – an ideology implies, manipulates, produces a pre-ideological enjoyment structured in fantasy. (Žižek 1989: 124–5)

If, however, here we have agreement and a careful and fruitful negotiation between negative and positive, formal and substantive, as far as the analysis and critique of ideology is concerned, this is not the case with Žižek's more recent polemical/revolutionary writings. The passage from theory to politics, from reflecting to acting, is not an easy one. A thorough examination of the terrain designated in this text as that of the Lacanian Left demands that we turn our attention to this issue now – and is there a better starting place than Žižek's theoretico-political interventions on the act, the undisputable nodal point of his recent work?

Notes

1. See, for example, Stavrakakis 2000a.
2. In Stavrakakis 2004 and 2005b I am evaluating the importance of the category of the 'nodal point' – the signifier 'the people' – in the analysis of populist discourse, with reference to the Greek experience.
3. See Stavrakakis 1999a: 75–82, where I elaborate on the operationality of all these concepts and logics in discourse analysis with reference to a variety of concrete examples.
4. As shown in the previous chapter, it is this dialectics which is ultimately disavowed in Castoriadis' work.
5. In terms of the Freudian conceptual constellation to which *jouissance* relates, one should keep in mind that 'in German, jouissance translates faithfully as *Genuss*, a term used with some frequency by Freud; but here we should point out that in Freud, *Lust* and, sometimes, *Libido* are equivalent to jouissance' (Braunstein 2003: 103). Lacan himself has pointed out that libido is 'the jouissance implied by Freud' (Lacan 1990: 9).
6. As Fink formulates it in a more recent text: 'Lacan translates Freud's fundamental distinction between representation and affect as the distinction between language and libido, between signifier and jouissance' (Fink 2004: 142).
7. For a detailed Lacanian critique of the more or less naïve constructivism implicit in some versions of culturalist theory, see Belsey 2005.
8. In Stavrakakis 2000b I am offering a detailed application of the logic of dislocation in the analysis of ideological discourse with reference to the formation of Green ideology. In San Martin 2002, Pablo San Martin is using the same logic in his analysis of Asturian nationalism.
9. This link is clearly visible in my analysis of Green ideological fantasy. See Stavrakakis 1997c.
10. See, for example, Lane 1996, where it is argued that Laclau and Mouffe have generally emphasised 'contingency and discourse at the expense of *jouissance*' (p. 112) and that, as a result, they 'have not adequately engaged with the impediments and irruptions that jouissance manifests in the social field' (p. 114). Lane, in effect, argues that Laclau and Mouffe's early work is marked by a 'foreclosure of the subject's *jouissance*' (ibid.). Also see, in this respect, Lane 2001. I shall examine in latter sections of this chapter how this situation is gradually changing.

11. Introductory but quite detailed presentations of the various definitions and nuances of *jouissance* in Lacanian theory can be found in Braunstein 2003, Declercq 2004, Evans 1998, Miller 2000b, Nasio 1998 and Patsalides and Malone 2000.
12. Also see, in this respect, Stavrakakis 1999a: 45–54 and 81–2.
13. In clinical terms, one should not comtemplate eliminating the symptom: an 'analysis which starts with a symptom will also end with the symptom – hopefully transformed' (Soler 2003: 90).
14. For a discussion of the relation between politics and ethics from a deconstructive and psychoanalytic perspective, see Glynos 2000c.
15. Incidentally, doesn't that sound rather incommensurable with his basic thesis of an all-encompassing 'discourse', which gives the impression that no further theorisation is necessary in this field, that everything is already in place?
16. The problem here is not that discourse cannot be conceptualised in a way which incorporates the two dimensions. In fact, Lacan's conceptualisation of discourse, at least in his latter teaching, does manage to do exactly that (XVII), but this is achieved precisely because it is not defined at the level of meaning and signification/representation, as is clearly the case with Laclau's 'discourse'. This is why, in Laclau's case, to incorporate *jouissance* into the picture requires substantial work and cannot rely on an automatic retroactive ascription.
17. This is not far from Castoriadis' observation that our experience is marked by the workings of a *vis formandi* (a power of creation), which is, however, accompanied by a *libido formandi* (a desire for formation). This formation takes place at the level of meaning and signification, but 'signification here is not a simple matter of ideas or representations, for it must gather together – bind in a form – representation, desire and affect' (Castoriadis 1997b: 343).
18. Among others, Judith Butler has also referred to 'the force of language' in the beginning of her *Excitable Speech* (Butler 1997: 1). It is clear, however, that Laclau uses force in a way closer to that of Marshal Alcorn, as a 'libidinal force': 'the libidinal power of language is found in its potential for attachments, attractions, organizations, repulsions, and bindings that create relatively stable sites of identification' (Alcorn 2002: 20–1). In a similar vein, André Green entitles one of the sections in his study of affect in psychoanalysis 'The economic and the symbolic: force and meaning' (Green 1999: 203).
19. In Green's view this rejection has the paradoxical effect of bringing together Lacanian theory and Ego-psychology: 'That Hartmann and Lacan say nothing of affect is hardly surprising, since, for the first, affect is what challenges the supposed autonomy of the ego; for the second, affect is subjected to the play of the signifier' (Green 1999: 196).

20. Ironically, as shown in the previous chapter, it was Castoriadis who was led in such a direction by positing a pre-symbolic meaning.
21. See, from the secondary literature, Gallagher 1997 and Harari 2000.
22. Indeed, as Michel Henry has pointed out, Freud's stress on the status of anxiety as the ultimate transformation of affect constitutes his most crucial addition to the history of affectivity (Henry 1993: 305).
23. In this instance he seems to be arguing against conceptualising affect in terms of energy (if, that is, energy is defined as something 'numerically expressed', a 'numerical constant', as in the natural sciences), or using the 'crude metaphor' of a 'life-force'. Instead, he gives priority to a formulation with reference to the category of *jouissance* (p. 19), to the 'power' of the drive (p. 25). In *The Four Fundamental Concepts of Psychoanalysis*, however, when discussing the fundamental concept (*Grundbegriff*) of the drive, he will again employ an energetic jargon. Although the drive cannot be reduced to a purely organic force or assimilated to a purely biological function – which is the case with instinct – it does entail an investment which, as Lacan observes, 'places us on the terrain of an energy . . . a constant force' (XI: 164).
24. And even this will not be enough: 'Lacan does not stop at *petit a*. Why? He explains it in his Seminar XX, at the end of his second stage of teaching. *Petit a* is still a *sense joui* inscribed in the *fantasme*' (Miller 2003: 16). In other words, *objet petit a* remains linked to an imaginary representation of *jouissance* as fullness, which ultimately masks other modalities of the real.
25. This comparison is particularly instructive precisely because the two texts were published within the same year.
26. Something not surprising for someone who even went so far as to try to consider psychoanalysis from the outside, as something that is likely to become outdated at a certain juncture – a clear indication of his boldness as a theorist: 'Well considered, Lacan's teaching would be missing something if it had not gone that far, had not made a step outside the bath we are in . . . Lacan's teaching would be remiss if it hadn't taken this step outside psychoanalysis' (Miller 2003: 6).
27. Ironically, it seems that Saussure himself has taken a similar risk, although this is not visible in the standard transcription of the *Cours* (Saussure 1983). There is, however, another Saussure beyond the dry Cartesian clarity and the insistence on linguistic structure: a Saussure that focuses on the 'dark alchemy of language', on the 'unconscious of digital language'. This other Saussure is present in his studies of anagrams, German myths, poetics and Indian philosophy (Christidis 2002: 18–19). These 'darker' studies, negotiating the dialectics between the cognitive and the affective, have been marginalised in the transcription of the *Cours* and in most post-Saussurean analyses (Bouquet 1997: 81). They came into light only in the 1960s and 1970s, with the publication

of previously unavailable notebooks collecting a multitude of anagrams – 'the letters of the name of a God scattered through the poem written in the god's honor, numerous kinds of homophony or echoes, and so forth – that he thought he could locate in archaic Latin poetry' – and showing how 'his integral and concrete entity of language [the whole structuralist tradition] is necessarily and extravagantly haunted by what it excludes' (Harpham 2002: 33–4), by the return of the foreclosed real of language (Milner 1990). Also see on this issue Starobinski 1979 and Lecercle 1985. Lacan himself refers to the publication by Starobinski of Saussure's anagrams in a footnote to his 'Agency of the letter in the unconscious or reason since Freud' added in 1966 (E1977: 177), and then again in *Encore* (XX: 19).

28. In fact, such an understanding of language as closure would be akin to the imaginary dimension which is always present in human experience but has very little to do with what is at stake here.
29. Of course, one has to notice that Laclau performs a certain displacement of the discussion from the real to the unconscious, which is hardly mentioned in our paper and is not, strictly speaking, at issue here.
30. See, in this respect, Laclau 2001a.
31. In Vanier's words, for Lacan ' "discourse" is a collective organization for managing jouissance' (Vanier 2001: 41), and this is the cornerstone of the socialisation process: 'a discourse will always give the child an idea of what one does or is supposed to do with jouissance' (Declercq 2004: 238).
32. Biased but not determined according to any logic of biologistic determinism insofar as there is no fixed, natural object guiding this process. The object of the drive constitutes what is most variable in it since it is not originally connected with it (Freud 1991b: 119). Indeed, as Lacan has formulated it, the Freudian drive 'has nothing to do with an instinct' (E2006: 721) since 'no object of any *Not*, need, can satisfy the drive' (XI: 167). But why exactly is that? First, because the aim of the drive is not to attain what 'from the point of view of a biological totalization of function would be the satisfaction of its end of reproduction', but simply to return into circuit (XI: 179). Second, this circuit of the drive can be formed and fixated around an infinite variety of objects, something that permits the drive to find satisfaction even when it is inhibited with regards to its supposed original aim, as in sublimation. Lacan offers a direct illustration of this point: 'In other words – for the moment, I am not fucking, I am talking to you. Well! I can have exactly the same satisfaction as if I were fucking' (XI: 165–6).
33. Before his metapsychological papers, Freud's views on the different fates of affect and representation follow a variety of shifts. In a 1894 letter to Fliess he argues that affect is subject to 'transformation' and 'displacement', while in *The Interpretation of Dreams* he presents the ideational

material as undergoing 'displacements' and 'substitutions', with affect remaining 'unaltered' (Green 1999: 18, 31). André Green also reminds us that, after his metapsychological contributions, in his 1927 paper on 'Fetishism', Freud seems to reverse his earlier position by arguing that repression primarily targets affect: 'Not only is the affect repressed, but repression operates specifically on the affect, whereas the representation falls under disavowal' (p. 56).

34. In the context of repression, it is also possible to distinguish emotions clearly from affect, something that, as already shown, Lacan also does in his *Anxiety* seminar, arguing against their use as synonyms. For example, if we turn to the current debate on emotions, especially to the whole bibliography on the social construction of emotions (Harré 1986; Billig 1999), we will encounter a distinction between (discursive, socially constructed) emotions and (energetic) affect. In Billig's schema, where emotions are conceptualised as 'discursive phenomena' incarnating 'social relations', the implication is that emotions can be repressed. But is that any different from the dominant Freudian/Lacanian conception of repression recounted here? Not really, and precisely because, even in this case, what is pushed from consciousness (emotions, which presuppose symbolisation, a conscious narrativisation) does not denote an embodied intensity beyond the control of consciousness (affect), 'a bodily feeling, but a means of interpretation' (Billig 1999: 187), corresponding to the Freudian ideational representatives of the drive.

From a Deleuzian perspective, Brian Massumi has also elaborated a similar distinction between emotion and affect. According to Massumi, 'emotion and affect – if affect is intensity – follow different logics and pertain to different orders' (Massumi 1996: 221). Affect there is understood as an unassimilable intensity, while emotion entails the 'insertion of intensity into semantically and semiotically forced progressions, into narrativisable action–reaction circuits, into function and meaning' (ibid.). In this sense, emotion marks a '*capture* and closure of affect' within a primarily symbolic structure (pp. 228, 220), and initiates a dialectics similar to the one between real and symbolic in Lacan.

3

Žižekian 'Perversions': The Lure of Antigone and the Fetishism of the Act

Žižek's revolutionary act: a vanguard for the Lacanian Left?

My engagement with the work of Laclau has focused on the importance of combining a Lacan-inspired awareness of lack and of the limits of discourse (the Lacanian conceptualisation of negativity qua encounter with the real) with a more substantive dimension, crucial for understanding political life and especially the affective aspect of identification processes: the axis of enjoyment in its different modalities and in its continuous interaction with the discursive constitution of our social and political reality, with the materiality of the signifier. As we have seen, such an articulation requires a delicate balancing act between negativity and positivity. If the chances of succeeding in this endeavour seem rather promising in the case of reorienting critical political theory, things become blurred when at issue is the ethico-political impetus of the Lacanian Left, when, that is, 'what is to be done?' and 'how?' come to the forefront as the central questions. In an effort to avoid the supposed reformist direction implicit in every politics which registers the unavoidable encounter with the negative, two major figures, absolutely central in this emerging terrain, Alain Badiou and Slavoj Žižek, have generally opted for a different strategy.[1] Through their various formulations of the 'event' and the 'act' respectively, they have consistently attempted to reintroduce the dimension of radical – even *ex nihilo* – socio-political change into the admittedly complacent horizon of existing democracies. Obviously, this can be quite appealing today, when the post-political consensus attempts to de-politicise the democratic process in the West and to impose models of domestic and international governance (the signifier of de-politicisation *par excellence*) which discourage active participation and passionate identification, marginalise democratic antagonism and foreclose the possibility of formulating any real alternatives.[2] Although such a move is to be commended on the grounds that it keeps alive the prospect of a transformation in power structures and social arrangements, as part of an effort to formulate new forms of political agency, it nevertheless poses important questions as far as the proper way of achieving this is concerned.

With respect to Žižek's work, the crucial problem I perceive here is the following: Žižek's politics of the act seems to be overstressing the unlimited (real) positivity of human action beyond any serious registering of lack and finitude. It privileges the moment of a political praxis, which transcends altogether the discursive (spatial) limits of the symbolic and, operating as a cataclysmic real creation, opens itself onto the void of eternity. Thus it entails a very clear danger of ultimately disavowing the dialectics between positive and negative central to Lacanian theory, replacing it with a positive politics of the event/act as miracle. In political terms, my hypothesis is that the problem here is the opposite from the one diachronically associated with discourse theory (too much stress on negativity, on the real qua negative, as shown in Chapter 2) – a problem analogous with the one which marks the work of Castoriadis (too much emphasis on positivity qua unlimited creation, as demonstrated in Chapter 1). The crucial question, of course, is whether the resulting circularity is vicious or not.

In this chapter – which focuses on Žižek's work – and in the excursus that follows – in which my attention shifts to Badiou – my aim will thus be to assess the theoretical constitution and the ethico-political implications of the two projects, with emphasis on their location within the Lacanian Left. This exploration will also reveal the convergences and divergences between them – which are equally obscured when the two projects are reduced/collapsed into a single unified argument and in the symmetrically opposite operation of magnifying and highlighting often misconceived tensions between them – as well as the language games implicit in their appropriation of Lacanian theory.

In trying to illuminate Žižek's 'revolutionary' desire and to evaluate its consequences for the Lacanian Left, I will be discussing as thoroughly as possible his recent work on the act. Although I will also be commenting on the overall development of Žižek's argumentation over the years, this chapter will not provide a comprehensive introduction or analysis of all aspects of Žižek's prolific and multidimensional work, a task which, if at all possible, would require a separate monograph.³ First, I will try to substantiate my claim that Žižek is guilty of a disavowal of the constitutive dialectics between negative and positive. I will argue that, contrary to his claims, this theoretico-political orientation is inconsistent with Lacan's understanding of the act. Furthermore, it does not take into account the dimension of temporality beyond the moment of this miraculous occurrence, it neglects the dialectics between time and space, and, as a result, it disregards the problem of the form institutional arrangements can and should take following the act, including the possibility of experimenting with new post-fantasmatic types of ordering. What the Lacanian Left needs is to move in the direction of articulating an alternative conception of the act, one which may link Lacan's insights (operating at both the real and symbolic levels) with a radical democratic project, able to promote the idea of a continuous *re-enacting of the act* as well as to imagine and construct a (conceptual, affective and material) space where such re-enacting becomes possible.

Ambiguities of the act in Lacan and Žižek

Given a certain fluctuation or indeterminacy typical of Slavoj Žižek's mode of argumentation as it evolves over time – to which I shall return shortly – I will start my critical approach to his politics of the act by focusing on one particular text which provides an exemplary summary of his position, inclusive of a discussion of his favourite example, that of Antigone. This text, entitled 'From "passionate attachments" to dis-identification', was first published in *Umbr(a)* (Žižek 1998a) and then reprinted in *The Ticklish Subject* (Žižek 1999), one of Žižek's most important books. A much earlier and less developed version of my critique of Žižek has also appeared in *Umbr(a)* and triggered Žižek's response in the same issue of the journal and in his recent book on Iraq (Žižek 2004a). Dealing with his responses will further illuminate what is wrong with Žižek's politics of the act. But let's take one step at a time.

In his *Umbr(a)* essay, a reply to Judith Butler's criticism of Lacan, Žižek's argument revolves around the radical character of Lacanian ethics and aims at demonstrating its radical political potential. What is at stake in Žižek's argument is not only the possibility of resisting, but also of undermining or displacing the existing socio-symbolic network, of radically transforming a given power structure. He distinguishes between an imaginary form of resistance, a 'false transgression' that ultimately serves to maintain and reproduce the law, and 'the effective symbolic rearticulation *via* the intervention of the real of an *act*' (Žižek 1998a: 5). Such a conception is consistent with Lacan's work precisely because it involves both a real and a symbolic dimension. Both these axes are central to Lacan's seminar of 1967–8, *L' acte psychanalytique*,[4] where the paradoxical status of the act as *un fait de signifiant*, as a language and division effect, is illuminated in depth. The act presupposes a given symbolic order, which is dislocated and, following an encounter with the real, rearticulated again in different – but still predominantly symbolic – terms. So there has to be an *after* the act, an after which should be different from the before if the act is to be awarded any real transformative potential.

Surely if the Lacanian Left purports to function as a facilitator of critique, a catalyst enabling social change, then this argument needs to be thoroughly evaluated, if not directly embraced. In fact, as we have seen towards the end of the first chapter, this move is absolutely crucial for the Lacanian Left. But how exactly should it be further conceptualised and developed? Where does one go from here? One would perhaps expect a thorough treatment of what form this rearticulation should take: encircling the lack in the Other and inscribing the possibility of continuous re-acts, for example. This is the direction Lacan's seminar of 1967–8 highlights when it describes the psychoanalytic act as an assertion that permits continuous 're-acts' (seminar of 20 March 1968). Following this direction and drawing its ethico-political implications, I have already attempted – in this book and elsewhere[5] – to articulate Lacanian theory and a certain conceptualisation of radical democracy. But this is not the direction followed by Žižek in his recent work. Is Žižek's recent formulation of a politics of the act consistent with this orientation of Lacan's teaching? Does he really 'prescribe suicide as the supreme ethical act' and in what exact sense? (Belsey 2005: 57) And if so, does this really offer a plausible way forward for the politics of social transformation?

First of all, it is necessary to highlight – and problematise – a certain *displacement* characteristic of Žižek's argumentation. Instead of grounding his supposedly Lacanian elaboration of the act on Lacan's seminar on the *Act* (1967–8), he chooses to concentrate on Lacan's *Ethics* seminar (1959–60), where Lacan addresses Antigone's act, an act pushing to the limit 'the realization of something that might be called the pure and simple desire of death as such', given that Antigone 'incarnates that desire' (VII: 282). This choice is far from innocent or coincidental; the distance between the two seminars in terms of the development in Lacan's teaching is considerable. In particular, this displacement provides Žižek with an opportunity to embrace the assumption of the death drive as 'the elementary form of the *ethical act*' (Žižek 1998a: 6). It also allows him to endorse the heroic example – the model – of Antigone, arguing that she 'effectively puts at risk her entire social existence, defying the socio-symbolic power of the city embodied in the rule of Creon, thereby "falling into some kind of death" – i.e., sustaining symbolic death, the exclusion from the socio-symbolic space' (pp. 6–7).[6] On Žižek's reading of Lacan, there is no ethical act proper without the 'risk' of a 'momentary' suspension of the big Other. Furthermore, only such a 'radical *act*' can engender 'a thorough reconfiguration of the entire field which redefines the very conditions of socially sustained performativity' (p. 8).

This is, then, where the political significance of Antigone's act lies: 'Lacan's wager is that even and also in politics, it *is* possible to accomplish a more radical gesture of "traversing" the very fundamental fantasy. Only such gestures which disturb this fantasmatic kernel are authentic *acts*' (p. 9). It is also here that Žižek locates a major difference between a deconstructionist ethics of finitude and a Lacanian ethics. In the case of the former, faced with a constitutive lack, the only ethical option is heroically to assume it: 'the corollary of this ethics, of course, is that the ultimate source of totalitarian and other catastrophes is man's presumption that he can overcome this condition of finitude, lack and displacement, and "act like God", in a total transparency, surpassing his constitutive division' (p. 16). By contrast, Žižek's Lacanian answer is that 'absolute/unconditional acts do occur' and that 'the true source of evil is not a finite mortal man who acts like God, but a man who disavows that divine miracles occur and reduces himself to just another finite mortal being' (p. 17). In that sense, Antigone's lure for Žižek has nothing to do with finitude, as some commentators of Alain Badiou have argued. For example, as opposed to Alain Badiou's celebration of infinity and immortality, Peter Hallward presents Žižek's stress on Antigone as 'guided by an ultimately morbid "fascination with the lethal Thing", a profoundly pessimistic conception of man [as] "nature sick unto death"' (Hallward 2003: 150). As we shall see in this chapter and in the excursus that follows – and as Žižek's outright dismissal of finitude implies – the problem is exactly the opposite: Antigone is chosen by Žižek because, although she embodies negativity, she does so in a solipsistic way, which transubstantiates an initial registering of lack into a glorious, total, perfect, unlimited act, *the only act that cannot misfire*. It is not a coincidence that this is exactly how Lacan defines suicide. The other side of Antigone's negative – morbid – desire is suicide as a purely positive radical act, an act that cannot fail. It becomes clear, then, that, although Žižek's conception of the act initially invokes a moment of rupture and negativity, it acquires its heroic gloss from repudiating the negative ontology characteristic of Lacanian theory, from re-founding the world without any registering of finitude. By transforming the pure negativity of her desire for death into a purely positive act, liberating her forever from the constraints of the symbolic order, Antigone functions as the primary example of such a strategy.

However appealing this passionate promise of miraculous change may be, particularly in an era of cynical apathy and/or pessimism, Žižek's schema raises a number of important theoretical and political questions. In what follows, I will attempt to highlight some of the tensions inherent in his argument in order to help clarify the Lacanian ethical position and its implications for contemporary critical theory, transformative political action and the Lacanian Left.

Antigone idealised

By identifying Antigone as one of the primary examples of the ethical act Žižek seems to situate his argument in the long tradition of what Simon Critchley has described as the 'tragic–heroic paradigm' (Critchley 1999: 231). There are at least two important issues one needs to address in evaluating this position. The first is related to Žižek's particular reading of Antigone. The way he presents Antigone seems to bypass important aspects both of the tragedy itself and of Lacan's commentary. The second concerns the general value of the heroic paradigm in Lacanian theory and in politics.

First of all, can Antigone really be presented as a model for progressive ethico-political action? According to Žižek, such an example can be offered only by someone who 'risks' an encounter with death in order to 'momentarily' suspend the symbolic/legal network and effect a shift in the existing power structure. Does Antigone fulfill these criteria? Even a cursory glance at Sophocles's text and Lacan's commentary seems to point to the opposite. Antigone does not merely 'risk' an encounter with symbolic death, a 'momentary suspension' of the laws of the city. In opposing the laws of the city, Creon's ethics of the good(s), she incarnates a pure desire, she achieves an *autonomy* so radical that it can only be associated with death in its most radical sense (both symbolic and real). In the words of the chorus, 'a law to yourself, alone, no mortal like you, ever, you go down to the halls of Death alive and breathing' (Sophocles 1984: 102, lines 912–14). According to Lacan, Antigone's position is the following: 'I am dead and I desire death' (VII: 281). In that sense, hers was never a case of 'risk' or 'suspension'. Risk entails a minimum of strategic or pragmatic calculation, which is something alien to Antigone's pure desire. Suspension presupposes a before and an after, but for Antigone there is no after. In that sense, this was never a case of an act effecting a displacement of the status quo. Her act is a *one-off* and she couldn't care less about what will happen in the polis after her suicide.

Antigone knows her fate from the beginning, she is involved in a game whose outcome is known in advance, a detail that does not escape Lacan's attention: in almost all of the seven tragedies of Sophocles, as he points out, 'there isn't even the suggestion of a perepetia. Everything is there from the beginning; the trajectories that are set in motion have only to come crashing down one on top of the other as best they can.' Moreover, as Lacan adds, 'tragic heroes are always isolated, they are always beyond established limits, always in an exposed position and, as a result, separated in one way or another from the structure' (VII: 271). Such a position can, of course, function as a radical critique of the social order as such. It is difficult to see, however, how the 'inhuman' position of Antigone could point to an alternative formulation of the same socio-political order. The 'suicidal heroic ethics' implicit in Lacan's reading of Antigone implies a total neglect of the socio-political world; as Žižek suggests in an earlier text, the motto of such an ethics can only be *fiat desiderium pereat mundus* (Žižek 1994: 69). Antigone's intransigence, her deadly passion, may thus be what creates her tragic appeal, but, even by Žižek's own standards, one has to conclude that this makes her unsuitable as a model for ethico-political action.

Unless, of course, she is reinterpreted in a substantial way. But then a certain paradox emerges: Antigone can only function as a model for radical political action on the condition that she is stripped of her radically inhuman (asocial and anti-political) desire. Brecht knew that very well, and this is what explains the need for his 'politicised' reworking of the play (in which Antigone explicitly offers herself as a model; Brecht 1965). Žižek's selection of certain terms ('risk', 'momentary suspension') seems to perform a similar function of *socialising/politicising* Antigone's pure desire.[7] Such a move, however, is unable to resolve an irreducible tension: a tension between the admiration for Antigone's pure desire and the simultaneous need to give way on her radical desire in order to make it relevant for politics. This is a tension that Žižek himself has accepted as far as his earlier work is concerned. Consider, for example, *The Metastases of Enjoyment*, in which he accepts, in a self-critical tone, that in the past he has yielded to the 'temptation' of complementing or moderating Lacan's ethics of persisting in one's desire (Žižek 1994: 84). Judging from his 1998 *Umbr(a)* article, one can conclude that the tension may be displaced and camouflaged, but not fully resolved. Such – necessary – moderation is still a taboo for Žižek, and thus immoderate Antigone retains her place within an ethico-political framework alien to her pure desire and demanding its reinterpretation. Yet, if Antigone is useful only if reinterpreted in such a way – a way almost antithetical to her profile in the play – why should one retain her as a paradigm of the ethico-political act?[8] *Wouldn't the truly radical act be to traverse the lure of Antigone altogether?* All in all, Antigone seems unsuitable as a model of the act and her lure leads Žižek to a position which contradicts its formal conditions, as he himself has outlined them.

Lacanian transformations

This is not to say, though, that the problem lies entirely with Žižek's appropriation of the Lacanian commentary and of the figure of Antigone. Things wouldn't be easier if one were to stick to Lacan's text in order to elevate *his* Antigone to a model of ethico-political action – fortunately, in opposition to Brecht and Žižek, Lacan himself does not seem particularly interested in doing that. To focus exclusively on Lacan's commentary on Antigone would amount to ignoring the radical shift in Lacan's own position following the *Ethics* seminar. Clearly, Antigone is not Lacan's last – or most insightful – word on the question of ethics and agency. His position continued to develop in a direction that undermined his earlier focus on Antigone's pure desire. As Alenka Zupančič has pointed out, this becomes evident, for example, in *The Four Fundamental Concepts of Psychoanalysis*, where the idea of 'pure desire' is radically questioned (Zupančič 2000: 3). Indeed, here Lacan not only denies the possibility of a pure desire of the analyst (XI: 276), but also highlights, in a very Hegelian/Kojèvian way, the alienating character of desire – '*man's desire is the desire of the Other*' (XI: 38, 115) – while also pointing to the interpenetration of law and desire (XI: 34). This shift needs to be taken into account when discussing the function of Antigone. Let us examine some of its implications in greater detail.

Lacan's reading of Antigone in the *Ethics* seminar is based on the antithesis between Creon's ethics of 'the good of all' (VII: 258) and Antigone's ethics, which is articulated around 'a good that is different from everyone else's' (VII: 270), a pure (and thus deadly) incarnation of the 'laws of desire.' But is this opposition as radical as it seems at first glance? What is the exact nature of the antithesis between Creon and Antigone in Lacan's account? Primarily, it is an opposition between the order (and the morality) of power and an ethics of pure desire. Creon's morality is the 'traditional' morality, also endorsed by Aristotle: it 'is the morality of the master, created for the virtues of the master and linked to the order of powers' (VII: 315). This order is not to become the object of contempt; Lacan makes it clear that his comments are not those of an anarchist, but simply of someone aware of the *limitations* of this order. It is clear that in the *Ethics* seminar these limitations are understood in terms of desire: what is opposed to the ethics of power is the pole of desire (VII: 314).

In this schema, Antigone's pure desire becomes the model of a radical transgression of the suppression or gentrification of desire implicit in every power structure and in the moral order sustaining it. More generally, desire is posited here as the complete antithesis to the sphere of the goods, as the transgression of power in all its different forms (traditional, capitalist or communist):

> Part of the world has resolutely turned in the direction of the service of goods, thereby rejecting everything that has to do with the relationship of man to desire – it is what is known as the postrevolutionary perspective. The only thing to be said is that people don't seem to have realized that, by formulating things in this way, one is simply perpetuating the eternal tradition of power, namely, 'Let's keep on working, and as far as desire is concerned, come back later.' But what does it matter? In this tradition the communist future is only different from Creon's, from that of the city, in assuming – and it's not negligible – that the sphere of goods to which we must all devote ourselves may at some point embrace the whole universe. (VII: 318)

While Lacan's insightful critique of power remains important, it is clear that his positing of desire as the antithesis of the order of power and of the service of goods cannot be sustained. It probably belongs to what Žižek has correctly criticised as a 'false transgression,' which ultimately reproduces the order it is supposed to undermine.

In fact, it is Lacan himself who provides the theoretical tools for such a critique of his earlier work, particularly of his comments on Antigone. It is Lacan who, echoing Saint Paul's first letter to the

Romans, eventually acknowledges the constitutive dialectics between law and desire (E2006: 103). In his seminar on *Anxiety*, delivered only two years after the *Ethics* seminar, one finds a revealing passage: 'desire and the law, which appear to be opposed in a relationship of antithesis, are only one and the same barrier to bar our access to the thing. *Nolens, volens*: desiring, I commit myself to the path of the law' (seminar of 19 December 1962). Desire not only loses its value as a pure force of transgression, but is also revealed as the ultimate support of power and the order of goods. No wonder that, as soon as *jouissance* acquires its central place in Lacan's theoretical universe, desire is revealed as a defense against enjoyment, as a compromise formation, while drive emerges as the nodal point of his ethical thought (Zupančič 2000: 235). Conceived this way, desire can never be a pure transgressive force. Even in perversion, where desire 'appears by presenting itself as what lays down the law, namely as a subversion of the law, it is in fact well and truly the support of a law' (seminar of 27 February 1963). In fact, Lacan will go so far as to argue that *desire is the law* (seminar of 27 February 1963). It is thus not surprising that Antigone eventually links her desire to a certain law, the laws of the Gods: 'These laws, I was not about to break them, not out of fear of some man's [Creon's] wounded pride, and face the retribution of the gods' (Sophocles, 1984: 82, lines 509–11). In that sense, Antigone remains ultimately obedient to the law of the Father (Grigg 2001: 119), which disqualifies her – once more, but now for a different reason – as a suitable example of a facilitator of radical social and political change:

> Antigone's act is not an act of absolute freedom in the required sense. . . . It is arguable that Sygne de Coufontaine's act is, but not Antigone's. And the reason why Antigone's is not is that she is acting, and sacrificing herself, blindly, in the name of the law – even if it is the fractured law of Oedipus. (Grigg 2001: 117)[9]

In actual fact, one could even argue that it is Antigone who should be seen as the guardian of traditional ethics here (of a sense of duty and sacred obligation towards the family and the bonds of blood). If this is the case, why not see Creon as the real rebel, the agent of autonomy and radical transgression, since it is he who disobeys the sacred laws and is eventually punished for it? (Politi 1997). And why ignore his own tragic appeal? Although Creon initially orders Antigone's entombment in a cave – with enough food just to 'keep the entire city free of defilement' – he eventually changes his mind and decides to release her, only to discover that it's too late, that she has committed suicide, with his beloved son, Haemon, and his wife, Eurydice, following her example.

Hence it is not only the order of power which is revealed as severely limited; desire also has precise limits (XI: 31). It is always conditioned by the structures of fantasy sustaining 'hegemonic' regimes – regimes of power, consumption, and even resistance and transgression. It is always stimulated by the imaginary lure of attaining *jouissance*, but it is also sustained by the constitutive inability to realise such a goal. In that sense, desire 'succeeds', reproduces itself, through its own failure, its own constitutive impurity. And such reproduction is never politically innocent. For example, as will be argued in the second part of this book, consumer culture is partly sustained by the continuous displacement of final satisfaction from advertisement to advertisement, from product to product, from fantasy to fantasy (Chapter 7). The important 'by-product' of this play is a specific structuration of desire which guarantees, through its cumulative metonymic effect, the reproduction of the market economy within a distinct consumer culture.

It is Lacan himself, then, who points the way to traversing the lure of Antigone by shifting his understanding of desire. This shift needs to be acknowledged as the radical break it truly represents. Any attempt to reconcile the 'pure' desire of Antigone with his latter conceptualisation and critique of *illusory* desire, as well as reconcile the ethics of desire with the ethics of the drive – what Zupančič seems to attempt in the last pages of her *Ethics of the Real* – needs to be re-examined and modified, if not abandoned.[10] To make my argument more clear, it seems to me that anyone taking seriously the important shift in Lacan's position has to abandon Antigone as a model of the ethico-political act, something that Žižek fails to do. It is this failure which ultimately justifies Grigg's conclusion: 'I believe that Žižek has a somewhat idealized view of desire' (Grigg 2001: 122). As a result, suffering from a similar idealisation, his conception of the ethico-political act does not fare any better.

Lack versus divine miracle

But let us return to Žižek's discussion of Antigone. His paradoxical idealisation of Antigone as a model of radical ethico-political action seems also to conflict with his own Lacanian account of the act as a non-subjectivist, non-intentional encounter with the real. For, at one level, Antigone's act is clearly presented as an act of subjective/voluntarist autonomy beyond the restrictions of the social world (if one accepts, that is, that Creon does embody these restrictions). Isn't it the case, then, that Antigone's 'heroic' act conflicts with Žižek's conceptualisation of the act as distinct from Will? (Žižek 1997: 223). In *L'acte psychanalytique*, Lacan himself points out that the act entails a certain 'renewal' of the subject (seminar of 29 November 1967) – the act is never an act of which anyone can claim to be the absolute master (seminar of 24 January 1968). Is this really compatible with Antigone's stance?

If Žižek's position is that 'absolute–unconditional acts do occur, but not in the idealist guise of a self-transparent gesture performed by a subject with a pure will who fully intends them' (Žižek 1998a: 16–17), then again Antigone seems to have no place in his schema. What is needed instead is a non-subjectivist *formal* model of the act. What would such a model look like? When Žižek juxtaposes deconstruction and psychoanalysis, it seems that he is indirectly attempting a reply. But how does Žižek conceptualise the distinction between the deconstructionist and the Lacanian position? In order to ground his ethics of the political, it seems that he introduces a criterion in terms of the oppositions passivity/activity and negativity/positivity and their philosophical/religious mutations: finitude/immortality and lack/miracle. In short, Žižek's point is that deconstruction prioritises lack and finitude as the limit of ethico-political action, locating the source of evil in any attempt to surpass the subject's constitutive division and act like God. In stark opposition to such a pessimistic, passive standpoint, Žižek's response is to reverse the argument and argue that the true source of evil is assuming finitude, mortality, and lack as such, ignoring the dimension of 'divine miracles': '[acts] occur, on the contrary, as a totally unpredictable *tuche*, a miraculous event which shatters our lives. To put it in somewhat pathetic terms, this is how the "divine" dimension is present in our lives' (Žižek 1998a: 17). But let us examine the exact terms of this crucial opposition.

First of all, it is not entirely clear why anyone would want to associate the logic of lack – of constitutive lack as the support and limit of desire, as its condition of possibility and impossibility – with deconstruction. Lack and its various synonyms, lack in its various guises, is clearly a Lacanian concept, as Žižek himself has pointed out repeatedly. For example, in *The Sublime Object of Ideology* one finds the following quotation with respect to the importance of lack, especially of the 'lack in the Other':

Today, it is a commonplace that the Lacanian subject is divided, crossed-out, identical to a lack in the signifying chain. However, the most radical dimension of Lacanian theory lies not in recognizing this fact but in realizing that the big Other, the symbolic order itself, is also *barré*, crossed-out, by a fundamental impossibility, structured around an impossible/traumatic kernel. (Žižek 1989: 122)

In his *Umbr(a)* text, however, lack and division paradoxically reappear as internal moments of a deconstructionist ethics of finitude. In Žižek's book on totalitarianism, what sounds like the lack in the Other is treated in a similar way: 'The deconstructionist political doxa goes something like this: the social is the field of structural undecidability, it is marked by an irreducible gap or lack, forever condemned to non-identity with itself; and "totalitarianism" is, at its most elementary, the closure of this undecidability' (Žižek 2001: 6).

It is difficult to understand, at least in theoretical terms, this willingness to hand over to deconstruction what Žižek himself has described as 'the most radical dimension of Lacanian theory', the lack in the socio-symbolic Other, as well as the Lacanian 'commonplace' of the subject as lack. One can only speculate that this move, visible in many of Žižek's recent texts, must be related to a general *political* strategy of juxtaposing negativity and positivity, passivity and activity, pessimism and optimism. If his version of radical politics is to be presented as an *optimistic politics of the miraculous act* – a politics of almost vitalist activity – and if Lacanian theory is to function as a support for this politics, then Lacanian theory has to be purified from its stress on negativity and lack, which is then conveniently projected onto deconstruction.

Even this purification, though, fails to guarantee the theoretico-political coherence of Žižek's argument. Passivity, for example, survives to haunt his politics of the act. Even if lack were to be associated with deconstruction, does that transform the supposedly 'Lacanian' politics of the miraculous act into a politics entirely beyond passivity? I doubt it, precisely because, as we have seen, the act is not purely subjective or subjectivised. In Žižek's own schema, our relation to acts is always a relation of assumption, of coming to terms with a radical break (Žižek 1998a: 15). What, then, is the difference between assuming lack and assuming the act, the event? The only difference seems to be located in the particular content of each experience. In the case of lack this is posited as being purely negative, while in the case of the act as purely positive.

Indeed, as already mentioned, Žižek's argument relies on staging a strict opposition between *lack*, denoting finitude and negativity, and *divine miracle*, denoting immortality and positivity. Moreover, this oppositional relation is conceptualised in terms of a zero-sum game. Is it possible, however, to sustain such a sharp distinction? I see at least two problems with a position of this kind: one theoretical, the other political. At the theoretical level, it is impossible to ignore the irreducible interconnection between negativity and positivity, lack and desire, death and resurrection. Even in Alain Badiou's work, which seems to be one of the inspirations for Žižek's conceptualisation of the act/event here, the event refers to a real break which destabilises a given discursive articulation, a pre-existing order.[11] It has, in other words, a negative/disruptive dimension. It relates to a lack in the pre-existing structure. But, like Ernesto Laclau's dislocation, it also has a positive dimension. In Badiou, the dislocating event is what (potentially) produces a new form of subjectivity. In that sense, the dimension of the 'miracle' – if one wants to use such religious jargon – is most visible in the continuous transformation of negative into positive, although, as we shall see, Badiou would not accept any dialectical relation between the two. This interconnection – as well as the opposite one: from positive to negative – is constitutive of social and political life, and this is not only an ethical but primarily an analytical/empirical observation.

Furthermore, by simplifying the terms of a complex relation, Žižek seems incapable of linking theory and political experience in a non-reductive way. Yet the destabilisation of the absolute frontiers between positive and negative is bound to contaminate the idea of miracle itself. The implication is that any prioritisation of the field of miracles has to face the question of how to distinguish between true and false, divine and satanic miracles.[12] We already know this from Christian theology, Church history, and everyday life in religious communities. We also know it from the critique of Badiou's work, by which Žižek's idea of the act/event seems to be influenced. In Jean-Jacques Lecercle's words:

> I can find hardly anything within [Badiou's] system to protect me from Heidegger's mistake, when he took the National Socialist 'revolution' for an event, and thought that a new process of truth had started. The risk is that the eventuality of the event will eventually be left to individual decision. (Lecercle 1999: 12)

Simon Critchley similarly asks: 'how and in virtue of what is one to distinguish a true event from a false event?' And he replies: 'I don't see how – on the basis of Badiou's criteria – we could ever distinguish a true event from a false event' (Critchley 2000: 23). In principle then, Badiou's 'event' and Žižek's 'act' seem to suffer from the same limitation: as soon as we accept a strict differentiation between positive and negative, good and bad, as soon as we prioritise one of these poles by disavowing the continuous interpenetration between positivity and negativity, we merely displace the problem into the realm of concrete ethico-political experience. We lose, however, at the same time, every theoretical/symbolic resource capable of supporting a proper ethical attitude in this unavoidable encounter with the real. I am not implying that one should look for a fullproof theoretical or metaphysical guarantee to guide such decisions *more geometrico*. I am merely suggesting that something is missing here: a space (partially) mediating between real and symbolic. There is no way to distinguish between true and false events, between events and simulacra, because Badiou's theoretical edifice does not offer a suitable space in which this operation would make sense: 'It is only by appealing to a third discourse which is not easily integrated into Badiou's theoretical system that the distinction truth/simulacrum can be maintained' (Laclau 2004b: 123). This is also true regarding Žižek's conceptualisation of the act: Antigone embodies the miracle of an automatic transubstantiation of negative to positive without any mediating mechanism apart from that of a 'pathological' disavowal of finitude and lack. Furthermore, precisely because the act is perceived as a one-off, the continuous interpenetration between negativity and positivity is never thematised. However, as will be argued in the 'Excursus on Badiou', Badiou seems to be aware of this problem, and there are attempts within his own theorisation to deal with it in a much more promising direction.

At this point, and since Žižek is so fond of passing the test of a concrete example (usually from popular culture and current politics), let me enlist one. *Time* magazine's person of the year for 2004 was no other than George Bush. One will inevitably ask: and what has George Bush to do with the risk entailed in genuine political acts that redefine the very framework within which they take place? But this is precisely the way George Bush, an 'American Revolutionary' as the title reads, is presented by *Time*. Why is he deemed worthy of such a title? 'For sharpening the debate until the choices bled, for reframing reality to match his design, for gambling his fortunes – and the world's – on his faith in the power of leadership, George W. Bush is *Time*'s 2004 *Person of the Year*'. And this is not only *Time*'s rendering of George Bush. It is also how the administration has been viewing itself:

> In the summer of 2002, after I had written an article in Esquire that the White House didn't like about Bush's former communications director, Karen Hughes, I had a meeting with a senior adviser to Bush. He expressed the White House's displeasure, and then he told me something that at the time I didn't fully comprehend – but which I now believe gets to the very heart of the Bush presidency.
>
> The aide said that guys like me were 'in what we call the reality-based community', which he defined as people who 'believe that solutions emerge from your judicious study of discernible reality'. I nodded and murmured something about enlightenment principles and empiricism. He cut me off. 'That's not the way the world really works anymore', he continued. 'We're an empire now, and when we *act*, we create our own reality. And while you're studying that reality – judiciously, as you will – we'll *act* again, creating other new realities, which you can study too, and that's how things will sort out. We're history's actors ... and you, all of you, will be left to just study what we do'. (Suskind 2004, emphasis added)

No wonder that Žižek's commentary following the 2004 American presidential elections, characteristically entitled 'Hurray for Bush!', can barely conceal a certain admiration (Žižek 2004d).

To conclude this part of my argument, Žižek's conceptualisation of a politics of the act seems to be premised on the idea that any inscription/assumption of lack and finitude within a political project of social transformation can only have disastrous or crippling results. Indeed, postmodern pessimism is a problem, but is it to be resolved through a reoccupation of quasi-religious faith? Is it to be resolved through the utopian disavowal of lack and negativity in political discourse? This option is clearly open to us, but it is difficult to see how it would be different from the 'false transgression' stigmatised by Žižek himself. It is also obvious that it would expose the politics of social transformation to an unacceptable risk of *absolutisation*. Thus, in opposition to Žižek's strict differentiation between the ethics of assuming lack and a politics of acts, why not see the *assumption/institutionalisation of the lack in the Other*, not as a limit but as the condition of possibility, or in any case a crucial resource, in ethically assuming the radical character of an act, of relating ourselves – as divided beings – to events? It is only here, on the basis of assuming this irreducible lack, that the difference between the Lacanian Left and the Utopian Left can be fully registered. Ironically, it is also here that the distance between a radical act (refusing its own idealisation and functioning as a terrain for future re-acts) and a reactionary act (like Bush's revolution) can be located.

Re-enacting the act: from event to event-ness

Badiou seems to be pointing in this direction when he designates an awareness of lack and finitude as the site where every event takes place. This is visible, for example, in the way he connects death and resurrection in his book on Saint Paul:

> Through Christ's death, God renounces his transcendent separation; he unseparates himself through filiation and shares in a constitutive dimension of the divided human subject. In so doing he creates, not the event, but what I call its evental site . . . death is an operation in the situation, an operation that immanentizes the evental site, while resurrection is the event as such. (Badiou 2003a: 70)

Of course, from the point of view of a particular event, of subjects engaged and produced through an event's truth procedure, the event itself – and fidelity to it – tends to erase and repress the traces of negativity. From this point of view, part and parcel of Badiou's understanding of the event is the elimination of any symbolic inscription of its evental site: 'Ultimately, for Paul, the Christ-event is nothing but resurrection. It eradicates negativity, and if, as we have already said, death is required for the construction of its site, it remains an affirmative operation that is irreducible to death' (p. 73). In this text Badiou ends up in a position similar to the one adopted by Žižek. Even Hallward agrees that, if truth is the result of post-evental implication, then 'there can be no clear way of distinguishing, before it is too late, a genuine event (which relates only to the void of the situation, i.e. to the way inconsistency might appear within a situation) from a false event (one that, like September 11th or the triumph of National Socialism, reinforces the basic distinctions governing the situation)' (Hallward 2004: 16).

Simply put, both Badiou and Žižek start by inter-implicating negative and positive. Žižek's references to 'risk' and 'suspension' initially function as the mediating mechanism between Antigone's apolitical desire and socio-political change. Similarly, for Badiou, the 'evental site' functions as a mediating apparatus. In Žižek's case this line of reasoning is abandoned in the end, with the divine miracle of the act completely overshadowing and eliminating lack and negativity. In Badiou, however, the picture is more complex – with signs of abandoning but also of further registering a non-dialectical negativity, depending on the texts examined. I shall return to this issue for a final commentary in the excursus that concludes the first part of this book. For the time being, however, let me insist a little on the question Žižek – and Badiou to a certain extent – never explicitly asks.

Isn't it impossible to avoid the constitutive and continuous interimplication between positive and negative? What happens, for example, when we fall in love, one of the privileged fields in which events take place in Badiou's schema? Although a degree of chance is always in operation, falling in love is never merely a chance event. It presupposes a certain preparedness. As Darian Leader reminds us, it has precise conditions of possibility linked to a sense of discontent, incompleteness, and lack (Leader 1997). In fact, Žižek himself has recently accepted that only a lacking being loves (Žižek 2003a: 115). Similarly, although the cases are not entirely symmetrical, even if 'the act as real is an event which occurs *ex nihilo*, without any fantasmatic support' (Žižek 1998a: 14), *assuming* this act nevertheless entails traversing the fantasy and coming to terms with lack. Ethically assuming the act can only become possible within such a symbolic matrix. In his early work Žižek had explicitly subscribed to such a symbolic conditioning of the real act:

> The real act is of a strictly symbolic nature, it consists in the very mode in which we structure the world, our perception of it, in advance, in order to make our intervention possible, in order to open in it the space for our activity (or inactivity). The real act thus precedes the (partial–factual) activity; it consists in the previous restructuring of our symbolic universe into which our (factual, particular) act will be inscribed. (Žižek 1989: 216)

Yet this is no longer the case, since 'by neglecting the importance of an act's involvement with the symbolic, Žižek seems to be saying that the real of an act happens without the symbolic' (Pluth and Hoens 2004: 187). But that can only mean that Žižek's act has very little to do with the way Lacan has conceptualised the psychoanalytic act: as an act that presupposes a certain reflexivity, an awareness of its own limits, of the fact that it will never lead to the full realisation of subjectivity (neither of the analyst nor of the analysand) (seminar of 20 March 1968). At the beginning of every new analysis, the analyst authorises and risks an operation – through the institution of the *subject supposed to know* – knowing well that it will end with his or her own rejection as excrement (seminar of 21 February 1968). Only thus can the analyst's (symbolic) assumption of castration and division be re-enacted in the subjective structure of the analysand(s).

In another text, Žižek has pointed out that '[t]here is ethics – that is to say, an injunction which cannot be grounded in ontology – in so far as there is a crack in the ontological edifice of the universe: at its most elementary, ethics designates fidelity to this crack' (Žižek 1997: 214). In order for a truly ethical fidelity to an event to become possible another fidelity is presupposed, a fidelity that cannot be reduced to the event itself or to particular symbolisations of the event and has to retain a certain distance from them: a fidelity to *event-ness* as distinct from particular events, a 'fidelity to the Real *qua* impossible' (p. 215).[13] Such a standpoint not only presents the necessary symbolic preparations for the proper ethical reception of the act/event, but also offers our best defense against the ever-present risk of being lured by a false event, a satanic miracle – against the ever-present risk of terror and *absolutisation* of an event, to use Badiou's vocabulary (Badiou 2001: 85). Of course, one should be aware that fidelity to event-ness, to what ultimately permits the emergence of the new and makes possible the assumption of an act, presupposes a betrayal, not of the act itself, but of a certain rendering of the act as an absolute and divine positivity. In that sense, fidelity to an event can flourish and avoid absolutisation only as an *infidel fidelity*, only within the framework of another fidelity – fidelity to the openness of the political space and to the awareness of the constitutive impossibility of a final suture of the social – within the framework of a commitment to the continuous political re-inscription of the irreducible lack in the Other.[14]

Needless to say, I am not offering these reflections as some kind of final statement regarding the issues discussed here. Bringing event-ness into consideration renders possible the restructuring of the formal requirements of an ethico-political conception of the act in what some would call a radical democratic direction, but it cannot bridge the gap between theory and politics. This irreducible aporia – the unbridgeable gap between theory and politics – is, I think, what ultimately explains Žižek's choice to persist in his references to Antigone as an *embodiment* of a particular ethico-political position within a formal framework essentially alien or even antithetical to her. As Joan Copjec has recently pointed out, the problem of embodiment is crucial in understanding and further developing the implications of Lacanian ethics (Copjec 1999: 237). But even if embodiment is necessary, even if embodiment constitutes not only the limit, but also the support of any formal model of the act, is the tragic–heroic model of Antigone ultimately unavoidable? I think not. From a point of view which acknowledges the importance of event-ness, the assumption of the lack in the Other as the symbolic prerequisite of a minimum – but not absolutised – ethical fidelity to acts/events is clearly not embodied by Antigone.

It is rather embodied by tragedy itself as a genre, as a social institution staging again and again the suspension of the socio-symbolic order and permitting a thorough self-reflection on the political order of the city and its moral foundations.[15] It is not Antigone but Sophocles, the tragedian, who fulfills the criteria set out at the beginning of Žižek's 1998 text. Antigone is important not in herself but because of the potentially ethical reaction she is bound to elicit from the audience of the play (Neill 2003: 355): 'The pertinent ethical question in Antigone is how we, the audience, the spectator, the reader, respond to the play and respond beyond the play. The only true act in Antigone is precisely not in Antigone, it is in response to Antigone' (p. 364). It is the playwright – whether of tragedy or comedy – who assumes and re-inscribes radical socio-political critique within the heart of the city, reproducing democratic society by re-examining again and again – through a series of aesthetico-political *re-acts* – its ethico-political premises. Costas Papaioannou rightly reminds us that Plato has captured this immense political importance of the theatre for democracy, of tragedy as an institution of democratic self-limitation (Castoriadis 1997b: 343). *Theatrocracy* may be another name for democracy (Papaioannou 2003). In that sense, I feel it is fitting to end this section exactly where Copjec begins one of her papers, citing the same quotation from Jean-Pierre Vernant:

> Tragedy is contemporaneous with the City and with its legal system. [O]ne can say, that what tragedy is talking about is itself and the problems of law it is encountering . . . What is talking and what is talked about is the audience on the benches, but first of all it is the City . . . which puts itself on the stage and plays itself . . . Not only does the tragedy enact itself on stage . . . it enacts its own problematics. It puts in question its own internal contradictions, revealing . . . that the true subject-matter of tragedy is social thought . . . in the very process of elaboration. (Vernant 1972: 278–9; Vernant in Copjec 1999: 233)

Žižekian 'perversions'

Let me recapitulate the basic points of my argument so far. I am not disputing the importance Žižek attributes to the idea of the act as the moment when a hegemonic regime, a sedimented crystallisation/positivisation of social meaning, is dislocated and what emerges is the prospect of its (radical) re-articulation. In fact, as we have seen at the end of Chapter 1 and in the previous sections of this chapter, democracy can be defined as the institutionalisation of a mechanism which enables such a continuous re-articulation of the symbolic field constituting society. I am also basically in agreement with Žižek when he designates the formal parameters of such an act – its non-intentionality, its risks, its function as a momentary suspension of the symbolic, and so on – although I would, much more than him, take seriously Lacan's emphasis on the symbolic aspect of acts. But I cannot understand how Antigone fits into this picture. Her suicidal attitude makes her unsuitable as a model of embodying the act. Instead, it is tragedy – a discourse, a particular type of symbolisation encircling lack – which could function as a model of that kind. In it we identify with Antigone, but we are also led to traverse her lure. I am also sympathetic to Žižek's initial attempts to politicise her, but I cannot help noticing the ultimate failure of this strategy. My impression is that he fails for the very reason that has led him to her in the first place: he cannot resist the lure of Antigone's pure desire for death. He seems to detect there something important for the type of politics he wants to advocate. But this is exactly what exposes him to a series of irresolvable paradoxes: in order to focus on the idealised purity of her desire, not only is he led to neglect Lacan's latter conceptualisations of desire and Antigone's own attachment to the law of Oedipus, he is also forced miraculously to transform her relentless striving towards death into a basis for a radical critique of lack and finitude.

How does Žižek respond to the line of argumentation I have just advanced? His response to my critical reading of his politics of the act unfolds at two levels. First he engages in a defence of his work, which apparently I misrepresent. Then he proceeds to a substantive discussion of what he sees as the crucial issues at stake, namely the proper understanding of the 'act' and the nature of democracy. A thorough discussion of both discursive instances will help me clarify and substantiate (even further) the basic claim I have made so far in this chapter: if in his *Umbr(a)* 1998 text Žižek engages in an ultimately failed attempt to articulate the risks, the implicit negativity, of politics with the apolitical model of Antigone, if her pure desire lures him to disavow what he himself has repeatedly highlighted as one of the cornerstones of Lacanianism, it is the same structure of *disavowal* that triumphantly re-emerges in his attempts to discard my critique.

This is the case both in terms of his defence of the integrity of his *oeuvre* and in terms of his stance on the act and democracy. I will deal in detail with these more recent arguments, not only because they seem to forget what is crucial about Lacanian theorisation, but also because they tend to obscure what is really at issue in critical political analysis and the Lacanian Left.

Žižek's first line of reasoning is to argue that I systematically misconstrue his positions. He points out a series of 'false attributions' that are supposed to invalidate my critique of his politics of the act and of his use of Antigone. Let us examine a couple of them. First of all, the crucial question of Antigone's pure desire. Consider this quotation:

> Stavrakakis writes, for example, '*Clearly, Antigone is not Lacan's last – or most insightful – word on the question of ethics*. His position continued to develop [after the *Ethics* seminar] in a direction that undermined his earlier focus on Antigone's pure desire.' Agreed, but why is this written as an argument against me? Did I not develop *in extenso* Lacan's shift from pure desire to drive? Did I not elaborate in detail a shift of 'primary examples' from Antigone to Sygne de Coufontaine (from Claudel's *L'otage*) and Medea? And how can the assertion of the identity of law and desire ('*Desire is the law*', he emphasizes) be an argument against me when I have made this point so often that I myself am already tired of it? (Žižek 2003d: 131)

Here it is necessary to dispel a certain misunderstanding. I am definitely not arguing that Žižek is not aware of the shift in Lacan's position pointing to the intimate relation between law and desire. And the reason I could never have argued anything of the sort is that – and I will not hesitate even for a moment to confess that – I have probably initially learnt it from him.[16] In any case, I have no intention to teach Žižek Lacanian commonplaces. I take it for granted that he knows them very very well, better than I do. *But this is exactly why it causes me great concern when Žižek himself seems to forget or abandon them*. It is not by coincidence that I have used the psychoanalytic term 'disavowal' to describe this attitude. As is well known, disavowal, as the fundamental operation of perversion,[17] involves the simultaneous recognition and denial of something – in the clinic, of castration. In fact, Žižek's response seems to come under this description. When interrogated on the prioritisation of one view of desire over another, and although these two views are clearly inconsistent with each other, he – paradoxically – perceives no tension between them, not even a productive one. He refuses to choose, to commit himself to one or the other. He seems to present his work as a unified whole without shifts and tensions, a theory of everything, absorbing all contradictions in a self-enclosed synthesis, immune to criticism – since every criticism is rendered an attack.

Let us go to a second quotation:

> Stavrakakis asserts that I am guilty of 'juxtaposing negativity and positivity, passivity and activity, pessimism and optimism', and that I thereby neglect the 'irreducible interconnection between negativity and positivity, lack and desire, death and resurrection', that is, the fact that the act has 'a negative/disruptive dimension', that it involves a 'continuous "transubstantiation" of negative into positive' – is this meant seriously? Is not the *title* of one of my books *Tarrying with the Negative*, that is, the notion that negativity should gain positive existence? Do I not reproach Badiou for neglecting the link between death and resurrection in his reading of Christianity, as well as for missing the point of the philosophical assertion of finitude as a transcendental category? Do I not emphasize how the act is, in its innermost negative, a 'No', a disruption of the existing sociosymbolic order? (Žižek 2003d: 131)

Again, I have no intention of disputing that Žižek is aware of the negative ontology underlying Lacanian theory. I know that in some of his texts he advances such a position, as in the example of love I have used in the previous section, where he argues that only a lacking being can love. He is also right to point, in this context, to his Lacanian reworking of the Hegelian 'tarrying with the negative': 'Therein resides the gist of the Hegelian notion of "tarrying with the negative" which Lacan rendered in his notion of the deep connection between death drive and creative sublimation: in order for (symbolic) creation to take place, the death drive . . . has to accomplish its work of, precisely, emptying the place and thus making it ready for creation' (Žižek 2004b: 167). Furthermore, in a recent interview, speaking about Europe's role in contemporary international politics, he advances the (related) view that a dislocated identity always functions as a prerequisite to act:

> Of course everyone was disappointed after the Iraq war: with all its protesting Europe didn't really live up to our expectations. But this might be a good sign; it is already a big step when you become aware that you failed. In a negative way you become aware of a task. The first step in every struggle is not to win, but to become aware of a failure. (Žižek 2004c: 298)

But what happens to this awareness afterwards? Is it supposed to be forgotten? Why something which has informed earlier publications of his – like *Tarrying with the Negative* – is today dissociated from Lacan and described as a defining characteristic of deconstruction? *And why, when confronted with a description of his own strategy, Žižek insists on having it both ways?* Can't he understand that, after elaborating in detail on the shift from Antigone to Sygne de Coufontaine, one can neither simply go back to an idealisation of Antigone nor pretend that Antigone's and Sygne's acts are perfectly compatible? The only way of making them compatible is to *disavow* the one in favour of the other. Likewise, the only way to make compatible the *pure desire* of the act and latter Lacan's stress on the *impurity of the act* and the symbolic conditioning of desire is to disavow the latter in favour of the former.

Now, if disavowal is indeed the basic discursive topos governing Žižek's theoretical and political conceptualisation of the act, then we are dealing here with nothing less than Žižekian 'perversions', since disavowal is the mechanism typical of perversion. But I have to make it absolutely clear that, in using terms like 'perversion', I am merely referring to the structure of his arguments. A short conceptual/clinical detour could be very illuminating at this point. Following Freud, what is at stake in perversion is the way castration is registered. The perverse subject – the fetishist – knows perfectly well that women do not have penis, but disavows the thought of castration (*Verleugnung*). It refuses to acknowledge this traumatising perception – the absence of a penis in the mother and in women generally – but in a way different from repression and foreclosure – the two other forms of negation typical of neurosis and psychosis. The difference lies in the fact that the fetishist knows about castration – which is neither repressed nor foreclosed – but, nevertheless, tries to forget all about it through the defensive strategy of elaborating a substitute formation for the lacking penis: the fetish (Dor 2001: 101).[18] The result is all too familiar to a reader of Žižek: 'Paradoxically, the fetishist is able to maintain simultaneously two intrapsychic components that at first seem incompatible: acknowledgment of the absence of the penis in women and the disavowal of this acknowledgment' (p. 102). The discursive imprint of such a position is the following formula: '*I am well aware . . . but nevertheless*' (p. 89, emphasis added). Can one think of a better account of Žižek's rhetorical strategy, both in the text I have been discussing and in his responses to my critical commentary? The way I read it, it always proceeds like that: I am well aware that the *Ethics* seminar was a 'point of deadlock' for Lacan . . . but nevertheless I want to stick to an idealised image of Antigone; I am well aware that negativity is our ultimate ontological horizon . . . but nevertheless I want to stick to a conception of the act as a miraculous intervention which acquires a thoroughly positive value; I am well aware that radical democracy is connected to Lacanian theory (I have even endorsed Stavrakakis' 1999 book saying exactly that) . . . but, nevertheless, 'whatever one wants to do with Lacan's theory, there is no way that one can claim that "radical democracy" is its direct implication' (Žižek 2003d: 134).[19]

This recital of absurdity reaches new levels in his recent book on Iraq. What one encounters here is – once more – the paradoxical effect of the mechanism of disavowal in its unmistakable purity. Consider the following two quotations. First, Žižek argues that, 'in a situation like today's, the only way really to remain open to a revolutionary opportunity is to renounce facile calls to direct action . . . The only way to lay the foundations for a true, radical change is to withdraw from the compulsion to act, to "do nothing" – thus opening up the space for a different kind of activity' (Žižek 2004a: 72). Three pages later he condemns the resistance to political acts and the obsession with 'radical Evil': 'It is as if the supreme Good today is that nothing should happen' (p. 75). What is one supposed to conclude from this? Surely 'to do nothing' does not make sense as a remedy against those who supposedly argue that 'nothing should happen'. However, it provides Žižek with an opportunity to retain the image of a sophisticated theorist, fully aware that in a world marked by the negative a total re-foundation of our positive reality is but a chimera, and at the same time to cultivate his image as the last revolutionary advocating this same (impossible) re-foundation.

But nowhere is this structure of disavowal revealed so clearly as in a recent interview in which I had the opportunity to debate some of these points with Žižek. Speaking about Laclau's work and radical democracy, he points out that 'the only difference it introduces is the fact that it makes us aware of contingency. For me this is definitely not enough as a ground for progressive politics.' Having in mind that elsewhere he directly repudiates this awareness of contingency, I ask him the following question: 'YS: Nevertheless, should this awareness be part of progressive politics? Žižek: Becoming aware of contingency? YS: Yes. Žižek: Frankly, if I approach this in naïve terms, at best, it is necessary but not sufficient' (Žižek 2004c: 294). Then he goes on to provide a multitude of examples in which 'being aware of contingency was on the wrong side' (ibid.). This is where the paradox of disavowal re-emerges. How can an awareness of contingency be a necessary condition for something which actually presupposes that we abandon it and is located beyond any conditionality: *the unconditional revolutionary act*? On the next page we have a similar instance. At stake is radical democracy as a way of articulating an element of hope, of radical new alternatives, with this awareness of contingency. What is Žižek's answer? The first part consists of this opening statement: 'For me, once more, this would be too formal. Of course, as an abstract guideline, I tend to agree; anybody would agree with it' (ibid., p. 295); which is then followed by a list of objections to Laclau's rendering of radical democracy. Isn't the logic of disavowal fully operative here? Isn't Žižek's position structured in a typically 'perverse' manner? I am well aware of contingency, I am well aware that one has to combine this registering of contingency and lack with the pursuit of radical alternatives, but nevertheless . . . this can only be an abstract guideline, too formal, necessary but not sufficient; and thus I can stick, at the same time, to my fetish: an idealised conception of an unconditional, miraculous act (perfectly embodied in Antigone). What is most problematic, of course, is that this disavowal precludes any serious reflection mediating between the two moments involved and between negative and positive more generally.

From structure to substance: the act and democracy

Let's move, however, from this first consideration of the structure of Žižek's discourse to the explicit content of his responses to this critical reading. 'What is truly at stake in his [my] attack?' Žižek writes: 'Two interconnected things, as far as I can see: the notion of the *political act* and the status of *democracy*.' Here he starts with a rendering of my position which needs to be questioned. What he argues is that, when I speak of an 'infidel fidelity' – designed to avoid the 'absolutisation' of an act/event – I surreptitiously introduce a difference between the unconditional–ethical and the pragmatic–political: 'the original fact is the lack, which pertains to human finitude, and all positive acts always fall short of this primordial lack. Thus we have what Derrida calls the "unconditional ethical injunction", impossible to fulfill, and positive acts or interventions, which remain strategic' (Žižek 2003d: 132). Žižek is clearly opposed to such a position. Well, he is not alone in that. I am also opposed to it, because it has very little to do with my argument. My starting point is not the impossibility of radical 'unconditional' acts, an impossibility leaving the road open only to strategic adjustments. On the contrary, I consider such 'unconditional' acts entirely possible and I have no reason to doubt their momentary 'success'. What I doubt is their ability to effect a radical re-foundation of the social in a progressive direction. I also contest their relevance for the Lacanian Left, their value as models of ethico-political action. This is because, in opposition to Žižek, I understand their success in a strictly Lacanian fashion. For Lacan, 'suicide is the only act which can succeed without misfiring' (Lacan 1990: 43); a totally successful, 'unconditional' act. I do not dispute that such acts can take place; what I dispute is their relevance for critical political theory and the radicalisation of democracy. When I point to the impossibility of utopia I do not doubt that suicidal or radically murderous acts can occur; what I doubt is their ability to effect a progressive transformation of the social. The reason why I insist in opposing political acts to radical suicidal gestures *à la* Antigone – questioning the equation Žižek attempts to establish between the two – is not that I adopt a Derridean position, but that I follow the strictly Lacanian opposition between the asocial madness of an acting out or a *passage à l'acte*[20] and the proper psychoanalytic/political act involving a distinct symbolic dimension. In other words, I could agree with Žižek that Antigone's 'act is not a strategic intervention that maintains the gap separating her from the impossible Void – it rather "absolutely" enacts the Impossible'. But, whereas this is what attracts Žižek to her – '*This* is why Antigone was of interest to me' he writes, adding that he is 'well aware of the "lure" of such an act' (Žižek 2003d: 132) – it is also exactly what makes me and others judge her unsuitable as a model.

Now, where exactly does Žižek look for supporting arguments for his position? His first claim is that he draws on Lacan's conception of the act: 'I claim that, in Lacan's later versions of the act, this moment of "madness" beyond strategic intervention remains' (ibid.). Well, this is something that has to be clarified once and for all. Is this idea of the supposedly unconditional real act, of an act unbound by any relation to the symbolic field, what defines Lacan's notion of the act? Surely, the place to look for an answer to this question is Lacan's seminar *L'acte psychanalytique*. But there is nothing there to support Žižek's argument.[21] This is not merely my reading, but also the conclusion drawn by other readers from the same seminar. There is no doubt, of course, that the act acquires its value precisely because it presupposes an encounter with the real. Yet this encounter only becomes conscious through the failure of the symbolic; and, in addition, it has to be expressed, articulated, registered within the symbolic. We only have an act when we respond to the encounter with the real with a registering of the lack in the Other: 'The Act is an act of saying (*un dire*) which responds to this point where the Other is lacking and it is thus linked to the real, even if its effects are sometimes in the symbolic' (Soler 1992: 53). In order to retain its ethical dimension, an act cannot be divorced from any re-inscription in the symbolic – this is the crucial point made by Lacan (Neill 2003: 339): 'An act does not just involve doing something: it involves doing something with signifiers' (Pluth 2004: 22).[22] It is in this sense that any socio-politically relevant fidelity to the act/event has to be an infidel fidelity, a symbolic recognition of the lack in the Other and of the irreducibility of the distance between the real and the symbolic it reveals.

A proper act, in other words, involves the production of a signifier of the lack in the Other and an attempt to institutionalise this empty signification, to pass, in other words, *from time to space* – in fact, to re-conceive space and spatiality in a way very different from what existed before the act.[23] The implication is very clear: there is no perfect act. The perfect act Žižek idealises – Antigone's suicidal gesture – may be an act which succeeds without misfiring, but this is precisely what excludes it from what, according to Lacan, would be a proper psychoanalytic act. Suicide

> is not, from the subjective perspective, reinscribed in the symbolic. There is in suicide no continuation, no possibility of recuperation by or to the symbolic . . . [This] is not to advocate suicide, it is, rather, to recognise the impossibility of other acts not misfiring . . . Suicide is the only act available to the subject which cannot result in a persistence of lack. Post-suicide, there is no subject to lack. And just as there is no subject, neither is there an Other for the subject, there is, that is, no symbolic order in which the act could be (re)inscribed. (Neill 2003: 349–53)

Although initially Žižek seems to accept this formal, symbolic conditioning of the act, Antigone's suicide lures him to disavow it in favour of the unconditional perfection of her act.

No doubt Žižek's disavowal is triggered by a very real and ever-present danger, the danger of the re-absorption of an act, of its co-optation: 'the Other is capable of absorbing any and every signifying creation. In other words, it is always possible for a signifying practice, no matter how act-like, to become a truism' (Pluth 2004: 31). It is this possibility that Žižek finds threatening for his politics of the act, and Antigone's death provides him with an opportunity to avoid, to *disavow* it. To be sure, when death does not intervene, all acts – even the most radical – are bound to encounter their own limit; their inevitable symbolisation is their condition both of possibility – without which they cannot claim any socio-political effectiveness beyond the *solipsistic* perfection of a suicidal act – and of impossibility – often taking the form of *banalisation*. In *The Human Stain* Philip Roth provides a paradigmatic artistic incarnation of these (ontological) limitations in their most radical aspect. The story is simple: Coleman Silk, Professor at Athena College, is accused of making racist remarks against some black students who fail to attend his class. This leads to his 'persecution' by the political correctness establishment and to a domino of other events triggering the unfolding of the story. What is of interest is the central reversal of the novel: *it is eventually revealed that he himself is black and not Jewish, as he was letting people believe.*

In fact, adopting a Jewish identity and changing completely his future prospects was his life's act. The precondition of this act – its 'evental site', in Badiou's vocabulary – was the contingency of Coleman's very light skin complexion. His lacking blackness permitted the misrecognition of his (black) identity by the Other's gaze. At some point Coleman fully assumes the passage from a black to a Jewish identity. However, this presupposes a very dramatic and traumatic encounter with his mother:

> [He was] murdering her on behalf of his exhilarating notion of freedom! It would have been much easier without her. But only through this test can he be the man he has chosen to be, unalterably separated from what he was handed at birth, free to struggle at being free like any human being would wish to be free. To get that from life, the alternate destiny, on one's own terms, he must do what must be done. (Roth 2000: 138–9)

Roth manages to capture all the violence, all the ontological weight carried by this shift in the parameters of life itself: 'It's so awful that all you can do is live with it. Once you have done a thing like this you have done so much violence it can *never* be undone – which is what Coleman wants' (Roth 2000: 139). What we have here is an act *par excellence*: 'This man and his mother. This woman and her beloved son. If, in the service of honing himself, he is out to do the hardest thing imaginable, this is it, short of stabbing her. This takes him right to the heart of the matter. *This is the major act of his life*, and vividly, consciously, he feels its immensity' (ibid., emphasis added). Furthermore, it is an act that radically alters all his social relations; it almost re-founds his whole life, it shifts his – and the (O)thers' – sense of space and time forever. In Roth's words, 'The act was committed in 1953 by an audacious young man in Greenwich Village, by a specific person in a specific place at a specific time, but now he will be over on the other side forever' (p. 145). This becomes evident when he is asked to pay the first price for assuming this new course, when his brother forbids him to have any contact with their mother in the future: ' "Don't you ever *try* to see her. No contact, No calls. Nothing. Never. Hear me?" Walt said. "*Never*. Don't you ever show your lily-white face around that house again!" ' (ibid.).

But this is not the end of the story. If it were, then Coleman Silk's act would be as successful as Antigone's, and Lacan's comment that suicide is the only act that does not misfire would be falsified; furthermore, Žižek's choice of Antigone's example would remain largely unexplained. Yet it is the merit of Roth's novel that it reveals how non-suicidal acts *do* misfire, how they are bound to misfire, how 'an act always misunderstands itself' (Lacan in Roudinesco 1997: 341):

> And yet, after that, he had the system beat . . . Yes, he'd had it beat for so very long, right down to all the kids being born white – and then he didn't. Blindsided by the uncontrollability of something else entirely. The man who decides to forge a distinct historical destiny, who sets out to spring the historical lock, and who does so, brilliantly succeeds at altering his personal lot, only to be ensnared by the history he hadn't quite counted on: *the history that isn't yet history*, the history that the clock is now ticking off, the history proliferating as I write, accruing a minute at a time and grasped better by the future than it will ever be by us. That we do that is inescapable: the present moment, the common lot, the current mood, the mind of one's country, the stranglehold of history that is one's own time. Blindsided by the terrifyingly provisional nature of everything. (Roth 2000: 335, emphasis added)

It is this unavoidable encounter with *contingency* and *negativity* – with the lack in the Other – that Žižek's perverse argument-structure is negating and his fetishism of the act aims to mask. Of course, Žižek does claim that his version of the act fully assumes the lack: 'In this precise sense, not only does the notion of the act not contradict the "lack in the Other", which, according to Stavrakakis, I neglect, it directly presupposes it. It is only through an act that I effectively assume the big Other's inexistence, that is, I enact the impossible, namely what appears as impossible within the coordinates of the existing socio-symbolic order' (Žižek 2003d: 132). What he hides is that his act can only assume the lack in the deeply solipsistic and apolitical form of suicide, collapsing symbolic and real death.

Indeed, it must have become abundantly clear by now that only the value attributed to death in Antigone's case can explain her lure for Žižek: it permits him to avoid dealing with 'the terrifyingly provisional nature of everything', in Roth's words. And this is another paradox inherent in Žižek's disavowal: in order to avoid dealing with the contingency/finitude of every socio-political construction, with the negative limits of every positivity, he is led to embrace the perfection of Antigone's suicide, to idealise the absolute positivity guaranteed by a wholly negative act. His sticking to Antigone can only be explained as a protective device against dealing with the decay of utopia, with the fact that the realisation of even the most perfect utopian dream is bound to encounter its own limits in the flow of historical time, which is impossible to control. Wouldn't it be nice to be able to freeze time, to enact a radical cut transposing us into another dimension? This is, for Žižek, Antigone's promise. Apart from that, there is nothing alluring and definitely nothing progressive in her. This is indirectly accepted even by Žižek himself, when he articulates the following view:

> So what about the reproach that Antigone does not only risk death or suspend the symbolic order – my determination of a political act – but that she actively strives for death, symbolic and real death, thereby displaying a purity of desire beyond any socio-political transformative action? . . . Is not, in certain extreme circumstances, such 'apolitical' defiance on behalf of 'decency' or 'old customs' the very model of heroic political resistance? Second, Antigone's gesture is not simply pure desire for death. If it were, she could have killed herself directly and spared the people around her all the fuss. Hers was not a pure symbolic striving for death, but an unconditional insistence on a particular symbolic ritual. (Žižek 2003d: 133)

Is it only my impression or is it indeed the case that, in order to defend the position that there is something other than death about Antigone, Žižek accepts that, even if there is, it is nothing progressive? On Žižek's own confession, that something ranges from the 'apolitical' to the conservative!

Now, if this is the case, the next question is, what transforms such apolitical or even conservative acts into radical political gestures? Again, there is nothing apart from the lure of Antigone's perfect death to explain this change. Moreover, Žižek's reply not only does nothing to shift the centre of gravity away from death, but also re-introduces a radical relativism in his conceptualisation of the act. If Antigone's apolitical or conservative act can be so easily characterised as radical and progressive, then *any* act can be characterised as radical or progressive. Not surprisingly, this is Žižek's own conclusion: 'An authentic political act can be, in terms of its form, a democratic one as well as a non-democratic one. There are some elections or referenda in which "the impossible happens" . . . On the other hand, an authentic political act of popular will can also occur in the form of a violent revolution, or a progressive military dictatorship, and so on' (Žižek 2004a: 88). But how is a progressive military dictatorship defined? Žižek's comments on Stalinism do not sound very promising: 'better the worst Stalinist terror than the most liberal capitalist democracy'; although, when compared in positive terms, 'welfare state capitalist democracy is incomparably better – what redeems Stalinist "totalitarianism" is the formal aspect, the space it opens up' (p. 84). Ironically, it is Žižek, the relentless critic of the supposed formalism of radical democracy, who introduces here his own formalism. And this is a formalism of a particular type, one that contaminates his argument with a radical relativism: Antigone dances with Stalin and *Time's* portrait of George Bush as a revolutionary suddenly acquires an uncanny aura![24]

Beyond fetishism: the missing link

But is Žižek's 'perversion' the only option left open to critical political analysis and to the Lacanian Left? As we have seen, this direction is Žižek's answer to the crucial problem of the temporality of the act and of the duration of its effects: 'Acts can always go on and make up part of an attempt to seek recognition by an Other "who knows". Thus, a question worth pursuing is the temporality or duration of an act' (Pluth 2004: 32). Here, by ignoring Lacan's stress on the symbolic aspect of the act, Žižek obscures another possible direction, consistent with the (socio-political) production of a signifier of the lack in the Other: the direction of radical democratic ethics, as developed by thinkers like Claude Lefort, Ernesto Laclau, Chantal Mouffe, and others.[25]

What is Žižek's principal objection to this other course? His position is that 'the justified rejection of the fullness of post-revolutionary Society does not justify the conclusion that we have to renounce any project of a global social transformation' (Žižek in Butler et al. 2000: 101). Laclau's response is predictable but justified: 'I agree entirely that this short circuit is illegitimate; the only thing I want to add to that is that it is only Žižek who is jumping into it' (Laclau in Butler et al. 2000: 197). Indeed, why should one deny the transformative potential of radical democracy? How can Žižek support his claim that the political promise of radical democracy is limited in such a severe and debilitating way?

Žižek's argument is that, although at the conceptual level the re-politicisation promised by radical democracy's stress on antagonism sounds quite radical, in practice hegemonic struggle is never played out at an ontological level, at the level of an ontology of negativity. For him, 'the Political' is split and thus seems to *'be operative only in so far as it "represses" its radically contingent nature, in so far as it undergoes a minimum of "naturalization"* . . . we are never dealing with the Political "at the level of its notion", with political agents who fully endorse their contingency' (Žižek 2000: 100). In other words, radical democrats cannot assume full responsibility for negativity; they have to rely on a certain positivisation. The price they pay for that is the naturalisation of capitalist relations. Such a view, however, can only be based on a significant omission, something pointed out by Laclau:

> [C]oncerning Žižek's assertion of the need for a minimum of naturalization and the impossibility of representing impossibility as such, my response is qualified . . . For in the endless play of substitutions that Žižek is describing one possibility is omitted: that, instead of the impossibility leading to a series of substitutions which attempt to supersede it, it leads to a symbolization of impossibility *as such* as a positive value . . . The possibility of this weakened type of naturalization is important for democratic politics, which involves the institutionalization of its own openness and, in that sense, the injunction to identify with its ultimate impossibility. (Laclau in Butler et al. 2000: 199)

In other words, Žižek seems to deny the very possibility of institutionalising lack and division, of articulating a *positive* political order encircling – but not neutralising – negativity and impossibility, which is exactly what radical democracy stands for. What is most astonishing here is that such a denial does not seem to be consistent with Žižek's Lacanian framework, insofar as Lacan has conceived psychoanalysis as a paradoxical enterprise leading to the traversing of fantasy. As is well known, Lacan has devoted considerable energy to inscribing the lack in the Other symbolically, in a non-totalisable, non-fantasmatic way. The empty place at the centre of (radicalised) democracy constitutes an attempt to discern – and encourage – the political equivalent of such a position within our political experience of (late) modernity. At this point, then, Laclau appears more Lacanian than Žižek, to the extent that a radical democratic argument can be seen as attempting to draw the political implications of a central Lacanian ethical attitude.

Furthermore, this significant omission highlighted by Laclau leads Žižek's politics into a certain ambiguity. Although at first he rejects the utopian promise of a 'post-revolutionary Society', he appears to end up supporting a form of utopian politics: '*Demandons l'impossible*' is the title of the closing section of his last intervention in the book. For him, today 'it is more important than ever to *hold th*[e] *utopian place of the global alternative open*' (Žižek in Butler et al. 2000: 325). This perverse paradox is the result of his inability to reflect on this middle ground of interpenetration between positivity and negativity, between revolution and conformism, fullness and lack; the result of disavowing the possibility of a non-reductive, non-neutralising positivisation/institutionalisation of lack. Paul Klee once said, speaking of Mondrian: 'To create emptiness is the principal act. And this is true creation, because this emptiness is positive' (Leader 2002: 90). In politics, this is the radical democratic strategy, and this is what Žižek seems unable to understand.[26]

This inability is also evident in Žižek's recent book on Iraq (Žižek 2004a). In that text he deals explicitly with the link I draw between radical democracy and Lacanian theory, which he describes as a short circuit between 'ontological openness–contingency–undecidability' – related to a Lacan-inspired 'politics of traversing the fantasy' – and democracy as 'the political form of this ontological openness' (p. 106). I am not going to discuss all his comments in the context of this chapter.[27] Yet one of Žižek's points does touch upon a real and important problem radical democratic argumentation has to deal with. What is his main objection? Simply put, that the radical democratic attempt to institutionalise social lack, to identify with non-identity, with the lack in the Other, leaves something out: the question of *jouissance*. This supposedly excluded *jouissance* returns to haunt the democratic order through the intensification of hatreds, the proliferation of fundamentalisms and destruction, the prospect of totalitarianism (p. 112). Although both Laclau and myself are considered by Žižek to be aware, in principle, of the intimate relation between democracy and totalitarianism, we are nevertheless presented as still missing the key point: 'that the "fundamentalist" attachment to *jouissance* is *the obverse, the fantasmatic supplement, of democracy itself*' (p. 113).

This problem is real and crucial for the prospects of radical democracy and of the Lacanian Left. However, it is by no means a new problem. In his *Freudian Left*, echoing some of Geza Roheim's observations, Paul Robinson argues that democracy may be 'highly problematic from a libidinal point of view' (Robinson 1969: 125). Furthermore, it is a problem already acknowledged and debated within radical democratic literature. For example, Jason Glynos has explicitly touched on this issue when he framed the difficulties facing a radical democratic project in the following terms:

> If this radical ethos exists as a possibility, what accounts for the apparently strong resistance to it? What accounts for the obvious reluctance fully to acknowledge as an experience the primacy of antagonism and political identification, or the resistance to transforming the limits of society into the ethical experience of the limit? What accounts for the difficulty with which the contingency involved in the political process is made visible and experienced as such, thereby making possible the emergence of a radically democratic ethos? . . . what resists efforts to produce a radical democratic ethos is the libidinal investment – what Lacan calls *jouissance*. (Glynos 2003a: 197–9)

What is needed, then, is to reconsider the place of enjoyment and of the body in democracy. Michael Sorkin is right when he points out that (radical) democracy is typically theorised in terms of disincorporation; the beheading of the monarch, the emptiness at the place of power, are often the dominant metaphors here (Sorkin 1999). This is also Ewa Ziarek's main point in her *Ethics of Dissensus* (Ziarek 2001). Yet, it is a mistake to stay at this level, 'to take disincorporation literally, as the mere excision of the physical body from space'. If democracy is to be relevant, it will have to be thought of as an invitation to invent the body anew (Sorkin 1999: 13). And to invent space anew, may I add. Žižek's concentration on the moment of the miraculous act, a moment which opens itself onto eternity, his fixation on Antigone's perfect suicide, an act without *after*, forecloses any real discussion of temporality and space after the act, especially of the way spatial configurations are altered by an event and of the extent to which the (infidel) fidelity to event-ness can be spatially embodied and (even partially) incorporated and enjoyed.

A word on space and spatiality is necessary here. Space is not necessarily conservative. On the one hand, of course, 'spatial configurations naturalize social relations by transforming contingent forms into a permanent landscape that appears as immutable rather than open to contestation' (Kohn 2003: 5). However, the manipulation of space by the state and other hegemonic powers – the role of the traditional monument, Haussmann's redesign of Paris and Bentham's Panopticon are just three well-known examples of such manipulation – is not the only existing possibility. As Margaret Kohn has convincingly argued, 'space is not just a tool for social control . . . spatial practices can contribute to transformative politics. All political groups – government and opposition, right and left, fascist and democratic – use space, just as they employ language, symbols, ideas and incentives' (p. 7). Thus, space has both a disciplinary and an emancipatory potential (p. 88).[28] This is clearly visible in the antithetical function of the square as a space of sedimentation as well as of contestation of power. For example, Kathrin Wildner has shown how the Zocalo, the main square in the historic centre of Mexico City, constitutes an 'empty' space which is again and again 'occupied, produced, negotiated and disputed'. An empty space reserved for the various manifestations of the state – such as parades and other military rituals – but also hosting oppositional movements and demonstrations (Wildner 2003). The same could be said about a multitude of similar spaces around the globe – from Tiananmen Square in Beijing to Syntagma in my native Athens.

Yet it is far from sufficient to point to the various spatialisations, incorporations, and investments associated with or (temporarily) covering over the emptiness around which every social configuration is structured. What about the (democratic) incorporation and investment of emptiness itself? Admittedly, this central issue needs to be researched and debated further, and there are no easy solutions here. However, this does not justify Žižek's final disavowal. His critique of radical democracy would indeed be devastating only if the field of *jouissance* was limited to that of phallic *jouissance* or to the mythical *jouissance* of utopian fantasies. Here, Žižek, the radical preacher of an act that changes the coordinates of reality, finds himself trapped within the terrain of 'really existing', phallic *jouissance*. Why does he bypass the whole Lacanian theorisation of another (feminine) *jouissance*? A *jouissance* that cannot be symbolically mastered but only encircled, that promises neither to compensate lack by fullness and accumulation nor to reduce truth to knowledge, but finds its bearings in a material acceptance of lack itself. Why foreclose a priori the possibility that what Lefort describes as emptiness at the locus of power may entail a certain *jouissance* of this type? This is implied in Renzo Piano's recent appraisal of the radicality of lack in urban planning and architecture, an appraisal evident in the distinction he draws between a *plaza* and a *piazza*: 'the plaza is the theme park of a piazza; the plaza is the commercial version. A piazza is an empty space with no function'. Yet such emptiness is tied to alternative forms of enjoyment: 'You don't have to struggle to give function to every single corner. You can just wait and see and enjoy' (Piano in Brokes 2005: 7). And the preceding analysis of democratic theatrocracy – of the role theatre (not only a distinct type of discourse, but also a mode of *jouissance*) played in democratic Athens – is indicative of this direction. Yet dealing in more detail with this whole problematic of radical democracy and *jouissance* will have to wait until the last chapter.

Notes

1. Although not without a certain ambivalence, visible here and there in their various interventions. More on that ambivalence in the excursus that concludes Part I, as well as in Chapter 8.
2. This post-democratic trend has led to an explosion of 'anti-systemic' activity taking a plurality of different forms, from the recent violent irruptions in France to the No in the French and Dutch referenda on the European Constitutional Treaty, not to mention generalised violence on the international scene. I will return to discuss 'post-democracy' and its domestic and global implications in the second part of this text, especially in Chapter 8.
3. A number of introductory books on Žižek are now available. See, for example, Parker 2004.
4. In this unpublished seminar the relation between psychoanalysis and politics occupies a prominent place. Not only does Lacan discuss the status of the political act with reference to, among others, Lenin and the 'days of October,' but the final sessions of the seminar are also disrupted by the events of May 1968. Respecting the strike called by the SNES (the Union of Teachers in Higher Education), Lacan would in fact suspend his teaching for two sessions of the seminar (8 and 15 May 1968) and offer instead a brief but extremely interesting commentary on the way analysts could become 'worthy of the events.' But this is also the seminar in which 'refusal to act' on the part of the analyst, thus frustrating the demand of the analysand within the clinical setting, is given appropriate attention.
5. Especially in the final chapter of Stavrakakis 1999a.
6. The example of Antigone is of considerable importance in Žižek's recent work. See, for example, his book on totalitarianism, Žižek 2001, especially ch. 4.
7. Notice how this strategy is repeated in another of Žižek's texts: 'we can rearticulate the symbolic space precisely insofar as we can, in an

authentic act, take the risk of passing through this liminal zone of *ate*, which only allows us to acquire the minimum of distance toward the symbolic order' (Žižek in Žižek and Dolar 2002: 187). But surely what is at stake in Antigone's suicidal act is the maximum of distance open to a human being, and its 'minimisation' is a rhetorical device designed to politicise her apolitical desire.
8. There are very precise reasons that explain why Žižek sticks to her and we shall return to this issue later on in this chapter.
9. Exploring the differences between Antigone and Sygne, Claudel's heroine also discussed by Lacan, constitutes a fruitful avenue for further research in this area. See, in this respect, Zupančič 1998.
10. Undoubtedly desire and drive are related, but their relation seems to me to escape any logic of reconciliation or supplementation, which is how Zupančič ultimately presents it. In particular, her aim seems to be to 'reconcile' desire with drive (Zupančič 2000: 238), something attempted through positing drive as a 'supplement' of desire (p. 239): 'at the heart of desire a possible passage opens up towards the drive; one might therefore come to the drive if one follows the "logic" of desire to its limit' (p. 243). What is not given appropriate attention here is that reaching this limit entails a *crossing* which radically transforms our relation to desire. In other words, the limit of desire does not connote the *automatic* passage into a supplementary field of reconciliation; it primarily signifies a rupture, precisely because 'desire never goes beyond a certain point' (Miller 1996: 423). Whereas Lacan's early work and his conceptualisation of desire as something 'always in violation, always rebellious and diabolical' (ibid.) – a position informing his reading of Antigone – leads to 'the confusion between the drive and desire' (p. 422), as soon as desire is reconceptualised as ultimately submissive to a law, a shift of almost 'gigantic' proportions is instituted (p. 423), and this shift needs to be thoroughly acknowledged.
11. Many of Žižek's theoretical choices and devices in this and other recent texts seem to be conditioned by a reading of Alain Badiou. The language of immortality and miracles, for example, is much closer to Badiou than to Lacan. It is true that some of Badiou's work comes very close to a Lacanian problematic and introduces a refreshing tone in contemporary philosophy, which explains the references to his work by Lacanian theorists such as Žižek, Zupančič, and Joan Copjec. However, there are still other areas where Badiou follows a direction that seems incompatible with Lacanian political theory. More on this issue in the 'Excursus on Badiou'.
12. In *L'acte psychanalytique*, Lacan indirectly raises this issue when he discusses the relation between the symptomatic and the psychoanalytic act (seminar of 22 November 1967).

13. 'Eventness' is present in Badiou's work but does not constitute a central concept, nor is it used in this exact sense. See, in this respect, Badiou 2005: 201, 219, 345.
14. This is how I translate in political terms Lacan's discussion of the psychoanalytic act as an assertion that institutes a space permitting continuous 're-acts' (seminar of 20 March 1968).
15. As far as Sophocles's *Antigone* is concerned, such a logic also seems to be embodied by the two figures, Haemon and Teiresias, who are strangely foreclosed in most discussions of the tragedy in order to sustain the seductive lure of the Creon–Antigone couple.
16. And from Thanos Lipowatz, of course, from whose mouth I first heard both the names 'Lacan' and 'Žižek'.
17. According to Lacan, the fundamental mechanism operating in psychosis is 'foreclosure', in neurosis 'repression' and in perversion 'disavowal'.
18. It must be emphasised at this point that Lacan will replace the Freudian reference to the penis with his whole problematic of the phallus, with the fetish substituting the absent maternal phallus.
19. Paradoxically, however, in the next paragraph of the same text he introduces a distinction between two different versions of political theory implicit in Lacan's work: a (radical) democratic one and a post-democratic one (with 'post-democracy' conceptualised in Žižek's own idiosyncratic way). There is a 'transcendental' Lacan accepting symbolic castration as the ultimate horizon of experience, emptying the place of the Thing and thus opening up the space for desire, a Lacan who can be made into a 'Lacan of democracy' (highlighting the empty place of Power, which can only be occupied temporarily, against the 'totalitarian' subject who claims to act directly for the Other's *jouissance*) and a Lacan 'beyond castration' pointing towards 'a post-democratic politics'. But even here one cannot fail to notice Žižek's preference for the second version of Lacan, a Lacan beyond the dialectics between lack and desire. And isn't this one more sign of disavowal, insofar as 'disavowal is the failure to accept that lack causes desire, the belief that desire is caused by a presence'? (Evans 1996: 44).
20. It is beyond the scope of this chapter to offer detailed elaborations of these two psychoanalytic concepts and of the types of action they are designed to encircle. It suffices to say that in both cases we are dealing with actions responding to a severe or total breakdown of the symbolic order. An *acting out* occurs when the big Other – the socio-symbolic world and its agents – is perceived as inaccessible and impenetrable to the subject's symbolic message or demand, which is thus forced to take the form of an action. In the second case, that of *passage à l'acte* (which is often associated with psychosis), the breakdown of the symbolic link is more radical, in the sense that the action is not addressed to the Other at all, but unfolds in the dimension of the real.

21. As we shall see, here Žižek is much more original than he admits. In general, it could be argued that, exactly because without Žižek much fewer people would have heard about Lacan – and because many of them know Lacan only through Žižek – quite often Lacanianism is defined by what Žižek says about Lacan's true position; he seems to be setting the tone. Obviously Žižek's work has been invaluable in bringing Lacanian theory to the fore and in developing the philosophical and political implications of Lacan's work, but the identification of Žižek with Lacan often conceals an easy reduction of Lacan to Žižek. It is important, then, to distinguish between the two. Here I tend to agree with Catherine Belsey's point: 'I should say at once that Žižek is brilliant: prolific, provocative, a thinker to be reckoned with in a world that needs such writers. I differ with him, however, in finding his work more original, more inventive, and less Lacanian, than he claims' (Belsey 2005: 53). However, I do disagree with her on the exact point where the difference from Lacan is located. She criticises Žižek as reoccupying a very un-Lacanian 'idealist position'. This sounds as a rather unfair criticism against someone who has explicitly stressed Lacan's difference from 'discursive idealism' and has repeatedly highlighted the centrality of the category of *jouissance* (Žižek 1993: 202–3). From my point of view, the difference is visible elsewhere, for example in the way the act is conceptualised.

    On the other hand, one should also avoid the symmetrically opposite danger of idealising Žižek's originality. This tendency has reached ludicrous highs in the case of the 'Glossary of Žižekian Terms' one can find in Sarah Kay's introductory book on Žižek – clearly a misleading heading when the terms in question are no other than the drive, enjoyment, fantasy, the big Other, etc. (Kay 2003: 158–72), that is to say, standard Freudian and Lacanian terms.
22. This is also how Lacan defines *praxis*, which originates from the Greek word for act: 'What is a praxis? . . . It is the broadest term to designate a concerted human action, whatever it may be, which places man in a position to treat the real by the symbolic' (XI: 6).
23. Spatial issues, related to the fields of architecture, planning, geography, etc., are increasingly being approached from a Lacanian perspective. See, for example, Holm 2000, Hillier and Gunder 2003, and Gunder 2005.
24. Things would be different, of course, if Žižek was advancing a descriptive account of the act. The problem arises because his aim is to highlight the importance of radical progressive acts.
25. For a concise account of this line of argumentation from a Lacanian perspective, see Stavrakakis 1999a, especially ch. 5. Also see the concluding chapter in this book.
26. Once more, this was not the case with Žižek's early work. Consider, for example, his comment on the way the negation of negation functions,

from the *Sublime Object*: 'The "negation of the negation" does not in any way abolish the antagonism, it consists only in the experience of the fact that this immanent limit which is preventing me from achieving my full identity with myself simultaneously enables me to achieve a minimum of positive consistency' (Žižek 1989: 176).

27. Unfortunately, some of them are not even worthy of serious discussion. This is the case, for example, when he highlights that my argumentation 'leaves out of the picture the main utopia of today, which is the utopia of capitalism itself' (Žižek 2004a: 109). This is simply untrue, to the extent that both in the text Žižek is discussing (Stavrakakis 2003b) and in other publications (Stavrakakis 2000c) I am explicitly addressing this dimension, especially in connection with consumerism and the post-democratic mutation of liberal democracies. Also see, in this respect, Chapters 7 and 8 of this text.
28. The *Casa del Popolo* is one of the important spatial sites of resistance studied in Kohn's book.

Excursus on Badiou

As seen in the preceding chapter, Žižek's act is conceptualised in a close dialogue with Alain Badiou's theorisation of the event. Before bringing the first part of *The Lacanian Left* to a close, it is thus important to deal more thoroughly with the relation between Žižek and Badiou, more precisely between Žižek's act and Badiou's event, and with the place Badiou's ethics occupy within the Lacanian Left.[1] The exact parameters of this relation are greatly obscured not only by the complexity of the two theoretico-political projects and their various reorientations over time, but also by the often contradictory comments of each one of the two philosophers towards the other (mainly Žižek vis-à-vis Badiou) and, last but not least, by the prevailing interpretations in the relevant secondary bibliography. For example – and this offers a good entering point to this whole issue – both Hallward and Bosteels, two of the most acclaimed Badiou scholars, while acknowledging the many influences of Badiou's work on Žižek, seem to diagnose a point of antithetical tension between the two projects, a tension conceptualised along the lines of 'positive versus negative'.

Indeed, Badiou is usually presented – by himself and others – as the philosopher of unlimited positivity, of infinity and affirmation. To give just one recent example, in view of current developments in international politics, his starting point is that 'philosophy must break with whatever leads it into the circuits of nihilism, with everything that restrains and obliterates the power of the affirmative . . . [with] the perpetual examination of limits, the critical obsession, and the narrow form of judgement . . . In a word, it is essential to break with the omnipresent motif of finitude' (Badiou 2003b: 162–3). In opposition to Badiou's celebration of infinity and immortality, Peter Hallward presents Žižek's work as guided by a morbid fascination with negativity. I have already discussed this argument briefly in the previous chapter. In particular, Hallward locates the origins of this position in the Lacanian conceptualisation of the death drive: 'In the end, all "drive [is] ultimately the death drive". And death, we know, is one occurrence that never qualifies as an event' (Hallward 2003: 151). In that sense, the stress on finitude, the 'morbid fascination with the abject' – exemplified in Žižek's attraction to Antigone's 'living death' – is what differentiates Badiou from Žižek (p. 261), precisely because Badiou does not accept this passage through negativity (p. 262). As a result, his approach is much more activist and interventionist (p. 150), when compared to the supposed passivity of Lacan-inspired approaches.

Clearly, what is at stake here is, once more, the relation between negativity and positivity. What is also (partly) at stake is the credibility of the commentary on Žižek's work articulated in Chapter 3. No doubt, Hallward offers a reading of Žižek very different from my own, and so the distance between the two interpretations needs to be spelled out and clarified. Let us determine, then, what exactly is involved here. For Hallward, Žižek's work is marked by a certain fixation on the negative, while Badiou manages to avoid this danger. And this fixation is due to Lacan's negative conceptions of the drive and the act. This understanding of the Lacanian act as purely negative is not typical only of Hallward's work. It is also present in Bosteels' argument (Bosteels 2002: 186; Bosteels 2005: 238). However, there are two problems with such a reading. First of all, as far as Lacan is concerned – and we have seen this throughout Chapters 2 and 3 – his language games with negativity and the act are much more subtle and complex than a first glance reveals. Pluth is right in summarising and stressing this exact point vis-à-vis the status of the act: 'the notion that an act is purely, and perhaps exclusively, negative does not give us a full account of Lacan's theory of the act. Acts use signifiers in a way that is not limited to negation' (Pluth 2004: 20). Recently, Žižek has also disputed this caricature of the Lacanian standpoint, which posits a symmetrical opposition between negativity (Lacan) and positivity (Badiou) (Žižek 2006: 64): 'Is Lacan really unable to think a procedure which gives being to the very lack itself? Isn't this again the work of sublimation?' (Žižek 2004b: 172) – and, may one add, the work of 'identification with the symptom'?[2] The second problem has to do with Hallward's – but, strangely, also Pluth's – reading of Žižek. I have tried to argue in the previous chapter that Žižek's argument is also much more complex than is initially visible. If Pluth is correct in pointing out the symbolic dimensions of the Lacanian act, he is however wrong in assuming that Žižek's references (in *The Ticklish Subject* and elsewhere) to the pure negativity of the act conclude his position on this matter. Likewise, Hallward's exclusive focus on Žižek's supposedly morbid fascination with finitude and death as an a priori non-event misses altogether an important dimension of his work. As I have argued, Žižek *disavows* his initial registering of finitude. Furthermore, his idealisation of Antigone's suicide performs a miraculous *transubstantiation of negative into positive* which – by ultimately eliminating negativity – presents suicide as the only perfect act, an act/event that cannot misfire.

To some, this shift of the centre of gravity from negative to positive may seem to be a move closer to Badiou's position, but such a conclusion would ignore the dynamic ways in which Badiou's work has itself been developing, as well as the complexity of his thought – a complexity often lost in some of his programmatic statements and in the religious–apocalyptic jargon employed in some of his texts. Simultaneously with Žižek's move towards disavowing negativity, Badiou has been increasingly drawn into a very delicate negotiation between negative and positive, much more nuanced than his glorification as the philosopher of infinity and immortality allows. It is necessary at this point to examine exactly how negativity is inscribed in Badiou's schema. However, in order to be able to do that we need first to familiarise ourselves with Badiou's conceptual apparatus, briefly but in a more systematic way than the sporadic use of some of his concepts in the previous chapter has permitted.

As is well-known, Badiou's theory is structured around his conceptualisation of the event. Simply put, 'the event' here refers to a real break, which destabilises a given discursive articulation, a pre-existing order, 'the situation' in Badiou's conceptual vocabulary. The event, which always involves a 'strictly incalculable emergence' (Badiou 2005: xiii), is described in a recent text by Badiou – his preface to the English translation of *L'être et l'événement*, in which he offers a telegraphic summary of his positions – in the following way: 'A truth is solely constituted by rupturing with the order which supports it, never as an effect of that order. I have named this type of rupture which opens up truths "the event" ' (p. xii). Badiou offers many examples of events, ranging from Cantor's invention of set theory to the French Revolution and Mallarmé's poetry (ibid.). Now, to move to another pivotal category in Badiou's conceptual constellation, 'ethics', in Badiou's sense, implies a particular type of relation to this destabilising event, a relation of 'fidelity': 'An eventful fidelity is a real break (both thought and practiced) in the specific order within which the event took place . . . I shall call "truth" (*a* truth) the real process of a fidelity to an event' (Badiou 2001: 42). Finally, 'subject', within this schema, is the bearer of such a fidelity, that is, the bearer of a process of truth – a truth procedure – and, in fact, it is constituted and emerges as a subject out of this process (p. 43): 'A subject is nothing other than an active fidelity to the event of truth' (Badiou 2005: xiii).

Now, how does negativity enter this picture? First of all, negativity is present in the beginning, that is to say, *before* the event. No event is possible without it, without what Badiou calls the 'evental site'. On the edge of the void crossing all situations (but masked within them), the evental site is presupposed in every emergence of the new: 'Every radical transformational action originates *in a point*, which, inside a situation, is an evental site' (Badiou 2005: 176). Badiou is not a determinist and thus the evental site does not determine or guarantee the occurrence of an event: 'The site is only ever a *condition of being* for the event' (p. 179). However, there is no event without such a historical conjuncture, even though such a 'historical situation does not *necessarily* produce events' (ibid.).[3] This becomes very clear with reference to Saint Paul, one of Badiou's favourite examples. Here Badiou is at pains to distance himself from a (Hegelian-style) dialectics between negative and positive where resurrection becomes the 'negation of the negation' of death, with the latter being thus elevated to the position of a decisive dialectical moment (Badiou 2003a: 65). Nevertheless, he cannot completely disengage the event of resurrection from death, construed – albeit non-dialectically – as some sort of pre-condition (of possibility). Thus death functions as an 'evental site', connecting the 'before' the event with the event itself and making possible and relevant its occurrence: 'The evental site is that datum that is immanent to a situation and enters into the composition of the event itself . . . Death is construction of the evental site insofar as it brings it about that resurrection (which cannot be inferred from it) *will have been addressed to men*, to their subjective situation' (p. 70). In that sense, although the event is supposed to eradicate negativity – and this is Paul's radical universal message – and is irreducible to death, nevertheless 'death is required for the construction of its site' (p. 73). As Ernesto Laclau has cogently formulated it, 'there would have been no resurrection without death' (Laclau 2004b: 134). This is especially the case in politics, where creation is often inextricably linked to destruction (Badiou 2003b: 176).

A final comment regarding the importance of the evental site for the overall evaluation of Badiou's schema. We have seen in the previous chapter how difficult it is to distinguish a true from a false event.

Oliver Feltham has correctly observed that the one safeguard present in Badiou's work to facilitate such a choice is his link between 'event' and 'evental site' (even if it cannot obviously offer a global guarantee). In his own words, although there can be no clear distinction

> between subjectivization in a truth procedure and ideological interpellation . . . Badiou has built in one safeguard to prevent the confusion of truth procedures and ideologies, and that is that the former is initiated by the occurrence of an event *at an evental site*. He recognizes that many practical procedures occur which invoke a certain fidelity – his example is Nazism – but he argues that they neither originate from an evental site, nor are they generic. (Feltham 2005: xxix)

In other words, the true positivity of a real event depends on its inextricable relation to the void of the evental site, to a registering of negativity.

But negativity is also present *after* the event, as the limit of truth procedures. Although often downplaying this aspect of his work, Badiou is not unaware of the dangers posed by the fidelity to an event, by what follows an event. The ways in which he attempts to guard against these dangers are multiple, but two feature as the most important ones. First, Badiou does acknowledge, in a very Lacanian way, the *unnameable* kernel of every truth procedure. There is something unnameable in every truth procedure, something which cannot be integrated into 'the realm of knowledge and objectivity' (Hallward 2003: 258) and has to be inscribed as such. Failure to inscribe it opens the door to evil. Which brings us to the second strategy he employs.

He does develop a whole typology of evil, in which evil is partly revealed as an excessive positivisation of the good, of the power of truth(s): 'Every absolutization of the power of a truth organizes an Evil', it entails 'a disaster of the truth induced by the absolutization of its power' (Badiou 2001: 85). One such manifestation of evil involves wanting, 'at all costs and under condition of a truth, to force the naming of the unnameable. Such exactly is the principle of disaster' (p. 86). In that sense, behind the strict dinstinction good/evil lies a delicate balancing act of determining the correct degree of positivisation. Too much positivisation, too much naming of the unnamable, absolutises the good and transforms it into evil. But if evil is an 'unruly effect of the power of truth' (p. 61), don't we have to acknowledge that the possibility of evil is inscribed in the very process of proclaiming our fidelity to a positive good, to an event? In other words, it is hard to see how '[t]he genuine militant, whose pursuit of truth is uncertain at every stage . . . who manages to avoid converting belief into a religion' (Barker 2001: 139), can succeed in this effort if the process of fidelity is conceived as driven 'by an intense faith on the part of the subject' (p. 84). In fact, it is debatable to what extent Badiou's effort to register and guard against the disastrous excesses of the ever-present risk of absolutisation is compatible with his own heroic and excessive, even quasi-religious, rhetoric.

At the same time, though, Badiou seems much more willing to inscribe these negative limits of positivity than Žižek is. Clearly, for Badiou, evil is a risk worth taking, in the sense that there can be no total defense against it:

> Since evil is something that happens to a truth or in proximity to truth, there can be no fail-safe defense against evil that does not simultaneously foreclose the possibility of truth. Preoccupied with the catastrophic effects of an absolute evil (Auschwitz, the Gulag, the Killing Fields), radical anti-philosophers from Adorno and Lyotard to Rancière and Lardreau have made a virtue of the political self-emasculation of philosophy . . . [for Badiou, however, who refuses to accept this direction] It is essential that philosophy provide reasoned grounds for the risk of truth. (Hallward 2003: 264)

However, that does not lead Badiou to a disavowal of evil and negativity. Quite to the contrary, and it is here that his approach differs from that of Žižek. Badiou does recognise the ever-present risk of an absolutisation of truth, of naming the unamable, that can only have disastrous consequences: 'A triple effect of the sacred, of ecstasy and terror thereby corrupts the philosophical operation, and can lead it from the aporetic void that sustains its act to criminal prescriptions. By which philosophy induces every disaster in thought' (Badiou 2003b: 168).

Most importantly, due to this constant danger, Badiou has often accepted the need to incorporate this recognition in the truth procedure associated with an event. Thus, an aporetic void must be continuously reinscribed in the philosophical/political terrain, a move related to Badiou's call for 'reserve' or 'restraint' (Badiou 2003b: 168). In Hallward's words, 'Since evil is the determination to impose the total power of a truth, to name everything in its situation, "the ethics of a truth derive entirely from a sort of restraint [*retenue*] with respect to its powers". The truth cannot and must not try to say everything . . . Only such restraint allows it to persevere in its forever ongoing self-elaboration' (Hallward 2003: 265).[4] It is here that the inscription of limits, of negativity, acquires its full force in Badiou's argument: 'whatever your truth, Badiou adds, one should not go all the way. One should continue in such a way as to be able to continue to continue' (ibid.).[5] An inscription that alters significantly the way an event and fidelity to an event are to be understood: Žižek 'mistakenly sums up Badiou's philosophy by speaking repeatedly of the miracle of a "Truth–Event". Even regardless of the awkward large capitals, this syncopated and apocryphal expression collapses into an instantaneous act what is in reality an ongoing and impure procedure' (Bosteels 2002: 199).

Now it becomes possible to formulate with some accuracy the differences between Žižek's act and Badiou's event. First, in Badiou there is an *after* the event, one could even argue that the event is its own after, to the extent that it implies a (primarily symbolic) procedure and cannot be equated with any one single moment. This is an element missing from Žižek's act, which is theorised as a miraculous moment of supposedly total refoundation.[6] Simply put, Žižek's act has a global character while Badiou's event is local: 'no event immediately concerns a situation in its entirety' (Badiou 2005: 178). Second – and this is extremely important for the overall orientation of the Lacanian Left – partly due to its local character, this after, this procedure, is impure and requires a continuous negotiation between negative and positive if disaster is to be avoided. Ernesto Laclau does not really depart from this logic when he points out that after the event 'some filling of the void – of a special kind which requires theoretical description – becomes necessary' (Laclau 2004b: 125). How can we have such a filling in a way that would also avoid absolutisation and evil? (p. 129). How can we articulate, without our articulations naming the unnameable? How can we institute, at the same time inscribing in what is instituted, the prospect of its continuous re-institution? Laclau here creates a new concept which can be of some relevance: 'a distinction has to be introduced between the *situation* and what we could call with a neologism the *situationness*, the former being the actually ontic existing *order* and the second the ontological principle of *ordering* as such' (p. 131). Laclau does not elaborate much on this but, for me, the question that follows has to be: how can the new post-evental state of affairs, constructed through a generic truth procedure following an event, incorporate this element of situationness as, perhaps, its own minimum level of symbolic/institutional consistency? Here, situationness would imply the need for a minimum of positivisation beyond the dislocated situation, while event-ness – as elaborated in the previous chapter – would graft within this new positivisation the principle of its own permanent renewal beyond the lure of the one miraculous act/event.

In this context, the following question posed by Badiou strikes me as extremely important: 'There is always one question in the ethic of truths: how will I, as some-one, continue to exceed my own being? How will I link the things I know, in a consistent fashion, via the effects of being seized by the not-known?' (Badiou 2001: 50). The implication seems clear enough. It is not enough to encourage fidelity to an event (in practice, any event), without cultivating an openness towards event-ness.[7] Such an openness, alert to the ever-present play between negativity, disaster, and the emergence of the 'new', will be more adequately equipped to allow and encourage the pursuit of a better future within a political framework founded on the awareness of the dangers of absolutisation; an absolutisation entailed in the glorification of an event, in collapsing the after of the act/event into its own miraculous fullness. In his seminal *Being and Event*, Badiou himself articulates a formulation that can be interpreted as an almost direct endorsement of such a view:

> *the possibility of the intervention* [the procedure through which something is recognised as an event within a situation that is changed as a result of its occurrence] *must be assigned to the consequences of another event.* It is evental recurrence which founds intervention . . . An intervention is what presents an event for the occurrence of another. It is an evental between-two. (Badiou 2005: 209)

What is the immensely important consequence of that? No intervention 'can legitimately operate according to the idea of a primal event, or a radical beginning'. Badiou calls 'speculative leftism' 'any thought of being which bases itself upon the theme of an absolute commencement' (p. 210), any thought that does not recognise evental recurrence – the dimension of event-ness – and thus remains trapped in the fantasy of Revolution or Apocalypse. Isn't Žižek's act the first association that springs to mind here?

Consistent with this schema, fidelity to event-ness is not a one-off, a unique occurrence. It is not tied to a great politics of nostalgia, but implies a *permanent democratic revolution* in our political ethos, a sceptical passion that will have to be re-inscribed in every political act. It cannot be reduced to a fidelity to particular acts, not even those associated with the democratic revolution, but extends its scope to an acknowledgment of the post-fantasmatic political potential opened by them in the direction of a continuous radicalisation of democracy.

Event-ness and *situationness* need to be acknowledged in their constitutive interrelation as the conditions of possibility/impossibility of all transformative political action: 'It is a matter of showing how the space of the possible is larger than the one we are assigned – that something else is possible, but not that everything is possible' (Badiou 1998: 121).[8] A position the Lacanian Left can and should directly embrace since it encapsulates and translates in cautiously positive terms the subversive orientation of psychoanalysis itself: 'Psychoanalysis is subversive – it encourages distrust in all official ideals and institutions – but not revolutionary, since it also distrusts idealistic notions of a bright post-revolutionary future' (Miller in Žižek 2004a: 103). An orientation inextricably linked with the invention of democracy and its ethos of the limit/restraint insofar as, in true democracy, 'people *can* do anything – and must know that they *ought not* to do just anything' (Castoriadis 1991b: 115).

Let me conclude by returning to the starting point of this excursus. If my readings of Žižek and Badiou are plausible, then the distance between the two theoretico-political projects does not lie where most of the commentaries have located it. In fact, a new picture of Badiou as more alert to negativity than Žižek, more faithful to the (non-Hegelian) negativity/positivity dialectics, politically innovative as far as the nature of an event's truth procedure is concerned, and even more Lacanian – *Left Lacanian* – slowly emerges.[9] And this is something we need to take seriously into account, not only in mapping but also in developing further the Lacanian Left.

Notes

1. Badiou's work is clearly operating within the Lacanian Left, although his use of Lacan is very idiosyncratic. His views on ethics provide a suitable example of what I mean. Obviously, I would be the last one to disagree with Badiou's insistence on the importance of Lacan for the development of a non-moralistic, political ethics. I entirely agree with his point that 'ethics must be taken in the sense presumed by Lacan' (Badiou 2001: 28) and I rejoice at his pointing out that 'the ethic of the truth . . . [i]s an ethic of the Real' *à la* Lacan (p. 52). My problem here is that I have a difficulty in making Badiou's prioritisation of the Good compatible with the Lacanian ethics of psychoanalysis, which is clearly an ethics very suspicious of the Good. Badiou's central thesis is that '[i]f Evil exists, we must conceive it from the starting point of the Good' (p. 60); but how can this be made compatible with Lacan's assertion that 'the good as

such – something that has been the eternal object of the philosopher's quest in the sphere of ethics' – is radically denied by Freud (VII: 96), and that, from an analytic point of view, not only does the analyst not have this Good that is asked of him, but 'he also knows that there isn't any' (VII: 300)?
2. See Stavrakakis 1999a: 131–40. In the concluding chapter a variety of such procedures will be discussed and their implications for radicalising democracy explored.
3. In other words, the site cannot name the event, but 'it serves to circumscribe and qualify it. For the site is a term of the situation, and its being-on-the-edge-of-the-void, although open to the possibility of an event, in no way necessitates the latter' (Badiou 2005: 203).
4. A view surprisingly close to Lacan's famous motto on the inability of language to say it all, mentioned in the introduction.
5. The practical/political correlate of this principle is an axiomatic commitment to non-violence, conceived of as offering the hope of a lasting break in the futile recycling of violences: 'Only such a principled commitment can both respond to the violent re-presentation of the state and, once this re-presentation has been suspended, block the creation or reassertion of new forms of violence' (Hallward 2003: 269).
6. Of course, as has been shown, the positive features of this refoundation are never thematised; the symbolisation of the real is never discussed. It remains obscured by the perfection of the suicidal act. If, for Badiou, the event – at first, a radical break conceptualised in quasi-religious terms – comes to be theorised as a procedure, if it constitutes a moment determined by its *after* (temporal and spatial), the (psychoanalytic) act – initially envisaged by Lacan as a procedure of symbolic rearticulation – is reduced by Žižek to a 'miraculous' transubstantiation of negative to positive, *a mere moment without after* or rather *a moment whose fullness coincides with its own after to the point of subsuming it completely*. If this is accurate, then it follows that, in this respect, Badiou's position is much more consistent with Lacan's version of the act than Žižek's; in fact, this is exactly the point made by Hoens and Pluth: here, 'Badiou is being more Lacanian than Žižek! For Žižek the act is a moment, whereas Badiou and Lacan show how an act is a process' (Pluth and Hoens 2004: 187).
7. In fact, is it not the case that signifiers like 'fidelity' and 'loyalty' (to an event) somewhat contradict this openness towards the not-known? From a semantic point of view, one could detect a rather conservative connotation insofar as they seem to imply a fixed, sedimented relationship, impenetrable to change. In Freud, for example, cathectic loyalty denotes an inability to detach an investment from one object and displace it to another. *Event-ness*, on the other hand, introduces an element of openness to change that is crucial for a democracy of alternatives and

may be able to make the idea of 'fidelity' more congruent with the procedural nature of Badiou's event.
8. This represents for me the best reply to Žižek's following statement: 'When the status quo cynics accuse alleged revolutionaries of believing that everything is possible, that one can change everything, what they effectively mean is that nothing at all is really possible, that we cannot really change anything, since we are basically condemned to live in the world the way it is' (Žižek 2003b: xii).
9. There is one final and decisive element which, at least in my view, justifies such a conclusion. What I have in mind is a part of Žižek's reaction to Badiou, which has not been discussed very much. If the reading of Badiou I have been offering is plausible, then Žižek should not be very satisfied with any of these ideas, especially with Badiou's willingness to take into account negativity in elaborating the *after* the event, in highlighting its procedural nature. However, is this really the case? Not surprisingly, he does choose to stigmatise Badiou on exactly this point, attacking his strategy of avoiding a 'Stalinist *désastre*' (Žižek 2004b: 173). What is also revealing is that he locates the problem in the way Badiou deals with finitude. Having elsewhere accused Badiou of a reduction of negativity, he now attacks its registering: 'Although Badiou subordinates the subject to the infinite truth procedure, the place of this procedure is silently constrained by the subject's finitude. Significantly, Badiou, the great critic of the notion of totalitarianism, resorts to this notion here in a way very similar to the Kantian liberal critics of "Hegelian totalitarianism"' (Žižek 2004b: 173; also see Žižek 2006: 324–5, 327).

Part II

Analysis: Dialectics of Enjoyment

4
What Sticks? From Symbolic Power to *Jouissance*

In the movement that leads man to an ever more adequate consciousness of himself, his freedom becomes bound up with the development of his servitude.

Jacques Lacan

Theories and practice

Throughout the first part of this book I have discussed central aspects of the work of major figures associated with the Lacanian Left. Engaging in a dialogue with the theoretico-political projects of Castoriadis, Laclau, Žižek and Badiou, I have tried to highlight the major contributions Lacanian theory has to offer to a critical understanding of political phenomena and to a much-needed ethico-political re-orientation. In the second part of *The Lacanian Left* I will be shifting my attention to a variety of concrete issues which can be fruitfully analysed and illuminated from the Lacanian viewpoint sketched in the preceding chapters. My main aim will be to address both what resists more traditional critical interpretations and what blocks the possibility of formulating and realising alternative political futures. How can one explain, for example, the grip of forms of identification and ideology that resist our conscious will to deconstruct or reconstruct them? Obviously, the Enlightenment signalled the dislocation of primordial attachments (objective reason) and their replacement by ideological attachments, changeable and constructed. We are now more than ever aware of the discursively constructed nature of social objectivity, of the central role of meaning in articulating, sedimenting and reproducing the various (material, economic, institutional) aspects of our social reality. But that does not mean that discourse is some neutral – transparent and immaterial – code, able to be recoded at will. It is still possible to develop 'pathological' attachments in discourse (Alcorn 2002: 6). Attachments that are often resistant to criticism and change. It may even be impossible for our socially constructed religious, cultural, ethnic and other identities to acquire any coherence, hegemonic appeal and long-term stability without being able to institute relations of attachment irreducible to our consciously controlled 'rational' choices.

How can we make sense of such attachments? Here, I share with Sara Ahmed an interest in clarifying the question 'What sticks?', which guides her recent study on the *Cultural Politics of Emotion* (Ahmed 2004). She understands this question as a recasting of other more familiar questions: '*Why is social transformation so difficult to achieve? Why are relations of power so intractable and enduring, even in the face of collective forms of resistance?*' (Ahmed 2004: 12, emphasis added). Kalpana Seshadri-Crooks asks a set of similar questions with reference to race:

> Even though it has now become commonplace to utter rote phrases such as 'race is a construct' or 'race does not exist', etc., race itself shows no evidence of disappearing or evaporating in relevance. It is common sense to believe in the existence of race. *Why do we hold on to race? What is it about race that is difficult to give up?* (Seshadri-Crooks 2000: 4, emphasis added)

As we shall see, the situation is similar with national identity, which offers one of the most challenging examples of *sticking*. It is clear that standard constructionist and post-structuralist methodologies are of limited use in this area: they can help us understand the contingent emergence of nations and nationalisms as historical constructions, but fail to account for the depth, the (often unconscious) persistence and the force national identifications have historically acquired, as well as for the difficulties in displacing or transforming them. How is it then possible to reach a more thorough understanding of these phenomena?[1]

The direction Ahmed takes, obvious already from the title of her book, is to focus on *emotion*.[2] To be sure, during the last two decades what the Enlightenment relegated to the stigmatised (irrational) periphery of human life – emotion, affect, passion, etc. – has gradually returned to centre-stage. In sociology and the social sciences, for example, most of the twentieth century was marked by an 'expulsion of emotion' mainly due to 'an almost exclusive emphasis on the cognitive bases of social action', an emphasis shared by functionalism, rational choice theories and even some conflict theories (Barbalet 2001: 16). This situation started to change from the late 1970s onwards, when emotions, the 'scandal' of reason, made a miraculous comeback through the establishment of the now thriving 'sociology of emotions' (Williams 2001: 1; Kemper 1990).³ The 2001 publication of a collective volume entitled *Passionate Politics* (Goodwin et al., 2001), and the 2002 special issue of *Soundings*, entitled *Regimes of Emotion*, both devoted to the 'politics of emotion', offer an indication of how this trend is now starting to encompass mainstream political science and political analysis. Indeed, by taking into account emotion, affect, and passion one may be able to reach a more thorough understanding of 'what sticks': both what fuels identification processes and what creates discursive fixity. Within this framework, it is now acknowledged that 'cognitive agreement alone does not result in action' (Goodwin et al. 2001: 6) and thus can neither facilitate new identification acts nor feed protest, political participation and/or other types of political activity. Furthermore, as a result of the centrality emotion acquires, 'what is difficult to imagine is an identity that is purely cognitive yet strongly held. The "strength" of an identity, even a cognitively vague one, comes from its emotional side' (p. 9).

This is a lesson valid not only for political scientists and sociologists but also for anyone politically active – especially for the various sub-sections of the 'rationalist' Left, Chomskians included. On top of pointing to the insufficiency of cognitive processes to function as foundations of identity, it also shows that knowledge and/or 'rational' argumentation are not enough as catalysts of change. And since the second part of this book will mainly focus on the analysis of concrete cases – employing a variety of examples – let me give one straight away. Wasn't it one of the lessons of the last US presidential elections that facts, knowledge and reason are not enough to effect change? As Stanley Aronowitz and Peter Bratsis have pointed out in a text discussing recent developments in American politics: 'Indeed, as Michael Moore's *Fahreneit 9/11* made its way across the United States leading up to the 2004 election, we saw that "the facts" did little to transform the realities of American society. As the epigraph from Gaston Bachelard argues, realism and "the facts" do not in themselves bring about a transformation of the real' (Aronowitz and Bratsis 2005: 12).

What is also crucial, at least from the point of view of the overall argument developed here, is that even forms of argumentation very critical of rationalism and realism – including many versions of post-structuralism and discourse theory – have generally failed to offer plausible alternatives. Why? Precisely because they remain attached to what Harpham has described as 'the critical fetish of modernity':

language. Although Harpham offers a caricature of post-Marxism – which he then submits to a series of ultimately unfair criticisms – his overall argument is worth considering seriously. It highlights the fact that, 'for thinkers in a wide range of disciplines, language has the status of . . . a "pilot science" capable of guiding all the rest' (Harpham 2002: 57). As a result of the linguistic turn in analytical/post-analytical philosophy and of Saussure's success in posthumously instituting semiotics as the basis of a variety of disciplines, language has become 'the critical fetish of modernity'. This has affected a variety of disciplines including the theory and critique of ideology, which has also become dependent on the study of language and representation (p. 71). However, focusing on the symbolic (and imaginary) aspects of political identity – although a necessary step, a step that, as already argued, Lacan has also taken – is not sufficient in order to reach a rigorous understanding of the drive behind identification acts and to explain why certain identifications (old or new) prove to be more forceful and alluring than others. In fact, post-structuralism has often employed models of subjectivity reducing it to a mere linguistic structure (reproducing a rationalist idea that control of talk means control of political belief) (Alcorn 2002: 97):

> When poststructuralist theory imagines a subject structured by discourse, it has great difficulty making sense of subjects caught in patterns of repetition unresponsive to dialectic. To understand discourse fully is to understand the limitations of discourse . . . its inability to persuade the anorexic to eat, and its inability to intervene in those mechanisms of subjectivity that drive actions inaccessible to dialectic. (Alcorn 2002: 101)

There is no doubt that post-structuralism has often 'oversimplified our understanding of signification' (p. 106). A paradoxical parallel is thus emerging between post-structuralism and more traditional (rationalist) perspectives: 'Classic perspectives on rhetoric undervalue emotion because it lacks reason. Postmodernists undervalue emotion because it seems merely an effect of discourse and social practice' (p. 109).

More reserved constructionists have not managed to overcome this problem either. And precisely for the same reasons: the almost exclusive reduction of emotion to representation and social construction. In their introduction to the innovative *Passionate Politics*, Goodwin, Jasper and Polletta cite Benford's self-critical note:

> Those operating within the framing/constructionist perspective have not fared much better than their structuralist predecessors in elaborating the

role of emotions in collective action. Instead, we continue to write as though our movement actors (when we actually acknowledge humans in our texts) are Spock-like beings, devoid of passion and other human emotions. (Benford in Goodwin et al. 2001: 7)

However, and this is clearly indicative of a broader difficulty, they end up reproducing the initial problem highlighted by Benford: associating politics with 'the more constructed, cognitive end of this [emotional] dimension' (p. 13). How is it possible to re-introduce emotion, affect and passion into the picture, avoiding, at the same time, both this rather instrumentalised, constructionist use of emotion and any return to an outmoded affective essentialism (of the type present in the Freudian Left and elsewhere)? This seems to be one of the most urgent tasks for contemporary socio-political theory and analysis.

What if we try to return to the psychoanalytic theorisations of affect, libido and *jouissance* touched upon in Chapter 2? It is along these lines that Marshall Alcorn has sketched an answer to the question 'What sticks?' This is the Freudian/Lacanian direction he takes:

> Because of a kind of adhesive attachment that subjects have to certain instances of discourse, some discourse structures are characteristic of subjects and have a temporal stability. These modes of discourse serve as symptoms of subjectivity: they work repetitively and defensively to represent identity . . . some modes of discourse, because they are libidinally invested, repeatedly and predictably function to constitute the subject's sense of identity. (Alcorn 2002: 17)

The libidinal character of these attachments – which, as has been shown, presuppose the mobilisation of *jouissance* – is also deeply implicated in processes of social change, which, under this light, can only be described in terms of a dialectics of dis-investment and re-investment. At this point, and although Lacan does agree with a certain social constructionism, he would probably add that 'to disinvest social constructions, one must do more than use language or be rational, one must do the work of withdrawing desire from representations. This work is the work of mourning' (Alcorn 2002: 117). Discursive shifts presuppose the 'unbinding of libido' and the re-investment of *jouissance* (p. 118).[4]

Accordingly, in this second part of *The Lacanian Left* I will be mainly focusing on *jouissance* as an important factor in explaining what sticks, in sketching why and how some forms of identification acquire long-term fixity and gain the allegiance of a plurality of social subjects. Yet, if indeed the Freudian/Lacanian problematic of affect/*jouissance* can illuminate the success of certain identifications – the nation will be the first empirical example here, examined in the next chapter – can it also explain why other forms of identity and identification – such as 'European identity', which will be discussed in Chapter 6 – have failed to institute themselves as desirable and, as a result, have not managed to acquire such a fixity? Obviously the plausibility of the Lacanian approach depends on its ability to cover both these angles, to explain both activity and inactivity, success and failure. And, as we shall see, this is exactly what the Lacanian theorisation of *jouissance* permits.

Needless to say, it is rather unproductive to approach this issue in terms of a dichotomy between old and new identifications: undoubtedly long-term social sedimentation tends to favour the reproduction of a hegemonic identity, but, on the other hand, this has never precluded the emergence of the new. Besides, the 'old' of today is always the 'new' of yesterday. Something new can also stick – especially within conditions of social and political dislocation of older identities.[5] But not everything new sticks. Along this line, my argument will be that, no matter whether we are dealing with old or new attachments, with passive or active forms of identification, sticking requires a particular form of relation or bond which, in terms of psychic investment, is of the same type: it requires the mobilisation and structuration of affect and *jouissance*.[6] And this is the case even when change is on the wrong side. Because obviously the new does not always imply progressive transformation; to use Badiou's vocabulary, it encompasses both 'authentic' and 'false' events. We all know, for example, that capitalism possesses a remarkable ability to alter reality radically and revolutionise itself constantly: 'all that is solid melts into air', as Marx and Engels have famously put it in the first chapter of the *Communist Manifesto* (Marx and Engels 1983: 17).[7] Is *jouissance* also implicated in the rapid colonisation of almost every aspect of social and political life by consumerism in late capitalism? Can it illuminate the elevation of consumption and advertising into the dominant discursive tropes of late capitalist modernity? These questions will guide my analysis in Chapter 7. And, as I will be asking in the last chapter of this book, how can democratic imagination deal with this troubling reality in our 'post-democratic' times?

National identification, European identity, consumerism in late capitalism, and democracy in a post-democratic world will thus be the topics of the next four chapters. But, before moving into a discussion of all these challenging subjects, I need to spell out in some greater detail what exactly it is that Lacan offers as a conceptual and analytical key to unlocking their secrets and why this is so relevant to political theory and praxis. Simply put, why is *jouissance* so important? And how exactly does it relate to the symbolic aspects of power and identification? Thus, in this chapter I want to discuss the relevance of *jouissance* to understanding the constitution of hegemonic orders and to effecting social change. Building on the relevant arguments articulated throughout Part I, my analysis will mainly focus on the nature of the attachment to power and authority in their broadest sense, which is one of the foundational problems of political study.

Authority and symbolic power

Moving beyond the banal level of raw coercion, which – although not unimportant – cannot form the basis of sustainable hegemony,[8] everyone seeking to understand how certain power structures manage to institute themselves as objects of long-term identification and how people get attached to them is sooner or later bound to encounter a variety of phenomena associated with what, since de la Boétie, has been labeled 'voluntary servitude' (de la Boétie 1942), the so-called problem of the 'contented slave' (Glynos 2003b). The central question here is simple: Why are people so willing and often enthusiastic – or at least relieved – to submit themselves to conditions of subordination, to the forces of hierarchical order? Why are they so keen to comply with the commands of authority, often irrespective of their content? And it is a question as old as political reasoning. The Freudian Left had already asked this question. Not only Marcuse and other members of the Frankfurt School – as mentioned in the introduction – but also Wilhelm Reich. As he puts it in his *Mass Psychology of Fascism*, 'What has to be explained is not the fact that the man who is hungry steals or the fact that the man who is exploited strikes, but why the majority of those who are hungry *don't* steal and why the majority of those who are exploited *don't* strike' (Reich in Rosen 1996: 1). The famous words of Rousseau from the second chapter of *The Social Contract* are heard echoing through Reich's statement: 'A slave in fetters loses everything – even the desire to be freed from them. He grows to love his slavery . . .' (Rousseau 1971: 172).[9] Obviously, the Oedipal structure implicit in the social ordering of our societies, the role of what Lacan calls 'the Name-of-the-Father' in structuring reality through the (castrating) imposition of the Law, predisposes social subjects to accept and obey what seems to be emanating from the big Other, from socially sedimented points of reference invested with the gloss of authority and presented as embodying and sustaining the symbolic order, organising reality itself. This central Freudian–Lacanian insight can still explain a lot. And this can be very well demonstrated through some recent examples.

Consider, for instance, the story of The Yes Men, two anti-corporate activist-pranksters who have set up a fake World Trade Organisation web-site.[10] Believing that the site is the official WTO site, many visitors have sent them invitations to speak addressed to the real WTO. Mike and Andy decided to accept some of the invitations and soon started attending business meetings and conferences throughout the world as WTO representatives. Although intending to shock and ridicule, they soon discovered that their ludicrous interventions generated other types of reaction. This is how they themselves describe their experience:

> Neither Andy nor Mike studied economics at school. We know very little about the subject, and we won't attempt to convince you otherwise; if you are of sound mind, you would see through us immediately. Yet, to our surprise, at every meeting we addressed, we found we had absolutely no trouble fooling the experts – those same experts who are ramming the panaceas of 'free trade' and 'globalization' down the throats of the world's population.
>
> Worse: we couldn't get them to *dis*believe us.
>
> Some of our presentations were based on official theories and policies, but presented with far more candour than usual, making them look like the absurdities that they actually are. At other times we simply ranted nonsensically. Each time, we expected to be jailed, kicked out, silenced, or at the very least interrupted. But no one batted an eye. In fact, they applauded. (The Yes Men 2004: 8)

Here are some lengthy but thoroughly rewarding excerpts from the keynote address for the 'Textiles of the Future' conference, held in Finland in August 2001, which the two friends prepared, dramatically revealing the absurdity/obscenity of our biopolitical age of domination and obedience. At some point the one delivering the address says:

> I am now about to show you an actual prototype of the WTO's solution [that] . . . can help even the most astute manager keep track of his workers . . . especially when they're remote.
>
> *Dr. Unruh steps out from behind podium so he is fully visible to the audience.*
>
> Mike, would you please?

Mike follows Dr. Unruh out. In one motion, he grabs the front of Dr. Unruh's suit at the chest and the crotch, gives a mighty yank that nearly pulls Dr. Unruh off his feet, and rips his suit right off. Dr. Unruh's gold lame body suit is revealed. After regaining his equilibrium, Dr. Unruh raises his arms to the crowd in a gesture of triumph. Applause.

Ah! This is better! This is the Management Leisure Suit. This is the WTO's answer to two central management problems of today: how to maintain rapport with distant workers, and how to maintain one's mental health as a manager with the proper amount of leisure. How does the MLS work, besides being very comfortable indeed, as I can assure you it is? Allow me to describe the suit's core features.

Nobody could predict what was going to follow, something that Lacan – having devoted many pages and seminars to the phallus – would greatly enjoy:

Dr. Unruh bends down, grabs a ripcord in his perineal region, and pulls hard. Nothing happens. He tries again. Still nothing. He pulls a second ripcord. This time, there is a violent hissing sound and a meter-long golden phallus inflates forcefully, snapping up and banging Dr. Unruh in the face. Dr. Unruh, now sporting a meter-long golden phallus, turns to the audience and again raises his arms in triumph. More applause.

This is the Employee Visualization Appendage – an instantly deployable hip-mounted device with hands-free operation, which allows the manager to see his employees directly, as well as receive all relevant data about them . . . The workers, for their part, are fitted with unobtrusive small chips, implanted humanely into the shoulder, that transmit all relevant data directly into the manager.

The MLS truly allows the corporation to be a corpus, by permitting total communication within the corporate body, on a scale never before possible. (The Yes Men 2004: 92–3)

Paradoxically, this presentation won the applause and the overall acceptance of the audience. In fact, to their astonishment, it was really hard for Andy and Mike to find even one person who didn't like the lecture.[11]

What could possibly lessen the hold of the current hegemonic order – the current blend of fixity and (capitalist) change, of the fixity of certain patterns of change at the expense of others – if such an intervention can't? What does this tell us about the way authority is still reproduced today, in our 'hyper-enlightened' age? Simply put, people seem to be ready to accept anything insofar as it is perceived to be transmitted from a source invested with authority: for businessmen and many academics the WTO is obviously such a source.

When I say anything I mean practically anything, and this is shown by the fact that when The Yes Men announce in another meeting the disbanding of the WTO and its re-foundation as an organisation promoting human rights and trade regulation, the audience is also positive – although, admittedly, much more surprised (The Yes Men 2004: 169). Although this sounds more encouraging as far as the concrete content of the announcement is concerned, it reveals even more clearly that there are no (fixed) limits to what can be accepted. In other words, *the content of the message is not as important as the source from which it emanates.* Likewise, the subject's autonomy in filtering and *consciously* managing their beliefs seems to be undermined by a dependence on symbolic authority per se.

Experiences like these bring to the forefront the general issue of acceptance of, and obedience to, authority structures. Here the obvious association is, of course, Stanley Milgram's famous social–psychological experiment of the early 1960s. Obedience was of particular relevance in Milgram's time: his work had been motivated by a need to explain how things like the Holocaust did happen, and it was explicitly inspired by Hannah Arendt's conception of *the banality of evil* (Milgram 2005: 7). Obedience is also of relevance today. We saw in the activities staged by The Yes Men how easily people are prepared to accept whatever is perceived as coming from an authority. Obviously, what is at stake here is not only acceptance but also obedience. In his foreword to the new edition of Milgram's book, Jerome Bruner highlights the treatment of Iraqi prisoners at Abu Graib as proof of this relevance (Bruner 2005: xi, xiii). As Jenny Diski has also put it,

> Milgram set out with the echoes of Nuremberg and the Eichman trial in his mind: perhaps it wasn't only Germans who did what they were told. But having discovered that Americans, too, valued obedience to authority, that indeed we were all inclined to do what we were told, there was as ever no automatic bridge between knowing and changing. We must learn from this, Milgram said; we all said. But no one said how we were supposed to learn from it . . . Tell people to go to war, and mostly they will. Tell them to piss on prisoners, and mostly they will. Tell them to cover up lies, and mostly they will. (Diski 2004: 8)

Clearly, the problematic of obedience must have something to do with difficulties in shifting relations *of* power as well as relations *to* power in our societies. But how exactly can it illuminate this whole terrain? Is it also capable of revealing the limits of knowledge in facilitating change?

The series of experiments directed by Stanley Milgram took place at Yale University between 1960 and 1963 and involved hundreds of volunteers ('subjects' in the jargon of social psychology). The aim was to study up to what point and under what conditions people were prepared to obey orders to 'punish' another person by subjecting that person to increasingly painful levels of electrocution. The results were described by Milgram as 'both surprising and dismaying': a substantial proportion continued to the last shock in the generator. In fact, out of forty men involved in the original experiment twenty-six administered the highest dose of electricity available in the fake generator. This was, then, the chief finding of the study: 'the extreme willingness of adults to go to almost any lengths on the command of an authority' (Milgram 2005: 7). Under the pressure of such a command – sanctioned by the authority of knowledge – people are inclined to disavow their openly stated values and to commit acts they themselves would previously deplore: 'Many subjects will obey the experimenter [the scientist giving the commands] no matter how vehement the pleading of the person being shocked, no matter how painful the [fake] shocks seem to be, and no matter how much the victim pleads to be let out' (ibid.). Milgram's experiment presents obedience as the psychological mechanism that links individual action to political purpose, as the 'dispositional cement that binds men to systems of authority' (p. 3). But how exactly is this 'binding' effected? What are the binding factors at play? This is not the place to discuss at length Milgram's hypotheses and their various shortcomings. However, one has to take very seriously his conclusion that *'it is not the substance of the command but the source in authority that is of decisive importance'* (pp. 94–5, emphasis added).

How can we make sense of this conclusion? First of all it seems consistent with the puzzling experience of The Yes Men. Most people, as is shown in their activities, are indeed prepared to accept and obey anything coming from a source of authority, irrespective of the actual content of the command. In fact, this structure of authority seems to be a frame presupposed in every social experience. As Milgram points out, already before the experiment starts, 'the subject enters the situation with the expectation that *someone* will be in charge'. Now, and this is the most crucial point, the role of this someone is structurally necessary, without such a figure the identity of the subject itself remains suspended and no functional social interaction can take place: 'the experimenter . . . fills a gap experienced by the subject' (Milgram 2005: 141). This quasi-Lacanian formulation reveals something essential. First of all, it lends support to the Lacanian understanding of the Name-of-the-Father, the signifier representing authority and order, as instituting the reality of the subject. In his brief Lacanian analysis of the Milgram experiment, David Corfield is right to point out that it 'reveals something of the super-egoical consequences of the establishment of the paternal metaphor in a clear, albeit brutal fashion' (Corfield 2002: 200).[12]

The founding moment of subjectivity, the moment when linguistic/social subjects come into being, has to be associated with symbolic castration, with the prohibition of incest that disrupts the imaginary relation between mother and child and permits our functional insertion into the social world of language. In other words, the command embodied in the Name-of-the-Father offers the prototype of symbolic power that structures our social reality in patriarchal societies.[13] Symbolic castration marks a point of no return for the subject. It is the command of prohibition and our subjection to it that institutes our social world as a structured meaningful order. Without someone in command reality disintegrates. What Lacan, in his 'Agency of the letter', describes as the 'elementary structures of culture' (E1977: 148), meaning a linguistically determined sense of ordering, is now also revealed to constitute elementary structures of obedience and symbolic power. The intersubjective effects of this logic are immense: 'It is not only the subject, but the subjects, caught in their intersubjectivity, who line up . . . and who, more docile than sheep, model their very being on the moment of the signifying chain that runs through them' (E2006: 21). Without such an elementary structure of obedience – instituted and reproduced in what Milgram calls 'antecedent conditions': the individual's familial experience, the general societal setting built on impersonal relations of authority – the experiment would collapse. And these antecedent conditions have to be understood in their proper Lacanian perspective: they refer primarily to the whole symbolic structure within which the subject is born: 'the subject . . . if he can appear to be the slave of language is all the more so of a discourse in the universal movement of which his place is already inscribed at birth, if only by virtue of his proper name' (E1977: 63–4).[14]

Beyond symbolic authority: fantasy and affect

If this structural and structuring role of the command provides the ontological nexus within which the subject learns to interact with its social environment – the symbolic pre-conditions of obedience – it cannot explain, however, why some commands produce obedient behaviour and others are ignored. Here, the Lacanian answer is simple. The performative, formal aspect of the command has to be supported by a fantasy scenario investing it with some supreme value at the level of enjoyment. When Milgram perceptively writes that 'the experimenter fills a gap experienced by the subject', the association with Lacan's formula of fantasy is unavoidable, since fantasy entails a link between the split (castrated) subject and his object-cause of desire, an object purporting to cover over lack and 'heal' or, at least, domesticate castration. The obvious question thus becomes: is there a fantasmatic frame that supports the symbolic command and binds the subject to the elementary structure of obedience revealed in the experiment? It is far from surprising that Milgram does isolate such a fantasmatic frame; he even highlights its *ideological* nature. This frame is science itself. What guarantees that the command of the experimenter will be taken seriously is that it is presented as part of a scientific experiment. Whatever happens in the experiment is commanded and justified by Science. As Milgram puts it, 'the idea of science and its acceptance provide the overarching ideological justification for the experiment' (Milgram 2005: 143).

Of course such a justification is always culturally specific: 'if the experiment were carried out in a culture very different from our own – say, among Trobrianders – it would be necessary to find a functional equivalent of science in order to obtain psychologically comparable results' (p. 144). It is also socially and politically specific: when The Yes Men, for example, make an outrageous WTO presentation to a group of students in New York, they are met with hostility and not with acceptance (The Yes Men 2004: 146–7). However, what is most important here is that this fantasmatic frame adds a *positive* dimension to the *negative/formal* aspect of the symbolic command, since science is obviously invested with a positive value: 'Ideological justification is vital in obtaining willing obedience, for it permits the person to see his behaviour as serving a desirable end' (Milgram 2005: 144). What seems to be involved is a particular form of attachment, which can only be thought of in terms of desire and positive investment. Thus, the experiment can function only because in the experimenter's face the empty gesture of symbolic power and the fullness of its fantasmatic support seem to unite. The other side of the negative force of castration implicit in the command is the fantasy channelling and sustaining in a much more positive and productive way the desire stimulated by this castration itself. In Milgram's words, 'once people are brought into a social hierarchy, there must be some cementing mechanism to endow the structure with at least minimal stability' (p. 149), and this mechanism involves a certain reward structure (p. 139), which can obviously be conceptualised in ways far more sophisticated than the ones Milgram himself could envisage.[15]

Only now can one begin to make real sense of the bond developed between experimenter and subject. The subject submits to the command not merely because it is a symbolic command but also because it is supported by a supreme knowledge projected onto the person of the experimenter; in this case, the experimenter is accepted as an agent of Science. This projection, however, does not depend exclusively on the particular fantasy present here: it also reveals a more general condition relating to the nature of the bond between authority and subject. In Milgram's own words, 'Because the experimenter issues orders within a context he is presumed to know something about, his power is increased. Generally, authorities are felt to know more than the person they are commanding; whether they do or not, the occasion is defined as if they do' (ibid., p. 143). My reading may be guided by my Lacanian bias, but isn't Milgram implying that the relation between experimenter and subject is a relation of *transference*? Isn't he demonstrating that the experimenter functions as a *subject supposed to know*? And, as we know from psychoanalysis, a transferential relation is never purely cognitive: it is primarily affective and libidinal; it also involves a certain enjoyment. Without such an emotional tie obedience cannot occur. Besides, how else can we explain the 'curious' feelings of compassion towards the experimenter, who issues the commands, and not so much towards the (supposedly) suffering person who receives the (fake) electric shocks, that Milgram detects in his subjects? The 'unwillingness to "hurt" the experimenter's feelings' is part of the 'binding forces inhibiting disobedience' (p. 152).

In that sense, two are the major points Milgram can contribute to this inquiry. First, obedience to authority has a lot to do with the symbolic source of the command and very little with its concrete (rational or irrational, factual or fictional) content. Second, our attachment to this symbolic source is, to a large extent, extimate to the symbolic itself. Beyond the formal force of the symbolic command, Milgram reveals a lot about the more positive aspects of attachment and obedience to power structures. Not only are these formal structures supported by a fantasy frame manipulating our desire, but this attachment itself is also of a libidinal, transferential nature. Symbolic power presupposes a particular type of relation between those who exercise the power and those who are subjected to it, a relation of *belief* which results in complicity. Such a belief cannot be cultivated and sustained without the mobilisation and manipulation of affect and enjoyment; it is clearly located beyond symbolic structure: 'What creates the power of words and slogans, a power capable of maintaining or subverting the social order, is the belief in the legitimacy of words and of those who utter them. And words alone cannot create this belief' (Bourdieu 1991: 170).

This is why it is so difficult – although, fortunately, not impossible – for subjects to withdraw from the experiment: 'Though many subjects make the intellectual decision that they should not give any more shocks to the learner, they are frequently unable to transform this conviction into action' (Milgram 2005: 150). In other words, resistance cannot rely on a shift in consciousness and knowledge. Resistance is not an intellectual issue precisely because obedience, also, is not sustained at an intellectual level. Even those who decide to ignore the command cannot do so without enormous emotional strain: 'As the subject contemplates this break, anxiety is generated, signalling him to step back from the forbidden action and thereby creating an emotional barrier through which he must pass in order to defy authority' (p. 154). It is here, I believe, that one encounters the most disturbing aspect of Milgram's experiment. It is clearly located in the difficulties encountered in passing from acceptance to dissent and from dissent to disobedience. In other words, the subject has to overcome two emotional barriers in order to resist the command. The first barrier is the one which leads to the expression of dissent. But dissent does not necessarily result in disobedience: 'Many dissenting individuals who are capable of expressing disagreement with authority still respect authority's right to overrule their expressed opinion. While disagreeing, they are not prepared to act on this conviction' (p. 163). Furthermore, even when disobedience is observed, when the second emotional barrier is also overcome, even then, how many subjects are led to a serious questioning or to a shift in their attachment to the whole fantasy structure involved? For example, how many of the disobedient subjects, after leaving the experiment, have done anything to prevent such experiments from happening? My fear is that, even when disobedience does occur, in most cases it is stimulated by a (local) de-legitimation of the experimenter as an agent of Science and not by a collapse of Science – and of the idea of *authority* in general – as a fantasy constitutive of the ideological horizon of the subjects involved.[16]

In view of this, it is not worth debating whether the percentages attributed by Milgram to obedient and disobedient subjects are accurate or not, precisely because even disobedience is often not enough to shake the overall circuit within which our psycho-somatic attachment to authority is reproduced, let alone to introduce fragments of the radically new. And isn't this one of the most striking characteristics of our current predicament: the inability to convert dissent and (local) disobedience into real transformation, reflexive knowledge into action? As Jenny Diski puts it in her perceptive analysis of Milgram's experiment:

> We were . . . the generation which believed that to know thyself was to be in a position to change . . . I suspect, however, that we failed to notice a missing term in the proposition. Between knowing ourselves and change, lay the chasm of how change may come about . . . Apparently, a majority of people in this country [UK] did not want to join the US in making war on Iraq. This country joined the US in its catastrophic adventure nevertheless. The dissenters marched and argued and put posters up in their windows, but . . . Great passions were aroused, and yet . . . It all happened and goes on. (Diski 2004: 8)

Let me summarise the conclusions of this discussion so far. Acceptance of, and obedience to, authority is not (primarily) reproduced at the level of knowledge and conscious consent, and thus a shift in consciousness through knowledge transmission is not enough to effect change. What is much more important is the formal (symbolic) structure of power relations that social ordering presupposes. Most crucially, the reproduction of this formal structure relies on a libidinal, affective support that binds subjects to the conditions of their symbolic subordination. Some further examples will help to demonstrate that the validity of these insights cross-cuts the micro- and the macro-level, clearly showing that cognitive transformations of consciousness – for example, through education – are never enough to change behaviours and attitudes, to un-block and displace identifications and passionate attachments.

This is the conclusion reached by Dragonas in her account of the achievements and obstacles encountered throughout the implementation of a multifaceted programme funded by the European Union and the Greek state and designed to eradicate the xenophobic stereotypes ingrained in the education of children in the Muslim minority in

Greece (Dragonas 2004). What is striking in this account, one written with much straightforwardness, is the detailed description of the failure of an approach based on the sharing of new information and knowledge to effect a displacement in the educational stance of Greek teachers in the area. The author locates the causes of this difficulty in the neglect of the unconscious and emotional aspects of the teachers' identifications. She even talks about strong resistance, in the psychoanalytic sense of the word, on the part of some groups of teachers. At best, the result of the programme's attempts to dissimulate the nationalist and xenophobic stereotypes of many teachers and replace them with a more open attitude towards the ethnic and religious Other have led to outbreaks of anger and affective ambivalence, which encroached even the facilitators themselves.

Julie Graham and Katherine Gibson, the two feminist critics of capitalism, relay a similar experience when they describe what led them to start writing their most recent book – the telling provisional title was *Reluctant Subjects*, but the book was eventually published as *A Postcapitalist Politics* (Gibson–Graham 2006). Starting from the premise that a variety of non-capitalist relations are possible, they initiated two action research projects in two separate geographical locations:

> Our goal was to build on our own theoretical understandings and the utopian aspirations of others to produce practical projects of non-capitalist community economic development. As we embarked on these projects we were surprised to encounter a lack of desire, both in ourselves and in our community collaborators, for non-capitalist economic alternatives and subjectivities. So pervasive was a sense of subjection to capitalist globalization and the market that we were forced to confront the embodied power of capitalist discourse at every step as we attempted practically to displace it. (Gibson–Graham 2002)

Drawing on the work of William Connolly, Judith Butler and others – and being increasingly alert to the dialectics between positive and negative – they point to the importance of affective regimes in explaining these difficulties and in facilitating a post-capitalist future: 'Capitalism is not just an economic signifier that can be displaced through deconstruction and the proliferation of signs. Rather, it is where the libidinal investment is' (Gibson–Graham 2006: xxxv).

What follows from these two examples is the realisation of the fact that social and political change is not a cognitive issue, an issue of providing politically correct or progressive information. What is at stake here, what fuels resistance to change, is the (often unconscious) subjective and collective investment of particular beliefs and attitudes. *Social and political change can only progress through processes of dis-investment and re-investment* (Dragonas 2004). It is one thing to oppose capitalism and a completely different one to begin to desire and create 'non-capitalism' (Gibson–Graham 2006: xxxv–xxxvi). And this is something that, due to its unconditional Enlightenment optimism, critical theory and progressive politics have not adequately taken into account.

So what exactly has been missing in most of our analyses, predictions and conclusions? As intellectuals, we overstated the political importance and explanatory force of processes of *conscious* deliberation and persuasion and we valued them much more than those of *unconscious* acceptance and obedience. We have generally stressed the content of ideological struggles and ignored the formal aspect of the 'identification–interpellation' loop. And even those of us who managed not to miss the symbolic foundations of hegemony have not always been alert to registering the way these formal foundations rely on the manipulation of emotion, on the mobilisation of transference, on processes of affective attachment and libidinal investment. Yet such a manipulation goes on everywhere we look. Not only in the preceding Lacanian interpretation of Milgram's experiment and in the puzzling experience of The Yes Men; not only in the *cul-de-sac* described by Dragonas and Gibson–Graham. It is present every day in our socio-political experience, and it is now registered more than ever in social and political analysis.[17]

This manipulation has never been so open, visible even by its own 'victims'. Already from his first book in English, Slavoj Žižek has been preoccupied with these questions, especially with the failure of various (classical) forms of ideology critique to shift power relations. In *The Sublime Object of Ideology* he discovers in Peter Sloterdijk's *Critique of Cynical Reason* something which helps a lot in illuminating this issue: the dimension of cynicism, which dissociates knowledge and consciousness from ideological praxis: 'The cynical subject is quite aware of the distance between the ideological mask and the social reality, but he none the less still insists upon the mask . . . Cynical reason is no longer naïve, but is a paradox of an enlightened false consciousness' (Žižek 1989: 29). Against such a cynical stance, any form of unmasking (serious or ironic, didactic or deconstructive) seems impotent. However, this does not indicate that ideology critique is dead or that we are living in a post-ideological era. On the contrary, it merely points out that we need to shift our attention from knowledge and consciousness to another level, to the level of an often unconscious enjoyment. The ideological operation does not take place merely at a cognitive level; it structures our reality itself and the way we act within it. Taking into account the enjoyment promised or (partially) experienced in that activity can decisively help to explain our sticking (even with some ironic distance) to symbolic constructions (ideals, rationalisations, and the like), which are obviously disabling and enslaving. The nodal point of the command reveals thus its reliance on the function of fantasy and the enjoyment of the *sinthome* emerges as the other side of the structuring operation of the Name-of-the-Father.

The politics of jouissance

One of my central hypotheses throughout this book is that the whole Lacanian problematic of *jouissance* – one that, as we have seen in Chapter 2, engages with the metapsychological legacy of the Freudian corpus and, at the same time, provides a sophisticated angle on the discussion of emotions and affects that is currently engulfing the social sciences – offers the best chance of articulating a thoroughly illuminating approach to phenomena such as these. Lacan's theorisation of *jouissance* – of this unconscious energy, difficult to displace, which invests displeasure with a pleasurable quality – is eminently qualified to shed light on our attachment to conditions of subordination and suffering, to the reproduction of structures of obedience and of ideological systems, insofar as 'today's politics is more and more the politics of jouissance, concerned with the ways of soliciting or controlling and regulating jouissance' (Žižek 2005a: 127). What sustains the social bond is not only symbolic power, but also affective investment. Apart from revealing the force of the Name-of-the-Father in structuring reality, our inability to escape or shift relations of subordination may indicate a particular structuration of enjoyment crystallised in a variety of practices, fantasies and (social) symptoms.

In Žižek's quotation, one should not interpret 'more and more' as implying that the politics of *jouissance* is a more or less novel phenomenon. In fact, what Lacan (and Freud, to a certain extent) elevate to centre-stage is an idea which has been surfacing here and there throughout history. Euripides' *Phaedra*, in Greek antiquity, also dissociates human misconduct and misery from knowledge: 'No, we know to recognise our good, but fail to act on the knowledge: either a kind of inertia obstructs us, or we are distracted from our purpose by "some pleasure"' (Dodds 1951: 187). No doubt, the conflict between knowledge, reason, rational will, on the one hand, and irrational passions, pleasures and appetites, on the other, constitutes a central theme throughout Western theological, philosophical and political reflection. Augustine was also preoccupied with this inability of reason – which he prioritises – to dominate 'our corporeal and appetitive nature', the only solution being 'the mysterious beneficence of divine grace' (Rosen 1996: 61). Typically, the passions are seen as obstacles to arriving at a stable and rational (divine or secular) order.

Nevertheless, order always exists. But what if this order itself is seen as irrational and unjust? What stops rational cognition and will from overthrowing such a regime? Here one is bound to return to the questions raised at the beginning of this chapter. Since de la Boétie we know that this must have something to do not only with a lack of courage, but also with a *lack of desire*: 'if a hundred, if a thousand endure the caprice of a single man, should we not rather say that they lack not the courage but the desire to rise against him, and that such an attitude indicates indifference rather than cowardice?' (de la Boétie in Rosen 1996: 63). One has to agree with Rosen that this question articulates, for the first time in terms so clear, the modern problematic of ideology and, may one add, of hegemony. No wonder that de la Boétie's work has exercised so much influence on the trajectory of someone like Claude Lefort.

Once more, what is most important here is the problematic of a paradoxical satisfaction which is implicated in the reproduction of authority, in power relations. Strangely enough, a connection with satisfaction is present even in the etymology of signifiers like the modern word 'passion'. Its ancestor, the Latin term *passio* (which derived from a Latin verb meaning 'to suffer') 'suggests something contrasted with an action – something that happens to a person, as opposed to what he initiates' (Cottingham 1998: 88). The ancient Greek *pathos* carries an equivalent meaning:

> The Greek had always felt the experience of passion as something mysterious and frightening, the experience of a force that was in him, possessing him, rather than possessed by him. The very word pathos testifies to that: like its Latin equivalent passio, it means something that 'happens to' a man, something of which he is the passive victim. Aristotle compares the man in a state of passion to men asleep, insane, or drunk: his reason, like theirs, is in suspense. (Dodds 1951: 185)

In addition to that, however, the verb *pascho*, from which *pathos* derives, has connotations of satisfaction, feeling or enjoyment during intercourse (Manthoulis 1999: 117). And this is the paradoxical and yet so revealing connection we also find at the conceptual root of Lacan's *jouissance*.

As strategies of domination will gradually shift their emphasis from the prohibition of the passions to their regulation and control, promoting certain desires (for example 'interest') in order to suppress others (Hirschman 1977), even to the point of instituting enjoyment as a social duty (in late capitalist consumer societies), it will become increasingly clear that hegemony and ideological supremacy cannot be achieved and sustained without manipulating the bodily dimension of *jouissance*. By pointing our attention to the passage from a *purely* 'negative' (repressive and coercive) to a *predominantly* – although not exclusively – 'positive' (productive and enabling), but no less alienating, type of power relations, Michel Foucault has also highlighted the importance of the axis of enjoyment. In his view, as put forward in his 'Truth and power' interview, power should not be understood as a Law that says 'No': power is accepted and reproduced precisely because of its productive dimensions, because it generates forms of knowledge, discourses, and things; because 'it induces pleasure' (Foucault 1991: 61). It is the same paradoxical satisfaction that psychoanalysis targets,[18] revealing – sometimes with surgical precision – its disturbing centrality: *jouissance* can be a purpose, a cause, much more potent than any knowledge, symbolic ideal or repressive apparatus. Furthermore, it often functions as one of the initially invisible foundations of such ideals and is thus directly implicated in our (libidinal) attachments to symbolic authority. In that sense, the Lacanian dialectics of enjoyment may be capable of greatly enhancing our understanding of processes of attachment which reproduce relations of subordination and obedience, stimulate ideological identification and sustain social organisation – the social bond in general. In the following three chapters an attempt will be made to explore in detail whether this is indeed the case with regard to nationalism, European identity and consumerism. Last but not least, it is now possible to do so in a way redressing the ' "cognitive" bias concerning the interplay between mind and body' characteristic of mainstream political science (Jenkins 2005: 2) without subscribing to the immanentism implicit in Foucault's – and Deleuze and Guattari's as well as Hardt and Negri's – projects.[19] But enough with all these declarations of intent. Can Lacanian theory – the Lacanian Left – really deliver, as far as the analysis of concrete issues is concerned? We can start answering this question by examining a particular example of passionate attachment, that of national identification.

Notes

1. As Slavoj Žižek has put it: 'In the "natural" course of events, things change, so the truly difficult thing to explain is not social change but, on the contrary, stability and permanence – not why the social order collapsed, but how it succeeded in stabilizing itself and persisting in the midst of general chaos and change' (Žižek 2003a: 41).
2. Since the authors discussed in this chapter do not uniformly subscribe to a clear differentiation between emotion and affect (of the type briefly mentioned in Chapter 2), these terms will be employed here in their broadest (overlapping) sense, as generally referring to the wide spectrum of affectivity.
3. If today it is still possible to speak of modern society as a 'postemotional society', it is not in the sense of a disappearance of emotions. According to Mestrovič, far from eliminating emotions, modernity has engaged in the production and proliferation of a series of 'mechanised' quasi-emotions initiating a period in which 'bondage' relies on a carefully crafted emotional manipulation (Mestrovič 1997: xi, xii).
4. More on this particular function of mourning will be elaborated in Chapter 8.
5. When Ahmed writes that emotions 'stick' as well as 'move' (Ahmed 2004: 4), she indirectly introduces a dichotomy between sticking and moving which is rather superfluous to the extent that, in such cases, moving is always moving towards something and conditioned by something – i.e. an object of identification – that sticks. In that sense *sticking* could describe both a passive attachment to an old, sedimented identification, and an active assumption of a new identity (the degree zero of a new sedimentation). In short, 'moving' and 'sticking' become almost synonymous.
6. In fact, already from an etymological point of view, emotion, affect and passion, which are often interchangeably used in the relevant literature, imply both movement, active identification, and passivity. As Ahmed has observed, 'the word "emotion" comes from the Latin, *emovere* [e + movere] referring to "to move, to move out"' (Ahmed 2004: 11). Affect, on the other hand, originating from *afficio* [ad + facio], entails a more passive connotation; it is linked to the concept of the passions. 'Passion' and 'passive' share the same root in the Latin word *passio*, meaning 'suffering' (p. 2). However, the situation is further complicated by the fact that both connotations (active and

passive) also mark every one of these concepts internally. Emotion, for example, apart from movement also implies passivity. To be emotional means to have one's rational judgement affected – 'to be reactive rather than active, dependent rather than autonomous' (p. 3). And vice versa: to be passionate about something connotes an *active* pursuit.

7. Here again what seems to stick is a certain paradigm of change driven by capitalism – and implicitly reproducing particular patterns of authority and power relations – that precludes many other possibilities of change in different directions.

8. Hardt and Negri are right to stress the 'limited utility of violence and force in political rule'. Drawing on a long tradition of modern political theory which stretches back at least to Machiavelli, they add: 'Military force can be useful for conquest and short-term control, but force alone cannot achieve stable rule and sovereignty . . . [which] also requires the consent of the ruled. In addition to force, the sovereign power must exert hegemony over its subjects, generating in them not only fear but also reverence, dedication, and obedience' (Hardt and Negri 2004: 332). For an overview of the two main traditions of theorising power within modernity – the Hobbesian and the Machiavellian – see Clegg 1989.

9. Deleuze and Guattari, who recognised Reich as 'the true founder of materialist psychiatry' (Deleuze and Guattari 1984: 118), refer directly to his assertion, relating it to the problematic of desire, the same desire we have just seen Rousseau highlighting:

> The fundamental problem of political philosophy is still precisely the one that Spinoza saw so clearly and that Wilhelm Reich rediscovered: 'Why do men fight for their servitude as stubbornly as though it were their salvation?' . . . As Reich remarks, the astonishing thing is not that some people steal or that others occasionally go out on strike, but rather that all those who are starving do not steal as a regular practice, and all those who are exploited are not continually out on strike: after centuries of exploitation, why do people still tolerate being humiliated and enslaved, to such a point, indeed, that they actually want humiliation and slavery not only for others but for themselves? . . . [N]o, the masses were not innocent dupes; at a certain point, under a certain set of conditions, they wanted fascism, and it is this perversion of the desire of the masses that needs to be accounted for. (Deleuze and Guattari 1984: 29)

In his preface to the *Anti-Oedipus*, Foucault locates this problematic at the centre of their explorations. In his view, the strategic adversary of Deleuze and Guattari is the fascist tendencies implicit in all of us, informing our judgement and behaviour: 'the fascism that causes us to love power, to desire the very thing that dominates and exploits us' (Foucault 1984: xiii).

10. I would like to thank Chantal Mouffe for pointing my attention to the activities of The Yes Men.

11. But there was one, although not of the kind they were expecting: 'A few minutes later we finally met her. She had not enjoyed the lecture . . .' (The Yes Men 2004: 111):

> 'Look guys,' the woman said. 'I'll tell you what was wrong with your presentation. You don't want to hear it, but . . .'
> 'Yes we do!' we both said at once.
> 'Well,' she said, 'I think your performance was clear. It was brilliant, in fact . . . But the way you presented it was not fair . . . females can be factory owners too'.
> Our hearts sank. 'Of course,' Mike said.
> 'It's just the . . . metaphor?' Andy managed.
> 'Exactly.'
> 'If we changed the . . . metaphor . . .' Andy made big circular motions around his chest, as if to show where big golden breasts might be placed. (The Yes Men 2004: 112)

12. For another Lacanian analysis of Milgram's experiment, see Alcorn 2002: 42–53.
13. More on symbolic power from a Lacanian perspective can be found in Stavrakakis 1999a: 21, 33.
14. In his book, Milgram presents a caricature of a supposed psychoanalytic explanation of the phenomena he is observing. In particular, he reduces the psychoanalytic input to a consideration of 'sadism', of the 'dark and evil part of the soul', in order to distinguish it from his own perspective. I am not sure that he is entirely right when arguing that 'aggressive tendencies' don't have much to do with 'the destructive obedience of soldiers in war' (Milgram 2005: 167). Consider, for example, the recent statement of an American three-star Marine general who, referring to Afghanistan, remarked that 'it's a hell of a lot of fun' killing some people (http://www.cnn.com/2005/US/02/03/general.shoot/). But even if we agree that 'the act of shocking the victim does not stem from destructive urges but from the fact that subjects have become integrated into a social structure and are unable to get out of it' (p. 167), he is obviously mistaken in thinking that psychoanalysis has nothing to say on that crucial issue. At least this is not the case with Lacanian theory.

    In empirical terms, the vast bibliography on life in the Nazi death camps seems to support the idea of an impersonal bureaucratisation of extermination while simultaneously offering many examples of sadistic cruelty. In fact, Milgram's biographer does concede that, by focusing primarily on dispassionate obedience based on duty and not malice, Milgram does not provide a wholly adequate account of the Holocaust (Blass 2004: 276). As Hanna Arendt, Milgram's main source of inspiration, has put it, commenting on the Auschwitz SS trial (Frankfurt,

1963–5): 'No one issued orders that infants should be thrown into air as shooting targets, or hurled into the fire alive, or have their heads smashed against walls' (Arendt in Blass 2004: 275).

Also see, in this respect, Chandler 1999, for a discussion of the Cambodian example – focusing on the story of the S-21 secret prison – which is of related interest.

15. Thus, although it is true that Milgram subscribes to a primarily hierarchical conception of power (Rushton 2003: 60), his observations can also shed light on the wider disciplinary conditions making possible such hierarchical structures and on the productive aspects of our attachment to authority, which continue to exert their influence even when a particular (local) hierarchy is resisted.

16. Likewise, the new environmental and health threats marking *risk society* do not de-legitimise science even when they are revealed as its by-products: 'Even if science appears to have suffered in the popular imaginary . . . institutional and popular faith in science effectively remains intact; and when it suffers set-backs, such faith is merely displaced on to the future, just as it was in the early days of the 17th century scientific revolution' (Glynos 2002: 14). As far as the Milgram experiment is concerned, it has to be noted that, after their participation in it, subjects were debriefed and informed that this was a scientific experiment; they were subjected to a 'postexperimental procedure designed to correct misperceptions and reassure participants' (Blass 2004: 112). In that sense, the experiment itself wanted to make sure that people did not lose faith in knowledge and science as a result of taking part in it.

17. To cite just one further example, Aronowitz and Bratsis have recently attributed the fact that progressive movements such as the environmental movement have been unable to mobilise protest and resistance against life-threatening policies of Western governments to the ability of the right to capture the politics of hope by manipulating the libidinal economy of Western peoples (Aronowitz and Bratsis 2005: 14).

18. Saul Newman is right to argue that the question of the relation of power to enjoyment and pleasure is the one on which Foucault and Lacan seem to come closer than on any other: 'Indeed, for both thinkers, there is an inextricable link between pleasure and the forces that would seem to restrict it' (Newman 2004b: 160).

19. Even when they share an interest on the same issue, Foucault and Lacan usually differ in the way they approach it. For example, although they both insist on keeping open the question of truth, Foucault's interest in truth is reduced to an attempt to reveal its socially constructed character, to show how socially and politically produced discourses are invested with truth-value. In Lacan, on the contrary, truth is directly related to an encounter with the impossible,

with what is beyond discourse and disrupts the field of social construction. Similar is their differentiation with respect to enjoyment. My hypothesis is that in all these cases what creates the distance between Lacan and Foucault is that Foucault's project remains trapped within a theoretical and analytical logic of *immanence*. Although, for example, Foucault accepts the crucial relation between (productive) power and enjoyment, he is ultimately unable to account for the exact mechanisms through which we become attached to – desire and enjoy – certain forms of subjection; his schema is also incapable of accounting for the occasional failure of such processes. Drawing on Butler's work, Newman points out that this is precisely because Foucault does not allow for dimensions (such as unconscious or real *jouissance*) that go beyond the discursively constructed limits of subjectivity and subjectivation (Newman 2004b: 153).

5

Enjoying the Nation: A Success Story?

As a matter of fact, the modern idea of the nation is not even on the horizon of classical thought, and it is not merely the fortunes of a word that demonstrate this to us.

Jacques Lacan

All that is elaborated by the subjective construction on the scale of the signifier in its relation to the Other and which has its root in language is only there to permit the full spectrum of desire to allow us to approach, to test, this sort of forbidden jouissance *which is the only valuable meaning that is offered to our life.*

Jacques Lacan

Approaching the nation[1]

Although our contemporary world is marked throughout by the importance of questions of identity, something increasingly reflected in the directions of contemporary social–scientific research, in the general field of nationalism studies the issue of the attraction and salience of national identities has not been sufficiently examined. This is partly due to the hegemonic position of modernist and constructionist approaches in the relevant literature.[2] In opposition to the common doxa reproduced by nationalist myths, contemporary research on the nation tends to stress the constructed character of national identity: the nation is primarily understood as a modern social and political construction. Thus, more emphasis is placed on the production of nationalism under specific historical conditions than on its *reproduction*, that is, on the remarkable continuity marking the identification with nations – a continuity observed in various geographical, social and historical milieus. The constructionist and modernist paradigms either tend to overemphasise the economic and structural conditions necessary for the emergence of nationalism[3] or, influenced by post-structuralism and the so-called 'postmodern turn' in the social sciences, tend to focus on the historicity and contingency of national identities.[4] However, none of these features of nationalism seems to be able to explain the longevity and sustained hegemonic appeal, or, in other words, the *force* – in Laclau's sense – of national identifications. As a result, the critique of nationalism and of its excesses remains at a rather superficial level. Psychoanalytic theory may be able to offer substantial help on this front. My aim in this chapter will be to articulate a psychoanalytic perspective on the phenomenon of nationalism, with special emphasis on the perplexing issue of the depth and relative durability of national identification.

Hence my main hypothesis will be that the longevity of national identifications, beyond any variation in the particular diachronic content of nationalist discourses, can only be indicative of the depth that certain attachments have historically acquired. The complex dialectics of *jouissance*, Lacan's way of recasting the Freudian problematic of libidinal investment, seem to offer a rather promising line of explaining the nature of these attachments. Although this direction of research has already been partially explored by some Lacan-inspired social and political theorists – including Slavoj Žižek – no systematisation of the particular way Lacan's arguments can intervene in these debates, interact with other arguments,[5] and orient the analysis of concrete empirical cases has been articulated up until now. Such an – admittedly incomplete – systematisation is attempted in this chapter.

The paradox of national identity and the limits of constructionism

If we can analyse nationalism today as an identity construction, it is mainly because modernity – and especially late modernity – introduces a sustained awareness of the contingent and socially produced character of all identity. Some have concluded that this sustained awareness of the socially and politically constructed nature of identity entails a picture of our world predominantly governed by fluidity and multiplicity: 'Our world is being remade . . . flexibility, diversity, differentiation, mobility, communication, decentralization, and internationalization are in the ascendant. In the process our own identities, our sense of self, our own subjectivities are being transformed'.[6] Zygmunt Bauman, for example, has repeatedly used 'fluidity' and 'liquidity' as fitting metaphors for the present phase of modernity (Bauman 2000). Today, the ostensibly firmest foundations of identity are revealed as 'irreparably fluid, ambivalent and otherwise unreliable'

(Bauman 1993: 234). Within such a framework it is sometimes argued that reality 'is more or less what we make it', that identity is purely cultural and performative (Belsey 2005: 16).

There is no doubt that modernity – late modernity in particular – has signalled a greater autonomy in the way people construct and reproduce aspects of their identities. Yet anyone who subscribes to the idea of identity as an invariably fluid, multiple construction must surely be challenged by the persistence of certain patterns of identification.[7] For how can one explain, then, the existence, rejuvenation and sustained reproduction of certain religious, cultural and national identities, with all their ambivalent effects in international and national politics? Furthermore, how can one account for the difficulty – even the impossibility – in shifting or displacing particular cultural, religious and national identifications? To a certain extent, the recent 'No' in the French and Dutch referenda on the European Constitutional Treaty may be seen as indicative of this difficulty.

This apparent paradox is crucial to the study of national identity. On the one hand, then, there is a wide consensus that there is no nation outside the universe of modernity; that national identity is one of the forms, in fact the dominant one, that the social bond acquires within modernity (Demertzis 1996). There is no doubt, in other words, that the nation is a contingent product of history, in fact of our relatively recent history. Yet, at the same time and throughout modernity, the nation has functioned as a relatively unshakable unifying principle for human communities. It is usually taken for granted. People believe in it in an almost religious manner and love it as an eternal essence conferring meaning to their existence. They are still ready to die and kill for it.

These are, then, the terms of our paradox: although socially and politically conditioned, national attachments function as an unshakable foundation that resists the 'laws of fluidity'. How can this be so? Above all else, and given the constructed character of national identity, how can we explain the fact of its remarkable resistance to various attempts to 'reconstruct' or 'deconstruct' it over the past two centuries? How come nationalism is still the primary locus – together with consumerism, which will be discussed in Chapter 7 – of individual and collective identifications in late modernity? How can this paradox be explained?

Anthony Smith has managed to register this paradox in a very productive way. In his *Ethnic Origins of Nations* he points out that the modernists, that is, those who share 'a belief in the contingency of nationalism and the modernity of the nation', must be right (Smith 1986: 11). Nevertheless, the modernists do miss something. They cannot explain the durability and salience, the depth and longevity, of national identifications: 'Hence the need for a type of analysis that will bring out the differences and similarities between modern national units and sentiments and the collective cultural units and sentiments of previous eras, those that I shall term *ethnie*' (p. 13). What is thus needed, in Smith's view, is an 'intermediate position between . . . "perennialism" and "modernism", [able to capture] . . . the often subtle relationships between modern nations and older ethnie' (p. 17). Indeed, one has to agree with Smith that the modern nation is constructed out of a selective articulation of materials that originate from pre-existing ethnic and cultural identifications and practices.

However, this valuable insight merely displaces the terms of the paradox. Surely these ethnic and cultural elements are also the products of social and historical construction – a construction that took place in earlier centuries and went through a successful process of sedimentation and/or re-activation. In that sense we seem to need something more if we are to make sense of the attachment of people *both* to the nation and to its ethnic fabric. *This something must be sought in the exact nature of the bond between people and nation – a bond which seems to exhibit the characteristics of psychic investment – and not so much in the content and origins of national identification.* This is a hypothesis consistent with the conclusions of the previous chapter. Furthermore, this means that, apart from studying the *form* nationalist identifications take (the semiotic and other 'laws' governing the social construction of the nation), one has also to take into account the particular type of investment which confers on the nation its *force* as a desirable and often irresistible object of identification (Laclau 2004a). It is here that psychoanalysis can be of some help.

Form and force

Clearly, then, a crucial element of all identity formation – including the one attempted through national identification – is its discursive, semiotic basis: identity relies on *difference*. In David Campbell's words, 'the constitution of identity is achieved through the inscription of boundaries that serve to demarcate an "inside" from an "outside", a "self" from an "other", a "domestic" from a "foreign" ' (Campbell 1998: 9). Identities are never fully positive. This is especially the case when it comes to nationalism: 'National identity is the form, *par excellence*, of identification that is characterized by the drawing of rigid, if complex, boundaries to distinguish the collective self, and its other' (Norval 2000: 226). Nationalism illustrates the importance of drawing political, social, and cultural frontiers between 'us' and 'them' in constituting individual and collective identities. Apart from nation-building,[8] this is also true of international politics[9] and of the construction of supra-national entities such as the European Union.[10]

There is no doubt, then, that nations are discursive constructs with particular historical and semiotic conditions of possibility. To what extent, however, is this a sufficient explanation of the pervasive nature of national identification? In Benedict Anderson's words, 'it is doubtful whether either social change or transformed consciousness, in themselves, do much to explain the attachment that peoples feel for the inventions of their imagination [or] . . . why people are ready to die for these inventions' (Anderson 1991: 141). The crucial question here concerns the level at which one locates the play of (national) identification. What exactly is at stake in identification processes? Is identity construction merely a semiotic play? Is the transformation which takes place in a subject through identification a process of an exclusively cognitive nature? And, most crucially, what accounts for the pervasive character, the long-term fixity of certain identifications?[11]

It is possible to illuminate these questions by paying some attention to Freud's comments on identification and group formation. It is also from here that a passage from form to force can begin. Undoubtedly, Freud's account bears the marks of its own historicity. It alerts us, however, to something which is often foreclosed or downplayed in discussions of identity and identification. What I have in mind is the crucial Freudian insight that what is at stake in assuming a collective identity is something of the order of affective libidinal bonds. As Freud points out in *Group Psychology*, 'a group is clearly held together by a power of some kind: and to what power could this feat be better ascribed than to Eros, which holds together everything in the world?' In that sense, what is at stake in collective identification is not only symbolic meaning and discursive fullness but also 'the libidinal organization of groups' (Freud 1991e: 140). Furthermore, true to Freud's commitment to the duality of the drives, every passionate affective investment also entails a more sinister dimension, that of hatred and aggressiveness: 'it is always possible to bind together a considerable number of people in love [to create, in other words, a libidinally invested shared 'identification'], so long as there are other people left over to receive the manifestations of their aggressiveness' (Freud 1982:

51). It is only repression that makes the sediment of hostility, which is present in every collective formation, escape our perception (Freud 1991e: 130). Hence, what is at stake in politics is not merely linguistic or semiotic differentiation: 'At the level of the symbolic, there can be a perception of abstract difference, but no "real" ground for antagonism toward the other' (Alcorn 1996: 87). Psychoanalysis suggests that the persistence of political antagonism can be explained only when we become aware of the (libidinal and other) investment of political discourse, of the real of enjoyment. Here – in the passage from form to force – the pair identity/difference takes on a second, much more sinister dimension. Difference becomes antagonism and hatred: the antagonistic force threatens or is construed as threatening my identity but, at the same time, it becomes a presence whose active exclusion maintains my consistency. From this point of view, one can agree with Berezin's formulation that 'modern nation–states serve as vehicles of political emotion. Patriotism and nationalism, political love and political hate, define friends and enemies' (Berezin 2001: 86).

Gerard Delanty has described very well the dangers involved in such a process: 'Identification takes place through the imposition of otherness in the formation of a bipolar typology of "Us" and "Them". The purity and stability of the "We" is guaranteed first in the naming, then in the demonisation and, finally, in the cleansing of otherness' (Delanty 1995: 5). Yet he is wrong to limit this only to a 'pathological' version of identity. He is doing that by introducing a sharp distinction between positive and negative difference: in the first case identity is founded on the positive recognition of otherness (leading to solidarity), in the second it is based on the negation of difference (leading to exclusion) (ibid.). A similar conclusion is reached by Marcussen et al. in an article on Europe and nation–state identities: 'apart from being defined by a set of shared ideas, the sense of community among members of a social group is accentuated by a sense of distinctiveness with regard to other social groups' (Marcussen et al. 2001: 102). According to Marcussen et al., these other social groups can be portrayed *either* as friendly out-groups (on the example of Europe and its function for the British) or as out-groups embodying the enemy (such as communism and the Soviet Union for the West during the Cold War).

These accounts fail, however, to take fully into consideration the paradoxical character of identification, the constitutive incompleteness of identity and the importance of the pair identity/difference in its two interrelated dimensions, the formal/semiotic and the substantive/affective. First of all, no positive sense of identity can be separated from its condition of possibility, difference. Difference does not only *accentuate* the sense of identity; nor does it exist *apart* from a positive sense of identity. If it is there, it is because it is crucial for identity formation. Identity and difference are two sides of the same coin, sustained in their paradoxical relation through the inherent ambiguity of identification acts.[12] Nor is it possible to draw a strict distinction between a positive (benign) and a negative, exclusionary (malignant) form of difference, implying that it is possible to cultivate the former and abolish the latter. As Neumann has put it, 'integration and exclusion are two sides of the same coin, so the issue here is not that exclusion takes place but how it takes place' (Neumann 1999: 37). Besides, even when this is not obvious, even where negativity is latent, the positive continuously turns into the negative (and vice versa). Even relatively stable identity formations, when encountering a dislocatory event, when entering a state of crisis or a 'critical juncture', often lose the appearance of stability and fullness. Under such conditions they can only attempt to retain their hegemonic status by blaming someone else, even a previously friendly out-group. Far from being a mere matter of (un)reflexivity and symbolic rearrangement, identity construction – this process of managing the semblance of a stable and complete identity – ultimately depends on the ability of a discourse to explain (and/or mask) its lack of fullness and completeness. This is why scapegoating, the sinister type of difference as exclusion and demonisation, always remains a real possibility inscribed at the core of any identity claim.

Freud's account, then, points to a crucial dimension beyond standard constructionism, which is constitutive in identification: the dimension of passion, of affective attachment and libidinal investment, something which presupposes the mobilisation of the energetics of the body, of libido (Freud 1991e: 118–19). As already mentioned in previous chapters, Lacan will redirect this Freudian focus on the affective side of identification processes onto the obscene paths of *jouissance*. In Lacan's work, *jouissance* – a satisfaction so excessive and charged that it becomes painful – seems to occupy a place partly overlapping with what is associated with the libido in Freud. In that sense, it could be argued that Lacan prefers to 'reconceptualise sexual energy [Freud's libido] in terms of *jouissance*' (Evans 1996: 101). As a result, identification has to be understood as operating in both these distinct but interpenetrating fields: discursive structuration/representation and *jouissance*. In fact, as I have already discussed in Chapter 2 and we shall also see in the following paragraphs, Lacan has attempted to rejuvenate and further develop all these crucial Freudian insights by articulating them into a unified theoretical and conceptual framework – organised around the novel and deeply paradoxical category of *jouissance* – with noteworthy implications for the study of political identity in general and nationalism in particular.

Typologies of jouissance

The problematic of enjoyment can help answer in a concrete way what is at stake in socio-political identification and identity formation, suggesting that support for particular identifications is partially rooted in fantasmatic *jouissance* as well as in the *jouissance* of the body. What is at stake in these fields, according to Lacanian theory, is not only symbolic coherence and discursive closure but also enjoyment, the *jouissance* animating human desire. In order to illuminate this connection between desire and enjoyment it is necessary to distinguish between different types of *jouissance* present in Lacan's work. I have already presented a typology of *jouissance* in the first part of this book in terms of the conceptual pair fantasy/symptom, but here this typology will be recast from a slightly different angle.

In Lacan, the emergence of desire is primarily related to the process of symbolic castration: desire presupposes the sacrifice of a pre-symbolic *jouissance* qua fullness, which is prohibited upon entering the social world of linguistic representation. It is only by sacrificing its pre-symbolic enjoyment that the social subject can develop desire (including the desire to identify with particular political projects, ideologies and discourses). The fact, however, that this enjoyment is excised during the process of socialisation does not mean that it stops affecting the politics of subjectivity and identification. On the contrary; it is the imaginary promise of recapturing our lost/impossible enjoyment that provides, above all, the fantasy support for many of our political projects and choices. Almost all political discourse focuses on the delivery of the 'good life' or a 'just society', which are, both, fictions of a future state in which current limitations thwarting our enjoyment will be overcome. It is, of course, the politics of utopia which provides the exemplary case of the structure described here.[13] But this is not the full story. Apart from the imaginarised *jouissance* promised in fantasy, what sustains desire, what drives our identification acts, is also our ability to go through limit-experiences related to a (partial) *jouissance* of the body. Otherwise, without any such experience, our faith in fantasmatic political projects – projects which never manage to deliver the fullness they promise – would gradually diminish and eventually evaporate. In his *Identification* seminar, for example, Lacan will argue that the subject can momentarily experience something akin to an attainment of his or her identification: 'at this unique instant demand and desire coincide, and it is this which gives to the ego this blossoming of identificatory joy from which *jouissance* springs' (seminar of 2 May 1962). A national war victory or the successes of the national football team are examples of such experiences of enjoyment at the national level. However impressive, this *jouissance* remains partial: ' "That's not it" is the very cry by which the jouissance obtained is distinguished from the jouissance expected' (XX: 111); its momentary character, unable to satisfy desire fully, fuels dissatisfaction. It re-inscribes lack in the subjective economy, the lack of another *jouissance*, of the sacrificed *jouissance* qua fullness, and thus it reproduces our attachment to the fantasmatic promise of its recapturing, which forms the kernel of human desire.

Let me recapitulate this complex dialectics: desire – and social life as we know it – is founded on the impossibility of fully re-capturing our lost *jouissance*; at the same time its appeal depends on the possibility of partial *jouissance* (encountered in momentary limit-experiences and in desiring itself). This paradox is also reflected in the peculiar structure of fantasy itself. What is crucial to understand here is that fantasy sustains desire by performing a delicate balancing act. This has been very well highlighted by Slavoj Žižek. On the one hand, fantasy promises a harmonious resolution of social antagonism, a covering over of lack. Only in this way can it constitute itself as (offering) a desirable object of identification. On the other hand, this beatific dimension 'is supported by a disturbing paranoiac fantasy which tells us why things went wrong (why we did not get the girl, why society is antagonistic)' (Žižek 1998b: 210). This second – obscene – dimension, which 'constructs the scene in which the *jouissance* we are deprived of is concentrated in the Other who stole it from us' (p. 209), is instrumental in perpetuating human desire and in reproducing the centrality of identification. By focusing on the 'theft of enjoyment', by conveying the idea that somebody else – the Jew, for example, or the national Other – has stolen our enjoyment, it succeeds on both fronts. It preserves our faith in the existence and the possibility of recapturing our lost enjoyment – a faith enhanced by the partial enjoyment we get from our experience – but projects its full realisation onto the future, when we will manage to get it back from the Other who has stolen it from us. This way enjoyment is kept at a 'healthy' distance, not too far but not too close either; close enough to support the appeal of an object of identification but far enough from letting us entertain the vision of full satisfaction as an imminent possibility – something that would kill desire, induce anxiety and put identification processes in danger.[14]

Nevertheless, there is an important by-product in this balancing act: the exclusion/demonisation of a particular social group. If identity itself is a slippery, ambiguous and insecure experience, then the political creation and maintenance of the ideological appearance of a true, natural identity can only depend on the production of scapegoats (Connolly 1991: 67). Only thus I can be persuaded that what is responsible for the impossibility of realising my (universalised) identity, what is limiting my identity, is not the inherent ambiguity and contingency of all identity, its reliance on processes of identification, its social and political conditioning, but the existence or the activity of a localisable group: the Jews, the immigrants, the neighbouring nation, and so on. If my identifications prove incapable of recapturing my lost/impossible enjoyment, the only way these can be sustained is by attributing this lack to the 'theft of my enjoyment' by an external actor. If, the ideological argument goes, this group, this 'anomalous' particularity, is silenced or even eliminated, then full identity could be enjoyed. This is when difference as antagonism reaches its most disturbing and unsettling political form.

It becomes now possible to understand the relevance of Lacanian theory for broadening the scope of the Freudian idea of identification and for enriching a constructionist approach to identity formation and nationalism. First, by elaborating his complex problematic of *jouissance*, Lacan points to the irreducible connection between love and hate, libido and death drive, in accounting for the complexity of identification: 'to understand the concept of *jouissance* in Lacan as unique, is to understand that it concerns at the same time libido and death drive, libido and aggression, not as two antagonistic forces external to each other, but as a knot forming an internal cleavage' (Miller 1992: 25–6). As has been shown, this connection is also reflected in the limit-experiences of (partial) *jouissance* – uniting satisfaction and dissatisfaction – as well as in the paradoxical (dual) structure of fantasy: that is, of a fantasmatic, imaginarised *jouissance* that can stimulate desire only insofar as it is posited as lacking/stolen and thus causing hatred of the Other.

Let me clarify a little further the implications of this abstract line of thought for the understanding of national identification. Romantic nationalist histories are often based on the supposition of a Golden Age (Ancient Greece and/or Byzantium for modern Greek nationalism, the Jewish Kingdom of David and Solomon in many versions of Jewish nationalism, and so on). During this imaginary period, which one could call 'the original state', the nation was prosperous and happy. However, this original state of innocence was destroyed by an evil 'Other', someone who deprived the nation of its enjoyment. Nationalist propagandas are based on the assumption that the desire of each generation is to try to heal this (metaphoric) castration and restore the lost full enjoyment. The evil 'Other' who prevents the nation from getting it back varies in different historical circumstances. It may be a foreign occupation, the Jews who 'always plot to rule the world', some dark powers and their local sympathisers 'who want to enslave our proud nation', the immigrants 'who steal our jobs', etc. The enemy may be different, but the logic is usually the same. The source of all evil for our community is someone out there – even if it is one of us, an internal enemy, the 'traitor'. Someone who is using all his powers to prevent our nation from realising its potential, from fulfilling its destiny, from getting back its lost enjoyment.

In the meantime, national solidarity is maintained through the ritualisation of practices which offer some limited enjoyment (celebrations, festivals, consumption rituals, and the like), as well as through the reproduction of the above-mentioned myth of national destiny in official and unofficial public discourse. Needless to say, the lost Golden Age of absolute enjoyment and the possibility of a return to it is a chimera. However, the existence of this fantasy fosters the solidarity of the community, consolidates national identity, and animates national desire.

National (lack of) enjoyment

Hence, from a Lacanian point of view, in order to account in a coherent and effective way for identification, it is necessary to redirect our attention from the formal to the substantive/affective dimension, from the symbolic to enjoyment, from a dryer to a stickier conception of the politics of subjectivity. Lacan's sophisticated reformulation of Freudianism seems to offer the possibility of doing that in a way that enriches constructionism without reoccupying the ground of an outmoded essentialism, in a way that incorporates into the same theoretical/analytical logic discursive construction and *jouissance*, as well as desire and aggressivity. Although not exclusively designed to address the intricacies of nationalist ideology, this Lacanian approach seems to be particularly suited for analysing nationalism. It permits to formulate the hypothesis that it must be the affective bonds underlying national identification that account for its persistence and hegemonic success.

The need to move in such a direction has not escaped the attention of some theorists and analysts of the nation. Freud's Eros, which plays a key role in the construction of every collectivity, seems to be crucial in understanding nationalism: 'it is useful to remind ourselves that nations inspire love, and often profoundly self-sacrificing love' (Anderson 1991: 141). As Jenkins and Sofos have argued, no doubt nationalisms are produced through complex social and political processes, but these processes are 'premised on the activation of social and cultural relationships and emotional attachments' (Jenkins and Sofos 1996: 11; also see Billig 1995: 18). In other words, the mobilisation of symbolic resources has to be coupled with an affective investment grounded in the body in order for national identity to emerge: 'References to sentiment, attitude, and loyalty underscore the very visceral dimension of identity. Nationalism works through people's hearts, nerves and gut. It is an expression of culture through the body' (Jusdanis 2001: 31). The force of national identity – or of any other identity for that matter – is not wholly attributable to the structural position of the nation as a nodal point (or of other signifiers and discursive elements). The discursive dimension is certainly important in structuring national desire – something also captured in certain Lacanian analyses of nationalism (Easthope 1999); but it is not enough. There is also a much more 'substantive'[15] – but not essentialist – dimension that has to be taken into account: 'The element which holds together a particular community cannot be reduced to the point of symbolic identification: the bond linking together its members always implies a shared relationship toward . . . Enjoyment incarnated', an enjoyment structured in fantasies and directly linked to the hatred of Others (Žižek 1993: 201). In Mark Bracher's words, 'the bedrock of a group's sense of identity . . . might be said to lie in the unique way in which a group finds enjoyment, the unique combination of particular partial drives that, like a unique blend of spices, gives each group's enactments of libido and aggression a unique particularity' (Bracher 1996: 5). The atmosphere in a London pub during a football game between England and Germany perhaps epitomises the way in which enjoyment operates as the ambivalent foundation of national solidarity.

This latter remark brings me to the next question, which is: How exactly can we recognise the presence of this aspect of enjoyment? Žižek's answer is that 'all we can do is enumerate disconnected fragments of the way our community organizes its feasts, its rituals of mating, its initiation ceremonies, in short, all the details by which is made visible the unique way a community organizes its enjoyment' (Žižek 1993: 201). In Kieran Keohane's rendering of Žižek's point,

> If you ask me what it is that makes me Irish, or I ask you what it is that makes you Canadian, we find that 'it's hard to say, exactly', so we resort to listing to each other unique aspects of 'our way of life': our food, our music, our customs, our festivals, our forms of recreation, and so on. What we relate to one another are the ways in which our enjoyment is organized; the unique things that we enjoy, that others do not have. (Keohane 1992: 20)

In any case, the symbolic aspect of national identification is not sufficient: 'A nation exists only insofar as its specific [partial] enjoyment continues to be materialized in a set of social practices and transmitted through national myths that structure these practices' (Žižek 1993: 202). Admittedly, Žižek's analysis leaves a lot of questions unanswered, especially as far as the precise interface between the discursive and enjoyment is concerned (Easthope 1999: 221). It highlights, however, a dimension which is central in accounting for the permanence of (national) identification. It draws our attention to the fact that the mechanism most effective in structuring subjectivity in relation to discourse may not be exclusively or primarily symbolic, but is linked to the real of enjoyment: 'Lacanian theory, unlike post-structuralist theory, posits linguistic meaning as operating not simply in the logic of a system of differences that structure the symbolic, but in relation to the effects of the real' (Alcorn 1996: 83).

Hence, even in our eclectic, globalised world, where, as Lyotard has famously put it, 'one listens to reggae, watches a western, eats McDonald's food for lunch and local cuisine for dinner, wears Paris perfume in Tokyo, and "retro" clothes in Hong-Kong' (Lyotard 1984: 76), national identities remain powerful determinants of human behaviour, often resist change, and, clearly, cannot be exchanged like last year's clothes: 'Perhaps the postmodern consumer can purchase a bewildering range of identity-styles. Certainly, the commercial structures are in place for the economically comfortable to change styles in the Western world . . . One can eat Chinese tomorrow and Turkish the day after . . . But being Chinese or Turkish are not commercially available options' (Billig 1995: 139).

Moreover, due to the fact that enjoyment reveals a knot between libido and the death drive, by virtue of its excessive nature – either too little or too much – every identification is bound to produce its obscene Other. Hence the fantasies of the Other's special enjoyment: 'the black's superior sexual potency and appetite . . . the Jew's or Japanese's special relationship with money and work' (Žižek 1993: 206). The Other is hated because he is fantasised as stealing our lost enjoyment.[16] This is what accounts for the ever-present potential for violence, aggressiveness, and hatred marking national identification: nationalism is 'both Pandora's box and Hephaestus' hammer, capable of unlatching evil and chaos while also creating novel forms of social life'. It can inspire people to seek justice, autonomy or other noble ideals, but it can also 'incite them to murderous violence' (Jusdanis 2001: 13).

Nationalist hatred can be explained, then, as a way societies or social groups attempt to deal with their lack of enjoyment, attributing this lack, this structural impossibility, to the action of an external force, the national enemy or the Other, who is fantasised as enjoying more (having stolen what is thought to have been 'essentially ours') (Žižek 1993: 203–6). This also explains the fact that in most nationalist or racist literature the demonised Other is usually accused and hated for his excessive enjoyment. One of the examples Žižek offers to illustrate this dynamics is late Yugoslavia, especially the relation between Serbs and Slovenes. Here one could witness a detailed network of 'thefts' of enjoyment:

> Every nationality has built its own mythology narrating how other nations deprive it of the vital part of enjoyment the possession of which would allow it to live fully . . . Slovenes are [representing themselves as] being deprived of their enjoyment by 'Southerners' (Serbians, Bosnians . . .) because of their proverbial laziness, Balkan corruption, dirty and noisy enjoyment, and because they demand botomless economic support, stealing from Slovenes their precious accumulation of wealth by means of which Slovenia should otherwise have already caught up with Western Europe. The Slovenes themselves, on the other hand, allegedly rob the Serbs because of Slovenian unnatural diligence, stiffness, and selfish calculation. Instead of yielding to life's simple pleasures, the Slovenes perversely enjoy constantly devising means of depriving Serbs of the results

of their hard labor by commercial profiteering, by reselling what they bought cheaply in Serbia. (Žižek 1993: 204)

A similar network seems to be operating in the Canadian case. Quebeckers are often accused of an excessive enjoyment – associated with their 'French' culture – they refuse to share with the rest of Canada. The argument here goes like that: 'If Quebec's excess enjoyment was shared, if Quebec would accept that the other provinces were as equal as itself, then we would be happy' (Keohane 1992: 5). On the other hand, Quebeckers themselves resent not enjoying the political power which supposedly benefits the (Federal government of) the Rest of Canada in excess. Furthermore,

> both Quebecois and rest-of-Canadians say, if we all only had that special relationship with the land which we suspect Natives of enjoying, even though the same Natives deny us our enjoyment of golfing at Oka . . . then we would all have a sense of place. If only we had the prosperity of the Americans, even though that prosperity is stealing our jobs, guzzling our resources . . . there would be no problem. (Keohane 1992: 5)[17]

Let me give another example demonstrating the importance of enjoyment in structuring national identification, this time from Greece. Consider the way the Greek sociologist Constantine Tsoukalas describes the shared feeling of 'Greekness': 'Greeks think they are Greek when they sing, dance, dream, laugh, feel, make love or fight, eventually when they are shrewd and individually successful, but never when they compulsively pursue unidimensional, collective, rational goals'. In other words, what is important is how 'communion, pathos, honor, pleasure, or even "contradiction" are sought, tasted and *enjoyed*: this is their cultural "uniqueness"; they are apt to boast of their vocation for *enjoying* life in ways aliens cannot hope to understand' (Tsoukalas 1993: 75–6, emphasis added). Needless to say, this is obviously not a Greek prerogative, nor is 'theft of enjoyment' operative only in the examples offered by Žižek and Keohane. Every national community is tied together by similar links and differentiated in similar ways from its 'Others'. Likewise, as Peter Bratsis (2003) has rightly argued, driving a Chevy, watching baseball, and eating hotdogs are experienced and *enjoyed* by Americans as distinctively American national practices, and every national identification is reproduced along similar axes.

Let me conclude this section with a systematic codification of the Lacanian contribution as it has been developed to date in the literature reviewed and in the arguments elaborated in this chapter, providing at the same time some further empirical illustrations. An approach to nationalism focusing on the enjoyment factor highlights at least three dimensions:

1. What gives consistency to the discursive construction of the nation is a fantasy promising our encounter with the fullness of enjoyment located/projected at the roots of national history.[18] This fantasy is often reproduced through official channels: education, national myths, ritualised practices like army parades, and so on. The Greek irredentist *Megale Idea* is paradigmatic of this fantasmatic promise. For nineteenth and early twentieth-century Greek nationalists, the 'liberation of unredeemed Greeks', the creation of a 'greater Greece of two continents and five seas' and the 'recapturing of Constantinople' offered the promise of an absolute fullness which would ameliorate all the problems of the newborn state.
2. Such imaginary fantasmatic promises acquire the gloss of the real through the partial enjoyment obtained from certain practices, unofficial for the most part: an enjoyment reproduced through characteristic everyday family rituals, customs, culinary preferences and traditions (especially in cases where what is consumed is considered unedible or disgusting in other cultures), and the like.[19] To continue with the Greek example, if official state ideology focusing on the (fantasmatic) continuity of Greek civilisation dominated the opening ceremony of the 2004 Athens Olympic Games, the closing ceremony revealed an underside infused with types of (predominantly somatic) enjoyment (such as very particular types of singing and dancing) rarely depicted in official discourses and practices. It is always such a dialectics between officially sanctioned ideals (imaginarised promises and illustrations of *jouissance*) and largely unofficial practices (partial encounters with a *jouissance* of the body) that structures an effective national identification.
3. This dialectics, however, is never enough. Precisely because the partiality of this second type of enjoyment threatens to reveal the illusory character of our national fantasies of fullness, the credibility and salience of the nation as an object of identification relies on the ability of nationalist discourse to provide a convincing explanation for the lack of total enjoyment. It is here that the idea of a theft of enjoyment is introduced, an idea also typical of

national myths and inextricably tied with the construction of national enemies (for instance Greece for Turkey or Turkey for Greece).

In this way psychoanalysis, and especially Lacanian theory, alerts us to the fact that nationalism cannot be reduced to rational self-interested motivations, economic conditions, and institutional dynamics. As important as the aforementioned factors may be, the play of identifications should be at the heart of any effort to study group actions and human agency in nationalist movements. However, highlighting the discursive/semiotic aspect of identification processes is not enough. The ecumenical appeal of discourses like nationalism rests on their ability to mobilise the human desire for identity and to promise an encounter with (national) enjoyment. The study of nationalism should therefore emphasise the workings of the processes of identification and the way in which the dialectics of enjoyment – of the different types of *jouissance*: of fantasy, of the body, and so on – is played out in different national contexts.

Censoring the affective dimension

If, however, the dimension of affect and enjoyment is so crucial in collective identification, why has it gone unnoticed by so many social theorists, political analysts and modern politicians? As I have already implied in the previous chapter, Enlightenment philosophy and political theory – as well as politics itself – have largely seen their role as drawing a sharp distinction between the symbolic dimension of identification and its affective/obscene support. In the age of reason and rational administration there was no room for 'irrational' forces and libidinal bonds. The aim was either to control or, even better, to eliminate passion, affect and enthusiasm, to drain out the *jouissance* of the body from political practice and political theory. In its attempt to ground politics on reason and nature, the Enlightenment was 'led to present an optimistic view of human sociability, seeing violence as an archaic phenomenon that does not really belong to human nature' (Mouffe 2000: 130). Passion and enthusiasm were also seen as dangerous pathological conditions, to be eradicated through the progress of human civilisation (Ruby 1996). Elements of such a stance are still implicit – among others – in certain traditions of democratic theory (including some aggregative and deliberative models) and even in versions of postmodernism (Mouffe 2000).

There are, however, serious problems with such a strategy. It is very difficult to sustain a strict separation between affect and reason, to disengage the symbolic aspect of discursive organisation and identification from libidinal investment and enjoyment. Let us return to the preceding analysis of national identification. It must have become obvious by now that both dimensions are crucial here. Nevertheless, literature on nationalism is replete with attempts to distinguish a benign, drier form of nationalism (or, even better, 'patriotism', as in Habermas' 'constitutional patriotism') from the malignant nationalism of hatred and affective cathexis. Hence the prominent dichotomies between civic and ethnic, political and cultural, Western and Eastern, benevolent and malevolent nationalism. At least twenty different formulations of such a dualism have been counted up to now (Spencer and Wollman 1998: 257). All these moralistic dichotomies are as many attempts to exorcise the obscene dimension of national identification. Many rationalists, liberals and cosmopolitans consider this aspect of it as anathema, 'straitlaced, illiberal and vulgar' (Jusdanis 2001: 28). For these politicians and academics, 'nationalism can be seen almost anywhere but here' (Billig 1995: 15); their motto is 'Our patriotism – Their nationalism' (p. 55).

Such a view obviously ignores the fact that 'benevolent nationalism frequently turns into ugly hypernationalism' (Mearsheimer 1990: 36). As Jenkins and Sofos have argued, it is wrong 'to see nationalism in terms of simple dichotomies – "good" and "bad", "open" and "closed", "Left" and "Right", "French" and "German". The reality is much more nuanced and complex, and in practice the two "models" are not mutually incompatible' (Jenkins and Sofos 1996: 15). The antithesis between cultural and political nations, between civic and ethnic nationalism, seems to be based on an idealisation of the histories of France, England and the United States, which are conceptualised as embodying the principles of the Enlightenment (Jusdanis 2001: 136; also see Smith 1995: 16). Such an idealisation presupposes the disavowal of the fact that, in the final analysis, 'all nationalism takes on a cultural dimension' (Jusdanis 2001: 162). As Spencer and Wollman have put it, 'political nationalism cannot itself exist without a vivid and strong sense of its own cultural identity' (Spencer and Wollman 1998: 261). In Anthony Smith's words, 'every nationalism contains civic and ethnic elements in varying degrees and different forms' (Smith 1991: 13), to the extent that, in practice, territorial nations also have to be cultural communities (Smith 1986: 136; 149) – communities that structure in their own distinct way their modes of enjoyment. From a Lacanian point of view, the possibility of 'a purely civic (uncultural) conception of nationalism – that a nation-state can be based on an idea, that it can flourish in a purely political sense, that it can be held together by its constitutional documents and democratic institutions' (Jusdanis 2001: 10) has to be put into question simply because no identity with the durability characteristic of nationalism can be constructed without effectively manipulating libidinal investment and *jouissance*. As Chantal Mouffe has put it, 'to make sense of nationalism one has to understand the role of "passion" in the creation of collective identities' (Mouffe 2001: 11).

This is not to say, however, that it is impossible to construct political projects with minimal affective content; it is merely to point out that such projects will be unable to mobilise popular support on a large scale and form the basis of pervasive identifications (as has been the case with national identification). The example of the underdevelopment of a strong European identity, which is discussed in the next chapter, will amply demonstrate this point. It is also not to say, and this has to be stressed, that the nation is an a priori privileged locus for affective investment and the administration of *jouissance*. In fact, the preceding analysis does not preclude the possibility of postnational developments. It points, however, to the fact that these cannot succeed merely on the basis of their signifying and cognitive dimension, nor can they rely exclusively on their institutional or economic impetus; they will have to effect a displacement of the energy currently invested in the national constellation. Accordingly, the challenge for the Lacanian Left is to construct equally forceful points of identification, able to sublimate the obscene aspect of national identification and to channel the ever-present hatred and resentment involved in every identity construction in a democratic agonistic direction.

Notes

1. I would like to acknowledge the invaluable help of Nikos Chrysoloras in drafting an earlier version of this whole chapter (Stavrakakis with Chrysoloras 2006).
2. These terms are widely used in nationalism studies to denote the mainstream current of thought in the discipline, which views nations as social constructions of modernity. As it has been emphasised by Anthony Smith, the assertion that marks out the essence of modernism is that 'nationalism is a product of modernity, nothing less . . . But it is not only

that nationalism is modern. So are nations, national states, national identities, and the whole "inter-national" community' (Smith 2001: 46–7). Most of the seminal figures in the field (Kedourie, Gellner, Hobsbawm, Anderson) seem to accept this assertion despite other significant theoretical differences between them.
3. See Gellner 1997.
4. See, for example, Anderson 1991.
5. This is important because, obviously, other factors still remain operative here.
6. Introduction to the special issue on 'New Times', *Marxism Today*, October 1988. Cited in Callinicos 1989: 4.
7. This paradox is registered in Bauman's work when he concedes that the awareness of contingency does not eliminate the demands for 'objective' foundations. In fact, since these are articulated within an environment of generalised uncertainty, they are bound to produce even more 'aggression and intolerance' (Bauman 1993: 235). The endemic precariousness of identity, coupled with a demand for this impossible object, is bound to produce a type of community which is 'neurotic about matters of security' and 'paranoic' about the hostility emanating from its environment, and, as a result, 'bellicose and intolerant' (ibid.). The question is, why does this demand for identity – in particular national identity – remain so strong? Why does national identity stick? Is it only coercion, custom, inertia, etc. that help explain this outcome?
8. Greece provides a good example of the importance of the 'us/them' binary opposition during the nation building process; see Chrysoloras 2004b. The oppositional character of national identity becomes even most apparent in the political discourse of right-wing, populist and nationalist movements; see Chrysoloras 2004a and Stavrakakis 2002a: 29–52.
9. Campbell's analysis of security is crucial here: 'The constant articulation of danger through foreign policy is thus not a threat to a state's identity or existence: it is its condition of possibility' (Campbell 1998: 13).
10. Neumann has shown in a lot of detail how 'representations of the other were used to reinforce and strengthen the collective of Europe' (Neumann 1999: 45).
11. These questions do not presuppose a strict distinction between a material (real) and an immaterial (linguistic/semiotic) field of construction. Lacan does not dispute the materiality of the signifier and even reminds us of Stalin's formulation that 'language is not a superstructure' (E1977: 167; also see E2006: 344). At issue here is the interaction between different registers of materiality (symbolic and affective).
12. For a detailed account of identity along these lines, see Stavrakakis 2001. The similarities with the pair creation/alienation examined in Chapter 1 are more than obvious.

13. See more on that in Stavrakakis 1999a, especially ch. 4.
14. For Lacan, anxiety – the paradigmatic affect – appears when we come close to fulfilling our desire, to attaining *jouissance*. It is not the signal of a lack; it emerges when the preservation of the lack, which sustains desire, seems to be threatened:

    > It is not nostalgia for what is called the maternal womb which engenders anxiety, it is its imminence, it is everything that announces to us something which allows us to glimpse that we are going to re-enter it . . . What provokes anxiety? It is not, contrary to what is said, either the rhythm or the alternation of the presence–absence of the mother. And what proves it is that the infant takes pleasure in repeating this game of presence and absence . . . What is most anxiety-provoking for the child, is that precisely this relation of lack on which it establishes himself, which makes him desire, this relation is all the more disturbed when there is no possibility of lack, when the mother is always on his back, and especially by wiping his bottom, the model of the demand, of the demand which cannot fail. (seminar of 5 December 1962)

15. In this text I am employing the word 'substance' not as referring to the content – as opposed to the form – of nationalist discourses, but in order to delineate the presence of a dimension – that of affect and enjoyment – beyond the formal rules governing signifying processes of identity construction.
16. Stealing our *mojo*, this precious something that encapsulates all our energy and potency, as Austin Powers – among others – would put it. In Austin Powers movies the story unfolds around the loss, the theft, of this mysterious *mojo*.
17. On the particularity of Canadian official identity and multiculturalism, see, from the perspective deployed here, apart from Keohane's work, Day 1994.
18. Drawing on Žižek and Kristeva, Ziarek argues that 'national affiliation cannot be sustained by merely symbolic and imaginary identifications; it requires a supplementary function of phantasmatic enjoyment, transforming the emptiness of the symbolic into the substance of national community' (Ziarek 2001: 125). She is of course right in highlighting the affective 'surplus value' involved in national affiliation (p. 126). However, by explaining libidinal attachment only in terms of fantasy (ibid.), she manages to take into account only the most elementary (imaginarised) aspect of the dialectics of *jouissance* involved in the reproduction of national identification.
19. Here we need to distinguish between three different levels. There is, first, the banal biological background that tells us that a number of calories is needed daily in order to survive. In Lacanian jargon, this would probably correspond to the level of need. Second, there is the level of socially acquired taste that permits us to find pleasure in the different cuisines on offer in our cosmopolitan societies. This is the level of symbolic

demand. But there is also a third level of (obscene) enjoyment – which is not extra-social, but requires a surplus investment – associated with desiring, preparing and consuming foods unique to our communities, foods that strangers might not find that appetising or might have difficulties in understanding our attachment to. What else makes the Greek student pack his or her suitcase with Greek food when going abroad to study?

Yet this point should not be understood in an essentialist manner. *Jouissance* here does not necessarily depend on the content of the food or the exclusive ingredients of the national cuisine. For example, *jouissance* may have much more to do with size than with taste, as in the American case: 'The enjoyment operant from the excess of the size itself is purely American' (Bratsis 2006: 101). Accordingly, what also distinguishes Greek–American food from Greek food is not the ingredients, but its size: 'The gyro is so big that it is hard to handle, the grease runs down your hands, it is messy, probably not too good for you, but, nonetheless, very pleasurable' (ibid.).

6
Lack of Passion: European Identity Revisited

Europe in focus

I started the previous chapter with an observation regarding the importance that questions of identity have gradually acquired. It would be bizarre if the broad field of international relations were to stay untouched by this trend. In fact, no one is surprised any more by the fact that 'the discipline of international relations (IR) is witnessing a surge of interest in identity and identity formation' (Neumann 1999: 1). The same applies to the sub-discipline of European Studies – affecting both marginal and mainstream approaches. As Anthony Smith has pointed out, one of the fundamental reasons for the current interest in 'European unification' is, undoubtedly, 'the problem of identity itself, one that has played a major part in European debates over the past 30–40 years. At issue [among other themes] has been the possibility and legitimacy of a "European identity", as opposed to the existing national identities' (Smith 1999: 226).

This development is hardly surprising given that, at least since the 1970s, processes of European integration have been explicitly linked with a problematic of identity. Already from 1973, when the member-states of the then European Community agreed to define European identity in a *Fundamental Declaration* released at the Copenhagen summit, the construction of European identity was officially recognised as a crucial policy issue in the process of strengthening the profile and safeguarding the future prospects of the European Community (European Commission 1974). Undoubtedly, the extent to which 'European identity' is something to be discovered or constructed (or both), something that should be viewed 'in opposition' to or 'side by side' with national identities (or even within a post-national framework), something to be celebrated or resisted (or, simply, ignored) is debatable: all these are still contentious points in the European public sphere(s). What is clear, however, is that identity is firmly positioned at the centre of intense European policy and research interest.

Yet this is not to say that the question of Europe (European integration, unification or identity) has been adequately addressed from a perspective focusing on processes of identity formation. As Gerard Delanty has put it in his book *Inventing Europe: Idea, Identity, Reality*, 'little thought is actually given to the meaning of the term Europe and its relationship to problems in contemporary political identity' (Delanty 1995: 1). For example, more than forty years after the European project in its current form began, 'it is striking how little we know about its . . . identity-shaping effects' (Checkel 2001: 50). This is not merely a matter of limitations in our empirical research; it has to be linked to the fact that it is rarely clear what such an identity approach implies. In this area, identity is becoming fashionable as a word, without, however, its meaning as a theoretical category and tool for analysis becoming more clear in the process. Such problems in conceptual clarity and theoretical rigour have serious analytical repercussions. For example, they make it extremely difficult to account in a sustained way for what may be the most pressing problem affecting the European Union today, namely that, although Europe now undoubtedly exists as an economic and increasingly as a political entity, identification with Europe has so far failed to acquire 'a wider cultural or affective meaning' for the different European peoples (Pagden 2002: 33). As has been observed, 'apart form a flag, a hymn and a few festivals . . . the European Union offers little that can inspire collective enthusiasm' (Chebel d'Appolonia 2002: 190) – a situation that seems to be corroborated by recent statistical data in the *Eurobarometer* (Dunkerley et al. 2002: 120) and by the difficulties which the ratification of the new Constitutional Treaty is facing.

The starting point of this chapter is that the paradoxical dimensions of political identity and identity formation discussed in the previous chapters, dimensions which are often neglected but remain essential if we want to arrive at a really thorough and rigorous conceptualisation of identity and identification, are crucial for rethinking questions around European identity and for the development of an appropriate set of research directions and hypotheses in this area. My main hypothesis here will be that the view of identity and identification resulting from a blend of discourse theory and Lacanian psychoanalysis and articulated around the analytical angle of *jouissance* can provide plausible and innovative explanations for the current difficulties in constructing European identity as a collectively appealing object of identification. It can thus redirect the (academic and political) debate around this issue in a largely uncharted but clearly promising direction.

In particular, two will be my central preoccupations in this chapter. Given the substantial input the Lacanian problematic of *jouissance* offers in analysing national affiliation, a relatively successful case of long-term collective identification, can we employ the same framework in accounting for the relative failure of European identity? Is one of the central reasons behind the obstacles identification with Europe is currently encountering its minimal affective appeal? Its inability to invest itself with this surplus enjoyment-value that is needed on top of symbolic attraction and imaginary gloss in order to create strong libidinal bonds and long-term attachments? On the basis of the overall theoretical/analytical schema developed in this text and tested in its second part, one would indeed expect a deficit at the level of *jouissance*, and the first section of the present chapter will explore whether this is the case or not.

The second section will focus on a related issue. When politics or theory manages to construct political projects almost devoid of affective substance, another problem appears – on top, that is to say, of the limited hegemonic appeal of the project in question. In most such cases one can observe the repression of signifiers cathected with libidinal and affective value. But this repression does not operate on affect itself. As I have already pointed out, on the dominant Freudian/Lacanian view, repression does not touch affects directly but only ideas (signifiers). Affects, however, are displaced and transformed as a result of repression: in repression affect and thought are dissociated from each other. As a result, representation is directed to the unconscious, while affect remains and gets attached onto another, substitute (often symptomatic) representation. It is not difficult to understand the political significance of this logic. It implies that, the more the affective dimension of political subjectivity and identification is repressed, the more a particular hegemonic project excludes signifiers associated or invested with political passion within a certain sociopolitical configuration, the more this dimension will seek expression through substitute political formations ('social symptoms').

An excellent example of this dynamics is provided by Mouffe's analysis of the rise of right-wing populism, one of the explosive political phenomena that challenged political analysis – and discourse theory – to broaden the scope of its analytical tools. According to Mouffe, the increasing appeal of right-wing populist parties in countries like Austria cannot be comprehended without exploring the link with the current de-politicisation of politics advocated by Centrist political projects (for instance Third Way politics). Putting the stress on a neutral 'politics without adversaries', on the de-politicised administration of what they accept as unavoidable – almost natural – forces and trends, such as globalisation, Third Way theorists and politicians have downplayed the 'primary reality of strife in social life' (Mouffe 1998: 13). This has significant effects on political identification: 'Major contemporary political passions cannot find an outlet . . . as there is no debate in which different forms of identification could be provided around which people could mobilise. We are therefore witnessing the growth of other forms of collective identification' (Mouffe 1999). In that sense, at the root of the rise of neo-populist parties one finds a refusal to recognise the political in its antagonistic dimension and 'the concomitant incapacity to grasp the central role of passions in the constitution of collective identities' (Mouffe 2002: 2).

Very often, right-wing populist parties are the only ones that try to mobilise passions and to construct collective forms of identification:

> Against all those who believe that politics can be reduced to individual motivations and that it is driven by the pursuit of self-interest, they are well aware that politics always consists in the creation of an Us versus a Them and that it implies the creation of collective identities. Hence the powerful appeal of their discourse because it provides collective forms of identification around 'the people'. (Mouffe 2002: 8)

This approach has been fruitfully applied in the case of Flanders (De Vos 2002). It is, however, the case of Le Pen in France which provides the best example so far, both in terms of the content and in terms of the style of his political discourse. Le Pen's discourse is marked throughout by 'passion, conflict, wit, playfulness, exaggeration, a willingness to name the enemy (or multiple enemies, in his case), and a mixture of literary references with pure vulgarity, physicality and action. By comparison, politicians of the Centre Left and Centre Right look cautious and wooden, devoid of genuine feeling, creatures of their respective machines' (Budgen 2002: 45). The inability of the political class and of political analysts to predict or comprehend Le Pen's success in the 2002 French presidential elections can safely be attributed to their neglect of the affective dimension, to the repression of the signifiers of political passion, and to the inability to realise that such a repression can only lead to a displacement of affective energy and to the 'return of the repressed' in a new (pathological) form, infused with obscene enjoyment and aggressivity. My hypothesis here is that a similar dialectics between repression and the return of the repressed is visible in the construction and dissemination of anti-European discourse.

Constructing European identity

FROM POLITICAL PRACTICE . . .

The basic argument I would like to put forward in this chapter is that political and academic debates on 'European identity' and Europeanisation often reproduce the problematic strategies of repression highlighted above. First, they purport to create a salient identification of European peoples with Europe, but they neglect the crucial role of affect and passion in this process. Second, by repressing this often obscene dimension of identification, by exclusively focusing on institutional arrangements and banal or passionless ideals, they force the expression of passionate attachment through a variety of anti-European discourses. In that sense, not only are they ineffective but they actually harm the prospects of constructing a strong European identification. In what follows I will treat political documents, scholarly texts, and – towards the end of the chapter – newspaper articles, three very different types of discursive instantiations, simply as surfaces for the inscription of discourse. Treating academic discourse as a privileged – more or less reliable – source would obscure the often unconscious 'complicity' between mainstream (European) politics and academia, two discursive domains which, in a typically modernist fashion, are inter-implicated in the formulation and reproduction of a particular, more or less technocratic, standpoint vis-à-vis European identity. As for the group of newspaper articles that will be discussed in the closing section, they merit our attention because they constitute the surface for the discursive inscription of the affective dimension, which is largely excluded from, or downplayed in, mainstream political and academic discussions. They thus provide a very good example of 'differential cathexis' (Chapter 2) in action.

Let us first explore the way 'European identity' is promoted and conceptualised in European political practice and theoretical analysis. There seems to be little doubt that the preoccupation with 'European identity' emerges as a primarily top-down strategy to foster popular support for the project of European integration and unification. During the early 1970s, when the EEC was faced with bleak economic prospects within a major international crisis (Strath 2000b: 401) and given the 'distinct lack of heartfelt support from ordinary Western Europeans' (Wintle 1996: 10), the issue of identity appeared to European institutions as a new recipe for fostering popular support and social legitimacy, for creating a sense of common belonging and identification with European institutions and the Europeanisation programme at all levels.

The fundamental declaration 'Concerning European Identity', agreed in the 1973 Copenhagen summit, was the first concrete discursive crystallisation of this strategy. It is impossible to analyse in detail this document within the limits of this chapter. We can focus, however, on one essential aspect. The way 'European identity' is envisaged and discussed in the document clearly draws on a dry, institutional, symbolic conception of identity. What are the 'fundamental' or 'essential' elements of European identity according to the document? They range from the rule of law, social justice and respect for human rights up to the common market, the customs union and all the other 'common policies and machinery for cooperation' (European Commission 1974: 492). Apart from these concrete but rather unimaginative references, the document is full of big words and boring jargon about a 'common European civilization', assurances of progress and international equilibrium, and the promotion of the 'deepest aspirations of [the European] peoples' (pp. 492–3). Even when it is accepted that identity presupposes asserting the difference of Europe in relation to other countries and parts of the world (see especially European Commission 1974: 496), this is expressed in a more or less naïve, neutral, 'objective' language: 'European unification is not directed against anyone, nor is it inspired by a desire for power. On the contrary, the Nine are convinced that their union will benefit the whole international community since it will constitute an element of equilibrium and a basis for cooperation with all countries, whatever their size, culture or social system' (p. 494).

Since Copenhagen, identity has appeared in a variety of official documents and declarations – including the 'Solemn Declaration of the European Union' (1983), the 'Single European Act' (1987), and up to the Maastricht treaty, where European identity is given an important role in the external relations of the Union but is conceived of as limited by the national identities of the member-states. During this period a variety of more practical reports were also produced: in 1975 the Tindemans report pointed to the importance of creating a European identity; in 1985 the Adonnino reports put forward the idea of introducing common symbols in order to enhance the identity of the EEC – hence the adoption of a standardised passport, an official European flag, and the like; in 1993 the De Clerq report discussed the importance of an effective communication of Europe to its citizens (Pantel 1999: 53; Strath 2000a; Strath 2000b). Of course, today, the Euro can be singled out as the most important development in this trend of unification. Simultaneously, sustained attempts have been made to promote European identity through education, with the introduction of a variety of student exchange and other educational programmes (such as Erasmus, Leonardo, Socrates, Tempus).

All these policies and actions have had considerable effects. By most accounts, however, *they failed to deepen popular identification with the European Union and European identity.* How can one explain this apparent failure? Many commentators have observed that all these processes and declarations, no matter whether premised on pragmatic concerns or a genuine Euro-enthusiasm, have been, to a large extent, 'contrived and shallow' (Wintle 1996: 10), focused on conscious knowledge and education, addressed to the subject of the signifier, limited to big words and a passionless institutional jargon: 'The impression therefore prevails that the policy of promoting European identity is no more than an effort to spread a more favourable image of Europe, without any substance backing it' (De Witte 1987). From a psychoanalytic point of view, this lacking substance can clearly be associated with the libidinal/affective dimension of identification. When this is missing, identifications cannot acquire any salience or deep hegemonic appeal. In that sense, one could argue that the problem lies in the fact that the stress has been clearly and exclusively on fostering 'identification with the EU as a political [and economic] entity' (Billig 1995: 125). Fortunately or unfortunately, however, as Delors has put it, 'you don't fall in love with a common market; you need something else' (Delors in Bideleux 2001: 25). Thus, it also 'seems unlikely that a European identity, with the EU as its political foundation, will generate the sorts of passions and loyalty that people feel towards their nations' (Billig 1995: 121). Indeed, the prospects will be bleak for Europe if it remains 'a patchwork, memoryless scientific "culture" held together solely by political will and economic interest' (Smith 1999: 245).

. . . TO ACADEMIC ANALYSIS

Let us now move to an exploration of the way academic analysis has dealt with these problems of European identity. Faced with the normative/formal/institutional and mostly top-down attempts of European institutions to foster a strong popular identification with Europe and with their poor results, most academics have been led to recognise the existence of the two crucial dimensions of identity formation: the procedural and the substantive, the *dryer* and the *stickier*. There is an increasing acceptance of the fact that 'Europeans do not recognize the EU as an appropriate sphere for politics, as they do the nation state', that the EU is deficient in terms of 'levels of affective attachment and identification', although this does not necessarily mean that the Europeans don't recognise it as a framework for politics alongside the national arena (Banchoff and Smith 1999: 1–2). Now, there are, broadly speaking, three ways to deal with the recognition of this split:

1. One can adopt a moralistic framework and attempt to abolish the darker side in favour of the brighter. A lot of research on European identity is predicated upon a strict distinction between a positive (benign) and a negative, exclusionary (malignant) form of identification, implying that it is possible to cultivate the former and abolish the latter. In other words, the situation is similar to the one examined in the previous chapter, which led to the ultimately unfounded distinctions between good and bad versions of nationalism. Delanty, for example, criticises 'the largely unreflective idea of Europe based on self-identity through negation and exclusion' – proposing its replacement 'with one based on autonomy and participation' (Delanty 1995: 15). He grounds this claim on the sharp distinction between positive and negative difference already mentioned in Chapter 5. In the first case identity is founded on a positive recognition of otherness leading to solidarity, while in the second, that of negative difference, it is based on a negation of difference producing exclusion (p. 5). Such a view has also affected what is known as the post-national agenda. As Shaw has put it: 'Postnationalism may be seen as . . . the attempt to recover and rethink some of the core values of nationalism as lending meaning to a particular community with shared practices and institutions, *without the necessary institutional baggage or ideological weight of the modern (nation) state or a negative sense of nationalism as exclusion*' (Shaw 2001: 74, emphasis added).

    As we have seen, this is an impossible strategy which, due to the inherent paradox of identification, is unable to produce any sustainable results. It is impossible to displace processes of social or political cathexis, to fight one form of exclusion, with another type of exclusion, with the theoretical or analytical *repression* of the 'obscene' side of identification.

2. One can, alternatively, adopt a 'multiple identity' or 'dual identity' framework which tries to keep the two dimensions present but strictly separate. This option is more alert to the irreducibility of the two dimensions involved in identification but fails to understand their close interconnection. For example, most of the theorists adopting a 'multiple identity' standpoint seem to subscribe to a quasi-relativist version of constructionism. They conceptualise identity as something in 'permanent flux where boundaries are constantly contested and negotiated': 'European – and national – identities are always fluid and contextual, contested and contingent' (Malmborg and Strath 2002: 5). According to such a view, 'the most essential part of identity is its multiple nature' (Wintle 1996: 22; also see Banchoff and Smith 1999: 7): 'the adjectives "European" and "national" are not alternatives but are articulated in the recognition of multi-identification' (Malmborg and Strath 2002: 6). But this is where the first problems enter the horizon.

'Multiple identity' or 'multi-identification' is typically predicated upon a model of peaceful co-existence between different but equally valid subject positions. Of course one can have multiple identifications at different levels, but that 'does not mean that such ties are entirely optional and situational, nor that some among them do not exercise a greater hold and exert a more powerful influence than others'. It was shown in the previous chapter how 'national identity does in fact exert today [within the modern context] a more potent and durable influence than other collective cultural identities' (Smith 1991: 175). Nationalism 'commands popular support and elicits popular enthusiasm. All other visions, all other rationales, appear wan and shadowy by comparison' (p. 176). Hence a series of legitimate questions appears on the agenda: what organises multiplicity? What determines the movement between different subject positions? Are all the components of a multiple identity of equal importance? The answer psychoanalytic theory provides is that there is always a fantasy scenario which organises and supports the apparent multiplicity of identity and determines the 'rules of engagement' between its different levels, a mapping which prioritises particular modes of enjoyment, particular libidinally invested components and nodal points (*points de capiton*) and not others, which remain structurally and emotionally peripheral.[1]

Two further points are crucial here. First, without the intervention of these nodal points, subjective structure can easily disintegrate into a psychotic state. This has to be taken very seriously into account by some 'chaotic' conceptions of 'multiple identity': 'the total disintegration of personal identity into identity atoms [components of a multiple identity] might not be psychologically manageable' and thus 'multiple identity' might not be the most promising solution for the Europeanisation of national identities (Wilson and van der Dussen 1995: 207). This also explains why, when a conflict of loyalties arises, certain components or levels are always assigned higher priority than others, which is precisely the process that has sustained most national identifications so far. As one reads in a textbook on Europe, 'people always were many things, but in the epoch of nationalism, one identity was the trump card . . . the national identity was the primary one in cases of conflict between loyalty to the different identities' (ibid.). Second, 'multiple identity' arguments often presuppose a fluid conception of identity, which is ultimately premised on a certain voluntarism. They seem, in other words, to imply that the particular profile of an identity is a matter of conscious, instrumental or even rational choice on the part of the subject, a matter of shopping around for interesting components for inclusion. Yet it is clear that discursive structuration and affective investment set precise – although historically contingent – limits to such movements.

3. As far as the 'dual identity' framework is concerned the model of the European citizen would comprise, in this respect, two distinct loyalties: one to a political entity (at European level) and the other to an ethnic nationality (Goldmann 2000: 42). In other words, every European citizen would be split between a political state identity (along the lines of the so-called 'French' model) and a cultural identity (along the lines of the so-called 'German' model) (Wilson and van der Dussen 1995: 208). I am using the term 'split' because, according to such a model, 'identity and politics are *delinked* and *refocused*' and what is introduced is 'a dualism, with Europe as the civic nation–state and our old nation–states as organic people–nations' (ibid., emphasis added). This split also constitutes one of the premises of certain versions of the 'post-national' agenda. Here again the link implied by nationalism between cultural integration (the ethnic, substantive aspect of

nationalism) and political integration (the formal, procedural aspect) is deconstructed (Curtin in Shaw 2001: 74).

Given my argument so far, it is very difficult to imagine how it would be possible to de-link politics from identity, discourse from enjoyment. Furthermore, even if it were possible to separate them, what would be the 'rules of engagement' between them? A conflictual scenario, that of a spill-over of aggressivity from the national to the European sphere, seems probable – even more probable than a peaceful one: 'the greater the distance between the models of different countries and the more emotionally involved the populations are with their respective models, the more unlikely it is that a common policy on a supranational level can be established, accepted and implemented' (Zetterholm 1994: 7). Furthermore, if such a contamination were unavoidable, then another question becomes crucial: Which one of the two dimensions would dominate the other? Given the deficiencies of a dry conception of 'European identity' or 'Europe', once more prospects look a bit gloomy. Engaged in such an unequal battle, it is difficult to see European identity ever acquiring a salient role in the lives of European citizens.

At this point, it is important to make it clear that this analysis is not premised on some sort of a priori privileging of national or state identity. Of course we can and should envisage a strong European Union beyond traditional statist and nationalist models, but such a development cannot materialise and will never succeed without dealing with the affective dimension of identification in a non-repressive way. This is the uncomfortable truth the Lacanian Left highlights. If theory and political analysis continue to repress or disavow this dimension, 'Europe' will, of course, develop in various directions but will never become a really salient identification winning the hearts and not only the pockets of European citizens. To put it in Georges Bataille's poetic language, 'the reduction to order fails in any case: formal devotion (devotion without excess) leads to inconsequence' (Bataille 1991: 161). Current research using a multiplicity of other methodologies seems to support these conclusions: feelings of national identity directly influence support for the European Union. In particular, 'there is a clear indication that a strong national identity leads to a decrease in support for the EU' and that the effects of national identification 'are at least as significant as utilitarian explanations, such as income, education, and subjective economic evaluations' (Carey 2002: 397, 407). However, this is not because national identity is a priori invested with such a privileged position. This differential cathexis is a contingent, historically determined reality associated with the shifts in collective identifications within modernity. It provides an opportunity to study the intricacies of the relation between affect, enjoyment and identity, but it does not preclude the possibility of articulating alternative administrations of enjoyment in the future.

Europe's obscene Other

What is even more crucial, repressing the dimension of enjoyment does not affect the future prospects of European unification alone. It also produces a series of indirect results of major political importance. As I have already argued, the repression of signifiers cathected with libidinal and affective value never leads to the disappearance but merely to the displacement of psychic energy and to the 'return of the repressed' through the emergence of symptomatic formations. We have seen the relevance of this logic in explaining political phenomena such as the rise of right-wing populism in Europe. If these hypotheses are correct, then a similar loop must be in operation in relation to discussions concerning European identity and integration. Indeed, it seems that the neglect of the affective side of identification leads to a displacement of cathectic energy which is now invested in anti-European political and ideological discourses, discourses that invite and value such a cathexis. In fact, a whole heated debate is mounted at a separate level, in which dry European identity, its institutional arrangements and big words, are seen as agents of castration, not only indifferent but hostile to the structures of enjoyment that operate in the various national contexts and engaged in a process of standardisation which has to be resisted. The discourses of resistance differ from the standard Euro-jargon not only in terms of their content but also in terms of their style: they are aggressive, visceral, and funny, ranging from the obscene to the violent, often via the grotesque. This may be, however, the secret of their success.

In fact, these discourses are so incommensurable with standard political and academic debates on Europe that both the political class and the research community have preferred to avoid taking them into account. This, however, will not make them disappear; quite the contrary. Hence it is more prudent to explore their constitution and functioning. A lot of very good examples are available: Le Pen again, religious populist discourse in Greece, and others. But the most graphic example is offered by some versions of British Euro-scepticism. I am particularly interested in the type of Euro-scepticism which attracts millions of people, that of the British popular press; this constitutes the last discursive reservoir to be analysed in this chapter.

In general, research on the treatment of European integration by the British media suggests that they are particularly negative and resistant to the idea of European integration and European identity (Cinnirella 1996: 263). What is most important, however, is that this hostility towards Europe typically takes a particular form. According to the main argument developed in this text, one would expect it to be articulated in a way antithetical to the dry, normative and detached form the debate takes in official political circles. Is this the case? Undeniably so. Resistance speaks a different language, it is played out at a completely different level, one founded on affect, passion, ridicule, obscenity. It is difficult to ignore the fact that, on 1 November 1991, when respectable politicians were discussing the pros and cons of federalism and national independence, one of Britain's most widely read national newspaper, *The Sun*, simply read 'Up yours Delors!' (ibid.). This type of discourse, characteristic of the right-wing popular press, has indeed become so successful that it now constitutes one of the major pillars on which Euro-sceptic influence is built (Forster 2002: 111).

What are the basic parameters of this resistance to Europe articulated in British popular press? Its most salient feature seems to be the depiction of the European Union as an alien regulating agency which somehow intervenes in the particular way we have organised our lives, in the particular way we have structured our enjoyment. In other words, the EU is primarily represented as an agent of castration. Some examples are in order here. 'Brussels bureaucrats' have been accused of wanting to scrap the traditional British loaf (*Daily Mail*, 27 October 1997: 29), of forcing Britain to change its three-pin plugs to the continental version, costing domestic electricity users a fortune in rewiring and allegedly jeopardising UK safety standards (*Daily Star*, 27 May 1994: 2), and of pushing Britain to replace the traditional British lavatory with the 'Euro-loo' (*The Sun*, 4 May 1999: 11). Other titles and news-flashes read: 'Eurocrats sparked outrage among the Welsh on St David's Day yesterday by ordering that all leeks sold in the future must look the same' (*Daily Express*, 2 March 2002: 36), 'EU Meddlers ready to outlaw smacking' (*The Sun*, 16 June 1998: 15), 'Brussels plan to scrap our passports' (*Mail on Sunday*, 29 October 2000: 1).

What is even more extraordinary from a psychoanalytic point of view is the abundance of sexual connotations and obscene metaphors which mark this discourse throughout. This is obvious, for example, when the EU is accused of deciding that 'bananas must not be excessively curved' (*The Sun*, 4 March 1998: 6) and that 'Cucumbers have to be straight' (ibid.), or when stories like these appear: 'Crackpot Euro chiefs have decreed British rhubarb must be straight' (*The Sun*, 24 June 1996: 11). Not to mention, of course, the alleged harmonisation of condom dimensions and the 'Euro threat to kill the British Banger'. One could go on recounting such stories ad infinitum. What is important is that these grotesque stories seem to provide the obscene support to a resistance towards a Europe that has failed to inspire passion and function effectively as an object of identification, a Europe that has neglected to engage with the visceral, obscene dimension of identification and is increasingly seen as devoid of affective substance and appeal.

Two further points are crucial here. First, one should be very careful before dismissing these stories as marginal or unimportant. Not only are they depicting the basic editorial line of some of Britain's major newspapers, they also surface occasionally in more serious newspapers and increasingly influence mainstream public discourse. In the first book-length account of British Euro-scepticism, Forster argues that, due to the predominance of pro-integrationists in the academic community, most discussions have 'routinely overlooked Eurosceptics and Euroscepticism and by design or default have often failed to treat it as a serious phenomenon or object of study' (Forster 2002: 3). If this is the case with respectable forms of Euro-scepticism, you can imagine what has been going on along the obscene axis of the debate. Fortunately this complacent indifference is slowly coming to an end. It is indicative that pro-European institutions – including the representation of the European Commission in the UK and the *Britain in Europe* campaign, an initiative supported by Tony Blair, Gordon Brown, Ken Clarke, Michael Heseltine and Charles Kennedy – are increasingly becoming aware of the need to deal somehow with this avalanche. Hence, a whole section of the European Commission British website had been devoted to the various Euro-myths I have presented (European Commission 2006), while the *Britain in Europe* campaign has produced a booklet characteristically entitled 'Straight Bananas? 201 Anti-European Myths Exposed'.[2] In both instances, however, the focus is on revealing how untrue these stories are. What is thus missed is that people do not enjoy these stories because of their truth-value but because they identify with the fantasy implicit in them, because 'European identity' does not offer them any other *real* choice.³ Why is the British press operating at this visceral level of argument? Why is the British public – as well as other European public spheres – still susceptible to such an obscene rhetoric? Mainstream social and political analysis should perhaps start entertaining the possibility that all these are the vicissitudes of a construction of European identity based on the exclusion of certain dimensions which are crucial in the reproduction of social and political identification: affect, enjoyment, passion. Following the No votes in France and in the Netherlands and the shelving of plans for a Euro-referendum in the UK, *Britain in Europe* ceased its campaigning. What better indication of the limits of a rationalist technocratic strategy to create strong bonds with Europe? This lesson needs to be urgently considered before it is too late.

What is to be done?

So, simply put, what is to be done? Readers unfamiliar with types of argumentation such as psychoanalysis employs could be easily led to the conclusion that it naturally follows from this analysis that people should surrender to aggressivity and obscene enjoyment, that European studies should re-focus their research attention on the shape of fruits and the castration fantasies of the European peoples, and that Europe will only become really appealing as an object of identification if it starts a sexual – if not an S&M – revolution! In actual fact, the conclusion I envisage is much more modest: European policy and European studies obviously don't have to reproduce the obscene reactions and identifications described in this chapter. It is, however, in their interest to take into account their causes and implications. *Only by taking seriously the dual nature of identification (discursive and affective, symbolic and libidinal) will they gradually become able to reflect on their own contribution – through their strategies of repression – to phenomena such as Euro-scepticism and the lack of pervasive popular identifications with 'Europe'.*

Both in terms of theoretical consistency and in terms of political productivity, it is important to accept that contamination from one dimension to the other is ultimately inevitable and that any viable European project must involve both, in a hybrid construction transcending them, a hybrid combining formal procedures with an administration of enjoyment capable of winning not only the political or academic argument but also 'the hearts' and 'the guts' of the peoples of Europe. At issue, then, is neither the elimination nor the glorification of antagonism, exclusion or *jouissance*, but a modified relation to these constitutive elements. Exclusion and antagonism may be unavoidable, but acknowledging this does not restrict our ability to influence their particular actualisations, to displace continuously the limits they impose. What is at stake is to find a way to *relate ethically to antagonism and jouissance*, as opposed to the unethical, unproductive and even dangerous standpoint of eliminating or mythologising them: to sublimate instead of repressing, to inject passion into the radicalisation of democracy and the reinvigoration of political discourse instead of channelling it into racist and nationalist aggression or reducing politics to the unattractive spectacle of the neutral administration of unavoidable necessities. This is the horizon the Lacanian Left opens for us.

Notes

1. This is especially the case when 'multiplicity' involves the articulation of apparently contradictory elements.
2. In fact, most of the examples cited above originate from these two invaluable sources.
3. Similarly, in a recent attempt to recast a pro-European agenda following the referenda in France and the Netherlands, Giddens and Beck describe the crisis of the European imaginary in affective terms: 'these feelings tend to stimulate an emotional return to the apparent safe heaven of the nation' (Beck and Giddens 2005: 6). However, this brief acknowledgment of emotional dynamics is followed by a list of 'rational' arguments in favour of Europe in which the affective side is ignored. Affect is presented in their argument as something associated with a regressive attitude of irrational sticking to the nation, which, although acknowledged at one level, cannot be really integrated in our way of thinking and negotiated on its own right.

7

The Consumerist 'Politics of *Jouissance*' and the Fantasy of Advertising

Desire is the very essence of man

Spinoza

Every political economy is libidinal

Jean-François Lyotard

Victorious consumerism?

The preceding explorations of nationalism and European identity reveal how much the fate and prospects of particular identifications and hegemonic projects rely on the affective dimension, on *jouissance* in its different modalities and interactions with the world of signification and social practice. Obviously the emergence of the 'new' cannot succeed if it ignores this important parameter, but this is not to say that sedimented, libidinally invested identifications are in any way privileged to retain their hegemonic position indefinitely. Processes of dis-identification and affective re-investment are, on the contrary, part and parcel of social and political life. In capitalist – especially late capitalist – societies it is the role of consumption and consumerism and the function of advertising, public relations and branding that offer perhaps the best example of how new interpellations and commands can re-shape social structure by imposing their hegemonic grip on individual and group identifications and behaviour. To be sure, nobody will be surprised if I argue that today consumerism constitutes one of the central aspects of social life or that advertising is one of the hegemonic discursive tropes in late modernity, staging the fantasy frame that ensures that our identity as consumers sticks. As Garry Cross has put it, consumerism, despite all the opposition, seems to be 'the "ism" that won' (Cross 2000:1). It did succeed where other ideologies and discourses failed. The question is, how? How was the act of consumption instituted as the undisputable nodal point of a whole culture, a whole way of life?[1] In this chapter

I will argue that the emerging hegemony of consumerism cannot be explained without taking seriously the axes of desire and enjoyment. Psychoanalytic theory can paradigmatically accomplish this task, revealing how the symbolically conditioned desire for consumption acts is stimulated by advertising fantasies and supported by the (partial) enjoyment entailed in desiring and consuming products as well as advertisements. Channeling desire in particular directions, consumer culture marks a significant shift in the way the social bond is structured in relation to enjoyment and reveals its central role in sustaining the current, late capitalist economic-political nexus.

First, however, it is important to clarify one preliminary but, in reality, quite central issue. Already from reading the title of this chapter, one would be entitled to ask: how does an analysis of consumption and advertising fit into a book of political theory and political analysis, even one of Lacanian inspiration? Yet it is one of the aims of this book – and of this chapter in particular – to explore the deep inter-implication between culture, economy and politics, which – like the three rings of the Borromean knot mentioned in the introduction – are tied together in this late capitalist *sinthome*: in a particular (capitalist) administration of *jouissance*, a unique crystallisation of desire marking consumerism and advertising.[2] Lacanian theory – and the Lacanian Left – can indeed offer substantial insights into the 'how' of this articulation, but its existence has not escaped the attention of contemporary consumption research. In a recent collection characteristically entitled *The Politics of Consumption*, the editors confidently argue that 'consumption has never existed outside of politics' (Daunton and Hilton 2001: 9). No doubt, during the last decade or so historians of consumption have amply demonstrated this point.

Throughout the twentieth century, consumption has been directly implicated in politics, both Left and Right. Here the paradigmatic case is the United States. Take, for example, the formulation of Roosevelt's *New Deal*: one of its principles was to take into account the rights of the consumer in government policy. During his 1932 presidential campaign Roosevelt had even predicted that 'in the future we are going to think less about the producer and more about the consumer' (Roosevelt in Cohen 2004: 24). As Lizabeth Cohen has correctly pointed out, although very often the identities of citizens and consumers are seen as opposites, with citizens defined within a political framework (with reference to broader social and national interests, duties and ideals) and consumers reduced to a private sphere of personal indulgence oriented towards the satisfaction of personal desires, this has not been the case for most of the twentieth century: 'Rather than isolated ideal types, citizen and consumer were ever-shifting categories that sometimes over-lapped, often were in tension, but always reflected the permeability of the political and economic spheres' (Cohen 2004: 8).

In the US especially, the symbiosis of consumption and politics has reached such a degree that Cohen speaks of 'a consumer's republic'. After the Second World War everybody, from big business to labour organisations, from the conservative to the progressive end of the spectrum, was 'mobilizing for abundance', for consumer spending as a vehicle for prosperity, as the title of a 1944 book by the New Deal economist Robert Nathan highlights (Cohen 2004: 115). Indeed, the end of the Great War was followed by a 'saturnalia of spending' (Cross 2000: 88). During this period, mass consumption was presented as essential in safeguarding mass production, their combination promising 'abundance for all' (Cohen 2004: 116). The prevalent idea was that mass consumption would create a more egalitarian society (p. 125): 'This yoking of free choice as consumers with political freedom was made frequently during the Cold War' (p. 126). Benefiting from such associations, consumerism thus became the underlying cultural factor to colonise politics and other social realms. As soon as this intimate link between consumerism and politics is acknowledged, one can even start recognising that the collapse of existing socialist regimes, much more than a victory of liberalism, marked, above all else, a victory of consumerism (Cross 2000: 8); it was the price state socialism paid for privileging production over consumption (Žižek 2006: 53).

Needless to say, this interconnection between capitalism and politics is not something new. Surprisingly enough, the first arguments in favour of capitalism were not of an economic but of a profoundly political nature, with interest-motivated human action being heralded as a force capable of subduing irrational passions and guaranteeing the stability of the social order (Hirschman 1977). Since then, self-interested behaviour has often been proclaimed a social duty by ideologies which elevated it into a true 'contribution to the common good' (Hirschman 2002: 67). Such ideologies cannot of course hide the fact that what is usually at stake here is the colonisation and de-contestation of signifiers like 'equality', 'prosperity', and 'the good' in ways that further capitalist hegemony.

Gradually, however, with the transition from mass to segmented markets, the justification of consumerism did not require such articulations any more; it moved farther away from social cohesion and into the realm of personal fantasy (Cross 2000: 193). In fact, after Reagan's era, the Consumer's Republic entered a stage of 'Commercialization of the Republic' (Cohen 2004: 396):

> Whereas from the 1930s to as late as the 1970s, to refer to the consumer interest was also to appeal to some larger public good beyond the individual's self-interest, the ubiquitous invocation of the consumer today – as patient, as parent, as social security recipient [may I add, as student] – often means satisfying the private interest of the paying customer, the combined consumer/citizen/voter whose greater concern is, 'Am I getting my money's worth?' (Cohen 2004: 397)

The point, then, is not only that consumer behaviour and citizen activities are not alien to each other (Hirschman 2002: 11). It is also – and more alarmingly – that the latter is increasingly being reduced to the former; that consumer culture imposes its rules on politics and other social realms and shapes the dominant forms the social bond is assuming. The reign of political advertising and 'spin doctors' in contemporary politics is only the last act in this long incestuous story.

On the other hand, however, radical politics and the protest culture have also influenced consumerism, sometimes imposing limits on its development. The consumer movement and the relevant organisations comprise a very diverse picture, ranging from consumer activism stimulated by a concern for animal welfare and anti-corporate protesters to organisations pressing for better quality controls and cheaper prices (Daunton and Hilton 2001: 2). Between the multifarious forces operating on this terrain and the industrial producers – as well as the state – interaction has been continuous. Already at the beginning of the twentieth century, the birth of corporate public relations was necessitated by the 'widespread public indignation at the prevailing practices of big business in the United States' (Ewen 1996: 400). This dialectics between forces of opposition and corporate forces has never stopped. Often, though, consumerism has been able to co-opt the influence of protesting groups and movements and to colonise the alternative 'ideals' they promoted. This was a risk already stressed by Marcuse (Marcuse 1966: xxiii). For example, mirroring the values underlying the social movements of the 1960s and 1970s, public relations were led to overcome ideals of conformity and homogeneity and learned to 'respect difference, dissension, conflict, and above all, individuality' (Finn in Ewen 1996: 403). All that in order, of course, to channel them in a particular direction: 'If the culture of the 1960s generation contributed to a new, fragmenting, individualistic consumption, the unfettered market ideology of the Reagan generation only furthered that trend' (Cross 2000: 193). Similarly, the identity politics of the 1980s and 1990s has been appropriated by a new form of 'identity marketing', changing to a certain extent but ultimately feeding – and not subverting – the system of corporate branding (Klein 2000: 1113). New movements opposing consumer culture are emerging every day, some of them in close association with so-called anti-globalisation activism, but, all in all, there is no question that consumerism has up to now remained victorious, that our culture has increasingly and predominantly become a 'promotional culture' (Wernick 1991). Exaggerating a bit, Cross – who appears fascinated by the story he is narrating – has nevertheless captured an important shift:

> At the end of the century, religious cults, nationalist violence, and political scandals still got the headlines. But such news was really on the fringes of modern American life, interesting as a sideshow. Identification with class, nation, and even high-minded social reform has declined sharply in the second half of the twentieth century . . . In sum, they seemed to be no moral equivalent to the world of consumption. (Cross 2000: 6)[3]

Psychoanalysing consumerism

At least from a historical point of view, then, it is very difficult to dispute the important political implications of the world of consumption. What needs to be illuminated is the exact mechanisms underlying this articulation between politics and consumerism and the increasing hegemonisation of our societies by the discourses of advertising, public relations and consumption. As will be argued, psychoanalytic theory is eminently qualified to capture, map and interpret these mechanisms in ways that more traditional analyses and the standard leftist critiques have been unable to envisage and/or fully develop.

What, however, legitimises this recourse to psychoanalytic theory? First of all, psychoanalysis was present at the 'birth' of public relations and continues to be an indirect resource for the advertising industry. Ironically, the so-called 'founder' of public relations, Edward Bernays – branded by his biographer 'The Father of Spin' – was no less than Freud's nephew. In his biography of Bernays, Larry Tye has included a chapter with the telling title 'Uncle Sigi', which recounts the quite close but at times bumpy relationship between Freud and Bernays; in fact, the latter had an active role in translating and publishing some of his uncle's first texts into English (Tye 1998).[4]

From the 1950s onwards, having gradually realised that it is not rational argumentation but emotional ties that bind, the advertising industry has adopted techniques of motivational research – a branch of research developed by Ernest Dichter, who was also influenced by Freud. These techniques target the unconscious motives of consumer behaviour and have often drawn on psychoanalysis. Hence the analogies between psychoanalytic free association, depth interviews and focus groups (Andersen 1995: 79).

If, on the one hand, a certain appropriation of psychoanalytic ideas took place in the development of some of the most important pillars of contemporary capitalism and consumer culture, on the other hand, advertising has also come to preoccupy psychoanalytic reflection. Lacan himself referred to advertising – to the slogan 'Enjoy Coca-Cola' – while speaking about *le sujet de la jouissance* in his Baltimore lecture in 1966. In this way he associated advertising and consumerism with the whole psychoanalytic problematic of enjoyment, a problematic deeply revealing of the foundations of capitalism (XVII: 123). Is not enjoyment, be it as a signifier, as an image or as a subtext, always at the kernel of the promise entailed in advertisements, a promise which stimulates consumer desire and reproduces consumer culture? Isn't real enjoyment what we expect from consumption acts? These days only the particular nature of this enjoyment is at stake, as for instance when some car manufacturer promises a surplus – a certain *plus-de-jouir* – of 'advanced enjoyment' against the supposedly average enjoyment offered by other cars. Similarly, a cigarette manufacturer had articulated its ad for a new cigarette brand around the promise of 'clean enjoyment' against the supposedly impure enjoyment offered by competitors. And isn't that enjoyment exhibiting all the paradoxical characteristics of Lacan's *jouissance*?

All these hypotheses inform the orientation of the present chapter. Such an orientation, however, is far from self-evident. For a long period, both the industry and the research on consumption – especially economic analyses – have largely been dominated by a rational choice model of consumer behaviour. Emanating from mainstream economics and premised on the ideal type of the 'rational economic individual', the utility maximisation paradigm severely restricted the scope of analysis to exploring merely 'the logical implications of man's rationality' (Scitovsky 1992: 15). As a result, 'the understanding of consumption by mainstream economics is shallow to the point of being paper thin' (Fine 2002: 125). What is astonishing is that many radical critics of advertising and consumption have adopted an equally essentialist position, blind to the limits of rationality and to the ambiguous structure of human desire. These critics have often seen advertising as a brainwashing activity which, by stimulating false desires, deepens our enslavement to consumerism and capitalist exploitation. Two are the main axes of such a critical approach. First, the claim that consumerism is founded on the distortion of real/natural human needs and on the creation and proliferation of 'false desires'. Second, the claim that these false desires are stimulated and disseminated through advertising discourse, which sustains the false consciousness required for their acceptance.

Ironically, the hypothesis of the 'rational consumer' has been falsified by the advertising industry itself. In fact, as early as 1923, Ivy Lee – one of America's prominent corporate public relations experts – had realised that, in order to be efficient, the sphere of public relations had to limit its reliance on factual argument and rational persuasion and target emotion and sentiment (Ewen 1996: 131–2). This realisation of the importance of often unconscious identification processes that escape the limits of rationality has led to the establishment of a class of 'public relations experts, advertising strategists, image managers, and architects of calculated spectacles' paid to 'manufacture the terms of public discourse' (p. 173), *crystallise public opinion* and *engineer consent* – to draw on the titles of two books by Edward Bernays. No doubt these ideas have not managed to displace completely the rationalist paradigm, and thus, while advertising practice has to take into account the non-rational character of desire and human motivation, advertising theory occasionally 'continues to pay lip-service to the traditional liberal philosophy of informed, rational consumers' (Qualter 1991: 89). However, as already mentioned, in its effort to reach an adequate self-understanding of its own operation and to develop more effective *strategies of desire* – and here I am drawing on the title of a book by Ernest Dichter – the advertising industry transformed itself into an advanced psychological laboratory (Packard 1991: 29) and did engage with certain aspects of psychoanalytic theory and method. If psychoanalytic insights are considered by the industry itself as able to provide a more adequate understanding of the mechanisms at work in consumption – even though what underlies this interest for psychoanalysis is a fantasy of an ultimately rational, instrumental control of the irrational forces operating on the masses by the *subjects supposed to know*: advertising executives – then surely no critique of advertising would be wise to ignore these insights and psychoanalytic theory more generally.

In this sense, psychoanalysis may be able to illuminate and overcome the limitations of more traditional approaches. Outside the advertising industry, these limitations are also being revealed through the inability of radical critiques of advertising to displace consumerist identifications and to lessen the ideological grip of advertising fantasies, to reintroduce the importance of the *political act* alongside the ubiquitous *act of consumption*. It is more than revealing that even people who are questioning the status of both market economy and advertising seem unable to organise their desire in an alternative way; thus advertising discourse enjoys a passive legitimisation that adds to its hegemonic hold. Despite the revival of the culture of constraint in the 1960s and 1970s – partly in the work of figures associated with the Freudian Left – no effective defence 'from the power and appeal of an ever-advancing consumerism' has been established (Cross 2000: 140). Furthermore, as a result of the difficulties in effectively dealing with the status of desire in a consumer culture, no real appealing alternatives have been created (p. 130). And the situation today is not markedly different.

The typical jeremiad form of critique has proved unable to reflect seriously on these failures. And the problem persists. A good case in point is Lodziak's recent book, where consumerism is castigated as a substitute for autonomy, able to satisfy 'only the most fickle'. Lodziak concludes: 'It is for the majority an inadequate compensation for the denial of a more meaningful life, but a compensation that has been tolerated in the absence of alternatives' (Lodziak 2002: 158). The obvious question here is: If consumerism is so inadequate, how does it manage to resist the unmasking operations of its critics, how does it retain its hegemonic grip? As I shall be arguing in this chapter, 'the jeremiad', the dominant type of radical critique, could never imagine the dynamics of *jouissance* underlying consumer culture, and was thus trapped within a 'false consciousness' paradigm which reduced what was a question of desire and enjoyment to a question of knowledge and rationality, being unable to offer any realistic alternatives. The result has been the defeat of the ultimately impotent culture of constraint. There is nothing to gain by denying that advertising is capable of *enchanting* us in a variety of ways. This is how it has managed to become a major force in structuring everyday life, our identifications, aspirations and imaginations; it is for the same reason that de-mystifying the normalising tendencies of advertising and consumerism presupposes that we learn to appreciate the affective mobilisation entailed by the presence or the promise of commodity consumption (Bennett 2001: 113–14).[5]

All this is not to say that there have been no economists aware of the constitutive antinomies of satisfaction which destabilise the ideal type of rational choice theories – consider, in this respect Scitovski's Lacanesque observation that 'the most pleasant is on the borderline with the unpleasant' (Scitovsky 1992: 34). Albert Hirschman has also highlighted the limitations of the rational choice model, and attempted to construct an enriched version of it drawing on a variety of sources, including Baudrillard (Hirschman 2002: 36). Obviously, there have been critics of advertising and consumerism, especially from a sociological perspective, who tried to move away from the naturalist/essentialist paradigm in order to take into account the plasticity, the metonymic character of desire. Already from Baudrillard's 1970 book *The Consumer Society* and up to more recent texts the problematic of desire is becoming more and more central.[6] With this trend, however, a new problem appeared, one associated with the increasing dominance of social constructionism and similar in many respects to the one examined in the chapter on nationalism: what was stressed was the symbolic, culturally conditioned aspect of human desire, sometimes at the expense of affect and real enjoyment. In what follows, I will be providing an overview of limitations in both the naturalist/essentialist and the constructionist/culturalist camp, mapping, at the same time, the radical implications of a Lacanian approach. If consumerism has been victorious, it is because it has managed – through the fantasmatic effects of advertising and experiences of partial *jouissance* – to register and re-shape the logic of desire, and no critique will ever be effective without acknowledging this fact and formulating an alternative administration of enjoyment.

Need, desire, fantasy . . . and beyond

During the last decades, we have been witnessing a gradual shift from a naturalist to a culturalist conception of need and desire, to the reign of *Homo Symbolicus*, which pushes the centre of gravity of the relevant discussion closer to certain insights of Lacanianism.[7] Drawing on traditions of thought that stress the predominance of the symbolic function over biological necessity and posit a 'radical discontinuity between culture and nature' (Sahlins 1976: 12–13), many consumption researchers have begun to realise that there is a fundamental material–symbolic correlate to human needing (Jhally 1990: 20). To put it more clearly: 'the recognition of the fundamentally symbolic aspect of people's use of things must be the minimum starting point for a discourse that concerns objects. Specifically, the old distinction between basic (physical) needs and secondary (psychological) needs must be superseded' (Jhally 1990: 4). Nevertheless, many radical critics of consumerism still remain stuck to the idea of universal basic needs, which may be culturally loaded but yet remain anchored in a certain type of (biological) necessity: 'there are universal needs relevant to an individual's survival and well-being, whereas wants tend to be associated with the mere preference of particular individuals' (Lodziak 2002: 4). Still common in mainstream economics and among leftist critics, an influential view remains that preferences 'are considered to be given . . . as a result of physiological needs and psychological and cultural propensities' (Hirschman 2002: 9).[8] How can Lacanian theory intervene at this point?

No doubt, the Lacanian understanding of the relation between need, demand and desire explodes the foundations of the obsolete criticism according to which consumerism would neglect genuine needs and create false needs or desires. I have already discussed this issue at some length in Chapter 1, but a brief rehearsal will do no harm. Entrance into the *symbolic*, the world of language, presupposes the sacrifice of all unmediated access to a level of 'natural' needs and of their quasi-automatic satisfaction. Needs have to be articulated in language, in a demand to the Other (initially the mother). As soon as the satisfaction of need enters this relation of dependence on the Other, every demand becomes, above all else, a demand for the Other's love. What we have here is 'a deviation of man's needs due to the fact that he speaks: to the extent that his needs are subjected to demand, they come back to him in an alienated form' (E2006: 579). This is an insight of value both to psychoanalysis and socio-political analysis: 'needs have been diversified and geared down by and through language to such an extent that their import appears to be of a quite different order, whether we are dealing with the subject or politics' (E2006: 687). There is something in need (a certain real) that cannot be symbolically articulated in demand, and 'appears in an offshoot that presents itself in man as desire' (E2006: 579). Alienated from natural need, incapable of any immediate access to 'real', 'natural' objects of satisfaction, human desire is always a desire for something else (E2006: 431), for what is lacking, for the part of the real impossible to articulate in demand. Desire has no fixed object; strictly speaking there is no object of desire, an object that could satisfy desire, but only an object-cause of desire: something that incarnates the lack and entails a promise of dealing with it. From this point of view desire and lack always go together, overdetermining the dialectical aporia of human life. In that sense, the reliance of consumerism on the continuous production and stimulation of new desires by advertising, on the manipulation of the dialectics between lack and desire, is not alien to the symbolic constitution of human reality. It does channel this reality in particular directions but, strictly speaking, neither distorts nor de-naturalises it. Subjected to drives and not to biological instincts, obliged to articulate need in demand, we are always already de-naturalised.

In that sense, there is no point in referring consumerist desire back to a notion of a prior or superior need. Constructing their own symbolic/imaginary reality, humans are able to ignore and/or transform such dichotomies. We know that we cannot survive without food, but the anorexic and the political prisoner on hunger strike follow their fantasies despite the pressure of biological necessity. As we have already seen (Chapter 2), the object of the drive is not the same as the object of biological instinct. Although from a biological point of view the anorexic, who refuses to eat, *does not eat*, from a psychoanalytic point of view, the anorexic *eats nothing*. Simply put, the anorexic 'employs his refusal as if it were a desire' (E2006: 524). 'Nothing' here functions as a perfectly legitimate object. The same applies to the political prisoner, whose hunger strike does not deny her access to an abundance of nourishing ideals, to the joy of fighting for a cause. In a certain sense – and here Lacan's neologism *parlêtre* is deeply revealing – symbolically conditioned desire is our most pressing biological necessity: 'A smoker's demand for cigarettes, for example, is no less inelastic than his demand for food' (Scitovsky 1992: 107). Doesn't that destabilise the simplistic dichotomy between natural needs and false desires? Marx would certainly agree with such a conclusion, as everybody who has gone through *Das Kapital* knows. On the first page of the first chapter he defines a commodity as 'an object outside us, a thing that by its properties satisfies human wants of some sort or another', only to add that 'the nature of such wants, whether, for instance, they spring from the stomach or from fancy, makes no difference' (Marx 1961: 35).[9]

Contrary to the traditional leftist critique, if consumerist hegemony is possible, it is precisely because human desire is not given or natural. And this hegemony remains a puzzle if symbolically conditioned desire is not sufficiently taken into account. But that does not mean that desire is easy to stimulate, cultivate and fix. Consumerism, however, effects a partial fixation of desire. What are the vehicles that perform this fixation? Although advertisements technically don't lie (at least not straightforwardly, which might in fact harm the product that is being advertised) they can stimulate and channel desire only by constructing a whole mythology around the product. Furthermore, they do so by using a multitude of rhetorical, imaginary and other devices. But even if advertisements were lying, this would not reveal much about the way their mythologies are accepted by the consumer. One would end up with a 'false consciousness' argument and a critique of advertising which has been proved both short-sighted and counterproductive: 'Consumer capitalism is not about false consciousness as such because many consumers are fully aware and critical of the sorts of inequalities and injustices that are associated with consumerism' (Miles 1998: 156). Žižek would probably formulate it like that: *they know very well what they are doing and they are doing it*. As Guy Cook has put it in *The Discourse of Advertising*, 'in many discourses, the underlying factual or logical content is either non-existent or of secondary importance; yet this does not deprive them of value'(Cook 1992: 206). In fact, 'the relationships of manufacture and consumption, and their discourses, of which advertising is one, are as real and natural (or, if you prefer, as unreal and unnatural) as those of any other discourse' (p. 208). For this reason, concentrating in the truth/falsity issue constitutes one of the bigger impediments to understanding the way advertising functions, the way it constructs and 'sells' its desirable mythologies and the way this whole organisation of desire guarantees the reproduction of market economy and capitalism. As Jean Baudrillard has put it in an early text with (what seem to me) a lot of Lacanian overtones, the aforementioned *Consumer Society*, 'the truth is that advertising . . . does not deceive us: it is beyond the true and the false . . . Advertising is a prophetic language, in so far as it promotes not learning or understanding, but *hope*' (Baudrillard 1998: 127, emphasis added).[10] *Now, how and where can one locate this element of hope, the promise which supports advertising, with reference to the Lacanian logic of desire? And what provides this hope with credibility?*

If advertising attempts to stimulate, to cause our desire, this can only mean that the whole mythological construction it articulates around the product is a social fantasy and, furthermore, that this product serves or functions as an object that causes desire, in other words as an object-cause of desire, an *objet petit a* in the Lacanian vocabulary. This fantasmatic dimension has been acknowledged by many critics of advertising, from Aldous Huxley to Raymond

Williams. More recently Baudrillard has highlighted the fact that what is actually bought and consumed in our consumer societies is not objects defined by their natural or physical properties, but the fantasies surrounding them, the fantasies articulated in advertising discourse (Baudrillard 1998: 33). In effect, products may even be absent from an advertisement. In the brand-age, with major companies sub-contracting their manufacturing operations, it is also not products, commodities, things, that are primarily produced, but mainly images of brands. This 'divestment of the world of things' now affects not only consumption but also the world of production. The real work of many large corporations lies not in manufacturing but in marketing their brand names (Klein 2000: 4). What we buy, above all else, is promises associated with these brands:[11] 'We buy advertising messages, which promise happiness, fun, popularity, and love' (Andersen 1995: 89). No wonder, then, that the truth value of ads becomes something of secondary importance: 'consumers seek much more than purely factual knowledge, because they do not look at things simply as factual objects' (Qualter 1991: 91), but as embodiments of the fantasmatic promise articulated in advertising discourse. What we buy is what we fantasise about, and what we fantasise about is what we are lacking: the part of ourselves that is sacrificed/castrated when we enter the symbolic system of language and social relations. As Lacan has formulated it, the subject is symbolically deprived of it for ever. This loss, however, the prohibition of *jouissance*, is exactly what permits the emergence of desire; a desire which is structured around the unending quest for the lost/impossible *jouissance*. Impossible because, if the subject does not have it, neither does the big Other, the socio-symbolic system. Both subjective lack and the lack in the Other are lacks of *jouissance*. Lost because, in its fullness, it is posited as lost, a process which thereby introduces the idea that it can be refound (through consumption acts).

Fantasy is a construction that stimulates or causes desire because it promises to cover for the lack created by the loss of *jouissance* with a substitute, a miraculous object, the *objet petit a*. In Lacan, the structure we always find in fantasy is this relation between the split subject, the lacking subject, and the *objet petit a*. The idea behind the category of *le sujet de la jouissance* is that the human condition is marked by this quest for a lost/impossible enjoyment. Fantasy offers the *objet petit a* as the promise of an encounter with this precious *jouissance*, an encounter that is fantasised as covering over the lack in the Other and consequently as filling the lack in the subject. Within such a framework, brand names become 'channels of desire, emblems of a world denied, embodiments of wishes unfulfilled' (Ewen and Ewen 1982: 46).

It is precisely a piece of this enjoyment that is promised in the slogan 'Enjoy Coca-Cola'. Advertising discourse functions as a fantasy, it can persuade and cause desire, because it promises to cover over our lack by offering us the product as an *objet petit a*, as the final solution to all our problems, as the creator of an ideal harmony. In other words, within the advertising universe, every experience of lack is projected onto the lack of the product that is being advertised, that is to say, onto a lack which can be eliminated through one simple move: the purchase of the product, the act of consumption. Advertising fantasy reduces the constitutive lack in the subject to a lack of the product which it simultaneously offers as an *objet petit a*, as a promise for the final elimination of this lack. Baudrillard gives a very 'poetic' description of this utopian element in advertising: 'The manifest presence of surplus, the magical, definitive negation of scarcity, the maternal, luxurious sense of being already in the land of Cockaigne . . . These are our Valleys of Canaan where, in place of milk and honey, streams of neon flow down over ketchup and plastic' (Baudrillard 1998: 26). A recent observation by Žižek summarises very well this argument:

> As we know from Marx, a commodity is a mysterious entity full of theological caprices, a particular object satisfying a particular need, but at the same time the promise of 'something more', of an unfathomable enjoyment whose true location is fantasy – all advertising addresses this fantasmatic space. (Žižek 2003a: 145)

However, what is not to be missed here is that, exactly because we are unable to recapture our lost/impossible pre-symbolic *jouissance* in its fullness, advertising fantasy attempts to exorcise the *malaise* of everyday life by reproducing the system to which this *malaise* is constitutive. Desire can only be sustained by the dialectics of lack and excess; in order to remain attractive, the promise of excess relies on the continuous renewal of experiences of lack. Thus capitalist society 'is geared both to *structural excess* and to *structural penury*' (Baudrillard 1998: 53, emphasis added). 'The system only sustains itself by producing *wealth* and *poverty* . . . as many *dissatisfactions* as *satisfactions*' (p. 55, emphasis added). This paradoxical dialectics has not escaped the attention of Albert Hirschman. Acts of consumption – and the same applies to active participation in public affairs – 'undertaken because they are expected to yield satisfaction, also yield disappointment and dissatisfaction' (Hirschman 2002: 10). One can certainly recognise here the true Lacanian definition of fantasy not only as a screen which promises to fill the lack in the Other, but also as what 'produces' this lack, what stages a domesticated scenario of castration. Only by staging a scenario of lack can fantasy move on to its promise of covering over this lack in some distant or not so distant future – only thus can the fantasmatic promise sound appealing: 'to produce desire is also to produce the lack or scarcity that will intensify desirousness and increase the anticipation of jouissance' (Goux 1990: 200)

As a result, the capitalist 'utopia' is predominantly a virtual 'utopia'. We all know that the harmony promised by advertising fantasy cannot be realised; the *objet petit a* can function as the object-cause of desire only insofar as it is lacking. As soon as we buy the product we find out that the enjoyment we get is partial, that it has nothing to do with what we have been promised. As already mentioned in Chapter 5 and as Lacan points out in *Encore*, 'That's not it! Is the very cry by which the jouissance obtained is distinguished from the jouissance expected' (XX: 111). With every such experience a lack is re-inscribed in the subject. But this resurfacing of the inability of fantasy to lead to a full satisfaction of desire is not enough to put in danger the cultural hegemony of advertising in late capitalist societies. It could even be argued that, exactly because the 'product never fails to reduce to a mere promise the enjoyment which it promises', it gets to rely even more on advertising; it needs it all the more because it 'cannot be enjoyed' to the extent that we expect it to be (Adorno and Horkheimer 1997: 162). As Slavoj Žižek has very successfully put it, the aim of fantasy is not to satisfy desire, something that is ultimately impossible. It is enough to construct it and support it as such: through fantasy we 'learn' how to desire. As far as the final satisfaction of our desire is concerned, this is postponed from discourse to discourse, from fantasy to fantasy, from product to product. Yet everything remains intact as long as new products are produced and new fantasies are advertised. The incapability to produce the satisfaction promised does not kill desire but, on the contrary, sets off a 'cyclical quest' (Andersen 1995: 90). It is this continuous displacement that constitutes the *formal kernel* of consumer culture.

Tim Burton's film *Charlie and the Chocolate Factory*, based on Roald Dahl's story, offers one of the most amusing illustrations of this fantasmatic play between lack and excess and of the cathectic displacements it generates. Willie Wonka, played by Johnny Depp, decides to allow five children into his impressive but secretive Chocolate Factory. The process of selection is random – it consists in finding one of the five 'golden tickets' hidden in Wonka's chocolate bars. One of the 'chosen' children turns out to be the utterly spoilt offspring of an English millionaire. Under hysterical pressure from Veruca, her father buys millions of chocolate bars, to ensure that his daughter will get one of the precious 'golden tickets' and to be spared all her screams: 'Where's my golden ticket? I want my golden ticket!' What is at stake, then, is obviously more than mere caprice: it is happiness and desire. As he himself points out: 'Well, gentlemen, I just hate it to see my little girl feeling unhappy like that – I vowed I will keep up the search until I could give her what she wanted!' Eventually the ticket is found and presented to the girl. Here we encounter the revealing twist which encapsulates the central paradox of consumption: she looks at it for a couple of seconds with joy painted all over her face, and then turns to her father exclaiming the following words: 'Daddy, I want another pony!'[12] Hirschman is absolutely correct when he concludes that the world we are trying to understand, the world we live in, *is one in which men think they want one thing and then upon getting it, find out to their dismay that they don't want it nearly as much as they thought or don't want it at all and that something else, of which they were hardly aware, is what they really want* (Hirschman 2002: 21). Spinoza and Immanuel Kant already knew that much. For Spinoza, desires were 'often opposed one to the other as the man is drawn in different directions and knows not whither to turn' (Spinoza 1993: 126), while Kant, in one of his letters, articulates the following view on desire: 'Give a man everything he desires and yet at this very moment he will feel that this *everything* is not *everything*' (Kant in Hirschman 2002: 11).[13] In our age, this metonymic status of human desire, so essential to consumerism, is acknowledged by authors so diverse as Richard Sennet[14] and Guy Debord.[15]

Yet it must have become clear by now that the symbolic conditioning of desire – the foundation of the culturalist paradigm – cannot adequately function without a real support. Albeit partial and not identical to the *jouissance* expected, there is nevertheless a certain enjoyment entailed in *consuming a commodity*, and also in *consuming an advertisement*. Without the unique bodily satisfaction of drinking a Coke – and I speak here as a connoisseur of Coke – the Coke fantasy would not be able to sustain itself. From a study of brand failures it becomes obvious that both the fantasmatic representations attached to a brand and the real (the bodily enjoyment-value) of the product are of paramount importance. When, in 1985 and on the basis of hundreds of thousands of blind taste tests, Coca-Cola decided to withdraw its original product and replace it with a new formula with a new name ('New Coke') the result was disastrous (Haig 2005: 12). This was obviously not a matter for 'objective' tasting; the original formula had been invested (at the symbolic, the imaginary and the real level) with a value that was impossible to displace. This is the revealing way – which, surprisingly, even includes a link with the preceding discussion of nationalism in Chapter 5 – in which industry executives accepted their blunder: 'The simple fact is that all the time and money and skill poured into consumer research on the new Coca-Cola could not measure or reveal the deep and binding emotional attachment to original Coca-Cola felt by so many people. The passion for original Coca-Cola – and that is the word for it, passion – was something that caught us by surprise. It is a wonderful American mystery, a lovely American enigma, and you cannot measure it any more than you can measure love, pride or patriotism' (Keough in Haig 2005: 12–13). Such attachments have very precise fantasmatic *and* real conditions of possibility. When these are threatened – try selling 'New Coke' or drinking warm Coke, for example – the mystique evaporates.[16] Similarly, ads themselves can be enjoyable; for example, they are often very funny, visceral, ambiguously obscene, and subversively entertaining. They can function as vehicles of the enjoyment in meaning Lacan calls *jouis-sens*. Simply put, advertisements are not only determinants of consumption, but also 'objects of consumption' (Baudrillard 1996: 189) – moreover, objects that can be enjoyed *gratis* (p. 187). We can discern here a mechanism similar to the one observed in the reproduction of the national fantasy: the symbolic aspect of motivation, identification and desire cannot function without a fantasy support and this in its turn – the imaginary promise entailed in fantasy – cannot sustain itself without a real support in the (partial) *jouissance* of the body.

Consumerism, however, also reveals the enjoyment entailed in desiring itself, an enjoyment of desiring and buying, as distinct from the enjoyment of the object of purchase or from the enjoyment entailed in consuming advertisements. Already in 1937, a Chevrolet public relations film emphasised 'the pleasure of buying' in itself, along with 'the enjoyment of all the things that paychecks can buy' (Cohen 2004: 20). It is here that the symbolic, inter-subjective conditioning of desire meets the problematic of enjoyment in the most unequivocal way. The partial enjoyment supporting fantasies of consumption is not only an enjoyment procured through consuming commodities and advertisements, but also through desiring itself. The desire implicit here is not only a desire for objects, but *a desire for desiring*: desiring itself functions as an *objet petit a*, as a cause of desire and a source of (partial) *jouissance*. This Lacanian insight was already captured in Kojève's reading of Hegel. According to Kojève, 'Human Desire must be directed toward another Desire' (Kojève 1980: 5):

> anthropogenetic Desire is different from animal Desire . . . in that it is directed, not toward a real, 'positive', given object, but toward another Desire . . . Desire directed toward a natural object is human only to the extent that it is 'mediated' by the Desire of another directed toward the same object: it is human to desire what others desire, because they desire it. Thus, an object perfectly useless from the biological point of view (such as a medal or the enemy's flag) can be desired because it is the object of other desires. Such a Desire can only be a human Desire, and human reality, as distinguished from animal reality, is created only by action that satisfies such Desires; human history is the history of desired Desires. (Kojève 1980: 6)[17]

We can see now how private acts of consumption are inextricably linked to an inter-subjective conditioning which marks fantasy, desire and enjoyment. The important by-product of all the processes and mechanisms described so far is a specific structuration of desire. It is this particular economy of desire, articulated around the advertised product and desiring itself qua *objets petit a* and supported by experiences of partial *jouissance*, that guarantees, through its cumulative metonymic effect and the fixations it creates, the reproduction of the capitalist market within a distinct 'promotional culture'. In other words, the hegemony of the capitalist market depends on the hegemony of this particular economy of desire, on the hegemony of this particular administration of enjoyment. The complex multi-directional relationships between all these moments demand all our attention, so this is what my argumentation will focus on in the last section of this chapter.

Consumption, enjoyment and the social order

Although the Lacanian problematic of enjoyment is not compatible with the classical leftist critique of advertising, it does offer a new angle from which to access market economy and a new understanding of what supports the institution of the social order in late capitalism. What we see emerging here is a variety of relations of *overdetermination*. I take my lead in this respect from the work of Jean-Joseph Goux – who, in *Symbolic Economies*, highlights the structural homology (or equivalence) between the way the monetary system is structured and the functioning of the phallus (Goux 1990) – and from the work of Alain Grosrichard, who has especially stressed such (over)determinations (Grosrichard 1998). For Grosrichard, for example, surplus value goes hand in hand with surplus enjoyment. He goes back to this Lacanian insight in order to show that these are two sides of the economy ('subjective' and 'objective', individual and collective) which 'serve mutually to mask one another as circumstances demand' (Grosrichard 1998: 138). This double structure is what one also finds at work in the functioning of advertising. Advertising fantasy supports capitalism and vice-versa. Consumerism registers the dialectics of desire and enjoyment characteristic of human society, but this registering entails a domestication of desire, a particular channelling of enjoyment:

> As soon as the intensity of desire . . . has become the subjective law that standardizes values, the libido becomes the silent hostage of the political economy and has no choice but to be manipulated by it. If market value is simply the effect of the libido, conversely the libido is reduced to a mere cause in the marketplace, and this is the (increasingly well-executed) design of the capitalist market economy in its political-economization of social life in general. (Goux 1990: 202)

Here, however, desire and enjoyment also emerge as political factors. In fact, it is Lacan himself who, in *The Ethics of Psychoanalysis*, connects an 'economic' analysis of the good(s) with power relations: 'The good is at the level where a subject may have it at his disposal. The domain of the good is the birth of power . . . To exercise control over one's goods, as everyone knows, entails a certain disorder, that reveals its true nature, i.e. to exercise control over one's goods is to have the right to deprive others from them' (VII: 229). In fact, Lacan even points to the political dimension of what governs consumerism and advertising, namely the metonymy of desire: 'The morality of power, of the service of goods is as follows: "As far as desires are concerned come back later. Make them wait"' (VII: 315).

In other words, as Mladen Dolar argues in his introduction to Grosrichard's work, any administration of enjoyment 'demands and presupposes a certain social organization, a hierarchy, which is in turn supported only by the belief in the supposed supreme enjoyment at the centre' (Dolar in Grosrichard 1998: xvii). Thus we have a tripartite nexus connecting *economy* (capitalist market economy), inter-subjective *desire* (a particular socio-cultural administration of desire), and *power* (a particular power regime). And what about consumerism and advertising? Together they constitute the element which holds together the three rings (economy, desire, power), the element – related to enjoyment – which knots together our present economic, cultural and political structures. From this point of view consumerism and advertising function as the symptoms, in Lacanian jargon the *sinthomes*, of our societies. What from one point of view is a fantasy, from another, macroscopic point of view can be described as a social symptom. If fantasy, advertising fantasy in this case, is what gives support to our particular socio-economic and political reality (Žižek 1989: 49), on the other hand this reality is always a symptom (Žižek 1992), it is knoted together by, among others, the *sinthome* of consumerism and the modalities of enjoyment entailed in it.

Recent Lacanian theorisations of consumer society have highlighted these political implications of consumerism, and especially its central role in instituting and reproducing the social order in late capitalism. Todd McGowan's recent book *The End of Dissatisfaction?* deserves much praise in this respect. McGowan starts by registering the enjoyment explosion surrounding us in consumer societies and develops the hypothesis that it marks a significant shift in the structure of the social bond, in social organisation (McGowan 2004: 1). In particular, he speaks of a passage from a *society of prohibition* to a *society of commanded enjoyment* (p. 2). While more traditional forms of social organisation 'required subjects to renounce their private enjoyment in the name of social duty, today the only duty seems to consist in enjoying oneself as much as possible' (ibid.). This is the call that is addressed to us from all sides: the media, advertisements, even our own friends. Societies of prohibition were founded on an idealisation of sacrifice, of sacrificing enjoyment for the sake of social duty; in our societies of commanded enjoyment 'the private enjoyment that threatened the stability of the society of prohibition becomes a stabilizing force and even acquires the status of a duty' (p. 3).

This emerging society of commanded enjoyment is not concomitant with capitalism in general; it characterises, in particular, late capitalism. In its initial phases, with its reliance on 'work ethic' and delayed gratification, 'capitalism sustained and necessitated its own form of prohibition' (p. 31). Simply put, early capitalism 'thwarted enjoyment to the same extent that [many] traditional societies did' (ibid.). Indeed, the classical bourgeois attitude – and bourgeois political economy – was initially based on 'postponement, the deferral of jouissances, patient retention with a view to the supplementary jouissance that is calculated. Accumulate in order to accumulate, produce in order to produce' (Goux 1990: 203–4). It is the emergence of mass production and a consumer culture that signifies the beginning of 'the turn to the command to enjoy', but it is only with late capitalist globalisation that the transformation is completed (McGowan 2004: 33). In *The System of Objects*, Baudrillard has also described this shift from an ascetic model of ethics organised around sacrifice to a new morality of enjoyment: 'the status of a whole civilization changes along with the way in which its everyday objects make themselves present and the way in which they are enjoyed . . . The ascetic mode of accumulation, rooted in forethought, in sacrifice . . . was the foundation of a whole civilization of thrift which enjoyed its own heroic period' (Baudrillard 1996: 172). In that sense, McGowan's – as well as Baudrillard's – analysis fits well with the historical accounts of the development of consumerism discussed in the first section of this chapter: its early association with socio-political ideals and the good of the community and its latter emancipation from these burdens of the society of prohibition.

In societies of commanded enjoyment, duty makes sense predominantly as a duty to enjoy: 'duty is transformed into a duty to enjoy, which is precisely the commandment of the superego' (McGowan 2004: 34). The seemingly innocent and benevolent call to 'enjoy!' – as in 'Enjoy Coca-Cola!' – embodies the violent dimension of an irresistible commandment. Lacan was perhaps the first to perceive the importance of this paradoxical hybrid when he linked the command 'enjoy!' with the superego: 'The superego is the imperative of *jouissance* – Enjoy!' (XX: 3). He was the first to detect in this innocent call the unmistakable mark of power and authority. Thus Lacan is offering a revealing insight on what has been described as the 'consuming paradox': while consumerism seems to broaden our opportunities, choices and experiences as individuals, it also directs us towards predetermined channels of behaviour and thus it 'is ultimately as constraining as it is enabling' (Miles 1998: 147). The desire stimulated – and *imposed* – by advertising discourse is, in this sense, the desire of the Other *par excellence*. Already in 1968, Baudrillard had captured this moral dynamics of an 'obligation to buy', and recent consumption research is becoming increasingly more alert to this *forced choice* of consumerism: 'It is now something of a duty to explore personal identity through consumption' (Daunton and Hilton 2001: 31).[18] In late capitalist consumer society this is the interpellating command that constructs us as social subjects: thus, apart from products and advertising fantasies, what is also manufactured is consumers (Fine 2002: 168). It is here that 'the triumph of advertising' is located, as Adorno and Horkheimer already knew: 'consumers feel compelled to buy and use its products even though they see through them' (Adorno and Horkheimer 1997: 167).[19]

Let me make it clear, however, that what we encounter here, albeit an important moral shift, is not some kind of radical historical break of 'cosmological' proportions. From a psychoanalytic point of view, the administration of enjoyment and the structuration of desire are always implicated in the institution of the social bond. Every society has to come to terms with the impossibility of attaining *jouissance* as fullness; it is only the fantasies produced and circulated to mask, or at least domesticate, this trauma that can vary, and in fact do vary immensely. Prohibition and commanded enjoyment are two distinct such strategies, designed to institute the social bond and to legitimise authority and power in different ways. Nevertheless, in both cases, certain things remain unchanged. What remains the same is, first of all, the impossibility of realising the fantasy: 'The fundamental thing to recognize about the society of enjoyment is that in it the pursuit of enjoyment has misfired: the society of enjoyment has not provided the enjoyment that it promises' (McGowan 2004: 7). We have seen throughout this chapter how dissatisfaction and lack remain firmly inscribed within the dialectics of late capitalist consumerism. But if this is the case, then the command to enjoy is only revealed as 'a more nuanced form of prohibition'; it continues – with other means – the traditional function of symbolic Law and power (p. 39).[20] This was something also observed by Baudrillard. In our consumer societies, authority and symbolic power are as operative as in 'societies of prohibition': the 'enforced happiness and enjoyment' is the equivalent of the traditional imperatives to work and produce (Baudrillard 1998: 80). In that sense, the structure of obedience discussed in Chapter 4 vis-à-vis the function of the command in Milgram's experiment is still relevant here. Indeed, McGowan uses the word 'obedience' to refer to our attachment to the enjoyment commandment. The command to enjoy is nothing but an advanced, much more nuanced – and much more difficult to resist –

form of power. It is more effective than the traditional model, not because it is less constraining or less binding but because its violent exclusionary aspect is masked by its vow to enhance enjoyment, by its productive, enabling *façade*: it does not oppose and prohibit but openly attempts to embrace and appropriate *le sujet de la jouissance*.[21] However, in opposition to what McGowan seems to imply, recognising the extent of our 'obedience' to this enjoyment commandment cannot be enough to 'find a way out of this obedience' (McGowan 2004: 194). Not only is this novel articulation of power and enjoyment hard to recognise and to thematise; it is even harder to de-legitimise in practice – to dis-invest consumption acts and dis-identify with consumerism. However, without such a dis-investment and the cultivation of alternative (ethical) administrations of *jouissance* no real change can be effected.

This predicament has not escaped the always alert sensors of literature. The suffocating/constraining character of the 'society of commanded enjoyment' and the difficulties in resisting or escaping it have been very graphically depicted in J. G. Ballard's recent book *Millennium People* (Ballard 2004). Here Ballard describes an upper middle-class London suburb, offering one of the most engaging mappings of the society of commanded enjoyment:

> Look at the world around you, David. What do you see? An endless theme park, with everything turned into entertainment. Science, politics, education – they're so many fairground rides. Sadly, people are happy to buy their tickets and climb aboard! (Ballard 2004: 62)

Behind the smiling faces, however, there is a relation of violence, an unending series of limitations: 'Live here and you're surprisingly constrained. This isn't the good life, full of possibility. You soon come up against the barriers set out by the system' (Ballard 2004: 86). And in another character's words:

> 'We bought its trashy dreams and now we can't wake up . . .'
> 'Right, but there's one problem about this trash society. The middle classes like it.'
> 'Of course they do' . . . 'They are enslaved by it. They're the new proletariat, like factory workers a hundred years ago.' (Ballard 2004: 63)

The new (affluent) proletariat Ballard is sketching cannot easily feel its chains. But even when it becomes aware of them, it cannot re-act against a system of desire whose reproduction is supposed to serve their own enjoyment. Every form of protest is eventually short-circuited: 'The interesting thing is they are protesting against themselves. There's no enemy out there. They know *they* are the enemy' (p. 109). The world of consumption can incorporate almost everything, even the mini-revolution Ballard recounts:

> 'An entire social class is peeling the velvet off the bars and tasting the steel. People are resigning from well-paid jobs, refusing to pay their taxes, taking their children out of private schools'.
> 'Then, what's gone wrong?'

Nevertheless, ' "Nothing will happen" . . . "The storm will die down, and everything will peter out in a drizzle of television shows and op-ed pieces" ' (p. 170). The end was more or less expected:

> The infantilizing consumer society filled any gaps in the status quo as quickly as Kay had driven her Polo into the collapsing barricade.
> At the junction with Grosvenor Place, two ten-year old boys played with their airguns, dressed in camouflage fatigues and military webbing, part of the new guerrilla chic inspired by [the insurrection in] Chelsea Marina that had already featured in an *Evening Standard* fashion spread. A Haydn symphony floated gently through a kitchen window, below a protest banner whose damp slogan had dissolved into a Tachiste painting. (Ballard 2004: 234)

Indeed, as long as no alternative structuration of enjoyment and desire emerges, the only options that remain open – even after one becomes conscious of the dialectics of power, domination and compliance grafted on consumerism – are basically three:

1. The cynical enjoyment of subordination, a 'cynical embrace' of the society of commanded enjoyment (McGowan 2004: 6–7). What we encounter here is a kind of *ideological reflexivity* that often takes the following perverse form: 'I know that consumerism is a trap, nevertheless . . . I enjoy it – in fact, I enjoy it even more now that I have already criticised it'. This is a stance that incorporates and, at the same time, annuls any *critical reflexivity*, reproducing thus the hegemonic economy of enjoyment.
2. The obsolete 'nostalgic attempt to return to a previous epoch' (McGowan 2004: 7) of real values based on sacrifice and prohibition, which informs a multitude of conservative and leftist projects to return 'back to basics'. We are all familiar, for example, with the standard conservative cultural critique: we live in an era of unprecedented permissiveness, children lack limits and prohibitions, and thus what we need is a firm limit set by a strong symbolic authority (Žižek 2006: 295).

3. The – equally dangerous and, besides, open to co-optation from the hegemonic system – violent *acting out*, acts of blind retribution without meaning, of the type described by Ballard and increasingly being observed in our cities.

Is it possible to escape this vicious circle? And how? We have seen in this chapter how our interpellation as consumers in the society of commanded enjoyment manages to translate an apparently benign call to consume, desire and enjoy into a structuration of desire and enjoyment that sustains late capitalism and reproduces obedience and cynicism – operating simultaneously at the symbolic, imaginary and at the real register: through social construction, fantasy, and partial enjoyment. Can this state of affairs be de-legitimised? What could help in this process and in charting alternative formulations of desire and enjoyment, able to restore our lost faith in radical criticism and in the political? More precisely, can a radicalisation of democracy perform this task? This is what I will be discussing in the final chapter of *The Lacanian Left*.

Notes

1. Throughout this chapter I will be using the word 'consumption' mostly to refer to the acts involved, while reserving 'consumerism' for the way of life founded on the centrality of consumption acts. In this sense, the category of 'consumerism' attempts to conceive the psycho-social implications of the consuming experience and to capture the interaction between personal appeal and ideological power underlying its success (Miles 1998: 4–5).
2. Needless to say, confined to this chapter, this exploration will have to obey strict space limitations, which impose the requirement to concentrate on particular central aspects of consumerism and advertising without discussing – at least not at length – related aspects of contemporary economy, including important developments in the sphere of production.
3. One should not forget of course that this world of consumption is accessible neither to everybody on the globe nor to the same extent and at the same price (from an economic, social, cultural, and ecological point of view). This was a point stressed by the Freudian Left. With some geographical additions and displacements, Marcuse's comment from 1966 still retains its relevance: 'But the truth is that this freedom and satisfaction [in the affluent society] are transforming the earth into hell. The inferno is still concentrated in certain far away places: Vietnam, the Congo, South Africa, and in the ghettos of the "affluent society": in Mississippi and Alabama, in Harlem. These infernal places illuminate the whole' (Marcuse 1966: iii).
4. On the pioneering role of Bernays, also see Ewen 1996.

5. It is worth noting that Bennett's understanding of enchantment is, in certain respects, extremely close to Lacan's *jouissance*. This is the case when she associates enchantment with a pleasurable feeling coupled with uncanny disruption (Bennett 2001: 5) or when she defines it as 'a mixed bodily state of joy and disturbance' (p. 111).
6. To give just one example, a recent collection of introductory texts characteristically entitled *The Why of Consumption* includes a text on desire which substantially draws on Lacanian theory (Belk et al. 2000).
7. I am referring to Lacan's social constructionism, discussed in Chapter 1.
8. For another example, see Guy Debord's analysis which does not escape the reference to 'pseudo-needs' entailing a 'falsification of life' (Debord 1995: 44).
9. Here Marx draws on Barbon's observation, made in 1696, that the appetite of the mind is 'as natural as hunger to the body' (Marx 1961: 35).
10. Another important book by Baudrillard, *The System of Objects*, employs a semiotic approach with an equally distinct Lacanian flavour and is characteristically concluded with this Lacanesque sentence: 'Consumption is irrepressible, in the last reckoning, because it is founded upon a *lack*' (Baudrillard 1996: 224).
11. As Klein has put it, 'Think of the brand as the core meaning of the modern corporation, and of the advertisement as one vehicle used to convey that meaning to the world' (Klein 2000: 5).
12. Exactly because the enjoyment experienced is never the enjoyment promised and expected – and thus a certain lack is bound to be re-inscribed – many brands have vowed to compensate for this lack in advance. Hence the preoccupation with products like the Kinder egg – a chocolate product that everybody buys for the non-chocolate gift found inside – and offers like the following: 'Buy this toothpaste and get a third extra for free' or 'Look on the inside of the metal cover and you may find that you are the winner of one of our prizes, from another free coke to a brand-new car' (Žižek 2003a: 146).
13. It is fair to conclude, then, that, while we can reach a formal understanding of the logic of desire, particular desires are imperfectly understood even by those who hold them (Qualter 1991: 90). This is what explains the ultimate failure of most new products advertised. 86% of the 85,000 new products advertised in the US in the 1980s did not survive beyond 1990, while in 1994 90% of the 22,000 products advertised failed (Fowles 1996: 19, 164). Of course this does not affect the cumulative economic, cultural and political effect of advertising discourse and consumerism as a whole.
14. Consider, for example, Sennett's observation that 'our desire for a dress may be ardent, but a few days after we buy and wear it, the garment arouses us less. Here the imagination is strongest in anticipation, grows ever weaker through use' (Sennett 2006: 138).

15. Debord states: 'Each and every product is supposed to offer a dramatic shortcut to the long-awaited promised land of total consumption. As such it is ceremoniously presented as the unique and ultimate product . . . But even this spectacular prestige evaporates into vulgarity as soon as the object is taken home by a consumer – and hence by all other consumers too'. Now, its inadequacy is revealed: 'For by this time another product will have been assigned to supply the system with its justification' (Debord 1995: 45).
16. Another example worth noting is the failure of Kellog's 'Cereal mates' due to the terrible taste of warm milk with which they were usually consumed (Haig 2005: 34).
17. As Bauman has recently put it, 'solely the desiring is desirable – hardly ever its satisfaction' (Bauman 2000: 88). Žižek has also highlighted this manipulation of 'desire to desire' by capitalism (Žižek 2006: 61).
18. Lodziak also cites Anthony Giddens' observation that 'in conditions of high modernity, we all not only follow lifestyles, but in an important sense are forced to do so – we have no choice but to choose' (Giddens in Lodziak 2002: 66). He concludes that 'we are compelled to consume', although he means this in a more structural sense and links it to the dependence on consumption through resourcing (income) and through constraining autonomy due to the under-resourcing of time and energy (Lodziak 2002: 89).
19. It is important to emphasise, however, that to accept the enjoyment command, to obey the new morality, was not an automatic process, especially for subjects socialised within societies of prohibition. Advertisers themselves became aware of this problem in the 1950s and 1960s:

> The problem confronting us now is how to allow the average American to feel moral even when he is flirting, even when he is spending money, even when he is buying a second or third car. One of the most difficult tasks created by our current affluence is sanctioning and justifying people's enjoyment of it, convincing them that to take pleasure in their lives is moral and not immoral. (Dichter in Baudrillard 1996: 202)

20. In the *Parallax View*, Žižek associates the society of prohibition with desire and the permissive society of enjoyment with demand. Even in this case, however, the difference between the two modes is not radical and a similar 'continuity in discontinuity' can be observed to the extent that both 'desire and demand rely on the Other' (Žižek 2006: 296). Moreover, one should not forget that the gesture of renouncing enjoyment, within a society of prohibition, can also 'generate a surplus-enjoyment of its own' and thus 'the superego injunction to enjoy is immanently intertwined with the logic of sacrifice: the two form a vicious cycle, each extreme supporting the other' (p. 381).
21. Foucault's discussion of the passage from a negative to a positive, productive, conceptualisation of power, is of much relevance at this point.

8
Democracy in Post-Democratic Times

Nobody can protect humanity from folly or suicide
Cornelius Castoriadis

Virtue, in a republic, is a very simple thing: it is love of the republic; it is a feeling and not a result of knowledge; the lowest man in the state, like the first, can have this feeling
Montesquieu

Democracy and the Lacanian Left: relations of ambivalence

Throughout this book, side by side with my critical explorations of the various theoretical projects associated with the Lacanian Left, side by side with the analyses of central socio-political phenomena undertaken from a Lacanian perspective, I have also been sketching – in an admittedly indirect way – some of the preconditions for a democratic ethics of the political, an orientation drawing on both Lacanian theory and theories of radical democracy. In fact, forging a link between the Lacanian ethics of psychoanalysis and radical democratic theory has already been one of the main aims of *Lacan and the Political*.[1] Today, in the emerging post-democratic context, this orientation remains as topical as ever. At the same time, however, the need for a more thorough elaboration of certain aspects of the radical democratic project has never been so pressing. In the few years since my earlier work was published, the world has witnessed an increase in democratic rhetoric coupled with an unprecedented assault on the two traditional pillars of modern democracy: equality and liberty. At first, this attack had targeted the democratic aspect of liberal democracy, the one associated with principles like popular sovereignty, political participation and equality: since the 1970s and 1980s decision making has been gradually de-politicised and, to a large extent, entrusted to supposedly neutral organisations and authorities (such as 'independent' central banks), market regulation has been abandoned or severely limited within an increasingly globalised horizon, business principles have invaded all aspects of public life, and centre-stage politics has entered the 'post-political' era of professionalised 'governance' beyond left and right.[2] Some celebrated this as a victory of liberalism which would signal the end of politics as we knew it and herald the dawn of a liberal–capitalist utopia. This view is not very widespread any more. A vibrant democratic life cannot rely solely on abstract rights, on formal legalism. Without the mobilisation of passions around strong democratic identifications, which only an egalitarian vision can productively achieve, without a proper political antagonism between real alternatives, the democratic spectacle sustained by the post-political consensus was bound to disintegrate whenever the first obstacle was encountered. This is exactly what happened post 9/11, with security overshadowing all other social and political priorities. The result has been a direct attack on the second pillar of liberal democracy, the one associated with rights and liberalism. When someone like Richard Rorty, in an article characteristically entitled 'Post-Democracy', predicts a 'cascade of governmental actions that would, in the course of a few years, bring about a fundamental change in the conditions of social life in the west', with the courts being brushed aside, authority transferred from locally elected officials to military commanders, and the introduction of media censorship (Rorty 2004: 10), then surely something important must be happening, something which demands serious attention.

It is not surprising that this trend has led to an increased suspicion towards the tropes of modern democratic rhetoric by many political theorists, including some associated with the Lacanian Left – namely Žižek and Badiou. The latter remains devoted to the activism of *l'organisation politique*, and warns us to refrain from the electoral game: abstain from voting and expect nothing from any political party is his message (Badiou 2001). The former, having run as a presidential candidate in his native Slovenia, tends to avoid such cataclysmic condemnations and often adopts an ultimately pragmatic view of things, an extimate relation to organised democratic politics. Nevertheless, this does not stop him from occasionally attacking 'democracy', even from concluding that democracy should now be considered as a political term belonging to the 'reactionary' vocabulary: democracy, for Žižek, is 'more and more a false issue, a notion so discredited by its predominant use that, perhaps, one should take the risk of abandoning it to the enemy' (Žižek 2001: 123). More importantly, Žižek's critique is not limited to 'existing democracies'; as already mentioned in Chapter 3, it also encompasses radical democratic arguments and, thus, needs to be urgently and thoroughly addressed.

Can, however, the current reduction of democracy to the reign of globalised capitalism and of fantasies of global hegemony justify the devaluation of the most important invention of our political imagination and experimentation? Hasn't the attempt to domesticate and neutralise the radicalism of democracy been with us all along, already from the inception of the democratic revolution? It was always against various attempts to co-opt the democratic invention that radical forces had to put forward their own articulation of freedom and equality – often with success. In reality, the history of modern democracy has been nothing but a continuous play of *sedimentations* – entailing an often suffocating fixation corrupting democratic openness – and *reactivations* of its radical potential. Needless to say, this play, another aspect of the negative/positive dialectics, is a defining characteristic of political struggles and social life in general,[3] something the Lacanian Left needs to take very seriously into account.

In this respect, Castoriadis is correct in some of the links he draws between ancient and modern forms of democracy. There is a common kernel, a common premise, which is located in both cases in the lack of any extra-social, extra-political foundation for society: in democracy the political community, the demos, constructs its own institutions and decides on everything, *knowing that it does so* (Castoriadis 2000: 129). This knowledge is also a knowledge of the inevitability of division and antagonism: if there is no God or other transcendental source to guarantee our constructions, then democratic antagonism has to be recognised as the only legitimate instituting moment of (limited, temporary, and never ideal) hegemonic crystallisations. However, this idea is never easy to swallow. It was quite difficult to accept it in ancient Athens, which is visible in the attacks mounted by the great critics of democracy (such as Plato). It is as difficult, if not even more difficult, to accept it today. As a result, the signifier 'democracy' is often hegemonised by non-democratic or post-democratic discourses. But is this a sufficient reason to discard democracy?

Our current post-democratic experience is just the last episode in a very long story of struggles around the meaning of democracy. But there is nothing here that forces one to abandon the theoretico-political horizon of what Chantal Mouffe calls the 'democratic paradox', this paradoxical registering of the constitutive play between positive (the need for sedimented social institutions and arrangements) and negative (the awareness of their contingent dislocations and political rearticulations), necessity and impossibility, situationness and event-ness. By recognising the irreducibility of political antagonism, (radical) democracy enables the emergence of blends of liberalism and democracy, of liberty and equality, capable of perpetually questioning the limits of community and of transforming existing hegemonic orders without resorting to the disaster-prone strategies of 'speculative leftism'. What emerges as a result is a truly *ethical* conceptualisation of democracy: not merely as an aggregate of different interests or a constitutional structure based on human and political rights, not only as 'rule of the people by the people', but – above all else – as an institutionalisation of lack and antagonism, as the possibility of instituting a sustainable and interminable questioning which permits the reflexive self-creation of society (Castoriadis 1991b). When discussing the (social and not subjective) autonomy characteristic of democracy, Castoriadis particularly stresses this dimension of self-institution. However, all human societies institute themselves. What, then, differentiates a democratic society? A democratic society institutes itself 'explicitly and reflectively' (Castoriadis 1997b: 340). This form of a self-institution aware of itself, of an 'explicit self-institution', emerges in its most emblematic form in the democratic Greek cities and re-emerges in Western modernity (ibid.). What is required today is a re-activation of this radical ethical potential of the democratic horizon: 'radical democracy' entails a recasting of 'autonomy', 'freedom', 'liberation' and 'emancipation'. These are not to be associated with utopian states where all domination and power relations have been banished, but with a critical opening of new ways to bring to consciousness, thematise, traverse and re-determine perpetually what is tolerable, acceptable, desirable and enjoyable in the manner in which politics is conducted, the social bond reproduced, and lives led.[4]

But is such a redefinition/re-activation of democracy still possible? Many theorists broadly associated with the Lacanian Left (from peripheral figures like Castoriadis to Laclau and Mouffe) would reply in the positive. As Oliver Marchart has put it, in a critique of Žižek's abandonment of democracy:

> it is possible to redefine the horizon because its currently hegemonic meaning . . . is the contingent outcome of a whole set of struggles which by definition is open-ended even as it seems to have 'won' for the time being. So there is no reason why it should be impossible to fight for a, let's

say, more radical, egalitarian, and participatory version of democracy. (Marchart 2002: 257)

At the conceptual level – both in political theory and in practical politics – such a renewal of the radical potential of democratic imagination can greatly benefit from seriously registering the deep transformations affecting contemporary existing democracies. I am obviously referring to the trends of de-politicisation and de-democratisation increasingly engulfing Western public spheres and to the dominance of a post-political consensus. Simply put, my argument here is the following: democracy can still function as the mobilising force, the common denominator, for a politics of alternatives, to the extent that existing Western regimes are re-evaluated and recognised by political theory and analysis as the 'post-democracies' they are increasingly becoming.

Besides, although democracy has been, and still is, invoked to justify some of the most barbaric political orders, one cannot dispute that the horizon of 'democratisation' remains one of the most forceful nodal points of political imagination, an inspiration articulating a multitude of radical demands throughout the world, and nothing else seems capable of replacing it – at least for the time being (Hall 2002: 23). This is perhaps what explains the ultimately ambivalent attitude of both Badiou and Žižek towards democracy. After firmly locating the signifier 'democracy' in the reactionary camp, Žižek does not hesitate to defend democracy, characteristically entitling one of his recent articles 'Today, Iraq. Tomorrow . . . Democracy' (Žižek 2003e). As for Badiou, one has to agree with Bensaid that democracy is a question not adequately addressed, and perhaps even repressed, in his work (Bensaid 2004: 97). Surely some explanation is needed to make sense of how someone who explicitly rejects democratic institutions can sustain the following position: 'The critique of democracy is something rather complicated. It is why sometimes I think that we must distinguish between true democracies and false ones . . . Democracies are the "real" of politics (*true* democracies) . . . You can say that the development of a new political field, the creation of something new, is democratic' (Badiou 2003c). If facilitating political creations embracing event-ness is democratic *par excellence*, indicative of a true democracy, then obviously another name is needed to describe the de-democratising political mutations we are currently encountering. It is to this problem that the introduction of new concepts such as 'post-democracy' attempts to respond.

The post-democratic trend

Starting from a view of democracy and its constitutive paradoxes like the one presented here, how is it possible to define post-democracy from a psychoanalytic standpoint? The focus will have to be on the particular negotiation between negative and positive embedded in its institutional arrangements and in the particular way it deals with the dimension of enjoyment. As already mentioned, there is no doubt that modernity has made us increasingly aware of the constitutivity of contingency and negativity in human life. This has permitted a philosophical registering of negativity as that 'which simply shows the limits of the constitution of objectivity and cannot be dialecticized' (Laclau 1990: 26). Indeed, we would not be aware of negativity without our social and political positivities – variable in time and space – being repeatedly destabilised and dislocated by 'something': by an encounter with the impossible, the uncanny, the unrepresentable, the unconscious, *the real*. The paradox of this sustained awareness of negativity is obvious. On the one hand, it encircles something which cannot be positivised per se – as Diana Coole has recently put it, 'to name it would be to destroy it; to render it positive, ideal, and thus to fail at the very moment of apparent success' (Coole 2000: 1). On the other, any ontology of negativity is limited by its reliance on – but not reduction to – the positive aspect of human experience: we can only acknowledge negativity by following its disruptive traces along the fabric of what societies construct as their positive world, by following the play between positivities and dislocations.

Furthermore, if negativity refers to the horizon of impossibility and unrepresentability that punctuates the life of linguistic creatures, this does not mean that it should be understood as a mere destructive force. In Coole's terms, negativity is also affirmative: 'a creative–destructive force that engenders as well as ruins positive forms. In this sense negativity does tend to operate as (a surrogate for) ontology, although it is far too mobile, too negative, to serve as a foundation for what follows' (Coole 2000: 6). Negativity, then, also indicates the dimension of 'becoming, a productivity that engenders and ruins every distinct form as a creative destructive restlessness' (p. 230). It is neither an object nor its negation: it is the condition of possibility/impossibility of the constitution of objects (Laclau 1990: 36). By inscribing a *lack* in our dislocated positivities it fuels the *desire* for new social and political constructions and identifications.

In that sense, the Lacanian dialectics between lack and desire becomes crucial in clarifying the status of an ontology of negativity. It is important to stress once more at this point that Lacanian theory does not consider lack in isolation, as a purely negative index of the real or some sort of primordial archetype of the psyche or the social. Lack is always inscribed in the fabric of our identifications as a lack of something: of the lost/impossible energy, of the fullness of *jouissance* which we retroactively project onto our existence before socialisation. Even if entering the world of language and social norms demands the castration of an excessive part of our bodily energy – or rather, precisely because of that – the 'nostalgia' and the associated promise of recapturing our sacrificed enjoyment persists and returns, to form the kernel of fantasies that stimulate our desire for new identifications. We have seen in much detail, throughout the second part of this text, how symbolic identity – as well as culturally conditioned desire – rely on this fantasmatic dimension in order to animate their formal structures. In their turn, however, the imaginarisations of fantasy cannot perform this function without some real support in experiences of (partial) *jouissance*. The *symbolic* of discursive articulation, the *imaginary* of fantasy and the *real* of *jouissance*, in their continuous interactions, constitute the backbone of identification processes, the irreducible registers on which the production and reproduction, the articulation and affective investment of our social and subjective realities largely depend.

In pre-modern societies religious imagination was the predominant discursive horizon for the inscription and administration of negativity. There is no doubt, however, that modernity has signalled a shift in our symbolic and imaginary administration of negativity and contingency. On the one hand, it has highlighted its constitutive nature: a world without God is a world visibly lacking the promise and the guarantee of a final resolution of negativity. On the other hand, unable to assume full responsibility for such a radical recognition, such a disruptive awareness, modernity has reoccupied the ground of a pre-modern ethics of harmony, often substituting God with reason.[5] What are the political and institutional implications of these developments? It seems that political modernity has oscillated between (at least) three responses vis-à-vis negativity, the lack of (total) *jouissance*: I will refer to them as the utopian, the democratic and the post-democratic response.[6]

The first response, one reoccupying the ground of pre-modern metaphysics, is best exemplified by some mutations in modern political utopianism. I use utopia here in the strong sense of the word, as a discourse that offers final political solutions from the point of view of a *subject supposed to know*, whose opaqueness and authority is never questioned per se. Fascism and Stalinism – notwithstanding their many important differences – are two obvious examples. What is dominant here is a fear to encounter negativity without recourse to the certainty of attaining another order (of limitless *jouissance*), a utopian society, a harmonious future eliminating negativity once and for all.[7] The young Trotsky, a twenty-two year old exiled in Siberia, has expressed through his writings this sentiment in the most revealing way: 'As long as I breathe, I shall fight for the future, that radiant future in which man, strong and beautiful, will become master of the drifting stream of his history and will direct it towards the boundless horizon of beauty, joy and happiness!' (Trotsky in Deutcher 1954: 54). A closer look, however, reveals that this desire to overcome negativity once and for all relies on the negative itself, it only makes sense within a society of prohibition. Societies of prohibition are marked throughout by such a polarisation between prohibition, sacrifice, the Law, and the dream of transgression incarnated in the desire for utopia. Without an explicit limitation, without the castrating command of the Law, utopia loses all its lure.[8] Moreover, utopia not only relies on negativity but is also likely to produce negativity: whenever a conscious attempt was made to realise such fantasies, to institute human reality according to a plan promising to resolve social contradiction, dissimulate political antagonism, and permit an encounter with the lost/impossible *jouissance*, the results were catastrophic, best described by 'the triple knotted effect, of ecstasy, the sacred and terror' that Alain Badiou has called 'disaster' (Badiou 1999: 133).[9]

If this is the case, then surely one of the most urgent political tasks of our age is to traverse the fantasy of utopia and reinvent transformative politics in a post-fantasmatic direction. As (early) Žižek had put it, the question of the *traversing of fantasy* – one of the aims of analytic treatment in Lacanian psychoanalysis – becomes 'perhaps the foremost political question' (Žižek 1996b: 118). But what does it mean to move in such a post-fantasmatic direction? Fortunately, it might not require a shift of Herculean proportions. One can encounter elements of such a political project in what is usually called the democratic invention or the democratic revolution. This brings us to the second response to negativity present in political modernity, the one closest to assuming – either consciously or unconsciously – the responsibility for its constitutive and irreducible character.

No final resolutions are promised here, no political *Aufhebung*; antagonism is and remains constitutive and the utopian dream of attaining the fullness of *jouissance* is relegated to the realm of impossibility, where it belongs. 'Democratic revolution' – an expression coming from de Tocqueville but radically refashioned by Lefort and others – marks a discontinuity from the heteronomous legitimacy of the pre-modern *ancien régime* to a new form of the political institution of the social, a society becoming aware of its own historicity, its own limits. A form of society that opens itself to a continuous process of questioning its own institutional structures and power relations, which detaches itself from fixed markers of certainty, including the body of the sovereign: 'The modern democratic revolution is best recognized in this mutation: there is no power linked to a body'. The place of power now appears as 'an empty place' which can be occupied only temporarily: 'There is no law that can be fixed, whose articles cannot be contested, whose foundations are not susceptible of being called into question. Lastly, there is no representation of a centre and of the contours of society: unity cannot now efface social division'. Democracy, according to Lefort, institutionalises 'the experience of an ungraspable, uncontrollable society', in which even the identity of the sovereign people 'will constantly be open to question' (Lefort 1986: 303–4).[10] This is clearly the boldest attempt to institute a political order on the lack of ultimate foundations (and total enjoyment) characteristic of a modernity worthy of its name.

Of course, this is not to say that all modern political forms claiming the name 'democracy' obey such a principle of organisation. One can clearly have an essentialist (pre-democratic) or a post-democratic conceptualisation of democracy, which would remain more or less blind to negativity. We all know that there is no dictator who has not tried to manipulate, at least once, the vocabulary of democracy. And no citizen of a Western liberal democracy would perhaps instantly identify their own political experience with the preceding picture of the guiding principles of the democratic revolution. This is not surprising. It is due to the fact that our current experience is marked by *a third way* of responding to negativity, characteristic of political modernity: the response of consumerist post-democracy, typical of the current articulation between the late capitalist consumerist order and the forms of political authority operating in societies of commanded enjoyment.

Now, what exactly are the characteristics of a consumerist post-democracy? How does it deal with negativity? If revolutionary and utopian imagination respond to the 'emptiness' of the democratic vision by promising the final elimination of negativity and the full encounter with our lost/impossible *jouissance* here and now, consumerist post-democracy follows a more nuanced strategy – the strategy of a *jouissance à venir*, to paraphrase Derrida's *démocratie à venir*. Commanded enjoyment may associate itself with the radical overcoming of prohibition and sacrifice but, nevertheless, the *jouissance* it promises is an infinitely deferred one. It is always already everywhere – since the command instituting the social bond openly endorses it – but at the same time it is nowhere as such, infinitely displaced from commodity to commodity, from fantasy to fantasy. This continuous displacement presupposes a dialectics between lack and desire, but this is limited to the world of consumption and advertising; it does not emerge as a political question since the command regulating the social bond – 'Enjoy!' – is posited as universal, uncontestable and irresistible. Hence politics loses all antagonistic connotations and becomes synonymous with administration. It is this reality that many political theorists and sociologists describe as 'post-democratic'.

Post-democracy is founded on an attempt to exclude the awareness of lack and negativity from the political domain, which leads to a political order that retains the token institutions of liberal democracy but neutralises the centrality of political antagonism. Jacques Rancière has been one of the political theorists who coined this term (Rancière 1995: 177). A whole chapter is devoted to consensus democracy or 'postdemocracy' in Rancière's *Dis-agreement* (Rancière 1999: 95–121). According to his schema, this is what post-democracy denotes:

> the paradox that, in the name of democracy, emphasises the consensual practice of effacing the forms of democratic action. Postdemocracy is the government practice and conceptual legitimisation of a democracy after the demos, a democracy that has eliminated the appearance, miscount, and dispute of the people and is thereby reducible to the sole interplay of state mechanisms and combinations of social energies and interests.
> (Rancière 1999: 101–2)

This diagnosis is congruent with the sociological observations of Colin Crouch: while the formal aspect of democratic institutions remains more or less in place, politics and government are gradually slipping back into the control of privileged groups in a way reminiscent of pre-democratic times (Crouch 2004: 6). Elections and electoral debate, which can still change governments, are transformed into a 'tightly controlled spectacle', managed by professional experts and restricted to a set of issues selected by them, with most citizens reduced to a passive, apathetic role. Behind this *façade* – but not beyond the terrain of visibility – 'politics is shaped in private by the interaction between elected governments and elites that overwhelmingly represent business interests' (p. 4). Although, in other words, the formal envelope of democracy survives, 'its substance is becoming ever more attenuated' (Marquand 2004: 4).

In some cases – and this is indicative of a more general trend – what accompanies the development of post-democracy is an outright identification of democratic form with the 'necessities' of globalised capital:

> From an allegedly defunct Marxism, the supposedly reigning liberalism borrows the theme of objective necessity, identified with the constraints and caprices of the world market. Marx's once scandalous thesis that governments are simple business agents for international capital is today an obvious fact on which 'liberals' and 'socialists' agree. The absolute identification of politics with the management of capital is no longer the shameful secret hidden behind the 'forms' of democracy; it is the openly declared truth by which our governments acquire legitimacy. (Rancière 1999: 113)

Chantal Mouffe has also contributed a lot to drawing our attention to the ideological characteristics of the emerging post-democratic imaginary and to demonstrating its effects on the way existing democracies represent, and deal with, dissent. In her last book, after sketching the characteristics of this post-political imaginary, she focuses on the dangers it entails at both domestic and international level (Mouffe 2005). In a world still marked – globally and domestically – by inequalities of various forms, the marginalisation of political antagonism and the hegemony of consumerist administrations of enjoyment, even though extremely successful, cannot fully absorb the potential for dissent. Unable to understand and reluctant to legitimise the centrality of antagonism in democratic politics, the post-political, post-democratic *Zeitgeist* forces the expression of this dissent – when it manages to articulate itself – through channels bound to fuel a spiral of increasingly uncontrolled violence: whereas a recognition of the adversarial nature of the political permits the transformation of antagonism into *agonism*, the taming of raw violence, a post-political approach leads to violent expressions of hatred which, upon entering the de-politicised public sphere, can only be identified and opposed in moral or cultural (and eventually military) terms. Indeed, when opponents are defined in an 'extra-political' manner, 'they cannot be envisaged as "adversary" but only as "enemy". With the "evil them" no agonistic debate is possible, they must be eradicated. Moreover, as they are often considered to be the expression of some kind of "moral disease", one should not even try to provide an explanation for their emergence and success' (Mouffe 2005: 76). Hence, at the international level, the preoccupation with 'axes of evil' and 'clashes of civilisations'. Hence, at the domestic level, the rise of racism, xenophobia and extreme right-wing movements and parties as well as the irruptions of youth violence in our cities *and*, most importantly, the difficulties in explaining and dealing with such phenomena politically.

What Mouffe does highlight is that, even in this case, a certain political frontier is drawn – since without an act of exclusion no identity can be constructed – but, at the same time, its political character is denied, so that the post-political imaginary can remain intact. Indeed, cultural and moral enemies are continuously constructed and demonised. This also helps to legitimise the assault on the two pillars of liberal democracy, namely equality and liberty, and to inject affective value into the post-political nexus. One needs to emphasise here that this stress on culture and morality is directly associated with the explicit elevation of the problematic of enjoyment into a nodal point of the social bond in late capitalist societies. What is the criticism of the personal morality of politicians, if not a(n often hypocritical and resentful) judgement of the Other's *jouissance*? What lies behind the 'clash of civilisations' – in both its current manifestations, terrorism and fundamentalism on the one hand, 'democratic' imperialism on the other – if not a hatred of the Other's enjoyment? In both cases, of course, it is the socially conditioned relation to our own (lack of) enjoyment that underlies these phenomena. McGowan has cogently captured the way this dialectics of *jouissance* was played out in the context of the Iraq war: 'Neither Bush nor any other American political figure discussed the war in political terms (as a struggle against Islamic fascism, against fundamentalism, etc.), except those of protecting American jouissance. In the society of commanded enjoyment, the politics of private enjoyment (and safeguarding it) becomes politics as such' (McGowan 2004: 149).[11] No wonder, then, that the average American was asked to react primarily at the level of consumerist *jouissance*. Throughout history a major catastrophe was followed by calls to sacrifice consumer pleasures in the interests of the common good. This was not what happened post 9/11: instead, 'government leaders hastened to urge people to keep their consumer activities going' (Stearns 2006: vii).

This is, then, the legitimating sophism of the post-democratic order: since the pursuit of enjoyment is not castrated but encouraged, then no antagonism is necessary to transgress the prohibitions sustaining the social order. Accordingly, the social space can be represented as a space in which people pursue their diverse private enjoyments and negotiate negativity through the (supposedly unlimited) channels offered by consumerism and advertising. Hence there is no need for a political (agonistic) registering of negativity. As a result, within the post-democratic political imaginary, antagonism is neutralised. In effect, negativity and its affective value are displaced from the political field and re-inscribed in – at least two – de-politicised ways. Either reduced to a 'clash of enjoyments' between different civilisations (at the global level),[12] or, in domestic terms, reduced to the lack of particular products; to a lack, in other words, that can be 'administered' through consumption acts: through the consumption of products, discourses, fantasies, even politicians.

The grip of these mechanisms is considerable. By commanding us to enjoy, consumerist post-democracy unarms the traditional utopian politics and spoils its attraction: not only is there no explicit prohibition to transgress, but the system itself is now supposed to bring us as close to *jouissance* as possible. No doubt, this is never the complete *jouissance* of the utopian promise, but did we ever really experience the utopian *jouissance*? Whenever one comes close to it, gold turns into shit. And the price to be paid is huge. Utopian fantasies lead to dystopian realities. But this realisation must not mask the fact that commanded enjoyment presupposes a function of authority not unlike the one operative in the society of prohibition, a structure of obedience which is as disabling and constraining as any other; that post-democracy entails dangers that should never be underestimated.[13] Moreover, within the post-democratic universe, this authority structure becomes increasingly immune from criticism. As shown in the previous chapter, any resistance is either reabsorbed into the Disneyland of consumerist *jouissance* in a more or less conformist/cynical way, channelled into obsolete reoccupations of a nostalgic type with anti-democratic implications but (fortunately) limited appeal, or pushed to violent acting outs or *passages à l'acte*, both internationally and domestically. The latter are easily discredited (why resist a supposedly 'benevolent' universal call to enjoy?) and, in any case, not only unable to shift the hegemonic administration of desire and enjoyment in any productive direction, but also triggering an escalation that denies the possibility of an agonistic negotiation and puts democracy at serious risk. The result is an increasingly complex and explosive short-circuit with a variety of serious parameters (personal, ecological, political, security, etc.) and no obvious solutions.

Paradoxes of democracy: ancient and modern

The question now is: How should one respond to the increasing hegemony of post-democracy, which after the demise of the utopian political imaginary is now eroding the achievements and the promise of the democratic revolution and makes our world a far riskier place? Can democracy resist the trend of de- or post-democratisation? Can it still function as a horizon within which true political acts are facilitated and encouraged? Through its sustained engagement with the ethical status of psychoanalysis and the end of analysis, Lacanian theory can provide crucial insights into current attempts to radicalise democracy, to re-activate the democratic revolution against the post-democratic trends implicit – and, alas, explicit – in contemporary international politics and in the meta-political consensus which dominates liberal democracies. A political theory determined to avoid the dangers entailed in the nostalgic politics of reoccupation and in violent acting-outs seems to have only one option: to insist on the radicalisation of democracy on a global scale, against de-politicisation and the domestication of negativity and antagonism within the 'imperialist' framework of consumerist post-democracy. The fact that capitalist consumerism has colonised democratic institutions should not make us *disavow* the radical potential of the democratic revolution within political modernity. In fact, it should only serve to reinforce the conviction that the democratic revolution remains the most advanced political invention vis-à-vis the recognition of the constitutive character of negativity and its translation into an organising principle for any politics of real transformation within communities or between communities. If democracy did not carry this potential, then there would be no need for the promotion of the post-democratic agenda on behalf of all those who benefit from the reproduction and globalisation of the present capitalist order. It is also true that most forms of democracy – liberal democracy included – still contain a kernel of that potential – often repressed and marginalised, and certainly in need of radical revitalisation and re-activation. I see such a re-activation as one of the most urgent tasks of contemporary political theory and praxis.

This is not to say, however, that it will be an easy task. On the contrary, it is something that becomes increasingly difficult. Moreover, there can be no guarantees here, no a priori source of creativity to rely on (Chapter 1). In Jason Glynos' words: 'How does one even begin to bring about this radical democratic ethos? What are the main obstacles to this? Is it sufficient to rely upon intellectualist–cognitivist strategies of persuasion?' (Glynos 2001c: 14). These are questions that require urgent attention. If something is clear, it is that, at least from a psychoanalytic point of view, persuasion and cognitive transformation are neither enough to shake ethical and political identifications nor capable of channeling resistance in a progressive democratic direction. As I have stressed throughout this book, what underlies such identifications, what helps to explain 'voluntary servitude' and accounts for the inability to transform local/temporary delegitimation into a sustained questioning and rearticulation of relations of authority, is a particular – often unconscious – relation to affect and enjoyment. In Europe, millions of people rallied against the war in Iraq, but did this lead to an erosion of the post-democratic consensus? The 'Nos' in the French and Dutch referenda could also be interpreted as a 'No' against the post-democratic climate of an unlimited consensus: they do not therefore say 'No' to Europe, they say 'No to the unquestionable Yes' (Baudrillard 2005: 24). For what the French and Dutch (and other European) peoples were asked was not merely to endorse the European constitutional treaty but to continue saying 'Yes to Yes'. From this point of view, however – and within a political framework that functions only 'from the authorities down, by means of a booby-trapped consultation and the circular game of questions and answers, where the question only answers Yes to itself' – the real puzzle is not how the 'No' outcome emerged but, on the contrary, why there has not been an even bigger and more sustainable 'reaction against this mindless yes-ism' (p. 25).[14]

One should be clear about this: a passionate endorsement of radical democracy would require the cultivation and hegemony of a different type of ethical relation to negativity and enjoyment (to what Lacan calls 'another *jouissance*'), an ethos beyond the politics of fantasy (in either of its forms: revolutionary, even fundamentalist, utopia or consumerist post-democracy). This relation cannot be a simple relation *with* negativity *and with* enjoyment; it also has to be a relation *between* negativity and enjoyment: an alternative relation to negativity will only be attractive if it manages to offer access to some enjoyment. What is needed, in other words, is *an enjoyable democratic ethics of the political*. And nobody should be surprised here by the weaving of enjoyment into the fabric of ethics. Jane Bennett is not mistaken when she singles out 'en-joying' the world as one of the tasks of ethics (Bennett 2001: 13). And this is absolutely crucial to the question of motivation which I am discussing here. An ethical stance – including radical democratic ethics – can be applied, enacted and institutionalised only when it manages to mobilise affective energy, when it entails a mode of enjoyment: 'to be transformed into acts, affects must be engaged, orchestrated, and libidinally bound to it [sc. to an ethical orientation]' (p. 131).

Let us first explore the issue of a distinct democratic negotiation of negativity. We know from the history of ancient Greek democracy that to accept and institutionalise division and antagonism, to keep open the prospects of permanent renewal, is not impossible. The polis undoubtedly knew that division and antagonism are central and have to be safeguarded and sustained. How else can one interpret Solon's famous law, discussed in Aristotle's *Constitution of Athens*:

> Solon realized that the city was often split by factional disputes but some citizens were content because of idleness to accept whatever the outcome might be; he therefore produced a specific law against them, laying down that anyone who did not choose one side or the other in such a dispute should lose his citizen's rights. (cited in Wolin 1994: 40)

Hence any citizen who will not take sides becomes *atimos* and is stripped of his political rights (Castoriadis 1991b: 107). It would be very difficult to find a more clear indication of the central idea at the core of democracy: 'democratic stability can be achieved through dynamic tensions. Indeed, in Athens, the never-resolved tensions between aristocratic values and demotic ideology, and between apparently contradictory but deeply held political values . . . lay at the heart of the democratic system' (Ober 1996: 31). Most importantly, these tensions are not only external to the demos; they are also internal: the demos is internally divided, it can make mistakes and has to be able to correct itself. A mechanism designed to allow exactly that can be discerned in what the ancient Athenians called *graphe paranomon* (indictment for unconstitutional proposal). Castoriadis describes this paradoxical procedure as follows: 'You have made a proposal to the *ecclesia*, and this proposal has been voted for. Then another citizen can bring you before a court, accusing you of inducing the people to vote for an unlawful law'. The judgement is formulated by a popular court in which hundreds of citizens drawn by lot participate. 'Thus, the demos was appealing against itself in front of itself: the appeal was from the whole body of citizens . . . to a huge random sample of the same body sitting after the passions had calmed, listening again to contradictory arguments, and assessing the matter from a relative distance'. In other words, 'the people say what the law is; the people can err; the people can correct themselves. This is a magnificent example of an effective institution of self-limitation' (Castoriadis 1991b: 117).[15]

Every citizen had to invest in these dynamic tensions and participate in democratic institutions. At the same time, the ancient Athenians knew that investment is never automatic and cannot rely exclusively on institutional principles, symbolic and imaginary ideals. No doubt, the encouragement of partisanship was also a means to stimulate the passions. In addition, in order to encourage democratic participation, the polis introduced an ingenious *reward structure*. Even in stringent financial circumstances, payment-for-participation was promoted (Ober 1996: 29). In fact, salary and lot were the two fundamental novelties of Athenian democracy (Vidal-Naquet 2002: 246), providing both a reward structure and an opportunity structure favourable to democratic participation. No wonder then that, as ancient sources reveal, the Athenians were willing to submit themselves to pain for the sake of Athens to the point of 'even enjoy[ing] it in an almost perverse equation of hardship and duty with pleasure' (Raaflaub 1994: 109).

Nevertheless, on the other hand, the unity of the polis had to be protected against extreme forms of political struggle. This principle explains, according to Castoriadis, the practice of *ostracism*: 'In Athens political division and antagonism should not be allowed to tear the community apart; one of the two opposing leaders must go into temporary exile' (Castoriadis 1991b: 112). Likewise, the polis could only come to terms with the risks involved in the antagonism it had itself sanctioned through a paradoxical inclusive exclusion of *stasis* or civil war. If the inscription of antagonism and lack is not impossible, even if it can be cultivated, enjoyed as well as endured, this does not mean that all that is easy. On the contrary, it requires a very delicate equilibrium. None has captured this paradoxical dialectics so vividly as Nicole Loraux in her *tour de force*, *La cité divisée* (Loraux 2001). She focuses her eloquent argumentation on the element of division and antagonism, the founding moment of the polis. Especially following the transition from the archaic to the classical period, the polis cannot reconcile itself with the ever-present possibility of civil war, *stasis*, implicit in division. Division and political antagonism are known to be always present but, at the same time, are stigmatised as disease, as a danger for the polis (Vidal-Naquet 2002: 271). While, on the one hand, division is acknowledged and politically instituted, the risks entailed in it lead to its disavowal,[16] through a variety of complex socio-political procedures. The polis can institute itself as a stable order only on the basis of regulating memory and forgetting its violent, antagonistic origins. However – and this is absolutely crucial – the rituals of forgetting never stop recalling to memory their disavowed origin: division. Thus, they remain essentially compatible with the democratic institutionalisation of lack and antagonism. This is, then, what constitutes the paradox at the basis of Athenian democracy; the ancient Greek way of exorcising the 'regression' of democratic agonism to raw antagonism.

A series of highly complex negotiations of conflict and unity, (political) disorder and (natural) order are employed to serve a desire for permanent reconciliation. But they ultimately fail to mask the fact that division is always the other side of unity; that the One can barely conceal the Two. This failure is even incarnated in the signifier at stake, *stasis*, which is etymologically associated with stability, continuity, calmness, but – at the same time – comes to denote revolt, revolution and civil war (Loraux 2001: 120). Only the first in a long series of ambiguous signifiers – *dialysis* is another one, meaning both destruction and reconciliation – *stasis* points to the founding aspect of division. The regulation of memory, even the prohibition of memory (of the memory of *stasis* and of division as founding moments), no matter how sophisticated, is only allowed to exclude and exorcise *stasis* and division by including them. This is, for example, the case when the Athenians ban one day from their calendar, the day commemorating the conflict between Athena and Poseidon that marks the foundation of the city (p. 241). To exclude, to prohibit any memory of this conflict – the archetype of all *stasis* – is envisaged as the best protection of the polis from extreme forms of division. But this is a mechanism with a variety of ambiguous consequences, indicative of the democratic politics of memory in the polis. What is supposed to be forgotten is marked, in the process of forgetting itself, through the visible absence of one day from the calendar: 'this repeated exclusion acquires the place of the most paradoxical reminder' (p. 266).

The predicament of modern democracy and the challenge of its radical refashioning is not that different. Today, antagonism and negativity seem hard to accept and their institutionalisation and sublimation unlikely to inspire and stimulate a new passionate attachment of a post-fantasmatic kind. The post-democratic trend and its interaction with anti-democratic identity claims (fundamentalist, nationalist, racist, and so on) create an explosive blend that threatens the radical kernel of democracy much more than its paradoxical negotiation in the ancient Greek politics of memory, which, at any rate, permitted an indirect but clearly visible registering of negativity and never threatened democratic institutions. In the past democracy has lost many battles with nationalism, racism and fundamentalism. It is now losing the war with consumerist post-democracy, since even 'the relatively open and undemanding goals of liberal democracy for public life have failed to compete with consumerism' (Cross 2000: 9). In general, the viability of democracy as a political/hegemonic project relies on its ability to compete with post-democratic and anti-democratic projects, projects that effectively manipulate affect and enjoyment, repress event-ness and antagonism, and displace negativity. By comparison, democratic citizenship seems to presuppose an 'emotional distance', a 'certain coldness' (Marquand 2004: 80–1). As for the radical democratic 'institutionalisation of lack', it looks like a rather pessimistic, negative attitude, 'unable to propose forms of popular democracy in place of the illusionary forms it criticises' (Simons 2005: 155). Such a view also underlies Ewa Ziarek's critique of the disincorporation and disembodiment implicit in the democratic visions of Lefort, Laclau and Mouffe (Ziarek 2001).

Radical democratic theorists themselves are not unaware of this problem. As Chantal Mouffe has recently conceded:

> People really need to be enthusiastic about political struggle, while at the same time being aware that there is no final goal – democracy is a process towards which we are continually working. So we are clearly facing a difficulty in terms of the way passion can be mobilised, in terms of an acceptance of the contingent nature of our struggle. (Mouffe in Laclau and Mouffe 2003: 74)

Lefort has also noted the alienating dimensions of democracy, the dangers inherent in the desacralisation of politics entailed in democratic emptiness. The results are obvious:

> [T]he democratic public sphere is continually vulnerable to the reinsertion of the private, or the resacralization of politics. The denial of emotion

embodied in democracy's refusal to incorporate the sacred into its institutions is the subterranean fault line that threatens to derail democratic ideals . . . The alienating effects of democracy create the void that anti-liberalism attempts to fill when it rejects the liberal separation of public and private and, ultimately, the democratic state. (Berezin 2001: 88)

What makes things even more difficult is the fact that, for democracy to create strong bonds of attachment, an awareness of the lack in the Other, of social division, needs to be coupled with an awareness of the lack in the subject, it has to be inscribed within political subjectivity. As Laclau has very recently put it, 'it is necessary to transfer the notion of emptiness from the place of power in a democratic regime – as proposed by Lefort – to the very subjects occupying that place'. We need to pass from the formal aspects of democracy to a consideration of a 'community's whole political way of life' (Laclau 2005: 169). Democratic creation needs to restore to society both its *vis formandi* and its *libido formandi* (Castoriadis 1997b: 343). Emptiness here has to be a 'political construction' (Laclau 2005: 170) passionately embodied in our own political identity. *Once more, the democratic citizen needs to be re-conceptualised not only as enduring but as enjoying social lack and emptiness.*

Matching the challenge: the Lacanian orientation

This is obviously a very complex problem and there are no easy solutions available. One option would be simply to accept that politics requires a suspension – a 'bracketing', if you will – of our awareness of contingency, of lack and division; to accept, in other words, that we can only be radical democrats in theory but not in practice. The Lacanian orientation cannot, however, endorse such a disavowal. But are there any other options available? Can we make lack stick? And how? Can the institutionalisation of lack contribute to the creation of a sustainable 'high-energy' (Unger 2005) or 'high-intensity' democracy (Santos 2005a)? Or does it contradict such aims? It is impossible, within the limits of this chapter, fully to illuminate this issue. I can, nevertheless, telegraphically highlight two important aspects that a psychoanalytic approach can offer in order at least to clarify what is at stake in it. There are two separate but related questions that need to be addressed here. The first concerns the conditions that would permit us to move beyond the lure of closure and identity, inscribe lack and event-ness, un-stick desire and enjoyment. Here, from a Freudian and a Lacanian point of view, it is a (thoroughly productive) process of *mourning* which is called for and an ability to mourn that has to be cultivated – a lesson particularly important for the Left. The second question is one related to the affective value of a radical democratic identification with lack. Here, Lacan's sketching of another *jouissance* may be of some help.

PRODUCTIVE MOURNING

With regard to the first question, Marshall Alcorn has very cogently shown how mourning – a process that in Freud is not only applicable in relation to a beloved person but also in relation to 'some abstraction' like 'one's country, liberty, an ideal, and so on' (Freud 1991d: 252) – constitutes the major precondition in shifting attachments, especially when these are invested with a symptomatic *jouissance*, an affective energy that makes them difficult to abandon or displace (Alcorn 2002: 2). As has been shown throughout this book, knowledge and 'rational' argumentation cannot easily displace such symptomatic formations (p. 37): 'the giving up of libidinal attachments [which show great durability] is always a form of mourning' (p. 27). Indeed, as Freud has indicated, in order to form new relations and attachments we need to go through such a process: to become possible, change requires a dis-investment in the form of experiencing and working through loss (p. 110). It does not depend on an instant permutation in relationships of signifiers. It requires slow changes in the libidinal/affective layer of identifications (p. 112).

It may sound initially rather surprising, but this is the case not only when we deal with identifications that are still, at some level, hegemonic – such as nationalism or consumerism – but also when we are dealing with dislocated identities. In fact, if Laclau is correct and all identities are always already dislocated, then what distinguishes the two cases is their success or failure in masking this ontological dislocation, the mark of negativity, the inherent division lying beneath their shining – or decomposing – veneer; their success or failure in offering compensations for their inherent lack (of total enjoyment) through fantasy and partial *jouissance*. Even in cases where the object of identification is lost, no new identification emerges automatically due to a melancholic '*immobilizing attachment* to injury' associated with 'feelings of hatred toward the self, the object of loss as well as the external obstacles held responsible for the loss' (Ozselçuk 2006: 227). In such cases resentful hatred may crystallise in symptomatic formations offering a compensatory *jouissance* to subjects who are then unable to move on to new identifications as they become libidinally attached to the vilified causes of their own defeat. Byrne and Healy discuss three paradigmatic cases (ideal types) from the economic field which exhibit such a structure. In the anti-capitalist's case, it is capitalism that obstructs the way to a 'Utopic true economy'; for those investing in the idea of a 'sustainable economy', what does not permit the reconciliation between human community and the environment is short-term gain; for the neo-liberal subject, what denies its Utopian vision is government regulation. In all three cases these subjects libidinally rely on their obstacles. In a truly Freudian fashion, Byrne and Healy observe that 'these individuals get a certain degree of pleasure or enjoyment out of the frustration of their fantasies' (Byrne and Healy 2006: 244). Yet melancholically sticking to these obstacles does preclude the exploration of other possibilities, the emergence of the new (p. 245): 'Whereas mourning frees the subject to move on, melancholia is stuck and isolated, looking backward rather than to the future, looking inward rather than seeking new alliances and connections' (Gibson–Graham 2006: 5). Change does presuppose the ability to un-stick such 'masochistic' identifications. *Something has to be lost/sacrificed even if it is only our (iron or golden) chains.*[17]

This is primarily the problem with disillusioned leftists who, unable to mourn 'proletarian revolution' and 'utopia', opt for a nostalgic return to the old – defeated and dangerous – politics of reoccupation. In fact, a substantial part of the Left has never managed to distance itself sufficiently from a particular version of political imagination, utopian revolutionary imagination. To put it in Freudian terms, for some, the process of mourning has not even started; or, rather, it has been interrupted and the object of mourning has been displaced to 'democracy' itself. Hence, it has become more fashionable to mourn democracy than utopian imagination. But if democracy has been discredited by its post-democratic use, is the situation any better with leftist utopianism, with the dream of a revolutionary radical re-foundation of the social? Are not the risks involved in the politics of reoccupation, in 'speculative leftism', substantially higher than those involved in the radicalisation of democracy? Are not the supposed benefits of an illusory and ambiguous nature? It seems that the politics of nostalgia presuppose a very selective memory. In the case of Žižek, as Laclau has observed, 'despite his professed Marxism, [Žižek] pays no attention whatsoever to the intellectual history of Marxism, in which several of the categories he uses have been refined, displaced, or – to encapsulate it in one term – deconstructed' (Laclau in Butler et al. 2000: 204). However, this is not only a question of memory or intellectual awareness and reflexivity. At issue is, above all else, a melancholic fixation that interrupts mourning and obstructs political reorientation.

In fact, these two moments (mourning and reorientation) are inextricably linked. A true process of mourning has important repercussions for the new identification it facilitates. In this sense, the identification at stake here is not just any type of identification; it resembles what in the Lacanian clinic is described as 'identification with the symptom'.[18] Simply put, it makes it possible to inscribe lack within the formation of the new. Drawing on Eric Santner's work, Ozselçuk highlights the fact that mourning should not be seen as entailing a complete forgetting of the loss. This is what distinguishes it from a nostalgic disavowal *à la* Žižek (Chapter 3). On the contrary, mourning articulates loss in a productive way: '*mourning* includes in its very definition an acceptance of its own practice, the practice of *mourning*, as the interminable dimension of human lives and the concomitant affirmation that the subject is ultimately a subject of loss' (Ozselçuk 2006: 230). According to this schema, inability to mourn forecloses transformation and fuels *ressentiment*. To be able to mourn, on the other hand,

> involves the flexibility and the desire to make such [new] concrete investments and the acceptance of the fact that any identification would never be complete. And in this sense, mourning is truly a process of resubjectivation, if, by becoming a subject, we refer here to nothing but the necessity of a movement and desire (or rather the drive) for change without any guarantees or predetermined ideals. (Ozselçuk 2006: 231)

DEMOCRATIC *JOUISSANCE*

Now, let's assume that a process of mourning makes possible a new identification and that this new identification is of a 'radical democratic' type, that it embodies a registering of negativity and lack. Yet, can such an identification be passionately endorsed? Can it really *attract*? As I have already pointed out, the problem revolves around the prospects of enjoying lack and emptiness. In his *Iraq* book, Slavoj Žižek has summarised what is at issue here with reference to Jacques-Alain Miller's formulation of democracy, which is quite close to a radical democratic position. For him, 'Democracy is Lacan's big S of the barred A, which says: I am the signifier of the fact that the Other has a hole in it, or that it doesn't exist' (Miller in Žižek 2004a: 110).[19] But Žižek also uses Miller in order to point to something that radical democrats allegedly 'do not see', namely that the subject of radical democracy, Lacan's barred subject, 'is as such foreign to – incompatible with – enjoyment' (Žižek 2004a: 111), and presumably unable to sustain its (radical) democratic identification. At this point, he cites Miller at some length:

> what we know is that, in actual fact, the more democracy is empty, the more it is a desert of enjoyment, and correlatively, the more enjoyment condenses itself in certain elements . . . The more the signifier is 'disaffected', as others have put it, the more the signifier is purified . . . the more passion builds up, the more hatred intensifies, fundamentalisms proliferate, destruction spreads, massacres without precedents are carried out, and unheard-of catastrophes occur. (Miller in Žižek 2004a: 112)

Not only then is (radical) democratic subjectivity untenable in itself but, incarnating emptiness in a purely formal way, it performs a *repression* that triggers a displacement of *jouissance*. As a result, affect can only be discharged through a multitude of 'pathological' outlets. In other words, what emerges is a vicious circle similar to the one outlined in the analysis of the ultimate failure/weakness of European identification and the (obscene) return of the repressed in anti-European discourse (Chapter 6), as well as in the post-democratic displacement of dissent examined in this chapter.

From Žižek's point of view, then, radical democracy seems to suffer from the same limitations that deliberative democracy faces: 'accounts of deliberative democracy, like most mainstream political theory, lack an account of affectivity' (Hoggett and Thompson 2002: 109). In the case of deliberative democracy, of course, this is due to excessive rationalism: 'whether the emotions are ignored or, if they are mentioned, it is only as dangerously destabilizing forces that need to be kept in check'. As a result of a restriction of deliberation to rational/reasonable argument – to be found in Habermas, Elster, and others – what is privileged is a model of dispassionate, disembodied speech premised on an identification of objectivity with calm and the absence of emotional/affective expression (pp. 109–10). The conclusion flows almost naturally: 'this sort of political theory is too abstract and rationalistic to be of practical use' (p. 107).[20] Hence, the astonishing implication of Žižek's critique of radical democracy's incompatibility with *jouissance* is that radical democracy becomes almost indistinguishable from deliberative democracy! Moreover, in terms of its consequences, it seems to flirt dangerously with aspects of post-democracy! In the first part of this text I have myself criticised Laclau's (and Mouffe's) earlier work as not taking sufficiently into account the problematic of affect and *jouissance*. But this is not the case with the way radical democracy has been formulated in their project – and especially in Mouffe's work during the last ten years. First of all, Chantal Mouffe has been the most vociferous critic of deliberative democracy on exactly this point: its excessive rationalism, which neglects the role of passions in the construction of political identity (Mouffe 2000). Furthermore, Mouffe has insisted on the importance of re-introducing the dimension of popular sovereignty, equality and antagonism into our gradually de-democratised democracies and we should not forget that in opposition to liberalism – the other pillar of liberal democracy, which relegates emotion to the private sphere (Berezin 2001: 87) – it is the democratic tradition associated with the struggles for equality that has historically exhibited a potential for arousing political passions and for enabling the construction of deep democratic identifications.

Pace Žižek, democratic lack can acquire a non-essentialist positive existence and an affective value able to attract and move. Indeed, 'we need not suppose that appeal to emotion belongs to those who strive in the direction of fascism [and other reactionary ideologies], while democratic propaganda [and ethics] must limit itself to reason and restraint' (Adorno et al. 1982: 480). Ironically, we can trace back to Žižek himself a very vivid illustration of how democratic lack and emptiness can unite and passionately inspire. His Romanian example can be found in his *Tarrying with the Negative*, but Oliver Marchart has connected it directly to the problematic of (radical) democracy:

> Within the framework of democratic politics what we identify with is precisely *the lack in the Other* . . . Žižek illustrates this point with a nice interpretation of the pictures that circulated in the media following Ceausescu's fall. What some of these pictures showed was the Romanian flag with a huge hole in the centre . . . the red star, the former ideological symbol . . . had been cut out by the insurgents. What was left was precisely a representation of the unrepresentable lack in the Other . . . Democracy then is nothing else than the – impossible, but necessary – attempt to institutionalize lack. (Marchart 2005: 24)

Far from being antithetical to *jouissance*, democratic subjectivity is capable of inspiring high passions. However, one needs to be aware of the fact that these passions are of a distinct type, which is necessary if we want to avoid, or at least minimise, the excesses of antagonism and the supposedly unconditional act, to sublimate hatred and deflate fantasy agonistically. They mobilise a *jouissance* beyond accumulation, domination and fantasy, an enjoyment of the not-all or not-whole. This is clearly the Lacanian orientation. Lacan directly connects the signifier of the lack in the Other – the radical, non-foundational foundation of democracy – with another (feminine) *jouissance*, situated on 'the side of the not-whole' (XX: 76, 84). While both prohibition and commanded enjoyment – in their very different ways – remain attached to the fantasy of complete enjoyment (McGowan 2004: 196), with all the socio-political side-effects discussed throughout this book, this alternative mode of *jouissance* traverses the fantasy and encircles its own partiality: 'partial enjoyment involves enjoying one's lack – what one doesn't have, not what one does have' (p. 195). It is only thus that it can ethically relate to the other: 'to embrace the partiality of one's own enjoyment is at the same time to embrace the enjoyment of the other' (ibid.). To move beyond prohibition/sacrifice and commanded enjoyment, we only need to combine them in the most unpredictable way: *we need to sacrifice the command*. Only by sacrificing our libidinal, fantasmatic/symptomatic attachment to symbolic authority (Chapter 4) can we really enjoy the signifier of the lack in the Other. Only the sacrifice of the fantasmatic *objet petit a* can make this other *jouissance* attainable (Fink 2004: 161).

In *Lacan and the Political* I have discussed identification with the symptom and sublimation as two of the Lacanian theoretical and conceptual innovations able to offer some guidance on this tricky terrain.[21] *Suppléance* is another way to think of enjoyment and the production of a signifier of lack in a democratic perspective: '*Suppléance* names a term that substitutes itself not (as in the case with other tropes) for another, but for an absence' (Copjec 2005: 123). It indicates the production of a supplemental (excessive) element, which takes place at the symbolic level without covering over the lack around which this level is structured. Thus the social bond is formulated in a way beyond repression (p. 126): '*suppléance* allows us to speak well of our desire not by *translating* jouissance into language, but by *formalizing* it in a signifier that does not mean but is, rather, directly enjoyed. This operation supplements the absence in language of a signifier that could translate jouissance with a signifier that marks this absence' (p. 127). Although Lacan's comments invite – as always – interpretation, it seems that *suppléance* involves the production of something beyond fantasy, something positive and enjoyable, that makes up for a lack, an impossibility, without reducing negativity, without functioning as an *objet petit a* (XX: 63). Fantasmatic desire substitutes 'object *a* in fantasy' for the signifier of the lack in the Other (E2006: 697); *suppléance* follows the opposite direction. The central task in psychoanalysis – and politics – is to detach the *objet petit a* from the signifier of the lack in the Other (XX: 83), to detach (anti-democratic and post-democratic) fantasy from the democratic institutionalisation of lack, making possible the access to a partial enjoyment beyond fantasy.

Judging on the basis of historical – or rather pre-historical – experience, we have to accept that such an alternative structuration of desire and a different ethical relation to *jouissance* are both possible. We know that the dialectics between lack and desire dates at least back to Plato's *Symposium*, we know that the dialectics between lack and the Law was known to Saint Paul, but we also know that earlier forms of society did not desire and enjoy in the same way with us. Here Marshal Sahlins' economic anthropology is quite revealing. Sahlins attacks the widespread idea that paleolithic communities, so called 'subsistence economies', were surviving on the verge of starvation and wretchedness. In a somewhat playful manner, he argues that these cultures have followed 'a Zen road to affluence' (Sahlins 1972: 2): by desiring little they have managed 'to enjoy an unparalleled material plenty – with a low standard of living' (ibid.). 'Want not, lack not' is the motto of what Sahlins calls 'the original affluent society' (p. 11). Drawing on a vast array of ethnological and anthropological material he draws a picture of hunter–gatherer societies as societies in which people 'work less than we do; and, rather than a continuous travail, the food quest is intermittent, leisure abundant, and there is a greater amount of sleep in the daytime per capita per year than in any other condition of society' (p. 14) – this is a society before the 'shrine to the Unattainable', of '*Infinite Needs*', was erected (p. 39). It is not necessary to idealise these societies, as the Freudian Left and others have done (Marcuse 1966: 151). These are societies deeply marked by the political, societies in which violence and war, on the one hand, and exchange, on the other, become the two aspects of a dynamic equilibrium (Clastres 1994: 45). Difference is also present, especially sexual difference. What is missing is the desire for accumulation (p. 38). There is no desire for, and production of, surplus to introduce inequality, exploitation, division (p. 39). These societies do not allow work, production, and consumption to devour them (Clastres 1974). Enjoyment seems to be had without the mediation of fantasies of accumulation, fullness and excess. Obviously, these societies do not constitute a lost Golden Age. They cannot function as a model or a blueprint. Yet they do show that another world may, in principle, be possible insofar as a detachment of (partial) enjoyment from dreams of completeness and fantasmatic desire is enacted. And although stone-age economics offers an example of dramatic proportions – but also of dramatic distance from contemporary societies – one does not need to escape late modernity in order to encounter enactments of such an orientation. Doesn't something similar happen in the psychoanalytic clinic? In traversing the fantasy, in identification with the symptom, even in *suppléance*? And isn't this also the challenge for radical democratic ethics?

But surely all that is pure philosophical, psychoanalytic and anthropological speculation. Well, not entirely. A variety of political theorists and analysts, economists, and active citizens – some of them directly inspired by Lacanian theory – are currently trying to put this radical democratic orientation to work in a multitude of empirical contexts. Ozselçuk and Madra, for example, attempt to reformulate a progressive agenda without recourse to utopianism as a fantasmatic support, and thus they extend the logic of the institutionalisation of lack to the economic field, something that was missing from theories of radical democracy (Ozselçuk and Madra 2005). In doing so they also utilise the Lacanian idea of a feminine 'non-all' that may 'enable us to move beyond the capitalist present and its masculine logic of "all"' (Ozselçuk and Madra 2005: 87).[22] Byrne and Healy start from a similar premise, that it is possible to institutionalise lack beyond fantasy in the economy (Byrne and Healy 2006: 243). A group of cooperative workers they have examined tried to restructure their enjoyment in a non-fantasmatic way, without recourse to the melancholic, fantasmatic and symptomatic fixation characteristic of the three modes of subjectivity discussed earlier in this chapter. In the co-operative firms, the communal production of goods and services destabilises the strict dichotomies between market and non-market exchange, paid and unpaid labour, capitalist and non-capitalist organisation in a way that acknowledges 'the overdetermined nature of the communal economic site'. Drawing on examples from Argentina and the United States, Byrne and Healy conclude that 'in the course of circling around the lack at the heart of the social and the economic, and engaging in the contingent processes of producing, appropriating, and distributing surplus, workers in cooperatives become ethical subjects, confronting their own relationship to the lack' (Byrne and Healy

2006: 254). One may be able to discern elements of the same logic in a variety of concrete proposals and arrangements recently put forward in order to re-democratise the economy, from the democratisation of Pension Funds (Blackburn 2002) and the passage from a family to a social inheritance system (Unger 2005: 80) to the introduction of a minimum citizenship income and experimentation – which is now widespread in Brasil and elsewhere – with projects of participatory budgeting and all the dynamic tensions inscribed in them (Santos 2005b: 357).

In any case, the difficulties which a radicalisation of democracy faces today are not due to lack of ideas and proposals. It is not an epistemic deficit which is the problem; it is rather an affective deficit. Libidinal investment and the mobilisation of *jouissance* are the necessary prerequisite for any sustainable identification (from nationalism to consumerism). This also applies to the radical democratic ethics of the political. But the *type of investment* involved has still to be decided. Emptiness and lack can indeed acquire a positive/institutional expression and can be enjoyed. Instead of functioning as a support for fantasy (for hegemonic fantasies), the partial drive can become the leading force towards a reorientation of enjoyment faithful to the positive/negative dialectics. Only thus shall we be able to really enjoy our partial enjoyment, without subordinating it to the cataclysmic desire of fantasy. Beyond its dialectics of disavowal, this is the concrete challenge the Lacanian Left addresses to us. In order to reorient and restructure the dialectics of enjoyment which is always implicated in the construction and reproduction of social and political identities and in sustaining relations of power and to power, each one of us will have to assume responsibility and respond to this challenge in one's own, unique way.

Notes

1. See Stavrakakis 1999a, especially chs 4 and 5. Although radical democratic arguments can and have been developed in a variety of different if inter-connected ways (Trend 1996; Tonder and Thomassen 2005), here I am mainly referring to the radical democratic project as formulated by Chantal Mouffe and Ernesto Laclau (Laclau and Mouffe 1985; Mouffe 2000; Mouffe 2005).
2. See Colin Crouch's *Post-Democracy* (Crouch 2004) for a detailed list of the symptoms of this post-democratic trend. Also see Marquand 2004.

3. I am using these Husserlian concepts in the politicised way introduced by Ernesto Laclau (Laclau 1990: 34–5).
4. I am rephrasing here a formulation by John Rajchman (1991: 113).
5. The concept of 'reoccupation' is used here in the sense introduced by Hans Blumenberg. See Blumenberg 1983.
6. I do not claim, of course, that this is the only possible way of construing the nuances of political modernity. Indeed, it would be possible to complexify this broad typology in a variety of directions. In any case, the ordering of the three directions presented here is logical and not chronological.
7. Before starting to flirt with utopia himself, Žižek had described utopia in the following manner: ' "utopian" conveys a belief in the possibility of a *universality without its symptom*, without the point of exception functioning as its internal negation' (Žižek 1989: 23).
8. In his *Parallax View* Žižek goes so far as to argue that 'the true function of the explicit limitation is thus to sustain the illusion that, through transgressing it, we can attain the limitless' (Žižek 2006: 296).
9. In ch. 4 of Stavrakakis 1999a, I am elaborating both a historical and a psychoanalytic grounding of this take on modern utopianism.
10. On the importance of the democratic revolution, also see Laclau and Mouffe 1985: 152–9.
11. The distance from a society of prohibition is also shown by the way loss of life 'on our part' – *sacrifice* – is not tolerated any more in the conduct of war. Military operations need to be concluded without casualties.
12. What the old argument, according to which consumption can be perceived 'as a preferable, peaceful alternative to violent clashes' (Bocock 1993: 112), does miss is precisely the fact that the clash of civilisations is a clash between modes of *jouissance*. And, as we have seen, our mode of *jouissance* is currently conditioned by consumerism and advertising.
13. As is the case with statements such as the following: 'as one of the main alternatives to the production of a sense of identity and purpose, being derived from ethnic, racial or national group membership, frequently linked with acts of violence . . . consumerism may well be judged to be preferable' (Bocock 1993: 111).
14. Nevertheless, there is no doubt that, much more than any other European country, France has witnessed a variety of popular mobilisations showing the limits of this consensus in many different fields (education, employment, etc.).
15. Wolin is correct when he points out that institutionalisation brings with it many well-known problems, including routinisation, professionalisation, ritualisation; it produces internal hierarchies and restricts experience (Wolin 1994: 36). On the other hand, one must also be aware of the opposite danger: 'A cold demobilized politics cannot serve as a means to reorganise society. A hot, mobilized politics is compatible with

democracy only when institutions channel its energies' (Unger 2005: 78–9). In order to avoid or at least limit these dangers democracy needs to experiment with anti-institutional institutions: 'institutions that subvert institutionalization' (Wolin 1994: 43). It is obvious that the ancient Athenians were masters at this craft, and there is still a lot to learn from them.
16. Loraux explicitly refers to psychoanalytic theory and psychoanalytic concepts such as 'disavowal' throughout her work.
17. Bill Mullen has very well expressed this paradox when he observed that 'the first step towards working-class emancipation is the recognition by workers that they must lose, not gain their "identity" and identification with capitalism, nationalism, imperialism, and other capitalist processes' (Mullen in Ozselçuk 2006: 228).
18. See Stavrakakis 1999a: 133–4.
19. From this Lacanian perspective, majority rule, the rule of the many – the starting point of democratic sovereignty – is not understood as premised on the idea that 'the people know better'. Not only is this a dry/cognitive conception of popular will that ignores that at stake here is not knowledge but the truth of desire, but such knowledge can be the result of manipulation, especially in today's spin-doctored 'propaganda-managed democracy'. Simply put, the central idea here is that 'no-one knows better' and this has to be accepted and taken into account every moment. In this democratic vision people do care about truth but know that – as argued in the introduction – it is mostly revealed when our knowledge is proven inadequate to master it.
20. Hoggett and Thompson try to remedy this imbalance by drawing on the psychoanalytic tradition, especially Melanie Klein's work, in articulating a view of cognition and affect as 'separate but interpenetrating dimensions of human experience' (Hoggett and Thompson 2002: 111–12). They devote most of their article to an attempt to inject the emotional potential into a new vision of democratic deliberation, trying, at the same time, to limit – to *contain* – the destructive potential of emotions: 'If sufficient thought is given to the emotional cultures of groups and the dynamics of inter-group encounters, then spaces can be created where politics can take account of people's feelings, and conflict can be contained but not suppressed. In such spaces people can argue, fight, laugh, and sometimes even agree in the knowledge that the situation is safe enough for relationships to endure while feelings are expressed' (p. 121). Although extremely refreshing and sharing some insights with Mouffe's version of agonism, this approach runs the risk of reducing political theory to therapeutic control. Addressing their argument to adherents of deliberative democracy, Hoggett and Thompson also fail to escape assigning to 'rationality' a supreme political value.
21. See, in this respect, Stavrakakis 1999a: 131–40.

22. This provides the best answer to feminist critics of Lacan who accuse him of allowing only one trope of desire, the male–patriarchal economy of one, forcing women 'to inhabit the tongueless zone of the imaginary' (McClintock 1995: 192). Even if we accept that the phallus is an 'impostor', 'does Lacan offer an escape route from the domain of the false monarch?' asks McClintock. And her answer is that 'no alternative is ever given; indeed the possibility of an alternative is explicitly denied. Lacan's politics, in the final analysis, is profoundly conservative and pessimistic' (p. 200). But is not feminine *jouissance*, the enjoyment of the not-whole, precisely such an alternative?

Bibliography

Adorno, Theodor (1973), *Negative Dialectics*, trans. E. B. Ashton, London: Routledge.
Adorno, Theodor and Max Horkheimer [1944] (1997), *Dialectic of Enlightenment*, trans. John Cumming, London: Verso.
Adorno, Theodor, Else Frenkel-Brunswik, Daniel Levinson and R. Nevitt Sanford [1950] (1982), *The Authoritarian Personality*, abridged edn, New York: Norton.
Ahmed, Sara (2004), *The Cultural Politics of Emotion*, Edinburgh: Edinburgh University Press.
Alcorn, Marshall (1996), 'Talking with Jesse Helms: The relation of drives to discourse', *Journal for the Psychoanalysis of Culture and Society*, 1:1, pp. 81–9.
Alcorn, Marshall (2002), *Changing the Subject in English Class*, Carbondale: Southern Illinois University Press.
Althusser, Louis [1964] (1999), 'Freud and Lacan', in *Writings on Psychoanalysis: Freud and Lacan*, trans. Jeffrey Mehlman, New York: Columbia University Press.
Andersen, Robin (1995), *Consumer Culture and TV Programming*, Boulder: Westview Press.
Anderson, Benedict (1991), *Imagined Communities*, London: Verso.
Aronowitz, Stanley and Peter Bratsis (2005), 'Situations manifesto', *Situations*, 1:1, pp. 7–14.
Ascherson, Neal (2004), 'Victory in defeat', *London Review of Books*, 2 December, pp. 3–6.
Badiou, Alain (1998), 'Politics and philosophy', interview with Peter Hallward, *Angelaki*, 3:3, pp. 113–33.
Badiou, Alain (1999), *Manifesto for Philosophy*, trans. Norman Madarasz, Albany: SUNY Press.
Badiou, Alain (2001), *Ethics: An Essay on the Understanding of Evil*, trans. Peter Hallward, London: Verso.
Badiou, Alain (2003a), *Saint Paul, The Foundation of Universalism*, trans. Ray Brassier, Stanford: Stanford University Press.
Badiou, Alain (2003b), *Infinite Thought: Truth and the Return to Philosophy*, trans. and ed. Oliver Feltham and Justin Clemens, London: Continuum.

Badiou, Alain (2003c), Interview with Tim Appleton, Joel Madore and David Payne, unpublished transcript, recorded 10 September at the University of Essex.
Badiou, Alain (2005), *Being and Event*, trans. Oliver Feltham, London: Continuum.
Ballard, J.G. (2004), *Millennium People*, London: Harper Perennial.
Banchoff, Thomas and Mitchell Smith (1999), 'Introduction', in Thomas Banchoff and Mitchell Smith (eds), *Legitimacy and the European Union*, London: Routledge, pp. 1–23.
Barbalet, J.M. (2001), *Emotion, Social Theory and Social Structure*, Cambridge: Cambridge University Press.
Barker, Jason (2001), *Alain Badiou: A Critical Introduction*, London: Pluto Press.
Barzilai, Shuli (1999), *Lacan and the Matter of Origin*, Stanford: Stanford University Press.
Bataille, George (1991), *The Impossible*, trans. Robert Hurley, San Francisco: City Lights Books.
Baudrillard, Jean [1968] (1996), *The System of Objects*, trans. James Benedict, London: Verso.
Baudrillard, Jean [1970] (1998), *The Consumer Society*, London: Sage.
Baudrillard, Jean (2005), 'Holy Europe', *New Left Review*, 33, pp. 24–5.
Bauman, Zygmunt (1993), *Postmodern Ethics*, Oxford: Blackwell.
Bauman, Zygmunt (2000), *Liquid Modernity*, Cambridge: Polity.
Beck, Ulrich and Anthony Giddens (2005), 'Nationalism has now become the enemy of Europe's nations', *The Guardian*, 4 October, p. 6.
Belk, Russell, Guliz Ger and Soren Askegaard (2000), 'The missing streetcar named desire', in S. Ratneswar, Glen Mick David and Cynthia Huffman (eds), *The Why of Consumption: Contemporary Perspectives on Consumer Motives, Goals and Desires*, London: Routledge, pp. 98–119.
Belsey, Catherine (2005), *Culture and the Real*, London: Routledge.
Bennett, Jane (2001), *The Enchantment of Modern Life: Attachments, Crossings and Ethics*, Princeton: Princeton University Press.
Bensaid, Daniel (2004), 'Alain Badiou and the Miracle of the Event', in Peter Hallward (ed.), *Think Again: Alain Badiou and the Future of Philosophy*, London: Continuum, pp. 94–105.
Berezin, Mabel (2001), 'Emotions and political identity: Mobilizing affection for the polity', in Jeff Goodwin, James Jasper and Francesca Polletta (eds), *Passionate Politics: Emotions and Social Movements*, Chicago: University of Chicago Press, pp. 83–98.
Berlin, Isaiah [1965] (2002), *The Roots of Romanticism*, trans. Yannis Papadimitriou, Athens: Scripta (in Greek).
Bernays, Edward [1923] (2004), *Crystallizing Public Opinion*, Whitefish: Kessinger.

Bernays, Edward (ed.) [1955] (1969), *The Engineering of Consent*, Norman: University of Oklahoma Press.
Bideleux, Robert (2001), 'What does it mean to be European?', in Martin Smith and Graham Timmins (eds), *Uncertain Europe*, London: Routledge, pp. 20–40.
Billig, Michael (1995), *Banal Nationalism*, London: Sage.
Billig, Michael (1999), *Freudian Repression*, Cambridge: Cambridge University Press.
Blackburn, Robin (2002), *Banking on Death*, London: Verso.
Blass, Thomas (2004), *The Man Who Shocked the World: The Life and Legacy of Stanley Milgram*, New York: Basic Books.
Blumenberg, Hans (1983), *The Legitimacy of the Modern Age*, trans. R. Wallace, Cambridge, MA: MIT Press.
Bobbio, Norberto (1996), *Left and Right: The Significance of a Political Distinction*, trans. with intro. Allan Cameron, Cambridge: Polity.
Bocock, Robert (1993), *Consumption*, London: Routledge.
Booker, Christopher (1996), 'Europe and regulation – The new totalitarianism', in Martin Holmes (ed.), *The Eurosceptical Reader*, London: Macmillan, pp. 186–204.
Boothby, Richard (1991), *Death and Desire*, New York: Routledge.
Boothby, Richard (2001), *Freud as Philosopher*, New York: Routledge.
Bosteels, Bruno (2001), 'Alain Badiou's theory of the subject: The recommencement of dialectical materialism? (Part I)', *Pli: The Warwick Journal of Philosophy*, 12, pp. 200–29.
Bosteels, Bruno (2002), 'Alain Badiou's theory of the subject: The recommencement of dialectical materialism? (Part II)', *Pli: The Warwick Journal of Philosophy*, 13, pp. 173–208.
Bosteels, Bruno (2005), 'Badiou without Žižek', in Matthew Wilkens (ed.), *The Philosophy of Alain Badiou. Special issue of Polygraph: An International Journal of Culture and Politics*, 17, pp. 223–46
Bouquet, Simon (1997), *Introduction à la lecture de Saussure*, Paris: Payot.
Bourdieu, Pierre (1991), *Language and Symbolic Power*, Cambridge: Polity.
Bracher, Mark (1996), 'Editor's Introduction', *Journal for the Psychoanalysis of Culture and Society*, 1:1, pp. 1–13.
Bratsis, Peter (2003), 'The Constitution of the Greek-Americans', *Discussion Paper No. 9*, Hellenic Observatory, LSE, August.
Bratsis, Peter (2006), *Everyday Life and the State*, Boulder: Paradigm Publishers.
Braunstein, Nestor (2003), 'Desire and jouissance in the teachings of Lacan', in Jean-Michel Rabaté (ed.), *The Cambridge Companion to Lacan*, Cambridge: Cambridge University Press, pp. 102–15.
Brecht, Bertolt (1965), *Die Antigone des Sophokles*, Frankfurt: Suhrkamp.

Breckman, Warren (1999), *Marx, The Young Hegelians and the Origins of Radical Social Theory: Dethroning the Self*, Cambridge: Cambridge University Press.
Britton, Howard (2004), 'Contemporary symptoms and the challenge of psychoanalysis', *Journal for Lacanian Studies*, 2:1, pp. 54–62.
Brockes, Ema (2005), 'Q: What can be done to improve the suburbs of Paris? A: People are starting to understand that the real challenge is to turn peripheries to cities', *The Guardian*, 21 November, pp. 7–8.
Bruner, Jerome (2005), 'Foreword', in Milgram 2005, pp. xi–xv.
Budgen, Sebastian (2002), 'The French fiasco', *New Left Review*, 17, pp. 31–50.
Butler, Judith (1997), *Excitable Speech: A Politics of the Performative*, New York: Routledge.
Butler, Judith, Ernesto Laclau and Slavoj Žižek (2000), *Contingency, Hegemony, Universality: Contemporary Dialogues on the Left*, London: Verso.
Byrne, Ken and Stephen Healy (2006), 'Cooperative subjects: Toward a post-fantasmatic enjoyment of the economy', *Rethinking Marxism*, 18:2, pp. 241–58.
Cacciari, Massimo (1999), *Archipelago*, trans. Nasos Kyriazopoulos, Athens: Travlos (in Greek).
Callinicos, Alex (1989), *Against Postmodernism: A Marxist Critique*, Oxford: Polity.
Campbell, David (1998), *Writing Security: United States Foreign Policy and the Politics of Identity*, Minneapolis: University of Minnesota Press.
Carey, Sean (2002), 'Undivided loyalties: Is national identity an obstacle to European integration?', *European Union Politics*, 3:4, pp. 387–413.
Castoriadis, Cornelius (1978), *The Imaginary Institution of Society*, Athens: Rappas (in Greek).
Castoriadis, Cornelius (1984), 'Psychoanalysis: Project and elucidation', in *Crossroads of the Labyrinth*, trans. Kate Soper and Martin Ryle, Brighton: Harvester Press, pp. 46–115.
Castoriadis, Cornelius (1987), *The Imaginary Institution of Society*, trans. Kathleen Blaney, Cambridge: Polity.
Castoriadis, Cornelius (1991a), 'The social–historical: Mode of being, problems of knowledge', in *Philosophy, Politics, Autonomy*, trans. and ed. David Ames Curtis, New York: Oxford University Press, pp. 33–46.
Castoriadis, Cornelius (1991b), 'The Greek *Polis* and the creation of democracy', in *Philosophy, Politics, Autonomy*, trans. and ed. David Ames Curtis, New York: Oxford University Press, pp. 81–123.
Castoriadis, Cornelius (1991c), 'Power, politics, autonomy', in *Philosophy, Politics, Autonomy*, trans. and ed. David Ames Curtis, New York: Oxford University Press, pp. 143–74.

Castoriadis, Cornelius (1997a), 'Radical imagination and the social instituting imaginary', in *The Castoriadis Reader*, trans. and ed. David Ames Curtis, Oxford: Blackwell, pp. 319–37.
Castoriadis, Cornelius (1997b), 'Culture in a democratic society', in *The Castoriadis Reader*, trans. and ed. David Ames Curtis, Oxford: Blackwell, pp. 338–48.
Castoriadis, Cornelius (1997c), 'Psychoanalysis and philosophy', in *The Castoriadis Reader*, trans. and ed. David Ames Curtis, Oxford: Blackwell, pp. 349–60.
Castoriadis, Cornelius (1997d), 'Done and to be done', in *The Castoriadis Reader*, trans. and ed. David Ames Curtis, Oxford: Blackwell, pp. 361–417.
Castoriadis, Cornelius (2000), *Lectures in Greece*, Athens: Ypsilon (in Greek).
Chaitin, Gilbert (1996), *Rhetoric and Culture in Lacan*, Cambridge: Cambridge University Press.
Chandler, David (1999), *Voices from S-21: Terror and History in Pol Pot's Secret Prison*, Berkeley: University of California Press.
Chebel d'Appolonia, Ariane (2002), 'European nationalism and European Union', in Anthony Pagden (ed.), *The Idea of Europe*, Washington: Woodrow Wilson Center, pp. 171–90.
Checkel, Jeffrey (2001), 'Social construction and European integration', in Thomas Christiansen, Knud Erik Jorgensen and Antje Wiener (eds), *The Social Construction of Europe*, London: Sage, pp. 50–65.
Christidis, Anastasios-Fevos (2001), 'The nature of language', in Anastasios-Fevos Christidis (ed.), *A History of the Greek Language*, Thessaloniki: Institute for Modern Greek Studies, Manolis Triandaphyllidis Foundation, pp. 21–52 (in Greek).
Christidis, Anastasios-Fevos (2002), *Aspects of Language*, Athens: Nisos (in Greek).
Chrysoloras, Nikos (2004a), 'The political discourse of the Greek Orthodox Church', *The Journal of the Hellenic Diaspora*, 30:1, pp. 97–119.
Chrysoloras, Nikos (2004b), 'Why Orthodoxy? Religion and nationalism in Greece', *Studies in Ethnicity and Nationalism*, 4:1, pp. 40–61.
Chryssochoou, Xenia (1996), 'How group membership is formed: Self categorisation or group beliefs? The construction of a European identity in France and Greece', in Glynis Breakwell and Evanthia Lyons (eds), *Changing European Identities: Social Psychological Analyses of Social Change*, Oxford: Butterworth Heinemann, pp. 297–314.
Ciaramelli, Fabio (1999), 'Human creation and the paradox of the originary', *Free Associations*, 7:43, pp. 357–66.
Cinnirella, Marco (1996), 'A social identity perspective on European integration', in Glynis Breakwell and Evanthia Lyons (eds), *Changing European Identities: Social Psychological Analyses of Social Change*, Oxford: Butterworth Heinemann, pp. 253–74.

Clastres, Pierre (1974), *La société contre l'état*, Paris: Les éditions de Minuit.
Clastres, Pierre (1994), *Archaeology of Violence*, Athens: Erasmos (in Greek).
Clegg, Stuart (1989), *Frameworks of Power*, London: Sage.
Cohen, Lizabeth (2004), *A Consumer's Republic: The Politics of Mass Consumption in Postwar America*, New York: Vintage.
Connolly, William (1991), *Identity/Difference: Democratic Negotiations of Political Paradox*, Ithaca: Cornell University Press.
Connolly, William (2002), *Neuropolitics*, Minneapolis: University of Minnesota Press.
Cook, Guy (1992), *The Discourse of Advertising*, London: Routledge.
Coole, Diana (2000), *Negativity and Politics*, London: Routledge.
Copjec, Joan (1994), *Read my Desire: Lacan Against the Historicists*, Cambridge, MA: MIT Press.
Copjec, Joan (1999), 'The tomb of perseverance: On Antigone', in Joan Copjec and Michael Sorkin (eds), *Giving Ground: The Politics of Propinquity*, London: Verso, pp. 233–66.
Copjec, Joan (2005), '*Gai Savoir Sera*: The science of love and the insolence of chance', in Gabriel Riera (ed.), *Alain Badiou: Philosophy and its Conditions*, Albany: SUNY Press, pp. 119–35.
Copjec, Joan (2006), 'May '68, the emotional month', in Slavoj Žižek (ed.), *Lacan: The Silent Partners*, London: Verso, pp. 90–114.
Corfield, David (2002), 'From mathematics to psychology: Lacan's missed encounters', in Jason Glynos and Yannis Stavrakakis (eds), *Lacan and Science*, London: Karnac, pp. 179–206.
Cottingham, John (1998), *Philosophy and the Good Life: Reason and the Passions in Greek, Cartesian and Psychoanalytic Ethics*, Cambridge: Cambridge University Press.
Critchley, Simon (1999), *Ethics, Politics, Subjectivity*, London: Verso.
Critchley, Simon (2000), 'Demanding approval: On the ethics of Alain Badiou', *Radical Philosophy*, 100, pp. 16–27.
Critchley, Simon and Oliver Marchart (eds) (2004), *Laclau: A Critical Reader*, London: Routledge.
Cross, Gary (2000), *An All-Consuming Century: Why Commercialism Won in Modern America*, New York: Columbia University Press.
Crouch, Colin (2004), *Post-Democracy*, Cambridge: Polity.
Curtis, David Ames (1999), 'Cornelius Castoriadis: Philosopher of the social imagination', *Free Associations*, 7:43, pp. 321–30.
Daly, Glyn (1999), 'Ideology and its paradoxes: Dimensions of fantasy and enjoyment', *Journal of Political Ideologies*, 4:2, pp. 219–38.
Daunton, Martin and Matthew Hilton (2001), 'Material politics: An introduction', in Martin Daunton and Matthew Hilton (eds), *The Politics of Consumption*, Oxford: Berg, pp. 1–32.

Day, Richard (1994), 'Constructing the official Canadian', *Topia*, 2, pp. 42–66.
de la Boétie, Étienne [1548] (1942), *Discourse on Voluntary Servitude*, trans. Hary Kurz, New York: Columbia University Press.
de Vos, Patrick (2002), 'The sacralisation of consensus and the rise of right-wing populism in Flanders', *Studies in Social and Political Thought*, 7, pp. 3–29.
de Witte, Bruno (1987), 'Building Europe's image and identity', in A. Rijksbaron, W. H. Roobol and M. Weisglas (eds), *Europe from a Cultural Perspective*, Amsterdam: Nijgh en Van Ditmar, pp. 132–9.
Debord, Guy (1995), *The Society of the Spectacle*, trans. Donald Nicholson-Smith, New York: Zone Books.
Declercq, Frederic (2004), 'Lacan's concept of the real of jouissance: Clinical illustrations and implications', *Psychoanalysis, Culture and Society*, 9, pp. 237–51.
Delanty, Gerard (1995), *Inventing Europe: Idea, Identity, Reality*, London: Macmillan.
Deleuze, Gilles and Guattari, Félix (1984), *Anti-Oedipus: Capitalism and Schizophrenia*, trans. Robert Hurley, Mark Seen and Helen Lane, London: Athlone.
Demertzis, Nicos (1996), *The Discourse of Nationalism*, Athens: Sakoulas (in Greek).
Descartes, René [1649] (1985), *The Passions of the Soul*, in *The Philosophical Writings of Descartes*, trans. John Cottingham, Robert Stoothoff and Dugald Murdoch, Cambridge: Cambridge University Press.
Deutcher, Isaac (1954), *The Prophet Armed, Trotsky: 1879–1921*, Oxford: Oxford University Press.
Dichter, Ernest [1960] (2002), *The Strategy of Desire*, New Brunswick: Transaction Publishers.
Diski, Jenny (2004), 'XXX', *London Review of Books*, 18 November, pp. 7–8.
Dodds, Eric Robertson (1951), *The Greeks and the Irrational*, Berkeley: California University Press.
Dor, Joël (2001), *Structure and Perversions*, New York: The Other Press.
Dragonas, Thalia (2004), 'Educating the uncanny "Other": The case of minority education', *Psychology*, 11:1, pp. 20–33 (in Greek).
Dunkerley, David, Lesley Hodgson, Stanislaw Konopacki, Tony Spybey and Andrew Thompson (2002), *Changing Europe: Identities, Nations and Citizens*, London: Routledge.
Easthope, Anthony (1999), *Englishness and National Culture*, London: Routledge.
Elliott, Anthony (1992), *Social Theory and Psychoanalysis in Transition*, Oxford: Blackwell.

Elliott, Anthony (1999), 'Psychoanalysis and the politics of postmodernity: A conversation between Sean Homer and Anthony Elliott', *PS: Journal of the Universities Association for Psychoanalytic Studies*, pp. 55–65.
European Commission (1974), 'Concerning European Identity', in *Seventh General Report on the Activities of the European Communities in 1973*, Brussels–Luxemburg.
European Commission (2006), 'Euromyths', http://ec.europa.eu/unitedkingdom/press/euromyths/index_en.htm, previously at http://www.cec.org.uk/press/myths/index.htm.
Evans, Dylan (1996), *An Introductory Dictionary of Lacanian Psychoanalysis*, London: Routledge.
Evans, Dylan (1997), 'The lure of the already there and the lure of the before: Psychoanalytic theory and historiography', *Journal for the Psychoanalysis of Culture and Society*, 2:1, pp. 141–4.
Evans, Dylan (1998), 'From Kantian ethics to mystical experience: An exploration of jouissance', in Dany Nobus (ed.), *Key Concepts of Lacanian Psychoanalysis*, London: Rebus, pp. 1–28.
Ewen, Stuart (1977), *Captains of Consciousness: Advertising and the Social Roots of the Consumer Culture*, New York: McGraw-Hill.
Ewen, Stuart (1996), *PR!: A Social History of Spin*, New York: Basic Books.
Ewen, Stuart and Elizabeth Ewen (1982), *Channels of Desire*, New York: McGraw–Hill.
Fel, David (1993), 'The "real" since Freud: Castoriadis and Lacan on socialization and language', *American Imago*, 50:2, pp. 161–95.
Feltham, Oliver (2005), 'Translator's Preface', in Alain Badiou, *Being and Event*, trans. Oliver Feltham, London: Continuum, pp. xvii–xxxiii.
Feltham, Oliver and Justin Clemens (2003), 'An introduction to Alain Badiou's philosophy', in Alain Badiou, *Infinite Thought: Truth and the Return to Philosophy*, trans. and ed. Oliver Feltham and Justin Clemens, London: Continuum, pp. 1–38.
Ferrell, Robyn (1996), *Passions in Theory: Conceptions of Freud and Lacan*, London: Routledge.
Fine, Ben (2002), *The World of Consumption*, 2nd edn, London: Routledge.
Fink, Bruce (1995), *The Lacanian Subject: Between Language and Jouissance*, Princeton: Princeton University Press.
Fink, Bruce (1997), *A Clinical Introduction to Lacanian Psychoanalysis: Theory and Technique*, Cambridge, MA: Harvard University Press.
Fink, Bruce (2002), 'Knowledge and science: Fantasies of the whole', in Jason Glynos and Yannis Stavrakakis (eds), *Lacan and Science*, London: Karnac, pp. 167–87.
Fink, Bruce (2004), *Lacan To the Letter*, Minneapolis: University of Minnesota Press.

Forster, Anthony (2002), *Euroscepticism in Contemporary British Politics*, London: Routledge.
Foucault, Michel (1984) 'Preface', in Gilles Deleuze and Félix Guattari (1984), *Anti-Oedipus: Capitalism and Schizophrenia*, London: Athlone, pp. xi–xiv.
Foucault, Michel (1991), 'Truth and power', interview given to Alessandro Fontana and Pasquale Pasquino, in *The Foucault Reader*, ed. Paul Rabinow, London: Penguin, pp. 51–75.
Fowles, Jib (1996), *Advertising and Popular Culture*, London: Sage.
Freud, Sigmund [1900] (1991a), *The Interpretation of Dreams* (The Penguin Freud Library, 4), trans. James Strachey, London: Penguin.
Freud, Sigmund [1915] (1991b), *Instincts and their Vicissitudes*, in *On Metapsychology* (The Penguin Freud Library, 11), trans. James Strachey, London: Penguin, pp. 105–38.
Freud, Sigmund [1915] (1991c), *Repression*, in *On Metapsychology* (The Penguin Freud Library, 11), trans. James Strachey, London: Penguin, pp. 139–58.
Freud, Sigmund [1917] (1991d), *Mourning and Melancholia*, in *On Metapsychology* (The Penguin Freud Library, 11), trans. James Strachey, London: Penguin, pp. 245–68.
Freud, Sigmund [1921] (1991e), *Group Psychology and the Analysis of the Ego*, in *Civilization, Society and Religion* (The Penguin Freud Library, 12), trans. James Strachey, London: Penguin, pp. 91–178.
Freud, Sigmund [1929] (1982), *Civilization and its Discontents*, trans. Joan Riviere, rev. and ed. James Strachey, London: The Hogarth Press and the Institute of Psychoanalysis.
Gallagher, Cormac (1997), ' "Despair, despair, despair . . . spare!" – affect in Lacanian theory and practice', *The Letter*, 11, pp. 108–29.
Gellner, Ernest (1997), *Nationalism*, New York: Weidenfeld and Nicolson.
Gibson-Graham, J. K. (2002), 'Autobiographical statement', http://www.nd.edu/~econrep/bios/jkgg.html.
Gibson-Graham, J. K. (2006), *A Postcapitalist Politics*, Minneapolis: University of Minnesota Press.
Gilbert, Jeremy (2004), 'Signifying nothing: "Culture", "discourse", and the sociality of affect', *Culture Machine*, 6, http://culturemachine.tees.ac.uk/frm_f1.htm.
Glynos, Jason (1999), 'From identity to identification: Discourse theory and psychoanalysis in context', *Essex Papers in Politics and Government: Subseries in Ideology and Discourse Analysis*, 11.
Glynos, Jason (2000a), 'Sex and the limits of discourse', in David Howarth, Aletta Norval and Yannis Stavrakakis (eds), *Discourse Theory and Political Analysis*, Manchester: Manchester University Press, pp. 205–18.
Glynos, Jason (2000b), 'Sexual identity, identification and difference', *Philosophy and Social Criticism*, 26:6, pp. 85–108.

Glynos, Jason (2000c), 'Thinking the ethics of the political in the context of a postfoundational world: From an ethics of desire to an ethics of the drive', *Theory & Event*, 4:4, http://muse.jhu.edu/journals/theory_and_event.

Glynos, Jason (2001a), 'The grip of ideology: A Lacanian approach to the theory of ideology', *Journal of Political Ideologies*, 6:2, pp. 191–214.

Glynos, Jason (2001b), ' "There is no Other of the Other": Symptoms of a decline in symbolic faith', *Paragraph*, 24:2, pp. 78–110.

Glynos, Jason (2001c) 'Radical democracy: Democratic theory from an anti-essentialist perspective', *Essex Papers in Politics and Government: Sub-series in Ideology and Discourse Analysis*, 17.

Glynos, Jason (2002), 'Theory and evidence in the Freudian field: From observation to structure', in Jason Glynos and Yannis Stavrakakis (eds), *Lacan and Science*, London: Karnac, pp. 13–50.

Glynos, Jason (2003a), 'Radical democratic ethos, or, What is an authentic political act?', *Contemporary Political Theory*, 2, pp. 187–208.

Glynos, Jason (2003b), 'Self-transgression and freedom', *Critical Review of International Social and Political Philosophy*, 6:2, pp. 1–20.

Glynos, Jason and Yannis Stavrakakis (2001), 'Postures and impostures: On Lacan's style and use of mathematical science', *American Imago*, 58:3, pp. 685–706.

Glynos, Jason and Yannis Stavrakakis (2003), 'Encounters of the real kind: Sussing out the limits of Laclau's embrace of Lacan', *Journal for Lacanian Studies*, 1:1, pp. 110–28.

Glynos, Jason and Yannis Stavrakakis (eds) (2002), *Lacan and Science*, London: Karnac.

Goldmann, Kjel (2001), *Transforming the European Nation-State: Dynamics of Internationalization*, London: Sage.

Goodwin, Jeff, James Jasper and Francesca Polletta (2001), 'Why emotions matter', in Jeff Goodwin, James Jasper and Francesca Polletta (eds), *Passionate Politics: Emotions and Social Movements*, Chicago: University of Chicago Press, pp. 1–24.

Goux, Jean-Joseph (1990), *Symbolic Economies*, Ithaca: Cornell University Press.

Green, André [1973] (1999), *The Fabric of Affect in the Psychoanalytic Discourse*, trans. Alan Sheridan, London: Routledge.

Grigg, Russell (1994), 'Dualism and the drive', *Umbr(a)*, 1, pp. 159–64.

Grigg, Russell (2001), 'Absolute freedom and major structural change', *Paragraph*, 24:2, pp. 111–24.

Grosrichard, Alain (1998), *The Sultan's Court*, trans. Liz Heron, London: Verso.

Gunder, Michael (2005), 'The production of desirous space: Mere fantasies of the utopian city?', *Planning Theory*, 4:2, pp. 173–99.

Habermas, Juergen (1987), *The Philosophical Discourse of Modernity*, trans. Frederick Lawrence, Cambridge: Polity.
Haig, Matt (2005), *Brand Failures*, London: Kogan Page.
Hall, Stuart (1988), 'The toad in the garden: Thatcherism among the theorists', in Gary Nelson and Lawrence Grossberg (eds), *Marxism and the Interpretation of Culture*, London: Macmillan.
Hall, Stuart (2002), 'Democracy, globalization and difference', in Okwui Enwezor et al. (eds), *Democracy Unrealized*, Kassel: Hatje Cantz, Documenta 11, Platform 1, pp. 21–35.
Hallward, Peter (2003), *Badiou*, Minneapolis: Minessota University Press.
Hallward, Peter (2004) 'Consequences of abstraction' (Introduction), in Peter Hallward (ed.), *Think Again: Alain Badiou and the Future of Philosophy*, London: Continuum, pp. 1–20.
Hansen, Lene and Ole Waever (2002), *European Integration and National Identity: The Challenge of the Nordic States*, London: Routledge.
Harari, Roberto (2000), *Lacan's Seminar on Anxiety: An Introduction*, trans. Jane Lamb-Ruiz, ed. Rico Franses, New York: The Other Press.
Hardt, Michael and Antonio Negri (2001), *Empire*, Cambridge, MA: Harvard University Press.
Hardt, Michael and Antonio Negri (2004), *Multitude: War and Democracy in the Age of Empire*, London: Hamish Hamilton.
Harpham, Geoffrey Galt (2002), *Language Alone: The Critical Fetish of Modernity*, New York: Routledge.
Harpham, Geoffrey Galt (2003a), 'Doing the impossible: Slavoj Žižek and the end of knowledge', *Critical Inquiry*, 29, pp. 452–85.
Harpham, Geoffrey Galt (2003b), 'Response to Slavoj Žižek', *Critical Inquiry*, 29, pp. 504–7.
Harré, Rom (ed.) (1986), *The Social Construction of Emotions*, Oxford: Blackwell.
Hegel, G. W. F. [1807] (1977), *Phenomenology of Spirit*, foreword John Findlay, trans. Arnold Miller, Oxford: Oxford University Press.
Henry, Michel (1993), *The Genealogy of Psychoanalysis*, trans. Douglas Brick, Stanford: Stanford University Press.
Hillier, Jean and Michael Gunder (2003), 'Planning fantasies? An exploration of a potential Lacanian framework for understanding development assessment planning', *Planning Theory*, 2:3, pp. 225–48.
Hirschman, Albert (1977), *The Passions and the Interests*, Princeton: Princeton University Press.
Hirschman, Albert [1982] (2002), *Shifting Involvements: Private Interest and Public Action*, Princeton: Princeton University Press.
Hoens, Dominiek and Ed Pluth (2002), 'The *sinthome*: A new way of writing an old problem?', in Luke Thurston (ed.), *Re-inventing the Symptom: Essays on the Final Lacan*, New York: The Other Press, pp. 1–18.

Hoggett, Paul and Simon Thompson (2002), 'Towards a democracy of the emotions', *Constellations*, 9:1, pp. 106–26.
Holm, Lorens (2000), 'What Lacan said Re: Architecture', *Critical Quarterly*, 24:2, pp. 29–64.
Howarth, David (2000), *Discourse*, Buckingham: Open University Press.
Howarth, David, Aletta Norval and Yannis Stavrakakis (eds) (2000), *Discourse Theory and Political Analysis*, Manchester: Manchester University Press.
Howarth, David and Yannis Stavrakakis (2000), 'Introducing discourse theory and political analysis', in David Howarth, Aletta Norval and Yannis Stavrakakis (eds), *Discourse Theory and Political Analysis*, Manchester: Manchester University Press, pp. 1–23.
Howarth, David and Jacob Torfing (eds) (2005), *Discourse Theory in European Politics*, London: Palgrave.
Hutchinson, John and Anthony Smith (eds) (1994), *Nationalism*, Oxford: Oxford University Press.
Hutchinson, John and Anthony Smith (eds) (1996), *Ethnicity*, Oxford: Oxford University Press.
Jameson, Fredric (1978), 'Imaginary and symbolic in Lacan: Marxism, psychoanalytic criticism, and the problem of the subject,' *Yale French Studies*, 55–6, pp. 338–95.
Jay, Martin (2005), *Songs of Experience: Modern American and European Variations on a Universal Theme*, Los Angeles: University of California Press.
Jenkins, Brian and Spyros Sofos (1996), 'Nation and nationalism in contemporary Europe: A theoretical perspective', in Brian Jenkins and Spyros Sofos (eds), *Nation and Identity in Contemporary Europe,* London: Routledge, pp. 9–32.
Jenkins, Laura (2005), 'Corporeal ontology: Beyond mind–body dualism?', *Politics*, 25:1, pp. 1–11.
Jhally, Sut (1990), *The Codes of Advertising*, New York: Routledge.
Judt, Tony (1996), *A Grand Illusion? An Essay on Europe*, New York: Hill and Wang.
Jusdanis, Gregory (2001), *The Necessary Nation*, Princeton: Princeton University Press.
Kalyvas, Andreas (2000), 'Hegemonic sovereignty: Carl Schmitt, Antonio Gramsci and the constituent prince', *Journal of Political Ideologies*, 5:3, pp. 343–76.
Kay, Sarah (2003), *Žižek: A Critical Introduction*, Cambridge: Polity.
Kemper, Theodore (ed.) (1990), *Research Agendas in the Sociology of Emotions*, Albany: SUNY Press.
Keohane, Kieran (1992), 'Symptoms of Canada: National ideology and the theft of national enjoyment', *cineACTION*, 28, pp. 20–33.
Klein, Naomi (2000), *No Logo*, London: Flamingo.

Kojève, Alexandre [1947] (1980), *Introduction to the Reading of Hegel*, assembled by Raymond Queneau, ed. Allan Bloom, trans. James Nichols, Jr., Ithaca: Cornell University Press.

Kolakowski, Lessek (1978), *The Main Currents of Marxism*, vol. I, Oxford: Oxford University Press.

Kohn, Margaret (2003), *Radical Space*, Ithaca: Cornell University Press.

Kuhn, Thomas [1962] (1996), *The Structure of Scientific Revolutions*, Chicago: Chicago University Press.

Lacan, Jacques [1947] (2006), 'Presentation on psychical causality', in E2006, pp. 123–58.

Lacan, Jacques [1948] (1977), 'Aggressivity in psychoanalysis', in E1977, pp. 8–29.

Lacan, Jacques [1949] (1977), 'The mirror stage as formative of the function of the I', in E1977, pp. 1–7.

Lacan, Jacques [1951] (2006), 'A theoretical introduction to the functions of psychoanalysis in criminology', in E2006, pp. 102–22.

Lacan, Jacques [1953–4] (1988), *The Seminar of Jacques Lacan, Book I: Freud's Papers on Technique, 1953–1954*, ed. Jacques-Alain Miller, trans. and notes John Forrester, Cambridge: Cambridge University Press.

Lacan, Jacques [1954–5] (1988), *The Seminar of Jacques Lacan, Book II: The Ego in Freud's Theory and in the Technique of Psychoanalysis, 1954–5*, ed. Jacques-Alain Miller, trans. Sylvana Tomasseli, notes by John Forrester, Cambridge: Cambridge University Press.

Lacan, Jacques [1955–6] (1993), *The Seminar of Jacques Lacan. Book III: The Psychoses, 1955–56*, ed. Jacques-Alain Miller, trans. and notes Russell Grigg, London: Routledge.

Lacan, Jacques [1956] (1977), 'The function and field of speech and language in psychoanalysis', in E1977, pp. 30–113.

Lacan, Jacques [1956] (2006), 'The Freudian Thing, or the meaning of the return to Freud in psychoanalysis', in E2006, pp. 334–63.

Lacan, Jacques [1957] (2006), 'Seminar on "The Purloined Letter"', in E2006, pp. 6–48.

Lacan, Jacques [1957] (1977), 'The agency of the letter in the unconscious or reason since Freud', in E1977, pp. 146–78.

Lacan, Jacques [1958] (2006), 'The signification of the phallus', in E2006, pp. 575–84.

Lacan, Jacques [1959–60] (1992), *The Seminar of Jacques Lacan. Book VII: The Ethics of Psychoanalysis*, 1959–1960, ed. Jacques-Alain Miller, trans. and notes Dennis Porter, London: Routledge.

Lacan, Jacques [1960] (2006), 'The subversion of the subject and the dialectic of desire in the Freudian unconscious', in E2006, pp. 671–702.

Lacan, Jacques [1961] (2006), 'The direction of the treatment and the principles of its power', in E2006, pp. 489–542.

Lacan, Jacques (1961–2), *Identification* [*L'identification*], unpublished seminar transcript, trans. Cormac Gallagher.
Lacan, Jacques (1962–3), *Anxiety* [*L'angoisse*], unpublished seminar transcript, trans. Cormac Gallagher.
Lacan, Jacques [1964] (1979), *The Four Fundamental Concepts of Psychoanalysis*, ed. Jacques-Alain Miller, trans. Alan Sheridan, London: Penguin.
Lacan, Jacques (1965–6), *The Object of Psychoanalysis* [*L'objet de la psychanalyse*], unpublished seminar transcript, trans. Cormac Gallagher.
Lacan, Jacques [1966] (2006), 'Position of the unconscious', in E2006, pp. 703–21.
Lacan, Jacques [1966] (2006), 'Science and truth', in E2006, pp. 726–45.
Lacan, Jacques [1966] (1977), *Écrits: A Selection*, trans. Alan Sheridan, London: Tavistock/Routledge (=E1977).
Lacan, Jacques [1966] (2006), *Écrits*, trans. Bruce Fink, in collaboration with Héloïse Fink and Russel Grigg, New York: Norton (=E2006).
Lacan, Jacques (1966–7), *The Logic of Fantasy* [*La logique du fantasme*], unpublished seminar transcript, trans. Cormac Gallagher.
Lacan, Jacques [1969–70] (1991), *Le séminaire, livre XVII, L' envers de la psychanalyse*, ed. Jacques-Alain Miller, Paris: Seuil.
Lacan, Jacques [1972–3] (1998), *The Seminar of Jacques Lacan. Book XX: Encore, On Feminine Sexuality, The Limits of Love and Knowledge, 1972–3*, ed. Jacques-Alain Miller, trans. and notes Bruce Fink, New York: Norton.
Lacan, Jacques [1973] (1987), 'Television', *October*, 40, pp. 7–50.
Lacan, Jacques [1973] (1990), *Television, A Challenge to the Psychoanalytic Establishment*, ed. Joan Copjec, trans. Denis Hollier, Rosalind Krauss, Annette Michelson and Jeffrey Mehlman, New York: Norton.
Lacan, Jacques [1975–6] (2005), *Le séminaire, livre XXIII, Le sinthome, 1975–6*, ed. Jacques-Alain Miller, Paris: Seuil.
Lacan, Jacques and the École Freudienne (1982), *Feminine Sexuality*, ed. Juliet Mitchell and Jacqueline Rose, trans. Jacqueline Rose, London: Macmillan.
Laclau, Ernesto (1990), *New Reflections on the Revolution of our Time*, London: Verso.
Laclau, Ernesto (1991), 'God only knows', *Marxism Today*, Last Issue, pp. 56–9.
Laclau, Ernesto (1993), 'Ernesto Laclau: A theoretical trajectory', interview given to Yannis Stavrakakis and Dimitris Zeginis, *Diavazo*, 324, pp. 56–62 (in Greek).
Laclau, Ernesto (1994), 'Introduction', in Ernesto Laclau (ed.), *The Making of Political Identities*, London: Verso, pp. 1–8.
Laclau, Ernesto (1996), *Emancipation(s)*, London: Verso.
Laclau, Ernesto (2001a), 'Can immanence explain social struggles?', *Diacritics*, 31:4, pp. 3–10.

Laclau, Ernesto (2001b), 'Democracy and the question of power', *Constellations*, 8:1, pp. 3–14.
Laclau, Ernesto (2003), 'Discourse and jouissance: A reply to Glynos and Stavrakakis', *Journal for Lacanian Studies*, 1:2, pp. 278–85.
Laclau, Ernesto (2004a), 'Glimpsing the future: A reply', in Simon Critchley and Oliver Marchart (eds), *Laclau: A Critical Reader*, London: Routledge, pp. 279–328.
Laclau, Ernesto (2004b), 'An ethics of militant engagement', in Peter Hallward (ed.), *Think Again: Alain Badiou and the Future of Philosophy*, London: Continuum, pp. 120–37.
Laclau, Ernesto (2005), *On Populist Reason*, London: Verso.
Laclau, Ernesto (ed.) (1994), *The Making of Political Identities*, London: Verso.
Laclau, Ernesto and Chantal Mouffe (1985), *Hegemony and Socialist Strategy*, London: Verso.
Laclau, Ernesto and Chantal Mouffe (2001), 'Preface to the second edition', *Hegemony and Socialist Strategy*, 2nd edn, London: Verso, pp. vii–xix.
Laclau, Ernesto and Chantal Mouffe (2003), 'Hope, passion and politics: Interview with Chantal Mouffe and Ernesto Laclau by Mary Zournazi', *Soundings*, 22, pp. 70–86.
Lane, Christopher (1996), 'Beyond the social principle: Psychoanalysis and radical democracy', *Journal for the Psychoanalysis of Culture and Society*, 1:1, pp. 105–21.
Lane, Christopher (2001), 'Politics and the real: A reply to Yannis Stavrakakis', *(a): the journal of culture and the unconscious*, 2, pp. 68–75.
Laplanche, Jean and Jean-Bertrand Pontalis (1988), *The Language of Psychoanalysis*, trans. Donald Nicholson-Smith, London: Karnac and the Institute of Psychoanalysis.
Latour, Bruno (2004), *Politics of Nature: How to Bring the Sciences Into Democracy*, Cambridge, MA: Harvard University Press.
Leader, Darian (1997), *Promises Lovers Make When It Gets Late*, London: Faber and Faber.
Leader, Darian (2002), *Stealing the Mona Lisa: What Art Stops Us From Seeing*, London: Faber and Faber.
Lecercle, Jean-Jacques (1985), *Philosophy Through the Looking-Glass: Language, Nonsense, Desire*, London: Hutchinson.
Lecercle, Jean-Jacques (1999), 'Cantor, Lacan, Mao, *même combat*: The philosophy of Alain Badiou', *Radical Philosophy*, 93, pp. 6–13.
Leclaire, Serge [1968] (1998), *Psychoanalyzing*, trans. Peggy Kamuf, Stanford: Stanford University Press.
Lee, Jonathan Scott (1990), *Jacques Lacan*, Amherst: University of Massachusetts Press, 1990.
Lefort, Claude (1986), *The Political Forms of Modern Society*, ed. with intro. John Thompson, Cambridge: Polity.

Leledakis, Kanakis (1995), *Society and Psyche: Social Theory and the Unconscious Dimension of the Social*, Oxford: Berg.

Lewis, David (2000), 'The construction of "New Age travellers" in official and popular discourse', PhD Colloquium, Department of Government, University of Essex.

Lingis, Alphonso (1985), *Libido: The French Existential Theories*, Bloomington: Indiana University Press.

Lodziak, Conrad (2002), *The Myth of Consumerism*, London: Pluto Press.

Loraux, Nicole (2001), *The Divided City*, trans. Babis Lykoudis, Athens: Patakis (in Greek).

Lyotard, Jean-François (1984), *The Postmodern Condition*, trans. Geoff Bennington and Brian Massumi, Manchester: Manchester University Press.

Lyotard, Jean-François [1974] (1993), *Libidinal Economy*, trans. Iain Hamilton Grant, London: Athlone Press.

MacCabe, Colin (2002), 'Le Pen and European democracy', *Critical Quarterly*, 44:3, pp. 115–17.

McCarthy, Tom (2003), 'Between pain and nothing', in Steve Rushton (ed.), *The Milgram Re-enactment*, Maastricht: Jan Van Eyck Akademie, pp. 16–32.

McClintock, Anne (1995), *Imperial Leather: Race, Gender and Sexuality in the Colonial Context*, New York: Routledge.

McGowan, Todd (2004), *The End of Dissatisfaction? Jacques Lacan and the Emerging Society of Enjoyment*, Albany: SUNY Press.

McLellan, David (1969), *The Young Hegelians and Karl Marx*, London: Macmillan.

Malmborg, Mikael af and Bo Strath (2002), 'Introduction: The national meanings of Europe', in Mikael af Malmborg and Bo Strath (eds), *The Meaning of Europe*, Oxford: Berg, pp. 1–26.

Manthoulis, Roviros (1999), *Ancient Erotic and Symposiac Vocabulary*, Athens: Exantas (in Greek).

Marchart, Oliver (2002), 'Enacting the unrealized: Political theory and the role of "radical democratic activism"', in Okwui Enwezor et al. (eds), *Democracy Unrealized*, Kassel: Hatje Cantz, Documenta 11, Platform 1, pp. 253–66.

Marchart, Oliver (2005), 'The absence at the heart of presence: Radical democracy and the "ontology of lack"', in Lars Tonder and Lasse Thomassen (eds), *Radical Democracy: Politics Between Abundance and Lack*, Manchester: Manchester University Press, pp. 17–31.

Marcuse, Herbert (1966), *Eros and Civilization*, 2nd edn, Boston: Beacon Press.

Marcussen, Martin, Thomas Risse, Daniela Engelmann-Martin, Hans-Joachim Knopf and Klaus Roscher (2001), 'Constructing Europe? The evolution of nation–state identities', in Thomas Christiansen, Knud Erik

Jorgensen and Antje Wiener (eds), *The Social Construction of Europe*, London: Sage, pp. 101–20.
Marquand, David (2004), *Decline of the Public*, Cambridge: Polity.
Marx, Karl [1867] (1961) *Capital*, vol. 1, Moscow: Foreign Languages Publishing House.
Marx, Karl and Friedrich Engels [1848] (1983), *The Communist Manifesto*, London: Lawrence and Wishart.
Massumi, Brian (1996), 'The autonomy of affect', in Paul Patton (ed.), *Deleuze: A Critical Reader*, Oxford: Blackwell, pp. 217–39.
Mearsheimer, John (1990), 'Back to the future: Instability in Europe after the Cold War', *International Security*, 15:1, pp. 5–56.
Merleau-Ponty, Maurice [1963] (1988), *In Praise of Philosophy and Other Essays*, Evanston: Northwestern University Press.
Mestrovič, Stjepan (1997), *Postemotional Society*, London: Sage.
Miles, Steven (1998), *Consumerism – As a Way of Life*, London: Sage.
Milgram, Stanley [1974] (2005), *Obedience to Authority*, London: Pinter and Martin.
Miller, Jacques-Alain (1981), 'Encyclopédie', *Ornicar?*, 24, pp. 35–44.
Miller, Jacques-Alain (1990), 'Microscopia: An introduction to the reading of television', in Jacques Lacan, *Television: A Challenge to the Psychoanalytic Establishment*, New York: Norton, pp. xi–xxxi.
Miller, Jacques-Alain (1992), 'Ethics in psychoanalysis', trans. Jorge Jauregui and Marguerite Laporte, *Lacanian Ink*, 5, pp. 13–28.
Miller, Jacques-Alain (1996), 'Commentary on Lacan's text', in Richard Feldstein, Bruce Fink and Maire Jaanus (eds), *Reading Seminars I and II: Lacan's Return to Freud*, Albany: SUNY Press, pp. 422–7.
Miller, Jacques-Alain (2000a), 'The Experience of the real in psychoanalysis', trans. Jorge Jauregui, *Lacanian Ink*, 16, pp. 7–27.
Miller, Jacques-Alain (2000b), 'Paradigms of *jouissance*', trans. Jorge Jauregui, *Lacanian Ink*, 17, pp. 10–47.
Miller, Jacques-Alain (2000c), 'Biologie lacanienne et événement de corps', *La Cause Freudienne*, 44, pp. 7–59.
Miller, Jacques-Alain (2002a), 'What does it mean to be a Lacanian?', *Psychanalysi*, 5, pp. 33–42 (in Greek).
Miller, Jacques-Alain (2002b), 'Enjoyment as axis of Lacan's teaching', *Psychanalysi*, 5, pp. 43–51 (in Greek).
Miller, Jacques-Alain (2002c), 'Pure psychoanalysis, applied psychoanalysis and psychotherapy', trans. Barbara Fulks, *Lacanian Ink*, 20, pp. 4–43.
Miller, Jacques-Alain (2003), 'Lacan's later teaching', trans. Barbara Fulks, *Lacanian Ink*, 21, pp. 5–41.
Miller, Jacques-Alain (2004), 'Religion, psychoanalysis', trans. Barbara Fulks, *Lacanian Ink*, 23, pp. 8–39.
Miller, Jacques-Alain (2005), 'Chapter One, presentation of the year's theme: From fantasy to symptom and return', *(Re)-turn*, 2, pp. 11–38.

Milner, Jean-Claude (1990), *For the Love of Language*, Houndmills: Macmillan.
Montesquieu, Charles de Secondat, Baron de La Brède et de [1748] (1989), *The Spirit of the Laws*, trans. and ed. Anne Cohler, Basia Carolyn Miller and Harold Samuel Stone, Cambridge: Cambridge University Press.
Mouffe, Chantal (1998), 'The radical centre: A politics without adversary', *Soundings*, 9, pp. 11–23.
Mouffe, Chantal (1999), 'Ten years of false starts', *New Times*, 9.
Mouffe, Chantal (2000), *The Democratic Paradox*, London: Verso.
Mouffe, Chantal (2001), 'Democracy – Radical and plural', interview in *Centre for the Study of Democracy Bulletin*, 9:1, pp. 10–13.
Mouffe, Chantal (2002), 'The "end of politics" and the challenge of right-wing populism', unpublished paper.
Mouffe, Chantal (2005), *On the Political*, London: Routledge.
Nasio, Juan-David (1998), *Five Lessons on the Psychoanalytic Theory of Jacques Lacan*, Albany: SUNY Press.
Negri, Antonio (2003), 'Kairos, Alma Venus, Multitudo', in *Time for Revolution*, London: Continuum, pp. 139–261.
Neill, Calum (2003), *Without Ground: Lacanian Ethics and the Assumption of Democracy*, PhD Thesis, Manchester Metropolitan University.
Neumann, Iver (1999), *Uses of the Other: The 'East' in European Identity Formation*, Manchester: Manchester University Press.
Newman, Saul (2004a), 'Interrogating the Master: Lacan and radical politics', *Psychoanalysis, Culture and Society*, 9, pp. 298–314.
Newman, Saul (2004b), 'New reflections on the theory of power: A Lacanian perspective', *Contemporary Political Theory*, 3, pp. 148–67.
Nobus, Dany (2000), *Jacques Lacan and the Freudian Practice of Psychoanalysis*, London: Routledge.
Nobus, Dany and Malcolm Quinn (2005), *Knowing Nothing, Staying Stupid: Elements for a Psychoanalytic Epistemology*, London: Routledge.
Nola, Robert (1993), 'The Young Hegelians, Feuerbach and Marx', in Robert Solomon and Kathleen Higgins (eds), *The Age of German Idealism* (Routledge History of Philosophy, vol. VI), London: Routledge, 1993, pp. 290–329.
Norval, Aletta (1996), *Deconstructing Apartheid Discourse*, London: Verso.
Norval, Aletta (2000), 'Trajectories of future research in discourse theory', in David Howarth, Aletta Norval and Yannis Stavrakakis (eds), *Discourse Theory and Political Analysis*, Manchester: Manchester University Press, pp. 219–36.
Ober, Josiah (1996), *The Athenian Revolution*, Princeton: Princeton University Press.
Ozselçuk, Ceren (2006), 'Mourning, melancholy, and the politics of class transformation', *Rethinking Marxism*, 18:2, pp. 225–40.

Ozselçuk, Ceren and Yahya Madra (2005), 'Psychoanalysis and Marxism: From capitalist-all to communist non-all', *Psychoanalysis, Culture and Society*, 10, pp. 79–97.
Packard, Vance [1957] (1991), *The Hidden Persuaders*, London: Penguin.
Pagden, Anthony (2002), 'Europe: Conceptualizing a continent', in Anthony Pagden (ed.), *The Idea of Europe*, Washington: Woodrow Wilson Center, pp. 33–54.
Pantel, Melissa (1999), 'Unity–diversity: Cultural policy and EU legitimacy', in Thomas Banchoff and Mitchell Smith (eds), *Legitimacy and the European Union*, London: Routledge, pp. 46–65.
Papaioannou, Kostas (2003), *Mass and History*, Athens: Enallaktikes ekdoseis.
Parker, Ian (2004), *Slavoj Žižek: A Critical Introduction*, London: Pluto Press.
Parker, Ian (2005), 'Lacanian discourse analysis in psychology', *Theory & Psychology*, 15:2, pp. 163–82.
Passerini, Luisa (2000), 'The last identification: Why some of us would like to call ourselves Europeans and what we mean by this', in Bo Strath (ed.), *Europe and the Other and Europe as the Other*, Brussels: PIE–Peter Lang, pp. 45–66.
Patsalides, André and Kareen Ror Malone (2000), '*Jouissance* in the cure', in Kareen Ror Malone and Stephen Friendlander (eds), *The Subject of Lacan*, Albany: SUNY Press, pp. 123–33.
Pluth, Ed (2004), 'How acts use signifiers', *Journal for Lacanian Studies*, 2:1, pp. 18–33.
Pluth, Ed and Dominiek Hoens (2004), 'What if the other is stupid? Badiou and Lacan on "logical time"', in Peter Hallward (ed.), *Think Again: Alain Badiou and the Future of Philosophy*, London: Continuum, pp. 182–90.
Politi, Jina (1993), 'The written and the unspoken', in Robert Clark and Piero Boitani (eds), *English Studies in Transition*, London: Routledge, pp. 51–71.
Politi, Jina (1997), 'Antigone's letter', unpublished paper.
Porcheret, Bernard (2000), 'Hands off my symptom', *Psychoanalytical Notebooks*, 4, pp. 141–6.
Pupavac, Vanessa (2004), 'International therapeutic governance', *Centre for the Study of Democracy Bulletin*, 11:2, pp. 2–12.
Qualter, Terence (1991), *Advertising and Democracy in the Mass Age*, London: Macmillan.
Raaflaub, Kurt (1994), 'Democracy, power, and imperialism in fifth-century Athens', in Peter Euben, John Wallach and Josiah Ober (eds), *Athenian Political Thought and the Reconstruction of American Democracy*, Ithaca: Cornell University Press, pp. 103–46.
Rajchman, John (1991), *Truth and Eros: Lacan, Foucault, and the Question of Ethics*, New York: Routledge.

Rancière, Jacques (1995), *On the Shores of Politics*, trans. Liz Heron, London: Verso.
Rancière, Jacques (1999), *Dis-agreement*, trans. Julie Rose, Minneapolis: University of Minnesota Press.
Reich, Wilhelm [1942] (1975), *The Mass Psychology of Fascism*, 3rd edn, trans. Vincent Carfagno, London: Pelican.
Reich, Wilhelm [1948] (1980), *Character Analysis*, 3rd edn, trans. Vincent Carfagno, New York: Farrar, Straus and Giraux.
Reich, Wilhelm (1973), *Ether, God and Evil, Cosmic Superimposition*, New York: Farrar, Straus and Giraux.
Ricoeur, Paul (1986), 'Foreword', in Bernard Dauenhauer, *The Politics of Hope*, New York: Routledge and Kegan Paul, pp. ix–xvi.
Roazen, Paul (1969), *Freud: Political and Social Thought*, London: Hogarth Press.
Robinson, Andrew (2004), 'The politics of lack', *British Journal of Politics and International Relations*, 6, pp. 259–69.
Robinson, Andrew (2005), 'The political theory of constitutive lack: A critique', *Theory & Event*, 8:1, http://muse.jhu.edu/journals/theory_and_event.
Robinson, Paul (1967), *The Freudian Left*, New York: Harper and Row.
Rorty, Richard (2004), 'Post-Democracy', *London Review of Books*, 1 April, pp. 10–11.
Rorty, Richard (ed.) (1967), *The Linguistic Turn: Recent Essays in Philosophical Method*, Chicago: University of Chicago Press.
Rosen, Michael (1996), *On Voluntary Servitude*, Cambridge: Polity.
Roth, Phillip (2001), *The Human Stain*, London: Vintage.
Roudinesco, Elisabeth (1997), *Jacques Lacan*, trans. Barbara Bray, London: Polity Press.
Rousseau, Jean-Jacques [1762] (1971), *The Social Contract*, in *Social Contract: Essays by Locke, Hume, Rousseau*, ed. Ernest Barker, Oxford: Oxford University Press, pp. 167–307.
Rozanis, Stephanos (2001), *Studies on Romanticism*, Athens: Plethron (in Greek).
Ruby, Christian (1996), *L'enthusiasme. Essai sur le sentiment en politique*, Paris: Hatier.
Rushton, Steve (2003), 'Agentic States', in Steve Rushton (ed.), *The Milgram Re-enactment*, Maastricht: Jan Van Eyck Akademie, pp. 49–63.
Sahlins, Marshall (1972), *Stone Age Economics*, Chicago: Aldine–Atherton.
Sahlins, Marshall (1976), *The Use and Abuse of Biology*, Ann Arbor: The University of Michigan Press.
Salecl, Renata (1997), 'The satisfaction of drives', *Umbr(a)*, 1, pp. 105–9.
San Martin, Pablo (2002), 'A discursive reading of the emergence of Asturian nationalist ideology', *Journal of Political Ideologies*, 7:1, pp. 97–116.

Santos, Boaventura de Sousa (2005a), 'General introduction: Reinventing social emancipation: Toward new manifestos', in Boaventura de Sousa Santos (ed.), *Democratising Democracy: Beyond the Liberal Democratic Canon*, London: Verso, pp. xvii–xxxiii.

Santos, Boaventura de Sousa (2005b), 'Participatory budgeting in Porto Alegre: Toward a redistributive democracy', in Boaventura de Sousa Santos (ed.), *Democratising Democracy: Beyond the Liberal Democratic Canon*, London: Verso, pp. 307–76.

Saussure, Ferdinand de [1916] (1983), *Course in General Linguistics*, ed. Charles Bally and Albert Sechehaye with the collaboration of Albert Reidlinger, trans. Roy Harris, London: Duchworth.

Scitovsky, Tibor (1992), *The Joyless Economy: The Psychology of Human Satisfaction*, rev. edn, New York: Oxford University Press.

Sennett, Richard (2006), *The Culture of the New Capitalism*, New Haven: Yale University Press.

Seshadri-Crooks, Kalpana (2000), *Desiring Whiteness: A Lacanian Analysis of Race*, London: Routledge.

Shaw, Jo (2001), 'The "governance" research agenda and the "constitutional question"', in European Commission, *Governance and Citizenship in Europe: Some Research Questions*, Luxembourg: European Communities, pp. 70–81.

Shepherdson, Charles (1997), 'The elements of the drive', *Umbr(a)*, 1, pp. 131–45.

Simons, Jon (2005), 'The radical democratic possibilities of popular culture', in Lars Tonder and Lasse Thomassen (eds), *Radical Democracy: Politics Between Abundance and Lack*, Manchester: Manchester University Press, pp. 149–66.

Simopoulos, Kostis (2000), 'Imaginary autonomy or imaginary nowayout?', *Nea Estia*, 147:1722, pp. 576–606 (in Greek).

Smith, Anthony (1986), *The Ethnic Origins of Nations*, Oxford: Blackwell.

Smith, Anthony (1991), *National Identity*, London: Penguin.

Smith, Anthony (1995), 'The dark side of nationalism: The revival of nationalism in late twentieth-century Europe', in L. Cheles, R. Ferguson and M. Vaughan (eds), *The Far Right in Western and Eastern Europe,* London: Longman, pp. 13–19.

Smith, Anthony (1999), 'National identity and the idea of European Unity', in *Myths and Memories of the Nation*, Oxford: Oxford University Press, pp. 225–52.

Smith, Anthony (2001), *Nationalism*, Oxford: Polity.

Sokal, Alan and Jean Bricmont (1998), *Intellectual Impostures*, London: Profile Books.

Soler, Colette (1992), 'The real aims of the analytic act', *Lacanian Ink*, 5, pp. 53–60.

Soler, Colette (2003), 'The paradoxes of the symptom in psychoanalysis', in Jean-Michel Rabaté (ed.), *The Cambridge Companion to Lacan*, Cambridge: Cambridge University Press, pp. 86–101.

Sophocles (1984), *Antigone*, in *The Three Theban Plays*, trans. Robert Fagles, London: Penguin.

Sorkin, Michael (1999), 'Introduction: Traffic in democracy', in Joan Copjec and Michael Sorkin (eds), *Giving Ground: The Politics of Propinquity*, London: Verso, pp. 1–15.

Spencer, Philip and Howard Wollman (1998), 'Good and bad nationalisms: A critique of dualism', *Journal of Political Ideologies*, 3:3, pp. 255–74.

Spinoza, Baruch (Benedictus de) [1677] (1993), *Ethics*, trans. Andrew Boyle, London: Everyman.

Starobinski, Jean [1971] (1979), *Words Upon Words*, New Haven: Yale University Press.

Stavrakakis, Yannis (1997a), 'Green ideology: A discursive reading', *Journal of Political Ideologies*, 2:3, pp. 259–79.

Stavrakakis, Yannis (1997b), 'Field note on advertising', *Journal for the Psychoanalysis of Culture and Society*, 2:1, pp. 139–41.

Stavrakakis, Yannis (1997c), 'Green fantasy and the real of nature: Elements of a Lacanian critique of Green ideological discourse', *Journal for the Psychoanalysis of Culture and Society*, 2:1, pp. 123–32.

Stavrakakis, Yannis (1999a), *Lacan and the Political*, London: Routledge.

Stavrakakis, Yannis (1999b), 'Lacan and history', *Journal for the Psychoanalysis of Culture and Society*, 4:1, pp. 99–118.

Stavrakakis, Yannis (1999c), 'Theory and experience: The Lacanian negotiation of a constitutive tension', *Journal for the Psychoanalysis of Culture and Society*, 4:1, pp. 146–50.

Stavrakakis, Yannis (2000a), 'Laclau with Lacan: Comments on the relation between discourse theory and Lacanian psychoanalysis', *(a): the journal of culture and the unconscious*, 1:1, pp. 134–53.

Stavrakakis, Yannis (2000b), 'On the emergence of Green ideology: The dislocation factor in Green politics', in David Howarth, Aletta Norval and Yannis Stavrakakis (eds), *Discourse Theory and Political Analysis*, Manchester: Manchester University Press, pp. 100–18.

Stavrakakis, Yannis (2000c), 'On the critique of advertising discourse: A Lacanian view', *Third Text*, 51, pp. 85–90.

Stavrakakis, Yannis (2001), 'Identity, political', in Joe Foweraker and Barry Clarke (eds), *Encyclopaedia of Democratic Thought*, London: Routledge, pp. 333–7.

Stavrakakis, Yannis (2002a), 'Religious populism and political culture: The Greek case', *South European Society and Politics*, 7:3, pp. 29–52.

Stavrakakis, Yannis (2002b), 'Creativity and its limits: Encounters with social constructionism and the political in Castoriadis and Lacan', *Constellations*, 9:4, pp. 522–39.

Stavrakakis, Yannis (2003a), 'The lure of Antigone: Aporias of an ethics of the political', *Umbr(a)*, pp. 117–29.

Stavrakakis, Yannis (2003b), 'Re-activating the democratic revolution: The politics of transformation beyond reoccupation and conformism', *Parallax*, 27, pp. 56–71.

Stavrakakis, Yannis (2004), 'Antinomies of formalism: Laclau's theory of populism and the lessons from religious populism in Greece', *Journal of Political Ideologies*, 9:3, pp. 253–67.

Stavrakakis, Yannis (2005a), 'Passions of identification: Discourse, enjoyment, and European identity', in David Howarth and Jacob Torfing (eds), *Discourse Theory in European Politics*, London: Palgrave, pp. 68–92.

Stavrakakis, Yannis (2005b), 'Religion and populism in contemporary Greece', in Francisco Panizza (ed.), *Populism and the Mirror of Democracy*, London: Verso, pp. 224–49.

Stavrakakis, Yannis with Nikos Chrysoloras (2006), '(I can't get no) enjoyment: Lacanian theory and the analysis of nationalism', *Psychoanalysis, Culture and Society*, 11, pp. 144–63.

Stearns, Peter (2006), *Consumerism in World History*, New York: Routledge.

Stiglitz, Joseph (2002), *Globalization and its Discontents*, London: Penguin.

Strachey, James [1957] (1991), 'Editor's Note', in Sigmund Freud, *Instincts and their Vicissitudes*, in *On Metapsychology* (The Penguin Freud Library, 11), trans. James Strachey, London: Penguin, pp. 107–12.

Strath, Bo (2000a), 'Introduction: Europe as a discourse', in Bo Strath (ed.), *Europe and the Other and Europe as the Other*, Brussels: PIE–Peter Lang, pp. 13–44.

Strath, Bo (2000b), 'Multiple Europes: Integration, identity and demarcation to the other', in Bo Strath (ed.), *Europe and the Other and Europe as the Other*, Brussels: PIE–Peter Lang, pp. 385–420.

Suskind, Ron (2004), 'Without a doubt', *New York Times*, 17 October, www.ronsuskind.com/articles/000106.htm

Todorova, Maria (1997), *Imagining the Balkans*, Oxford: Oxford University Press.

Toews, John Edward (1980), *Hegelianism*, Cambridge: Cambridge University Press.

Tonder, Lars and Lasse Thomassen (eds) (2005), *Radical Democracy: Politics Between Abundance and Lack*, Manchester: Manchester University Press.

Trend, David (ed.) (1996), *Radical Democracy*, New York: Routledge.

Tsoukalas, Constantine (1993), 'Greek national identity in an integrated Europe and a changing world order', in Harry Psomiades and Stavros Thomadakis (eds), *Greece, the New Europe and the Changing World Order*, New York: Pella Publishers, pp. 57–78.

Turkle, Sherry (1992), *Psychoanalytic Politics*, 2nd edn, London: Free Association Books.
Tye, Larry (1998), *The Father of Spin: Edward Bernays and the Birth of Public Relations*, New York: Owl Books.
Unger, Roberto Mangabeira (2005), *What Should the Left Propose?*, London: Verso.
Urribarri, Fernando (1999), 'The psyche: Imagination and history. A general view of Cornelius Castoriadis's psychoanalytic ideas', *Free Associations*, 7:43, pp. 374–96.
Vanier, Alain (2001), 'Some remarks on the symptom and the social link: Lacan with Marx', *Journal for the Psychoanalysis of Culture and Society*, 6:1, 2001, pp. 40–5.
Verhaeghe, Paul and Frederic Declercq (2002), 'Lacan's analytic goal: Le sinthome or the feminine way', in Luke Thurston (ed.), *Re-inventing the Symptom: Essays on the Final Lacan*, New York: The Other Press, pp. 59–82.
Vernant, Jean-Pierre (1972), 'Greek tragedy: Problems of interpretation', in David Macksey and Eugenio Donato (eds), *The Languages of Criticism and the Sciences of Man: The Structuralist Controversy*, Baltimore: Johns Hopkins University Press, pp. 273–95.
Vidal-Naquet, Pierre (2002), *The Greeks, the Historians, Democracy*, trans. Anastasia Metheniti and Athanasios Stephanis, Athens: Patakis (in Greek).
Wernick, Andrew (1991), *Promotional Culture*, London: Sage.
Whitebook, Joel (1995), *Perversion and Utopia: A Study in Psychoanalysis and Social Theory*, Cambridge, MA: MIT Press.
Whitebook, Joel (1999), 'Requiem for a Selbstdenker: *in memoriam* Cornelius Castoriadis (1922–1997)', *Free Associations*, 7:43, pp. 331–56.
Wildner, Kathrin (2003), '*La Plaza*: Public space as space of negotiation', unpublished paper.
Williams, Caroline (1999), 'Reconstituting the subject of political discourse: From Lacan to Castoriadis', in Iain Mackenzie and Shane O'Neill (eds), *Reconstituting Social Criticism*, London: Macmillan, pp. 103–20.
Williams, Simon (2001), *Emotion and Social Theory*, London: Sage.
Williamson, Judith (1978), *Decoding Advertisements: Ideology and Meaning in Advertising*, London: Marion Boyars.
Wilson, Kevin and Jan van der Dussen (1995), *The History of the Idea of Europe*, London: Routledge and Open University Press.
Wintle, Michael (1996), 'Cultural identity in Europe: Shared experience', in Michael Wintle (ed.), *Culture and Identity in Europe*, Aldershot: Avebury Press, pp. 9–32.
Wolin, Sheldon (1994), 'Norm and form: The constitutionalizing of democracy', in Peter Euben, John Wallach and Josiah Ober (eds), *Athenian Political Thought and the Reconstruction of American Democracy*, Ithaca: Cornell University Press, pp. 29–58.

Yes Men, The (2004), *The True Story of the End of the WTO*, New York: Disinformation.
Zetterholm, Staffan (1994), 'Introduction: Cultural diversity and common policies', in Staffan Zetterholm (ed.), *National Culture and European Integration*, Oxford: Berg, pp. 1–12.
Ziarek, Ewa (2001), *An Ethics of Dissensus*, Stanford: Stanford University Press.
Žižek, Slavoj (1989), *The Sublime Object of Ideology*, London: Verso.
Žižek, Slavoj (1992), *Enjoy Your Symptom!*, New York: Routledge.
Žižek, Slavoj (1993), *Tarrrying with the Negative*, Durham: Duke University Press.
Žižek, Slavoj (1994), *The Metastases of Enjoyment*, London: Verso.
Žižek, Slavoj (1996a), *The Indivisible Remainder*, London: Verso.
Žižek, Slavoj (1996b), 'I hear you with my eyes', in Slavoj Žižek and Renata Salecl (eds), *Gaze and Voice as Love Objects*, Durham: Duke University Press, pp. 90–126.
Žižek, Slavoj (1997), *The Plague of Fantasies*, London: Verso.
Žižek, Slavoj (1998a), 'From "passionate attachments" to dis-identification', *Umbr(a)*, 1, pp. 3–17.
Žižek, Slavoj (1998b) 'The seven veils of fantasy', in Dany Nobus (ed.), *Key Concepts of Lacanian Psychoanalysis*, London: Rebus Press, pp. 190–218.
Žižek, Slavoj (1999), *The Ticklish Subject: The Absent Centre of Political Ontology*, London: Verso.
Žižek, Slavoj (2000), *The Fragile Absolute*, London: Verso.
Žižek, Slavoj (2001), *Did Somebody Say Totalitarianism?*, London: Verso.
Žižek, Slavoj (2003a), *The Puppet and the Dwarf*, Cambridge, MA: MIT Press.
Žižek, Slavoj (2003b), 'Hallward's fidelity to the Badiou event', Foreword in Peter Hallward, *Badiou*, Minneapolis: Minnesota University Press, pp. ix–xiii.
Žižek, Slavoj (2003c), 'A symptom – of what?', *Critical Inquiry*, 29, pp. 486–503.
Žižek, Slavoj (2003d), 'What some would call . . . : A response to Yannis Stavrakakis', *Umbr(a)*, pp. 131–5.
Žižek, Slavoj (2003e), 'Today Iraq. Tomorrow . . . democracy', *In These Times*, April, www.inthesetimes.com/site/main/article/565/
Žižek, Slavoj (2004a), *Iraq: The Borrowed Kettle*, London: Verso.
Žižek, Slavoj (2004b), 'From purification to subtraction: Badiou and the real', in Peter Hallward (ed.), *Think Again: Alain Badiou and the Future of Philosophy*, London: Continuum, pp. 165–81.
Žižek, Slavoj (2004c), 'Psychoanalysis, theory and politics: Yannis Stavrakakis interviews Slavoj Žižek', *Journal for Lacanian Studies*, 2:2, pp. 282–305.

Žižek, Slavoj (2004d), 'Hurray for Bush!', *London Review of Books*, 2 December, www.inb.co.uk/v26/n23/letters.htm.
Žižek, Slavoj (2005a), 'The politics of *jouissance*', *Lacanian Ink*, 24/25, pp. 126–35.
Žižek, Slavoj (2005b), 'Odradek as a political category', *Lacanian Ink*, 24/25, pp. 136–55.
Žižek, Slavoj (2005c), 'Some politically incorrect reflections on violence in France and related matters', www.lacan.com/zizfrance.htm.
Žižek, Slavoj (2006), *The Parallax View*, Cambridge, MA: MIT Press.
Žižek, Slavoj and Mladen Dolar (2002), *Opera's Second Death*, New York: Routledge.
Zupančič, Alenka (1998), 'Lacan's heroines: Antigone and Sygne de Coufontaine', *New Formations*, 35, pp. 108–21.
Zupančič, Alenka (2000), *Ethics of the Real: Kant, Lacan*, London: Verso.

Index

Abu Graib, 172
act, 12–13, 19, 57, 59, 103–4, 109–49, 118, 150, 151, 155, 156, 158, 166, 173, 234, 264, 269, 283n
  absolute/unconditional, 113
  vs activity, 12
  the after of, 112, 143
  and Antigone, 112–13, 114–20, 138–40, 150
  authentic, 113, 145–6n
  of *capitonnage*, 59–60
  of consumption, 23, 232, 234, 239, 249, 251n, 266
  and democracy, 59–60, 134–40
  ethical/ethico-political, 112–13, 114, 116, 119, 127
  and event, event/act *see* event
  genuine/true political, 123, 267
  heroic, 114, 120
  of identification, 25, 40, 165, 166, 195, 196
  of imagination, 57–8
  and lack, 125, 126, 134, 138
  miracle of, vs lack/negativity, 119–25, 133
  miraculous, 132–3, 143, 156–7; and optimism/vitalism, 121
  and negativity/positivity, 114, 120, 121, 123, 125, 127, 131, 139, 151–2
  and passivity, 120, 121
  perfect, 136–7, 152; and suicide, 137, 143
  politics of, 110, 111, 112, 121, 124, 129, 130; re-enacting of, continuous, 111, 125
  positive, 114, 121, 134
  psychoanalytic/in psychoanalysis, 15, 31n, 112, 126, 135, 146n, 147n, 159n
  radical, 18, 113–14, 116, 124, 134–5
  (as) real, 59, 126, 135; the real of, 59, 111–12
  and space, 13, 32n, 123, 143–5, 145–6n
  subjective/voluntarist, 119, 120
  and subjectivity, 121, 126
  and the symbolic, 126–7, 129, 135–6, 145–6n
  temporality of, 140, 143
  unconditional, 134–6, 278–9
  see also Lacan; psychoanalysis; Žižek
L'Acte psychanalytique (Lacan), 13–4, 31–2n, 112, 120, 126, 135, 145n, 146n
Adonnino reports, 216–17
Adorno, Theodor, 33n, 155, 241, 248, 278
advertising, 21–2, 168, 227–54, 263, 266, 283n
affect, 12, 15, 20–1, 70–1, 76, 84–7, 95–102, 104n, 105n, 106n, 107–8n, 164, 165, 167, 184n, 205–7, 209n, 213, 215, 221–2, 223, 225, 226n, 235, 277, 284n
  and enjoyment/*jouissance*, 16, 71–2, 85–95, 100–2, 167–8, 209n, 274, 278
  and fantasy, 174–81
  and repression, 100–2, 108n, 213–15
  and social transformation, 167–9
  and the unconscious, 101
  see also Freud; Lacan; representation
afficio, 184–5n
'The agency of the letter in the unconscious or reason since Freud' (Lacan), 107n, 174
aggressiveness/aggressivity, 193–4, 202, 214, 221, 222, 225

Ahmed, Sara, 100, 164, 184–5n
Alcorn, Marshal, 105n, 163, 166, 167, 186n, 194, 201, 274
alienation, 19, 27, 37, 47–9, 52–4, 57–9, 60, 63n, 64n, 208n
  constitutive, 52, 56
Althusser, Louis, 33n
analysis, 4, 5, 8, 9, 14, 16, 19, 21, 22, 25, 31n, 32n, 61n, 66, 70, 78, 88, 103, 104n, 105n, 126, 145n, 147n, 183–4, 186n, 190, 192, 212, 215, 228, 232
  academic, 217
  critical, 1, 3, 13
  economic, 245
  end of, 81, 267
  historical, 9, 61n
  political, 3, 15, 16–17, 18, 20, 61n, 65n, 67, 80, 81, 130, 140, 165, 180, 213, 221, 225, 228, 258
  socio-political, 81, 167, 236
  and theory, 30–1n; and experience, 5–14, 31n
  see also discourse analysis; psychoanalysis
analyst(s), 281
  of the nation, 200
  political, 205, 214
analytic theory, 31n
anti-humanism, 23
Anti-Oedipus (Deleuze & Guattari), 185n
Antigone, 18, 109–49, 151, 152
anxiety, 90–1, 100, 101, 102, 106n, 177, 198, 209n; *see also* Freud; Lacan
apophatism, 5
Arendt, Hannah, 32n, 172, 186–7n
Aristotle, 76, 117, 182, 269
Aronowitz, Stanley, 165; *see also* Bratsis
asbestos, 7
Athena, 271
Athens, 144, 204,
  (ancient), 145, 256, 269, 270
atimos, 269
Augustine, 182
authority, 6, 21, 79, 169–78, 182–3, 185n, 187n, 247–50, 255, 260–1, 262, 266, 268, 279; *see also* obedience; power

Bachelard, Gaston, 165
Badiou, Alain, 3, 15, 18–19, 109, 110, 113, 122, 123, 125–6, 127, 131, 137, 146n, 147n, 150–62, 163, 168, 255, 258, 261
Ballard, J. G., 249–51
banality, 7, 32n
  of evil, 32n, 172
  see also Arendt; normal science
Bataille, Georges, 27, 221
Baudrillard, Jean, 235, 238–40, 243, 247–8, 252n, 263, 268
Bauer, Bruno, 34n
Bauman, Zygmunt, 190–1, 208n, 253n
Bennett, Jane, 234, 252n, 269
Bentham's Panopticon, 144
Being and Event (Badiou), 152–4, 156–9
Bernays, Edward, 231, 233, 251n

312

INDEX

biologism, 27; *see also* Freud
de la Boétie, Étienne, 169, 182
Boothby, Richard, 73–4, 92, 93, 94, 101
Borromean knot, 11, 32n, 228
Bosteels, Bruno, 150–1
Bracher, Mark, 200
Bratsis, Peter, 165, 187n, 203, 210n; *see also* Aronowitz
Brecht, Bertolt, 115, 116
Breckman, Warren, 23, 24–5, 26
Bricmont, Jean, 5, 31n
Bruner, Jerome, 172
Burton, Tim, 241
Bush, George, 123–5, 140, 265
Butler, Judith, 4, 61–2n, 67, 105n, 111, 140–1, 142, 179, 188n, 276
Byrne, Ken, 275, 281; *see also* Healy

Campbell, David, 192–3, 208n
Cantor, Georg, 5, 152
capitalism, 18, 21, 22, 168, 179, 180, 185n, 229, 232, 238, 245, 246, 247, 251, 253n, 275, 284n
  American, 1
  critics of, 179
  globalised, 3, 256
  utopia of, 149n
capitonnage, 21, 59–60, 65n; *see also* Lacan; nodal point
Cartesian(ism), 53, 58, 106n
Castoriadis, Cornelius, 4, 15, 17, 18–19, 33n, 37–65, 66, 67–8, 69, 71–3, 88, 103, 104n, 105n, 106n, 110, 128, 158, 163, 254, 256, 257, 269–70, 273
castration, 77, 126–7, 130, 160n, 175, 199, 222, 223, 225, 241
  and perversion, 132
  symbolic, 47, 75, 95, 147n, 174, 196
cathexis/cathectic, 45, 84, 86, 99–100, 159n, 206, 213, 215, 218–19, 221–2, 241
Chaitin, Gilbert, 48, 65n
Chandler, David, 187n
Character Analysis (Reich), 27–8
Charlie and the Chocolate Factory, 241–2
Christian theology, 122
Christianity, 24, 131
Chrysoloras, Nikos, 207n, 208n
La Cité divisée (Loraux), 270–1
Claudel, Paul, 130, 146n
closure, 33n, 75, 96–7, 121, 273
  of affect, 108n
  discursive, 81, 196
  language as, 107n
  of the Other, 75
  theoretical, 11
Coca-Cola, 232, 240, 243, 247
Cohen, Lizabeth, 228–30, 243
Cohn-Bendit, Daniel, 2, 29n
Cold War, 194, 229
Coleman Silk, 137, 138
Coleridge, Samuel Taylor, 58
Collège de France, 5
Connolly, William, 97, 179, 198
Consilience: The Unity of Knowledge (Wilson), 31n
constructionism, 17, 19, 43, 44–5, 47–9, 71–3, 189, 190–2, 195, 199–200, 219
  social, 17, 41, 43, 167, 235, 252n
  see also Castoriadis; Lacan; Laclau
consumer culture, 22, 119, 228, 230–4, 241, 247
consumer's republic, 229–30
The Consumer Society (Baudrillard), 235, 238–40
The Communist Manifesto (Marx & Engels), 168
The Constitution of Athens (Aristotle), 269
consumerism, 16, 21, 22, 77, 79–80, 149n, 168, 183, 191, 227–38, 242–52, 266, 267, 272, 274, 282, 283n

consumption, 21, 23, 25, 32n, 119, 168, 199, 227–53, 263, 266, 280–1, 283n
Cook, Guy, 238
Coole, Diana, 259
Copjec, Joan, 43, 61n, 63n, 98–9, 101, 127–8, 146n, 279
Corfield, David, 174
Courbet, Gustave, 63n
creativity, 15, 17, 37–65, 69, 268; *see also* Castoriadis; Lacan
Creon, 113, 114, 117, 118–19, 120, 147n
Critchley, Simon, 114, 122–3
The Critique of Cynical Reason (Sloterdijk), 180
Cross, Garry, 227, 229, 231
Crouch, Colin, 263, 282n
The Cultural Politics of Emotion (Ahmed), 164, 184–5n

Dahl, Roald, 241
De Clerq report, 217
death drive, 28, 112–13, 131, 150–1, 198, 202; *see also* drive; Freud
Debord, Guy, 242, 252n, 253n
de-democratisation, 16, 22, 30n, 258, 278
Delanty, Gerard, 194, 212, 218
Deleuze, Gilles, 34n, 183, 185n
demand, 46–8, 63n, 95, 197, 209n, 236–7, 253n; *see also* desire; need
The Democratic Paradox (Mouffe), 67, 205, 256
démocratie à venir, 263; *see also* Derrida
democracy, 3, 16–17, 24–6, 42, 60, 65n, 66, 128, 129–30, 134–40, 142, 143, 157, 158, 159n, 168, 226, 251, 254–85
  of alternatives, 30n, 159–60n
  ancient (Greek) vs modern, 256, 267–73
  Athenian, 270, 271
  capitalist, 140
  deliberative, 277–8, 284n
  liberal, 254, 255, 262, 263, 265, 267–8, 272, 278
  passions in, 26, 278
  radical, 25–6, 66, 67, 112, 132–4, 140–2, 143, 144, 145, 254, 257, 267–8, 277, 281
  see also Badiou; Castoriadis; Lefort; Rancière; Vernant; Žižek
Derrida, Jacques, 134, 263
desire, 12, 27, 30n, 31n, 45, 72, 49, 53, 54, 56–7, 59, 62n, 63n, 69, 72, 74, 75, 77, 78, 87, 100, 102, 105n, 110, 112–14, 115–19, 125, 129–31, 132, 139, 146n, 147n, 175–6, 179, 182, 183, 185n, 188n, 189, 196–7, 198, 199–200, 205, 209n, 216, 227, 228–9, 233–4, 239–42, 243–4, 245–6, 247, 248, 249, 250, 252n, 253n, 259, 261, 267, 271, 273–4, 276, 279, 280, 282, 284n, 285n
  and consumerism/consumption, 228, 232, 234, 237–8, 244, 251
  and creation, 54, 56
  and drive, 119, 130, 146n, 276
  and enjoyment/*jouissance*, 13, 21, 196–7, 251
  ethics of, 119, 237–8
  false, 233; vs need, 237
  fantasmatic, 280, 281
  and fantasy, 75, 175
  and identification, 75, 243, 259, 260
  and impossibility, 63n, 69
  and lack, 40, 54, 60, 120, 122, 131, 147n, 237, 241, 280; dialectics of, 33n, 260, 263
  and law, 33n, 116–18, 130
  logic of, 22, 235, 238, 252n
  metonymic character of, 235, 242, 245
  national, 199, 200
  and need/demand, 46–7, 197, 237, 235–7; and the real/reality, 63n
  object of, 78; socio-political, 69
  object-cause of, 75, 78
  and the Other, 63n, 91, 247–8

desire (*cont.*)
  and representation, 52, 105n, 167
  and satisfaction, 198, 241
  and *suppléance*, 279–80
  unconscious, 72
  and utopia, 261
  see also Castoriadis; Kojève; Lacan; Other, the; Spinoza
dialectics, 33n
  positive/negative, 19, 72, 282
  see also desire; disavow(al); enjoyment; Lacanian; lack; negative dialectics
Dichter, Ernest, 232, 233, 253n
das Ding, 90, 94; *see also* Freud
Dis-agreement (Rancière), 263–4
disavow(al), 4, 56–7, 58, 108n, 133, 136, 139, 142, 144, 147n, 152, 155, 173, 271, 273, 284n
  dialectics of, 19, 35–160, 282
  of negativity/lack/finitude, 18–19, 58, 123, 124
  and perversion, 130, 132, 147n
  structure/mechanism of, 129–34
  see also Badiou; Castoriadis; Žižek
discourse/discursive, 4, 7, 10, 11, 13, 19, 20, 21, 22, 31–2, 43, 44, 58, 59, 66–108, 105n, 110, 129, 163, 166, 167, 168, 192, 193, 195, 196, 199, 200, 201, 204, 205, 206, 214–15, 216, 220, 221, 222, 224, 226, 227, 231, 238, 256, 260
  limits of, 11, 15, 18, 66–108, 109, 166
  see also Laclau
discourse analysis/theory, 16, 18, 31n, 44, 62n, 67, 69, 70, 71, 72, 82, 84, 85, 87, 95–104, 212, 213; *see also* Laclau; Mouffe
Le Discours vivant (Green), 88
The Discourse of Advertising (Cook), 238
Diski, Jenny, 172, 178
dislocation, 7, 53, 54, 55, 57, 59, 69, 70, 73–4, 75, 122, 259
Dolar, Mladen, 245, 246
Dora, 100
Dragonas, Thalia, 178, 179, 180
drive, 52, 63n, 71, 80, 886–7, 91, 92, 94–6, 100–1, 106n, 107n, 108n, 118, 119, 148n, 150, 151, 166, 200–1, 282
  and biological instinct, 107n, 237
  and desire, 119, 130, 146n, 276
  duality of, 28, 193
  and libido, 27
  see also death drive; Freud; Lacan

École Normale, 2
Ego-psychology, 105n
  American, critique of, 1
Elliott, Anthony, 60–1n, 63–4n
Emancipation(s) (Laclau), 66
enact(ing/ment), 10, 11, 12–13, 111, 125–8, 135, 138, 139, 269, 281
  of desire, 281
  of libido and aggression, 200–1
encircling, 10–13, 53–4, 64n, 81, 87–8, 95, 147n, 259
  and *jouissance*, 144, 279
  and lack, 129; in the Other, 112
  and negativity, 141
  and the real, 11, 32n, 53, 93–4
Encore (Lacan), 11, 43, 95, 106n, 107n, 241, 279, 280
Encyclopédie Française, 90
The End of Dissatisfaction? (McGowan), 246–50
Engels, Friedrich, 168; *see also* Marx
enjoyment, 1, 15, 16, 18, 19, 21, 22, 23, 27, 28, 40, 63n, 71, 77, 78, 80, 81, 83, 84, 90, 91, 96, 103, 109, 118, 143, 145, 148n, 161, 175, 176, 181, 183, 187n, 188n, 196, 197, 198, 199, 200, 201, 202, 203, 204, 205, 206, 207, 209n, 210n, 213, 214, 219, 221, 222, 223, 225, 228, 232, 234, 235, 239, 240, 241, 242, 243, 244, 245, 246, 247, 248, 249, 250, 251, 252n, 253n, 259, 260, 262, 264, 265, 266, 268, 269, 275, 277, 279, 280, 281, 282, 285n
  and affect, 90, 91, 177, 205, 209n, 268, 272
  commanded, 22, 246, 248, 249, 250, 262, 263, 265, 266, 279
  and desire, 13, 21, 22, 196, 228, 234, 244, 245, 250, 267, 273
  dialectics of, 161–285
  excessive, 203
  and fantasy, 200, 209n, 239, 279, 281
  impossible, 196
  and language, 80–1
  lost, 197, 202
  manipulation of, 22, 183
  and meaning, 91, 98, 243
  of the not-whole, 285n
  obscene, 209n, 214, 225
  partial, 197, 228, 244, 279, 280, 281, 282
  pre-symbolic, 74, 196
  the real of, 194, 201
  and *sinthome*, 181
  stolen, 197, 203, 204
  and symptom, 78, 80, 81
  total, 28, 204, 274,
  unconscious, 181
  see also jouissance; Lacan; lack; Žižek
Enlightenment, 8, 16, 64n, 163, 164, 180, 205, 206
L'Envers de la psychanalyse (Lacan), 1, 29n, 40, 94, 101, 232
essentialism, 18, 58, 76–7, 96, 97, 199–200
  affective, 167
  of emotions, 20
  humanist, 25–6
  subjective, 20, 47, 60
Ether, God and Devil: Cosmic Superimposition (Reich), 28
ethics/ethos, 113, 114, 115–16, 117, 118, 121, 122, 124, 126, 127, 128, 130, 150, 157, 158–9, 226, 257, 268, 279, 280
  democratic, 13, 22, 25, 60, 65n, 254, 257, 268, 269, 282
  of the event, 3, 15, 152
  of theorising, 10, 70, 87
  see also act; Badiou; desire; event; Lacan; Lacanian; political, the
Ethics of Dissensus (Ziarek), 26, 143
The Ethics of Psychoanalysis (Lacan), 48, 90, 112, 115, 116, 117, 118, 130, 132, 158–9n, 245
Ethics of the Real (Zupančič), 119
The Ethnic Origins of Nations (Smith), 191–2
Europe *see* European identity/identification; identification
Euripides, 181
European Community, 211
European Constitutional Treaty, 21, 145n, 191, 268
European identity/identification, 21–2, 77, 99, 168, 183, 207, 211–26, 227, 277
European Union, 178–9, 193, 212, 216–17, 221, 223
Euro-scepticism in British media, 223–5
Evans, Dylan, 61n, 95, 105n, 147n, 195
event, 7, 15, 32n, 44, 59, 97, 101–2, 122, 125–8, 143, 150–7
  and act, event/act, 18, 19, 59, 109, 110, 122, 124, 125–8, 134, 136, 137, 152, 156–8, 159–60n; and lack, 121
  the after of, 156, 160n
  dislocatory, 195
  ethics/ethical implications of, 3, 18
  fidelity to, 125, 127–8, 136, 152, 153, 154, 156, 157, 159–60n
  as miracle/miraculous, 18, 110, 120, 122, 156–7
  naming of, 155, 159n
  non-event, 151–2
  primal, 157
  true/real/authentic vs false, 122–3, 153–4, 168

INDEX

truth procedure of, 125, 152–3, 154, 155, 156, 158
Truth-Event, 156
see also act; Badiou; ethics; evental; event-ness; post-evental; Žižek
evental
 recurrence, 157
 site, 125, 137, 153–4
event-ness, 125–8, 143, 147n, 156–8, 159–60n, 256–7, 258, 272, 273–4
 fidelity to, 127, 143, 152–3, 157
ex nihilo (creation/creativity), 42, 48, 59, 109, 126
Excitable Speech (Butler), 105n
extimité, 55, 67; *see also* Lacan
existentialism, 57–8

Fahreneit 9/11 (Moore), 165
fantasy, 2, 6, 7, 12–13, 16, 27, 39–40, 78, 81, 94, 95, 96, 102, 103, 113, 119, 126, 141, 142, 148n, 157, 175, 176, 177–8, 196, 197, 199, 209n, 219–20, 224–5, 227, 230, 233, 235, 239–40, 241, 244, 245, 248, 251, 260, 261, 263, 266, 274, 279–80, 281, 282
 advertising/of advertising, 227–53
 and affect, 174–81
 and aims of analytic treatment, 261
 vs biological necessity, 237
 of castration, 225
 Coke, 242–3
 consumerist/of consumption, 227–53
 and desire, 175, 176–7, 197, 239, 280
 emotional dynamics of, 21
 and enjoyment/*jouissance*, 103, 200, 202, 205, 239–40, 244, 248, 260, 275
 function of, 75, 181
 Green ideological, 104n
 hegemonic/of hegemony, 256, 282
 and nation, 198–9, 200, 204, 243
 of normal science, 6
 paranoiac, 266
 politics of, 268
 social, 77, 238
 structure of, 197, 198
 and symptom, 78–82, 196, 246
 utopian/of utopia, 2, 22, 23, 144, 181, 261, 266
 of the whole/wholeness/fullness, 31n, 49, 204, 280–1
 in Ziarek, 26
 see also traversing
Fascism, 69, 185n, 261, 265, 278
Feltham, Oliver, 154
fetish(ist/ism), 109, 132, 134, 138, 140, 147n, 165, 166
'Fetishism' (Freud), 108n
Feuerbach, Ludwig, 23–4, 34n
Fink, Bruce, 31n, 34n, 45, 50, 62n, 71–2, 98–9, 101, 104n, 279
The Four Fundamental Concepts of Psychoanalysis (Lacan), 1, 8, 9, 43, 64n, 74, 101, 106n, 107n, 116, 119
force, 105n
 and form, 86, 192–6
 and language, 105n; libidinal, 105n
formalisation, 11, 64n, 81, 96
Foucault, Michel, 183, 185n, 187–8n, 253n
Frankfurt School, 34n, 169
French Revolution, 29n, 152
Freud, Sigmund, 1, 2, 11, 13, 24, 26, 27, 28, 33n, 34n, 37, 38, 50, 62n, 64n, 71, 73, 76, 78, 80, 86, 88, 89, 90, 91, 92, 94, 100, 101, 102, 104n, 106n, 107n, 108n, 132, 159n, 181, 193, 194, 195, 200, 231, 232, 274; *see also* Lacan, Lacanian
Freudian(ism), 16, 24, 26, 38, 41, 46, 70, 72, 74, 78, 99, 104n, 108n, 147n, 148n, 167, 170, 181, 190, 196, 198, 199, 213, 273, 275, 280; *see also* Lacan, Lacanian

Freudian Left, the, 26, 27, 28, 29, 143, 167, 169, 234, 251n
The Freudian Left (Robinson), 26, 143

Gallagher, Cormac, 88, 90, 106n
Gilbert, Jeremy, 70
Gibson, Katherine, 179, 180, 275; *see also* Graham
Glynos, Jason, 31n, 32n, 82–6, 105n, 143, 169, 187n, 268
Goedel's theorem, 5
Goux, Jean-Joseph, 241, 245, 247
Graham, Julie, 179, 180, 275; *see also* Gibson
graphe paranomon, 269
'The Greek Polis and the creation of democracy' (Castoriadis), 42
Greekness, 203–5
Green, André, 88, 105n, 108n
Green ideology, 59, 65n, 104n
Grigg, Russell, 92, 118, 119
Grosrichard, Alain, 245, 246
Group Psychology (Freud), 193
Guattari, Félix, 34n, 183, 185n

Habermas, Juergen, 49, 51, 206, 277
Haemon, 147n
Hallward, Peter, 113, 125, 150–1, 154, 155, 159n
Hardt, Michael, 64n, 97, 183, 185n
hatred, 193–4, 200, 206, 207, 265, 274, 277
 and group bonds, 194, 202
 nationalist, 202
Healy, Stephen, 275, 281; *see also* Byrne
Hegel, G. W. F., 23, 24, 26, 34n, 63n, 244
Hegelian Left, the, 23, 24, 25–6, 29, 34n
hegemony/hegemonic, 3–4, 15, 21, 22, 67, 76, 86–7, 99, 102, 119, 129, 163–4, 169, 171, 182, 183, 213, 227, 228, 231, 234, 237, 241, 244, 250, 256, 257, 267, 272
 theory of hegemony, 3, 67; *see also* Laclau
Hegemony and Socialist Strategy (Laclau & Mouffe), 62n, 66, 68, 84
Heidegger, Martin, 45, 65n, 122
Henry, Michel, 106n
Hirschman, Albert, 183, 229, 230, 235, 236, 240–1, 242
Hoens, Dominiek, 79, 81, 126, 159n; *see also* Pluth
Hoggett, Paul, 277, 284n; *see also* Thompson
The Human Stain (Roth), 137–8
humanism/ist, 20, 23, 25–6, 47, 48, 49
Huxley, Aldous, 238–9

identification, 16, 18, 19–20, 25, 40, 43, 47, 53, 63n, 66–7, 75, 79–80, 82, 94, 102, 105n, 109–10, 163, 165–9, 178, 179, 180, 183, 184n, 189–207, 209n, 212–25, 227, 231, 233, 234, 243, 255, 259, 260, 264, 274–82, 284n
 collective, 213, 214, 222
 consumerist, 234
 with lack, 274, 276
 libidinal/visceral/affective/obscene dimension of, 71, 217, 215, 219, 221, 222
 and mourning, 274–6
 national(ist), 21–3, 99, 164, 168, 184n, 189–207, 209n, 221
 political, 15, 20, 60, 77, 143, 214, 225, 268
 with the symptom, 82, 151, 276, 279, 281
identity formation *see* identification
ideology/ideological, 59, 65n, 70, 80, 81, 82, 103, 104n, 163, 166, 175, 180, 181, 182, 183, 198, 234, 250
imaginary, the, 32n, 33n, 40–1, 42–5, 62n, 63n, 73–5, 95, 98, 187n, 226n, 243, 251, 264–7, 285n
 radical instituting, 42
 see also Lacan; real, the; symbolic (the)
The Imaginary Institution of Society (Castoriadis), 45–6, 62n

315

immanentism, 57, 97–8, 183–4
impossibility, 5, 11–12, 27, 32n, 47, 58, 64n, 67, 69, 73, 93–4, 120–1, 127, 134–5, 136, 137, 141, 157–8, 191, 198, 202, 256–7, 259, 279–80
  and desire, 63n
  and fantasy, 248
  and *jouissance*, 197, 248, 262
  of society, 67, 69, 73, 76
  of utopia, 135
incommensurable/incommensurability, 9, 10, 28, 45, 47, 50, 51, 53, 55–6, 222; *see also* real, the
incompleteness, 11, 126
  of identity, 73, 194–5
  see also lack
inconsistency 11, 73, 125
Instincts and their Vicissitudes (Freud), 92
Intellectual Impostures (Sokal & Bricmont), 5
The Interpretation of Dreams (Freud), 107–8n
investment, 84–6, 96, 99–102, 106n, 144, 159n, 157–68, 175, 180, 192, 194, 209–10n
  affective, 100, 181, 193, 200, 207, 220, 227, 260, 270, 276, 282
  cathectic, 86
  libidinal, 21, 26, 99, 143, 179, 190, 195, 206, 207, 282
Iraq (Žižek), 111, 276

Jenkins, Brian, 183, 200, 206; *see also* Sofos
jouis-sens, 95, 243
jouissance, 1, 17, 20, 21, 26, 48, 66–108, 72, 74, 144, 163–88, 196, 197, 198, 209n, 213, 227, 227–53, 263, 274, 277, 279
  and affect, 71–2, 84, 87–103
  castrated, 74
  consumerist, 266
  democratic, 143, 276–282
  imaginarised, 198
  and language, 94–5, 97, 99
  and libido, 99, 104n
  partial, 197, 274
  phallic, 144
  and social transformation, 167–9
  see also enjoyment; Lacan; Lacanian
Journal for Lacanian Studies, 82, 83, 96

Kant, Immanuel, 242
Das Kapital (Marx), 237
Kay, Sarah, 148n
Keohane, Kieran, 201, 203, 209n
knowledge, 5, 6–7, 12, 13, 21, 25, 31n, 88, 144, 154, 165, 172, 173, 176, 177, 178–9, 180–1, 182, 183, 187n, 217, 239, 254, 256, 274, 282, 284n
  and consciousness, 180–1
  and desire, 14
  and experience, 5, 6, 8, 9, 10, 12
  and rationality, 234
Kohn, Margaret, 143–4, 149n
Kojève, Alexandre, 23, 34n, 62–3n, 244
Kolakowski, Lessek, 24, 26
Kuhn, Thomas, 6, 7–8, 10–11, 73

Lacan, Jacques, 1, 2, 3–4, 5, 9, 10, 11, 12, 13, 14, 15, 19, 23, 24, 25, 27, 28, 29n, 30n, 32n, 33n, 34n, 37, 38, 39, 40, 41, 42, 43, 45, 46, 47, 48, 49, 50, 51, 53, 54, 55, 56, 59, 60, 61n, 62n, 63n, 64n, 65n, 66, 68, 69, 71, 73, 74, 75, 76, 77, 78, 79, 80, 81, 88, 89, 90, 91, 92, 93, 94, 95, 96, 97, 100, 101, 102, 103, 105n, 106n, 107n, 108n, 113, 114, 115, 116, 117, 118, 119, 120, 126, 129, 130, 132, 135, 136, 138, 140, 145n, 146n, 147n, 148n, 158n, 159n, 163, 166, 167, 171, 174, 175, 189, 190, 208n, 239, 241, 247, 268, 276, 277, 279, 285n
  and (theory of) the act, 111–15, 119–20, 132, 135–6, 151; ambiguities of, 111–14

and advertising, 232, 245
and affect/affectivity, 88–91
and anxiety, 91, 209n
and Badiou, 3, 19, 150–60
and Castoriadis, 17, 33n, 37–65, 73
communist interest in, 33n
constructionism/constructionist arguments of, 17, 41–9, 67, 71, 73, 251
and desire, 34n, 40, 72, 102, 196, 238
ethics of, 115, 116
and *extimité*, 55, 67
and feminine 'non-all'/'not-whole', 281, 285n
and Foucault, 187–8n
and Freud(ianism), 1–2, 13, 27–8, 33n, 80, 88, 104n, 181, 190, 195–6, 199–200
and Hartmann, 105n
and Hegel, 23, 34n
and *jouissance*, 16, 28, 71–2, 76–7, 102, 181, 183, 195, 196, 198, 232, 274; feminine and partial, 279
and Kojève, 23, 34n
and Laclau, 18, 66–108, 142
and language, 38, 40, 43, 45, 51, 80, 89, 94–5, 96–7, 107n, 208n
and libido, 28, 91, 195
and Marx, 1, 29n
need/demand/desire in, 46–7, 237
negative ontology/negativity of, 17, 19, 70, 71, 151
and *objet petit a*, 67, 75, 76, 238
the Other in, 25, 33n, 39, 46, 47, 50, 52, 63n, 67, 69, 73, 74, 75, 76, 91, 97, 189, 236, 239–40, 279–80
and *parlêtre*, 237
and *point de capiton*, 59, 65n, 67, 68, 220
and politics, 1–3, 29n, 285n
and (category of) the real, 16, 18, 51, 53, 60, 72, 76; vs reality, 6–7, 44–5
and repression, 101–2, 108n, 213
and Scitovsky, 235
Seminars of, 17, 50; I, 88–9; II, 12; III, 39, 43, 50; VII, 48, 90, 112, 115, 116, 117, 118, 130, 132, 158–9n, 245; IX, 197; X, 90–1, 101, 108n, 118, 209; XI, 1, 8, 9, 43, 64n, 74, 101, 106n, 107n, 116, 119; XIII, 63n; XIV, 39; XV, 13–14, 31–2n, 112, 120, 126, 135, 145n, 146n; XVII, 1, 29n, 40, 94, 101, 232; XX, 11, 43, 95, 106n, 107n, 241, 279, 280; XXIII, 80
and sexual liberation, 27
and sublimation, 107n, 279
and *suppléance*, 279–80
and symptom/sinthome, 77, 78–81, 246
terms of art/neologisms/formulations/phrases of, 5, 7, 11, 17, 32n, 67, 173, 237
and Žižek, 4, 19, 109–49, 158
see also Freud; *jouissance*; Lacanian
Lacan and the Political (Stavrakakis), 15, 16, 17, 32n, 33n, 34n, 61n, 104n, 105n, 148n, 159n, 186n, 208n, 254, 279, 282n, 284n
Lacanian, 18, 19, 20, 22, 43, 44, 45, 46, 51, 53, 65n, 66, 67, 69, 70–1, 74, 83, 97, 98, 99, 104n, 108n, 111–14, 116, 130, 151, 167, 170, 174, 175, 180, 181, 183, 186n, 213, 228, 235, 236, 238, 241, 244, 245, 246, 252n, 260, 273, 276, 279, 284n
  approach to/analysis of nationalism, 200, 203–5, 207
  ethics, 67, 70, 111, 113, 114, 120, 121, 127, 142, 144, 146n, 148n, 254
  jargon, 209n, 246
  Left, the, 1, 4, 14, 15, 16, 17, 18, 19, 23, 24, 25, 26, 27, 28, 29, 33n, 37, 40, 41, 44, 48, 60, 66, 72, 77, 81, 83, 87, 88, 103, 109, 110, 111, 112, 114, 124, 130, 140, 143, 150, 156, 158, 163, 167, 168, 183–4, 207, 226, 228, 244, 254, 255, 256, 282
neologisms, 95
psychoanalysis *see* psychoanalysis

INDEX

radicalism, 1, 18, 27, 76
real, the, 16, 17, 33n, 54, 64n, 67, 70, 76, 82
semiotics, 16
theory, 1, 3, 10, 15, 16, 17, 18, 19, 20, 23, 30n, 31n, 33n, 37, 38, 39, 40, 49–50, 52, 54, 55, 58, 60, 61n, 67, 69, 71, 73, 74, 76, 77, 81, 87, 105n, 110, 112, 114, 121, 131, 133, 142, 183–4, 186n, 198, 201, 228, 236, 251, 254, 260, 267, 281; political, 4, 16, 17, 29n, 38, 40, 59, 146n, 205
triad real–symbolic–imaginary, 32n, 98
lack, 10, 11, 18, 22–3, 25, 39–40, 49, 51, 54, 57, 59, 64n, 66–7, 69, 71, 74–9, 87–8, 97, 109, 110, 113, 119–24, 129, 132, 134, 136, 138, 141–2, 144–5, 147n, 151, 175, 179, 197, 198, 199–208n, 209n, 236–7, 239–242, 252n, 257, 259, 260, 263, 270–4, 276–82
constitutive, 25, 29n, 79, 97, 113
and consumerism, 248, 252n, 266
and desire, 33n, 47, 60n, 63n, 147n, 237; dialectics between, 260, 263
of fullness/completeness, 195
of identity, 69
institutionalisation of, 10, 25, 124, 141, 142, 262, 272, 273, 278, 281
of (pre-symbolic/total) *jouissance*/enjoyment, 78, 97, 197, 199–208, 260, 265, 274
and love, 131
vs miracle, 119–24
in the Other, 39, 47, 67, 73, 74, 76, 97, 112, 124, 127, 128, 135–6, 138, 140, 141, 142, 239–41, 273, 278–80
of the real, 74–5
see also Castoriadis; Lacan; Žižek
Laclau, Ernesto, 3, 4, 14, 15, 17–18, 19, 29n, 31n, 44, 58–9, 61–2n, 64n, 66–108, 109, 122, 123, 133, 134, 140–2, 153, 156, 163, 190, 192, 257, 259, 272, 273, 274, 275–6, 278, 282n, 283n; see also discourse analysis/theory; Mouffe
Laclau: A Critical Reader, 82, 86
lalangue, 94, 95
lamella, myth of, 64n, 93–94
language, 12, 38, 39, 40, 42, 43, 45, 46, 50, 60n, 80, 81, 83, 84, 89, 95, 96, 97, 99, 102, 105n, 106n, 107n, 165–6, 167, 174, 208n, 216, 223, 236
and need and demand, 46, 236
status of, in modernity, 164–7
see also Lacan; need; representation; Saussure; signifier; symbolic (the); symbolisation
Lane, Christopher, 104n
Latour, Bruno, 6, 7, 10, 16
Le Pen, Jean-Marie, 214, 222
Leader, Darian, 63n, 126, 142
Lecercle, Jean-Jacques, 107n, 122
Leclaire, Serge, 8–9, 32n, 88–9
Lefort, Claude, 25, 26, 60, 140, 144, 182, 262, 272, 273
Left, the, 1, 3, 4, 21, 33n, 37, 206, 214, 228, 255, 274, 275
Left/Right division, 29–30n
'rationalist', 165
utopian fantasies of, 22
utopian vs Lacanian, 124
see also Freudian(ism); Hegelian Left, the; Lacanian
leftism/ist, 22, 231, 236, 237, 244, 250, 257, 275
Lévi-Strauss, Claude, 39
libidinal, 18, 19–21, 71–2, 105n, 143, 167, 176–80, 187n, 193–5, 213, 217, 222, 225, 227, 274
attachment, 183, 209n, 274, 279
bond, 193, 205, 213
energy, 71, 91, 92
investment, 21, 26, 99, 143, 179, 180, 190, 195, 206, 207, 282; and social link, 86
Libidinal Economy (Lyotard), 88
libido, 27–8, 64n, 71, 91–2, 103, 104n, 105n, 195–6, 198, 200–2, 245, 273

and affect-*jouissance*, 21, 99, 167
unbinding of, 167
see also Freud; Lacan
Lipowatz, Thanos, 147n
Little Hans, 100
Lodziak, Conrad, 234, 236, 253n
'Logos' (Heidegger), 65n
Loraux, Nicole, 270, 271, 284n
Lust 89, 104n; see also Freud
Lyotard, Jean-François, 57, 87–8, 100–1, 155, 201, 227

Maastricht treaty, 216
McClintock, Anne, 285n
McGowan, Todd, 246–50, 265, 269, 279
Machiavelli, Niccolò, 185n
Madra, Yahya, 281; see also Ozselçuk
Marchart, Oliver, 82, 257–8, 278
Marcuse, Herbert, 26–8, 169, 230, 251n, 280
Marcussen, Martin, 194
Marx, Karl, 1–2, 24, 29n, 34n, 168, 237, 240, 264
Marx, the Young Hegelians and the Origins of Radical Social Theory (Breckman), 24
Marxism/ist, 3, 29n, 33n, 59, 62n, 264, 275–6
Mass Psychology of Fascism (Reich), 169
Massumi, Brian, 108n
May 1968 (events), 2, 13–14, 145n
Medea, 130
Merleau-Ponty, Maurice, 5
metapsychology/metapsychological, 27, 71, 91–3, 101, 107–8n, 181; see also Freud
The Metastases of Enjoyment (Žižek), 116
Meyerson, Émile, 62–3n
Milgram, Stanley, 172–80, 186n, 187n, 248
Millennium People (Ballard), 249–50
Miller, Jacques-Alain, 13, 24, 30n, 61n, 76, 78, 79, 91, 94–5, 105n, 106n, 146n, 158, 198, 276–7
miracle, 18, 110, 113, 119–25, 146n, 156; see act; lack; Žižek
Moebius band, 15, 33n
Montesquieu, Charles de Secondat, Baron de, 254
Moore, Michael, 165
Mouffe, Chantal, 3–4, 17, 18, 26, 29n, 31n, 44, 59, 62n, 66–8, 69, 81, 104n, 140, 185n, 205, 207, 213–14, 256–7, 264–5, 272, 278, 282n, 283n, 284n; see also Laclau
mourning, 167, 273-6

Name-of-the-Father, 81, 169–70, 173–4, 181; see also Lacan
Nasio, Juan-David, 11, 12, 105n
Nathan, Robert, 229
nationalism, 16, 21, 60, 77, 104n, 164, 183, 189–96, 198–200, 202, 204–8, 218–21, 227, 235, 243, 272, 274, 282, 284n
need, 45–9, 52, 63n, 107n, 209n, 233, 235–44, 280
and demand–desire/*jouissance*, 46, 47, 48, 95
and language, 46, 236
see also demand; desire; Lacan
negative dialectics, 33n; see also Adorno; dialectics
negative ontology, 18, 19, 69, 71, 72, 114, 131; see also Lacan
negativity, 8, 10, 18, 58, 75, 132–3, 151–4, 158, 160n, 195, 259–61, 262–3, 266, 267–9, 272
as encounter with the real, 109
and enjoyment, 268, 269
and lack, 121, 124, 263, 276
and positivity, 11–12, 15–16, 17, 18, 19, 26, 76, 109, 114, 121, 122, 123, 131, 141, 151, 259
see also Badiou; Lacan; Lacanian; Žižek
Negri, Antonio, 57, 185n
Neo-Freudian, 27, 62n
Neuropolitics (Connolly), 97
neurosis, 28, 100, 132, 147n

317

New Reflections on the Revolution of our Time (Laclau), 66, 67, 73, 75
New Social Movements, 29–30n
Newman, Saul, 187n, 188n
nihilism, 17, 150
Nobus, Dany, 101, 102
nodal point, 21, 43, 59, 62n, 67, 68, 81, 102, 103, 104n, 118, 181, 200, 220, 227, 258, 265
normal science, 6, 7–8, 10, 31n
  banality of, 8, 10
  fantasy of, 6

obedience, 21, 118, 170, 172–87, 248–9, 251, 266; *see also* authority; power
objet petit a, 74–7, 82, 106n, 239
  and advertising, 238–41, 244
  and central task of psychoanalysis, 280
  and phallus, 92
  sacrifice of, 279
  see also Lacan
obscene, 205, 222–5, 243, 277
  enjoyment, 209–10n, 214–15, 225
  fantasy, dimension of, 197
  (national) identification, dimension/aspect of, 206, 207, 215–16
  jouissance, forms/paths of, 21, 195
  Other, 202, 222–6
Oedipal, 169
Orgone, 28
L'Origine du monde (Courbet), 63n
Other, the, 53, 56, 113, 121, 136, 137, 138, 140, 147n, 148n, 169–70, 197–9, 200, 202, 203, 253n, 276–82
  and advertising, 247
  desire of, 116, 247
  ethnic and religious, 179
  evil, 199
  jouissance of, 147n, 265
  lack in, 112, 120, 124, 127–8, 135–6, 138, 140, 141–2, 273, 278
  national, 197
  obscene, 202, 222–6
  see also Lacan
Ozselçuk, Ceren, 274, 276, 281, 284n; *see also* Madra

Papaioannou, Costas, 128
paradigm, 6, 7–8, 11, 29n, 114, 185n, 232, 234
  culturalist, 242
  heroic, 114
  modernist, 189
  naturalist/essentialist, 235
  rationalist, 233
  scientific, 30n
The Parallax View (Žižek), 253n, 283n
Paris, Haussmann's redesign of, 144
parlêtre see Lacan
passage à l'acte, 135, 147n
passion(s) 18, 157, 164, 205, 207, 211, 213, 214, 215, 217, 223, 225, 229, 272, 278
  pascho and *jouissance*, 183
  passio and *pathos*, 182–3, 184–5n
  see also Mouffe
Passionate Politics, 165, 166
perverse, 28, 132, 134, 138, 142, 202–3, 250, 270
perversion, 38, 118, 130, 132, 147n, 185n
  mechanism of, 132
Perversion and Utopia (Whitebook), 39
Phaedra (Euripides), 181
phallus, 46–7, 89–90, 92, 71, 245, 285n
  absent maternal, 147n
philosopher, 1, 14, 43, 63n, 150, 152, 155, 158–9n
philosophy, 5, 14, 26, 32n, 98, 146n, 150, 155–6
  analytical, 166
  Enlightenment, 205
  Indian, 106n

liberal, 233
political, 6, 18, 185n
Piano, Renzo, 144–5
Plato, 128, 256, 280
Pluth, Ed, 79, 81, 126, 136, 140, 151, 159n; *see also* Hoens
point de capiton see Lacan; nodal point
political, the, 4–5, 16, 37, 56–60, 64n, 69, 120, 141, 214, 264, 280
  ethics of, 22, 254, 269, 282
political theory, 1, 13, 14–15, 17, 20, 23–4, 33n, 37–8, 41, 53, 59–60, 66, 147n, 167, 168–9, 185n, 205, 228, 258, 267–8, 277–8, 284n
  anti-essentialist, 77
  critical, 20, 109, 135
  Lacanian, 4, 16, 17, 29n, 38, 40, 59, 146n
  post-structuralist, 20
politics, 1–2, 3, 10, 12–13, 15, 17, 18, 59, 61n, 72, 75–6, 77, 103, 105n, 109, 110, 113, 114, 115–16, 121, 123, 127, 129, 131, 142, 150, 153, 164, 165, 166, 167, 179, 181, 191, 193, 194, 205, 213–14, 215, 218, 220, 221, 226, 228, 229, 230, 231, 236, 249, 255–6, 257, 258, 263, 264, 267, 272, 273, 275, 283–4n, 285n
  affective dimension of, 20
  democratic, 3, 14, 18, 26, 58, 141, 255, 264, 271, 278
  of emotion, 165
  of the event/act, 18; and Žižek, 110, 111, 112, 121, 124, 129, 130, 136–7
  of fantasy, 268
  (ancient) Greek, 272
  of hope, 187n
  of identification, 196
  of imagination, 56–7
  of *jouissance*, 181–4; consumerist, 227–53
  of memory, 271
  of nostalgia, 157, 275
  post-democratic, 147n
  of private enjoyment, 265
  progressive, 60, 133, 180
  radical, 58, 121, 230
  relation positive–negative in, 38; and identity, 221
  revolutionary, 2of subjectivity, 196, 199
  symbolic dimension of, 20
  of transformation/transformative, 14–15, 112, 124, 144, 261, 267
  of traversing the fantasy, 142
  of utopia/utopian, 146, 196, 266
  see also Lacan
The Politics of Consumption, 228
On Populist Reason (Laclau), 66
positivisation, 8, 10–12, 26, 53, 75–6, 128–9, 141, 142, 154, 156–7; *see also* negativity
A Postcapitalist Politics (Gibson-Graham), 179
post-democracy, 22, 145n, 147n, 255, 258, 259–67, 277–8, 282n
  consumerist, 268, 272
  Post-Democracy (Crouch), 263, 282n
  'Post-Democracy' (Rorty), 255
  see also Žižek
post-eventual, 125, 156
post-Marxism/ist, 62n, 166
post-structuralism/ist, 20–1, 61n, 72, 73, 80–1, 164–6, 189–90, 201
power, 111, 119, 163, 169, 182, 185n, 187n, 216, 245, 247, 262, 282
  symbolic, 21, 169–74, 175, 176–7, 178, 181, 248–9
  see also authority; obedience
Powers, Austin, 209n
praxis, 4, 5, 8, 14, 19, 34n, 49, 110, 148n, 169, 280, 268; *see also* act
'Presentation on Psychical Causality' (Lacan), 61n

INDEX

prion, 7, 8
Project for a Scientific Psychology (Freud), 88
protest culture, 2, 230
proto-meaning, 52–3, 56–7, 59
Prusiner, Stanley, 8
psychic monad, 49–53, 56, 57, 59
psychoanalysis, 1, 2, 3, 8, 9, 10, 11, 13, 15, 24, 26, 29n, 30n, 31n, 34n, 38, 39, 41, 43, 61n, 64n, 67, 68, 69, 70–1, 74, 78, 79, 81, 83, 87, 88, 93, 105n, 106n, 120, 141, 145n, 158n, 176, 183, 186n, 192, 194, 205, 212, 225, 231, 232, 233, 234, 236, 254, 261, 267, 28; *see also* Castoriadis; Freud; Lacan
(psycho)analyst, 1, 8–9, 13–14, 31n, 32n, 39, 60, 116, 126–7, 145n, 159n
psychosis, 38, 59, 132, 147n

Quebec(kers), 203

radical imagination, 19, 37, 49, 52–3
  politics of, 17
'Radical imagination and the social instituting imaginary' (Castoriadis), 41
radicalism, 24
  anti-utopian, in Lacan, 1, 3
  of democracy, 256
  Freudian, 27
  Lacanian, 27
  sexual, 27
Rancière, Jacques, 155, 263, 264
the Rat-man, 100
Reagan era, 230
real, the, 4–14, 19–20, 25, 29n, 32n, 33n, 34n, 40, 45, 47, 48–9, 50, 51, 52–6, 58–60, 62–3n, 64n, 69–70, 71–2, 72–82, 90, 92–100, 102–3, 106n, 107n, 108n, 109, 111–12, 119–20, 123, 135–6, 148n, 158n, 159n, 165, 201, 204, 236, 243, 258, 260
  as/of enjoyment/*jouissance*, 16–17, 19, 77, 80, 81, 82, 83, 194, 260
  of experience, 7–8, 9–10, 11
  and lack, 74–5
  negative, 19, 72–7, 110
  positive, 78–82
  Real-Ich, 90
  and reality, 6–7, 12, 44–5, 47, 70
  see also imaginary, the; Lacan; Lacanian; symbolic (the)
reduction(ism/ist), 9, 10, 11–12, 20, 25, 26, 33n, 89–90, 91, 94, 95, 98, 148n, 160n, 166, 221, 256, 259
Regimes of Emotion, 165
Reich, Wilhelm, 26–8, 169, 185n
Reluctant Subjects, 179
representation, 6–11, 20, 25, 32n, 34n, 45–6, 48–9, 52, 53–6, 59, 64n, 69, 71–2, 73–6, 83–5, 91–3, 96–102, 105n, 167, 208n, 213, 242–3, 278
  and affect, 15–16, 72, 97, 98, 99, 100–2, 104n, 107–8n, 213
  and emotion, 166
  and *jouissance*, 97, 99, 102, 106n, 195
  and language, 99, 166, 196
  see also Castoriadis; symbolisation
repress(ion), 4–5, 7, 10, 19, 27, 28, 42, 56, 84, 93, 100–2, 108n, 125, 132, 141, 147n, 183, 193–4, 213, 214, 215, 218–19, 221, 222, 225, 267–8, 272, 277
  and anxiety, 101–2
  and displacement of the affect, 101–2, 213–15
  and representation/signifiers, 101, 213–14
  repressed, return of the, 8, 214–15, 222, 277
  vs sublimation, 226
  vs *suppléance*, 279
  see also Freud; Lacan
Repression (Freud), 92, 101

revolutionaries, 2
  vs cynics, 160n
  vs reformists, 4
Ricoeur, Paul, 58
Robinson, Andrew, 1, 4, 29n
Robinson, Paul, 2, 26, 27, 143
Roheim, Geza, 27, 143
romantic(ism), 48, 49, 53, 58, 60, 64n, 199
Rome discourse (Lacan), 1, 80, 89
Roosevelt's *New Deal*, 228
Rorty, Richard, 255
Roth, Philip, 137–9
Rousseau, Jean-Jacques, 169, 185n

Sahlins, Marshal, 280
Saint Paul, 117–18, 125, 153, 280
Saussure, Ferdinand de, 39, 106–7n, 166
science, role of in Milgram's experiment, 175–8
scientific experiment, 6, 175, 178
scientific theory, 5, 6, 7
  banality of, 7–8
  see also normal science
Second World War, 229
semiotic(s), 16, 21, 87–8, 192, 193, 194, 205, 208n;
  see also Lacanian
Sennet, Richard, 242, 252n
sentimentalism, humanist, 20
Serbs and Slovenes, 202–3
Shaw, Jo, 218
'The signification of the phallus' (Lacan), 46
signifier, 3, 4, 6–7, 11, 15, 30n, 33n, 34n, 42–3, 48, 50, 59, 60, 62n, 67, 68, 69, 71–2, 74–7, 78, 80–1, 89–90, 94–5, 98–102, 103, 104n, 105n, 109, 122, 136, 140, 151, 159n, 174, 179, 182, 189, 200, 208n, 213, 214, 217, 229, 232, 256, 258, 271, 274, 276–7, 279–80; *see also* Lacan; Laclau
sinthome, 80–1, 93–4, 181, 228, 246; *see also* enjoyment; Lacan; symptom
situationness, 156–68, 256–7
Sloterdijk, Peter, 180
Slovenia, 255
Smith, Anthony, 191–2, 206, 207n, 208n, 211, 217, 218, 219
social
  change/transformation, 15–16, 20–1, 81–2, 102, 112, 164, 167, 169, 184n, 193
  objectivity, 72–3, 163
The Social Contract (Rousseau), 169
socialisation, 42, 45, 49–56, 74, 78, 107n, 196, 260
Socialisme ou barbarie group, 37
society
  eidos of, 42
  impossibility of, 67, 69, 73, 76
  permissive, 253n
  of prohibition vs of commanded enjoyment, 22, 246–7, 249, 250, 253n, 261, 265–6, 283n
  and self-creation, 41–2, 257
Sokal, Alan, 5, 31n; *see also* Bricmont
Sophocles, 114, 115, 118, 128, 147n
Sorkin, Michael, 143
Spinoza, Baruch, 47, 48, 185n, 227, 142
Sofos, Spiros, 200, 206; *see also* Jenkins
Stalinism, 140, 261
Starobinski, Jean, 107n
stasis, 270–1
Stavrakakis, Yannis, 83, 85–6, 130–1, 133
Stirner, Max, 34n
Strauss, David, 34n
structuralism/ist, 20, 38–40, 48, 59, 61n, 71, 80–1, 89, 91, 96, 103n, 166–7
sublimation, 107n, 131, 151, 272, 279; *see also* Lacan
subject supposed to know, 6, 31–2n, 126, 176, 233, 261
The Sublime Object of Ideology (Žižek), 120, 148–9n, 180

319

'The subversion of the subject and the dialectic of desire in the Freudian unconscious' (Lacan), 46
suicide, 112–15, 118–19, 135–6, 138–9, 143, 152, 154
superego, 28, 247, 253n
suppléance, 279–81; *see also* Lacan
Sygne de Coufontaine, 118, 130, 132
symbolic (the)/pre-/post-/socio-, 4, 6–7, 8, 9–12, 17, 19, 20–1, 32n, 33n, 39–40, 42–3, 45, 46, 47, 48–9, 50–6, 57–60, 62n, 63n, 64n, 69, 71–5, 77, 78, 80–1, 83, 89, 91, 92–9, 101, 102, 105n, 106n, 108n, 110–14, 121, 123, 125, 126–8, 129, 131, 132, 135–6, 138, 139, 140, 145–6n, 147n, 148n, 151, 156–7, 159n, 163, 165, 166, 169–70, 172, 174–8, 180, 181, 183, 186n, 193–5, 196, 199–201, 205, 206, 208n, 209n, 213, 216, 225, 235–40, 242–3, 245, 248, 250, 251, 260, 270, 279; *see also* imaginary, the; Lacan; real, the
Symbolic Economies (Goux), 245
symbolisation, 6–7, 10–12, 48–9, 53, 55, 56, 64n, 93, 94, 96–7, 108n, 127, 129, 136–7, 159n
Symposium (Plato), 128
symptom, 11, 28, 77, 78–82, 84, 102, 105n, 167, 196, 246, 282n
advertising/consumerism as, 246
identification with, 151, 276, 279, 281
and *sinthome*, 80–1, 246
social, 77, 79, 80, 181, 213, 246
see also Lacan
symptomatic, 20, 78, 79, 81–2, 102, 146n, 213, 222, 274–5
attachment to authority, 279
fixation, 281
jouissance (unconscious)/enjoyment, 21, 81, 274
Syntagma Square, 144
The System of Objects (Baudrillard), 247, 252n

Tarrying with the Negative (Žižek), 131, 132, 278
Teiresias, 147n
Television (Lacan), 5, 91
tension, 45, 73, 77, 110, 115–16, 130–1, 150, 229, 269–70, 282
knowledge–experience, 5, 8, 10
theatre, 128
theatrocracy, 128, 145
theoria, 31n
Third Way politics, 213, 214
Thompson, Simon, 277, 284n; *see also* Hoggett
Tiananmen Square, 144
The Ticklish Subject (Žižek), 111, 151
Time magazine, 123–4
de Tocqueville, Alexis, 262
totalitarianism, 113, 121, 142, 145n, 160n
Stalinist, 140
transgress(ion), 30n, 111–12, 117–19, 124, 261, 266, 283n
transubstantiation, 122, 123, 131, 152, 159n
traversing, 7–8, 70, 94, 102, 116, 119, 129, 257
of discourse, 103

the fantasy, 12–13, 82, 94, 95, 96, 102, 113, 126, 141, 142, 261, 279, 281
Trotsky, Leon, 261
truth, 5–6, 8, 12, 53, 74, 89, 93, 99, 122, 123, 125, 144, 152–8, 187n, 221, 238, 239, 264, 28
ethic of, 157, 158n
and event, 125, 158
Truth–Event, 156
truth procedure, 153–6, 160n
see also Badiou; Foucault
'Truth and Power' interview (Foucault), 183
Tsoukalas, Constantine, 203
tuche, 120

Umbr(a), 111, 116, 121, 129
unconscious, the, 11, 21, 28, 60, 180, 213, 232, 233
and language, 89
and obedience, 21
see also Freud; Lacan
The Unconscious (Freud), 92
Unger, Roberto, 30n, 60, 273, 282, 283–4n
Université Catholique de Louvain, 2
utopia, 135, 139, 149n, 196, 255, 260–1, 268, 283n
Utopian Left, 124
utopianism, 16, 260–1, 275, 281, 283n

Vanier, Alain, 107n
Vernant, Jean-Pierre, 128
via negativa, 5
Vincennes, 2
voluntarism, 120, 220
imaginary, 59
political, 18
voluntary servitude, 27, 81, 169, 268

Whitebook, Joel, 38–9, 50–1, 53, 54, 58
The Why of Consumption, 252n
Wildner, Katherine, 144
Williams, Raymond, 88, 165, 238–9
Wilson, E. O., 31n
Winnicott, Donald, 2
Wolff, Françoise, 2
World Trade Organisation (WTO), 170, 171, 172, 175

Yale University, 173
The Yes Men, 170–2, 175, 180, 185n, 186n

Ziarek, Ewa, 26, 143, 209n, 272
Žižek, Slavoj, 3–4, 9, 12, 14, 15, 18–19, 24, 29n, 30n, 57–8, 59, 61n, 62n, 64n, 66, 67, 69, 73–4, 75, 80, 81, 83, 103–4, 109–49, 150, 151–2, 155, 156, 157, 158, 159n, 160n, 163, 180, 181, 184n, 190, 197, 200, 201, 202–3, 209n, 229, 238, 240, 241, 246, 250, 252n, 253n, 255–6, 257, 258, 261, 275–8, 283n
Zocalo, the, 144
Zupančič, Alenka, 116, 118, 119, 146n